Critical Reasoning

Understanding and Criticizing Arguments and Theories

SEVENTH EDITION

Critical Reasoning

Understanding and Criticizing Arguments and Theories

Jerry Cederblom
The University of Nebraska-Omaha

David W. Paulsen
The Evergreen State College

Australia • Brazil • Japan • Korea • Mexico • Singapore • Spain • United Kingdom • United States

Critical Reasoning: Understanding and Criticizing Arguments and Theories, Seventh Edition

Jerry Cederblom and David W. Paulsen

Publisher/Executive Editor: Clark Baxter

Acquisitions Editor: Joann Kozyrev

Assistant Editor: Nathan Gamache

Editorial Assistant: Michaela Henry

Media Editor: Diane Akerman

Marketing Manager: Mark Haynes

Marketing Communications Manager: Laura Localio

Content Project Management: PreMediaGlobal

Senior Art Director: Jennifer Wahi

Print Buyer: Rebecca Cross

Manufacturing Director: Marcia Locke

Senior Rights Acquisitions Specialist: Katie Huha

Cover Designer: Wing Ngan, Ink Design, Inc.

Cover Image: © Artifacts Images/ Getty Images

Compositor: PreMediaGlobal

Library of Congress Control Number: 2010932709

ISBN-13: 978-0-495-80878-7

ISBN-10: 0-495-80878-4

Wadsworth
20 Channel Center Street,
Boston, MA 02210
USA

Cengage Learning is a leading provider of customized learning solutions with office locations around the globe, including Singapore, the United Kingdom, Australia, Mexico, Brazil, and Japan. Locate your local office at **www.cengage.com/global**.

Cengage Learning products are represented in Canada by Nelson Education, Ltd.

To learn more about Wadsworth, visit **www.cengage.com/wadsworth**

Purchase any of our products at your local college store or at our preferred online store **www.cengagebrain.com**

Printed in the United States of America
1 2 3 4 5 6 7 14 13 12 11 10

CONTENTS

PREFACE TO THE SEVENTH EDITION

This text has evolved alongside an educational movement. When the first edition was written, it was one of very few texts designed to help students improve their ability to evaluate critically what they heard and read in a variety of everyday contexts. Most of the books in the field of logic did not address this need directly. In succeeding years, the importance of developing and applying analytical and critical skills in real-life contexts became widely recognized. Courses involving techniques of critical reasoning have become regular offerings in college and university curricula. In this era of increasingly polarized opinions and contentious disagreement, the cooperative approach to critical thinking and the formation of beliefs, which has been a hallmark of this text through its various editions, is even more compelling.

In this edition, we preserve the features that have appealed to users of previous editions: readability, the clear presentation of step-by-step procedures for reconstruction and criticism, and a diverse range of examples and exercises, including longer passages such as newspaper editorials and essays. These longer, real-life passages are aimed at enabling students to apply critical reasoning outside the classroom. We have found that students must be encouraged to move beyond short, artificially constructed passages if they are to benefit fully from a study of critical reasoning techniques. As any instructor who reads newspaper editorials will quickly find, actual argumentative passages of moderate difficulty are not readily available. We have provided a collection of these passages, but instructors and students should be encouraged to maintain their own portfolios of interesting readings. The wide array of resources available on the Internet, including columns and editorials from papers across the country, provides especially good places to look, but they have to be carefully culled.

As in previous editions, we supplement the text with an Instructor's Manual available from Wadsworth, Cengage Learning. It contains teaching tips and answers to exercises for each chapter. We have paid special attention to providing extensive commentary on the more difficult exercises in the later chapters of the text. In addition, we provide sample examination questions covering relevant sections.

NEW FEATURES IN THE SEVENTH EDITION

Whereas the aim of the last edition was to make the text more concise, in this new edition we have aimed at a balance between expanding the discussion of topics that require more detailed explanation and streamlining and compressing material that seemed to hinder the flow of ideas in the text. Additionally, the formatting of the text has been improved throughout, with clearer visual delineation of main and subordinate topics and clearer designation of examples, argument types, and alternative reconstructions of arguments. The organization of exercise sets and the numbering of exercises is easier to follow for the purposes of making assignments and checking answers. Examples and exercises have been updated throughout the text, and several longer passages of contemporary interest have been added as examples and exercises.

The following summary indicates the main changes in the text:

- Chapter 1: The section on the attitude of the critical reasoner has been integrated into the previous section on critical reasoning versus mere disagreement. A new exercise section has been added on identifying main points and supporting points in brief, real-life passages.
- Chapter 3: The sections on moving to real-world discourse and on finding an argument in a sea of words have been streamlined and reorganized so that the main techniques are easier to learn and to apply to examples and exercises.
- Chapter 4: The section dealing with arguments that we should or should not do something has been developed and tied to a new section that focuses on argument context, leading to new exercises at the end of the chapter.
- Chapter 6: The introductory material on the nature of fallacies, persuasiveness, and the categories of fallacies has been compressed and reorganized so that the reader is moved more quickly into the discussion of specific fallacies.
- Chapter 7: Several longer passages have been added on topics of current interest. The discussion of how conceptual theories can support premises of deductive arguments has been expanded.
- Chapter 8: The discussions of reconstruction and criticism of sampling arguments and of arguments with statistical premises have been expanded, with particular attention to internal validity, external validity, and construct validity of sampling arguments. New material has been added on the criticism of sampling arguments that make faulty generalizations from samples of properties that are temporally unstable.

- Chapter 9: The account of convergent arguments has been simplified so that counter-considerations are presented as criticisms of a convergent argument, rather than part of the argument.
- Chapter 12: Material at the beginning and ending of the chapter has been streamlined and compressed; discussion of dogmatism and the "true believer" is expanded.

SUGGESTIONS FOR USING THE TEXT

We doubt that many instructors will be able to cover this entire book and assign every one of the exercises in a one-semester course. In our own teaching, we omit several sections and exercises. The question, then, is *what to omit*. We believe students will benefit from doing some work in all of the chapters (with the possible exception of Chapter 5), rather than covering the early chapters thoroughly and then not reaching the later chapters.

Chapters 1 and 12 frame the text. The first chapter presents our account of critical reasoning as a cooperative enterprise for deciding what to believe. The final chapter traces some of the implications of attempting to reason our way to our own beliefs while living in a world of experts.

The main body of *Critical Reasoning* is divided into two parts: Chapters 2 and 3 focus on analysis and reconstruction of arguments; Chapters 4 through 10 concentrate on evaluating and criticizing arguments. Within this second section, Chapter 4 and the optional Chapter 5 focus primarily on argument structure, whereas Chapters 6 through 10 focus on evaluating premises. The techniques for understanding and evaluating arguments are tied together in Chapter 11. We believe that by putting together the individual techniques learned in previous chapters and applying them as a whole to real-life examples, students will become more inclined to transfer what they have learned to situations outside the classroom.

A main concern in selecting a text and planning a course in critical thinking is how much time to devote to more formal aspects of logic. We have sought to give users a maximum of flexibility. Chapter 4 introduces elements of formal logic by explaining that a successful argument must have a correct structure (validity) as well as true premises. This chapter presents some informal techniques for revealing faulty structure in an argument—ways of explaining that the conclusion does not follow from the premises. Chapter 4 also introduces some elementary symbolism by presenting some common successful argument patterns.

Chapter 5 provides a more detailed symbolism, definitions of truth functional connectives, and a discussion of truth tables and Venn diagrams, as well as comments about natural deduction. This chapter can be omitted, used in part (for example, as an introduction to symbolic notation), or treated as an introduction to a more elaborate discussion of symbolic logic, along with supplementary materials.

Instructors might consider varying the passages to be analyzed or criticized by asking students to select op-ed pieces from newspapers or magazines, or to take advantage of the Internet to search websites. Other ways of extending the text are presented in the *Critical Reasoning* Instructor's Manual. Additional resources can be obtained through the Wadsworth Internet site: http://philosophy.wadsworth.com.

ACKNOWLEDGMENTS

Special thanks are due to Joann Kozyrev, Wadsworth's philosophy editor, and to the Wadsworth staff for organizing reviewers' comments on the sixth edition. The current edition has benefited from the comments of colleagues at the University of Nebraska at Omaha as well as support from colleagues at The Evergreen State College. Numerous dialogues with Ralph Johnson of the University of Windsor and Donald Hatcher of Baker College have enriched the concept of argumentation that runs through the text, although we have no doubt that their own conceptions differ from ours. We would like to thank the critical reasoning students of UNO and Evergreen for their comments. We are also grateful for the many helpful comments from the following reviewers:

Bernita C. Berry, PhD., MSW; Savannah State University
Carla Ann Hage Johnson; St Cloud State University
John Justice; Randolph College
Joseph F Keeping; York University
Michael Nassif; Kent State University, Cleveland State University
Mark A Pfeiffer; University of South Florida
Glenn M Sanford; Sam Houston State University

CHAPTER 1

Deciding What to Believe

When you read a newspaper or book, listen to someone speak, or even just think to yourself, you face decisions about what to believe. Should you accept a newspaper columnist's position on the issue of gay marriage? Should you be persuaded by your professor's reasoning that plea bargaining in the criminal courts should be eliminated? Should you agree with a television commentator that certain drugs should be legalized? Should you alter your attitude toward abortion when a friend points out that it is inconsistent with some of your other beliefs? Should you accept the claims made on an internet blog that global warming is man-made and sufficiently serious to justify immediate worldwide action? Should you be led by your own considerations to the conclusion that assisted suicide should not be made legal? You already evaluate arguments about issues like these every day. In this sense, critical reasoning—the subject of this book—is not entirely new to you. But this book offers a collection of procedures that will enable you to carry out this activity more carefully and systematically. This should help you develop your own position on such issues more effectively.

Critical reasoning, then, is concerned with deciding what to believe, but this is not to say that critical reasoning alone can tell you what to believe. Critical reasoning is not a magical technique guaranteed to tell you whether to accept a particular belief in isolation. It does not operate in a vacuum. To decide whether certain drugs should be legalized, for example, you need supporting information. You would probably want to know the extent of drug use under present laws, the nature of illegal drug trafficking and the harm it produces, the probable effects of different plans for legalization (Would drug use increase? By whom? How much?), and so on. But in evaluating what appears to be information on these subjects and in judging whether this information justifies taking a particular position on the issue, critical reasoning should play a crucial role.

The techniques of critical reasoning that we describe in this book assume that you already have many beliefs and that you use these beliefs to decide whether to accept new arguments presented to you. For example, suppose that someone claims that drug use wouldn't increase significantly if medical use of marijuana were legalized. You will be inclined to accept or reject this, depending on your beliefs about people—how tempted they are to use drugs, whether they would treat this as a loophole even if they didn't have a legitimate medical condition, and whether they would become more inclined to use harder drugs if the threat of legal punishment for marijuana were eased. If you believe that the threat of legal punishment has little to do with whether people use drugs, this would support the claim that legalization at least for marijuana wouldn't result in higher drug use overall. Of course, you can always pursue the question further, asking whether the supporting belief is itself well supported. Why do you believe that the threat of punishment isn't what keeps people from using drugs? You could try to find out whether there is support for this belief, perhaps by looking at research done on why some people use drugs while others don't. Moreover, it is crucial for a critical reasoner to be willing to give up some previously held beliefs if those beliefs appear to be inconsistent with claims that have better support.

The techniques of critical reasoning that we present here are not techniques for generating beliefs or for cleverly presenting arguments. They are not techniques that tell you how to move from premises you now accept to conclusions you haven't yet considered. They are techniques for *evaluating* some beliefs in the light of others. By contrast, the detective in fiction is often depicted as deducing unexpected conclusions from a set of clues. Critical reasoning does not operate in this way. It is a procedure for judging beliefs, not for generating them.

Critical reasoning as we conceive it is both *active* and *open* to alternative points of view. We can describe our approach more clearly by contrasting it with two other kinds of activity: (1) *passive* reading or listening (as in the case of students who expect a lecturer to fill them with information) and (2) mere disagreement (as in the case of a combative person who is not willing to take seriously the reasons and opinions offered by other people).

CRITICAL REASONING VERSUS PASSIVE READING OR LISTENING

Sometimes, when we listen to a lecture or read a book or an essay, we take each statement as information to be remembered. Suppose you are listening to a professor lecturing on the criminal courts. If your main purpose is to prepare yourself for a multiple-choice test, you might simply try to remember as many of her statements as you can: "Most criminal cases don't go to trial." "About 90 percent of defendants plead guilty." "Most legal scholars account for this high rate of guilty pleas as being the result of plea bargaining. If this is so, then eliminating plea bargaining would swamp the courts with cases." You see the professor as presenting information and you see yourself as a passive recipient whose task is take in this information. If you are taking notes, your mind will be active only to the extent that you select some statements as worth writing down for the exam, and you might even group statements together under topical headings. But you are *passive* in the sense that you don't evaluate which of the professor's statements to accept and which to doubt or reject, and you don't consider the lecturer's pattern of reasoning.

By contrast, critical reasoning demands a more fully *active* approach. First, in order to evaluate the lecturer's reasoning, you must listen for structure: Are some statements presented as conclusions (for example, "eliminating plea bargaining would swamp the courts") and others as supporting reasons (for example, "plea bargaining results in guilty pleas")? Are some presented as explanations? (Is the availability of plea bargaining intended to explain the high rate of guilty pleas?) Next, you must examine the reasoning *critically*, that is, you must evaluate or assess it: Has this conclusion been adequately supported? Do I have reason to doubt the supporting statements? Does the conclusion follow from them? Is this explanation adequate? These are some of the questions this book will address.

CRITICAL REASONING VERSUS MERE DISAGREEMENT

In contrast to passive reading and listening, mere disagreement is both critical and active, but it lacks some essential features of critical reasoning. When we engage in mere disagreement, we are predisposed to reject that with which we disagree. We approach what we hear or read with our own established beliefs already in mind. We consider each statement presented to us and accept it, reject it, or hold it as uncertain, depending on how it squares with our prior set of beliefs. For example, if we are listening to a commentator discuss drug legalization and we hear her say, "Marijuana is no more harmful than alcohol and is sometimes used medically to relieve pain," we might think, "OK, I agree with that." As we hear the further claim that, if it were legalized, the buying and selling of marijuana could be regulated by law, we think, "Well, I guess so." But as we hear the commentator arrive at the conclusion that some drugs should be legalized, we might make the judgment, "No, that's too radical, I've always been against drugs."

This process is active in that, as each statement is considered, a judgment is made. And the process is critical insofar as the judgments are evaluative (some statements are accepted, some are rejected). But critical reasoning differs from mere disagreement in certain crucial ways.

Mere disagreement is applied to separate, individual statements, and they are judged solely against the background of the reader's or listener's own beliefs. Critical reasoning, by contrast, requires us to examine the argumentative structure of an entire commentary, taking some statements as justifications for believing others. Rather than judging someone's main thesis and evaluating it on the basis of our prior beliefs alone, critical reasoning requires that we be open to having our minds changed. Even if we would have disagreed with a particular claim initially, we might be persuaded by the remainder of the commentary to believe it. Critical reasoning opens us to changing our beliefs; it involves looking at reasons on which a claim is based, judging whether these reasons are strong enough to justify accepting the claim, and altering our beliefs if a better alternative is presented. If we have been against abortion, but someone points to other beliefs we hold that would rationally compel us to the view that a fetus in its early stages should not be considered a person, as critical reasoners we must take them seriously as providing potentially good reasons to embrace this view, even though it threatens our antiabortion position. And the same can be said if we are in favor of allowing abortion and we are given good reasons for taking the fetus to be a person. The object is not to save face by attempting to justify past beliefs, but to embrace whatever is most reasonable now. We are committed to being consistent and to following reason wherever it leads.

An issue such as abortion typically reduces potential reasoners to mere disagreers. Because the issue is heartfelt and because those on both sides tend to see their opponents as villains, it is difficult to accept a point that might give support to the opposing view, even if there is good reason to accept it. The object becomes "winning" the argument by making the opposition look or sound bad. Critical reasoning, by contrast, seeks to take reasoning out of the context of this competitive arena. If an arguer points out that reasons we ourselves would accept actually support an unanticipated conclusion, and therefore should compel us to give up some conflicting view we hold, we see this as a gain, not a loss.

As we conceive it, critical reasoning is more concerned with revising our own systems of beliefs than with being critical of other arguers. If we focus on the word "critical," it is easy to construe *critical reasoning* as finding fault with other people's arguments. But this is not our primary objective. We distinguish between the tasks of (1) interpreting and clarifying the arguer's thinking with the aim of helping the arguer see any mistakes that might have occurred and (2) using the presentation of an argument as an occasion for deciding what to believe. Although many of the techniques we discuss apply to both tasks, we will focus on the second.

CRITICAL REASONING AS A COOPERATIVE ENTERPRISE

Suppose two people begin a discussion and realize that they hold opposing views. Some would avoid pursuing the discussion because of the potential for unpleasant conflict. Others would proceed for bad reasons—seeking to show their superiority or relishing the opportunity to show their opponents' views to be wrongheaded. We suggest that if both participants approach this situation with the attitude of the critical reasoner, it is an opportunity to work cooperatively so that both can improve their sets of beliefs.

Suppose the issue under discussion is whether homosexuals should be permitted to marry. Both participants have reasons for taking the positions they do. One might think it would be harmful to society for gays to marry. The other might think that it follows from a principle of equality of rights that gays are entitled to marry. But it is likely that neither of them has tried to formulate a clear, complete argument that adequately supports a conclusion. Rather than rushing into debate, they could say, "Let's try to determine the most reasonable position to hold on this issue."

The procedure we will be sketching out in the following chapters calls for one of the participants to lay out a position and supporting reasons, and for both participants to work together at this point to refine the argument in order to make it as strong as possible. Obviously, this requires the opponent to set aside his or her point of view temporarily and share in the other person's role of constructing an argument. Together they can then proceed through the reasons given and ask whether each of them is acceptable, and whether the reasons add up to adequate support for the point of view being advanced. The same process can then be carried out in constructing the opposing position.

We suggest that both participants have nothing to lose and a lot to gain through cooperative critical reasoning. There is no danger that a well-supported belief will somehow become less so through this process. The person who held the belief can maintain it even more confidently after subjecting it to scrutiny. A more likely outcome is that both parties will discover their positions to be weaker and less clear than they initially thought. The process might reveal a way to clarify and strengthen a position on the issue, or it might lead one or both participants to take a more modest stance, admitting that they have not thought through the issue well enough to take a firm position. Either of these outcomes is better than continuing to hold uncritically a position that can be shown to be hazy and weak.

Another common outcome is that the two parties will continue to disagree about gay marriage because the course of discussion reveals a disagreement about a supporting reason for one of the positions. For example, they might disagree over whether gay marriage is likely to have bad effects on the children of gay couples. At least the cooperative process has clarified what information needs to be gathered in order to reach agreement—a roadmap has been laid out for further investigation and discussion. By contrast, if the participants enter the discussion in a combative way, attacking each other's conclusions and not seeking to understand the supporting reasons, it is likely that they will end up no more enlightened than they began.

The absence of this cooperative approach to critical reasoning is increasingly evident in contemporary exchanges about public policy by political figures and commentators. In a polarized political environment, it is all too common for critical reasoning to be replaced by biased or uninformed comments that are held to be immune from critical scrutiny. Political opponents are demonized, their comments are taken out of context, and criticism, when it is advanced, is not well grounded—half-truths and intentional misinterpretations abound.

The tradition of active, critical, and open discourse with others is associated with the philosopher Socrates.[1] Socratic method or Socratic dialogue involves constantly scrutinizing beliefs and asking whether they are justified by the reasons put forward in their support. We would add that this process is as important in our dialogues with ourselves as with others.

SOME COMMON MISCONCEPTIONS ABOUT CRITICAL REASONING

We believe there are certain misconceptions about critical reasoning that make some students leery of the enterprise. Perhaps the most common misconception is that critical reasoning locks us into rigidly structured patterns of thought. It is associated with "being logical," which calls up a picture of moving from proposition A to proposition B to proposition C in a mechanical, almost inhuman way. This linear way of thinking is sometimes contrasted with a spontaneous, creative, free-and-easy manner of thought that sounds much more appealing.

This picture of critical reasoning and its effects on the mind is a mistaken one. It is true that in learning to evaluate arguments you will begin to look at the patterns formed by the statements that make up arguments. But learning to do this will not suddenly make the thoughts that come into your head fit into patterns. You may get your ideas any way you want; critical reasoning won't have any effect on this. Your thoughts might float through your head in any order, mixed with the wildest fantasies and daydreams—critical reasoning has nothing to say about this. But if, on some later occasion, you wish to evaluate a certain thought that occurred to you, you might then need to fit it and certain other thoughts into a pattern. Critical reasoning doesn't tell

---

[1]Socrates (470–399 B.C.) was a Greek philosopher. The Socratic tradition of critical reasoning springs from a series of dialogues by his follower Plato (427–347 B.C.) in which Socrates is the central character.

you to spend a large portion of your mental life doing this, but if and when you want to evaluate a statement that you have considered or that someone else has offered, at that time you will need to consider whether there are other statements that adequately support the one in question. This involves looking at the pattern of the statements in the process of assessing and editing your beliefs.

The notion that a person thinks either logically or nonlogically all the time, and that learning to reason will transform you from doing the latter to doing the former, is preposterous. If thinking nonlogically means thinking spontaneously, freely, in no imposed order, then everyone thinks nonlogically a good deal of the time, and no one should want to stop doing so. But on some occasions, everyone needs to determine whether a certain belief is well supported and worth holding. On these occasions, there is really no choice about whether to do this logically or nonlogically. Critical reasoning, in other words, is something we all do some of the time. The question is, How to do it better?

Another common misconception about critical reasoning is that it supposes there is a right and wrong point of view. Some people are more attracted to the notion that each person has his or her own way of looking at things and one way is no better than another. Actually, engaging in critical reasoning doesn't force you to assume that there is always a single correct position on an issue. It could be that more than one position can be held equally reasonably. We do not assume that the truth can always be known, or even that it can ever be known with certainty. But to engage in critical reasoning is to assume that, at least sometimes, one point of view can be seen to be more reasonable than another. We also assume that it is sometimes more reasonable to doubt a certain position than to believe it.

Perhaps the notion that one person's opinion is always as good as another's seems the more humane and tolerant attitude. A more thorough assessment of this relativism will be given in the final chapter of this book. For now it is worth noting that this attitude has a profound and dangerous consequence: If one holds that there is no way of determining what is reasonable to believe—that one opinion is always as good as another—then, when it comes to deciding which belief to act on, what procedure is available for making this decision? If it is assumed that no opinion can be shown to be more reasonable than another, it is a short step to the view that the only final appeal in settling differences is an appeal to force.

BENEFITS OF CRITICAL REASONING

What is to be gained from approaching disputes as opportunities to improve your set of beliefs rather than as contests? Many people enjoy winning arguments, and they would be disappointed to learn that studying critical reasoning won't prepare them to win more arguments. Nevertheless, there are several points to consider in favor of critical reasoning.

First, not all disputes in which you engage are with other people. Perhaps the most important dialogues that occur in your mental development are the ones you have with yourself. If you have acquired the habit of arguing with others only for the purpose of winning, you have not prepared yourself adequately to reason well in these dialogues with yourself. There are sidetracks along which you alone can be drawn, just as a pair of people can be drawn away from reason and into competition. In a conversation with yourself, unless habits of reasoning have been well established, it is easy to choose the position that is the most comfortable or the most self-serving, rather than the one that is the most reasonable.

Second, from a broader perspective, the practice of critical reasoning can promote substantial social values. In an important way it can provide defense against our vulnerability as citizens in a society in which experts are increasingly important. This is most conspicuous in arguments that involve technical or scientific issues, such as whether we are facing global warming caused by our burning of fossil fuels. But it can help us as well in avoiding the pitfalls that arise from an overreliance on religious or political figures who claim to have special insight. Even though we might not be experts ourselves, we can mitigate our status as amateurs and avoid being seduced by the claims of ideologues by honing our reasoning skills. Moreover, our guiding assumption in promoting critical reasoning is that our beliefs form the basis for our actions, and the better justified our beliefs, the more appropriate to the world our actions will tend to be.

EXERCISE 1.1

Taking Notice of Disagreements and Reasoning

1. Write a short account of a dispute that you overheard or one in which you recently participated. State whether you think anyone's point of view was changed as a result of reasons presented by the opposition. If not, why not? To what extent did the exchange consist of mere disagreement, and to what extent was there reasoned criticism?
2. When you enter into a discussion, you are likely to find that there are many factors that might promote or discourage critical reasoning. For example, you might be more inclined to reason with a peer than with a parent, or with someone who acknowledges some of your points rather than someone who rejects everything you say. Your arguments might receive a better hearing if you're sitting across from someone than if you are standing above him or her.

   Make a list of the factors that tend to encourage critical reasoning and the factors that tend to discourage it. Next, underline which of these factors you can control. You might consider strategies for controlling these factors when you try to engage someone in a critical dialogue. (This is a good exercise for collaborative discussion in small groups.)
3. Consider the situations of a courtroom trial and a formal debate. Write a few paragraphs contrasting the procedures followed in these situations (as you understand them) to the procedures of reasoned criticism outlined in this chapter.

THE MAIN TECHNIQUES OF CRITICAL REASONING

Thus far we have claimed that critical reasoning is a process that emphasizes a rational basis for belief and provides a procedure for resolving disagreements by means of further inquiry. We have contrasted critical reasoning with a mere disagreement or quarrel in this respect. As an introduction to Chapters 2 through 12, consider briefly some of the ways critical reasoning can accomplish its ends.

We can illustrate the main techniques of critical reasoning by applying them to the following lecture fragment on the subject of plea bargaining. Suppose you have taken notes on this lecture, and you now want to critically evaluate what has been said. How do you structure what you have heard in a way that prepares you to evaluate it fruitfully? What should you accept of what has been said? What should you call into question? Why? These are the kinds of questions we hope to prepare you to answer for yourself in the chapters that follow.

Lecture Fragment on Plea Bargaining

First Argument

Plea bargaining (agreeing to plead guilty in exchange for a reduced sentence) generates problems. Innocent defendants who can't afford bail may plead guilty just to avoid jail time waiting for trial. The process makes no presumption of innocence. Guilt is not determined in an adversarial process, it is negotiated. It makes work easier for prosecutors, defense attorneys, and judges, but it sometimes results in dangerous offenders receiving less jail time than they otherwise would.

Second Argument

Given these problems, some have suggested that plea bargaining be eliminated. But this might create an even worse problem. Ninety percent of defendants plead guilty, and most of those do plea-bargain. Suppose plea bargaining were eliminated and the percentage of guilty pleas dropped to 80 percent. This would double the number of criminal trials, placing a staggering burden on the criminal justice system. The practice of plea bargaining should be continued if eliminating it might have this disastrous result.

The experience of Alaska, however, calls this fear into question. Alaska has virtually done away with plea bargaining. There was some increase in the number of trials, but not as much as expected. In the year before elimination of plea bargaining, there were seventy-two felony trials in Fairbanks. In the year after, there were ninety. This is only a 25 percent increase.

Why was the increase so small? The explanation of why defendants plead guilty could be because most of them are factually guilty, and they don't have a viable legal argument for their defense (i.e., they are legally guilty as well); so they believe it is unlikely that they would win in a trial. If this is the case, then, as Alaska's experience indicates, while it may be difficult to eliminate plea bargaining, it is not impossible.

What arguments can we find in the lecture fragment on plea bargaining? If we survey the passage, we can see that the first paragraph contains reasons in favor of the conclusion that plea bargaining should be eliminated. The second paragraph presents reasons supporting the opposite conclusion—that plea bargaining should not be eliminated. The third and fourth paragraphs cast doubt on the second argument; they suggest that the reasons given for keeping plea bargaining may be weak. The last statement of the passage ("... while it may be difficult to eliminate plea bargaining, it is not impossible") indicates that the lecturer is supporting the first argument and rejecting the second.

In applying critical reasoning to this passage, you will want to decide for yourself whether to accept the first argument and reject the second. To do this, you will first need to restate each argument clearly, listing all the reasons (premises) and the conclusion for each.[2] Often, this requires rewriting parts of the passage in a clearer, more direct manner. For example, the first argument might be stated in the following way:

FIRST ARGUMENT (AGAINST PLEA BARGAINING)

Premise 1: Plea bargaining may cause innocent defendants to plead guilty.
Premise 2: Plea bargaining makes no presumption of innocence.
Premise 3: Plea bargaining results in guilt being negotiated.
Premise 4: Plea bargaining sometimes results in dangerous offenders receiving less jail time than they otherwise would.
Conclusion: Plea bargaining should be eliminated.

SECOND ARGUMENT (FOR PLEA BARGAINING)

Premise 1: Eliminating plea bargaining might overwhelm the court system with criminal trials.
Premise 2: If eliminating plea bargaining might overwhelm the court system with criminal trials, then it should not be eliminated.
Conclusion: Plea bargaining should not be eliminated.

Notice that there is a difference between these two arguments. The first presents several independent reasons for its conclusion. Each premise by itself carries some weight in supporting the conclusion that we should eliminate plea bargaining. By contrast, the second argument gives two *linked* reasons for its conclusion. The first premise is a reason by itself in support of the conclusion, but the second is not. Rather, it links the first premise to the conclusion. We might represent the difference between these two kinds of arguments by diagramming the premises in two different ways—horizontally and vertically, as we do on the following page.

---

[2]Reasons offered in support of a claim are conventionally called "premises;" the position being supported is called the "conclusion."

Argument 1: Independent Premises

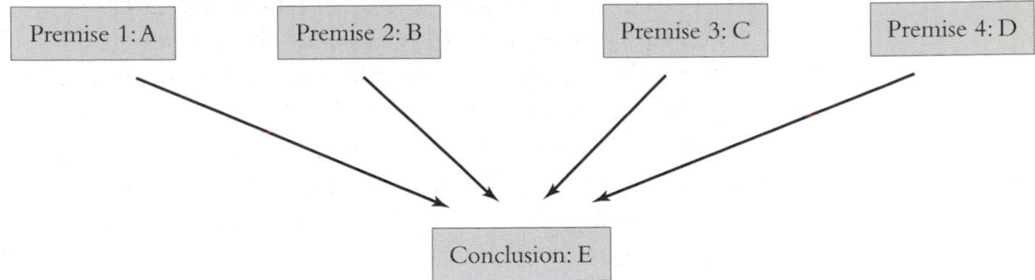

Argument 2: Linked Premises

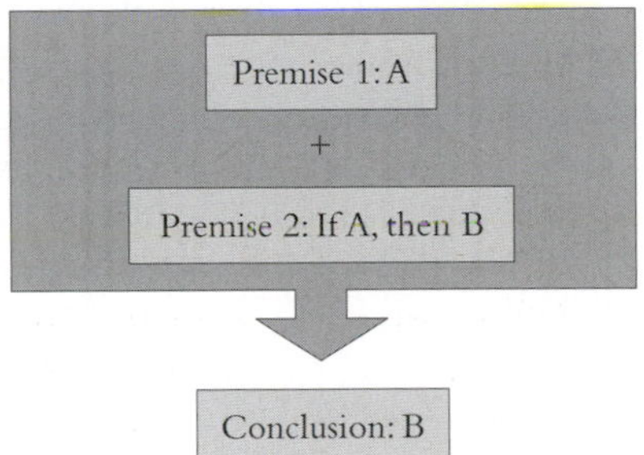

After a general discussion at the beginning of Chapter 2 on the nature of arguments and kinds of arguments, Chapters 2 through 7 will focus on arguments such as argument 2—ones with premises that are linked together so that (if they are linked in a correct pattern) the conclusion follows necessarily from all of the premises. These are called *deductive arguments*. These chapters discuss in detail how to reconstruct and evaluate them. We present evaluation as a two-step procedure of asking the following: (1) whether the conclusion follows from the premises and (2) whether the premises themselves should be believed. These basic steps are initially discussed in Chapter 4. Chapter 5 is a more detailed account of how we can determine whether an argument's conclusion follows from its premises. It introduces elements of reasoning studied by an area of philosophy called *logic* and taught in classes on symbolic logic. Our approach to critical reasoning downplays this formal approach. We offer a collection of procedures that will be useful in a variety of contexts, such as the identification of fallacies (Chapter 6) and an examination of how the soundness of arguments can depend on definition and meaning (Chapter 7).

Chapters 8 and 9 discuss arguments that are not deductive. The premises of these arguments provide some support for their conclusions, but the conclusions do not follow necessarily. Our discussion of nondeductive arguments covers those such as argument 1 (which we will call *convergent*), arguments by analogy, arguments based on statistical premises, and arguments based on data (traditionally called *inductive*). Paragraphs 3 and 4 of the lecture fragment on plea bargaining can be seen as generalizing from particular data. The particular case of Fairbanks, Alaska, in which felony trials increased only 25 percent when plea bargaining was eliminated, is used to suggest that it may not be impossible to eliminate plea bargaining generally (that is, in other states as well). Chapter 8 will give you a procedure for judging whether generalizations such as this are warranted.

Chapter 10 extends the discussion of critical inquiry to the topic of theories. Theories are often set forth either as premises of arguments or as explanations of why certain patterns occur in the observable world. Evaluating theories sometimes requires specialized knowledge, but we present some general procedures that are helpful in understanding many theories and provide a way to begin evaluating them.

The lecture fragment can be interpreted as presenting two theories, both intended to explain why most defendants plead guilty. The first theory (suggested in paragraph 2) supports the argument that plea bargaining should not be eliminated. According to this theory, most defendants plead guilty simply because they are offered a lesser sentence under plea bargaining than they would stand to get if they went to trial. The second theory is presented in paragraph 4. In essence, this theory claims that defendants plead guilty because they *are* guilty. The techniques described in Chapter 10 will help you reconstruct these theories more precisely and understand how to evaluate them. This reconstruction in turn will help you choose between the two opposing arguments presented in the lecture.

Sometimes we feel unqualified to judge what we hear and read because we lack expertise. In the case of plea bargaining, for example, we might feel tempted to leave the matter to specialists in the field of criminal justice and simply adopt the views of those specialists. However, taking this approach raises difficulties of its own. How do we know whom to count as experts in a particular field? What do we do if the experts disagree? How do we avoid being controlled by experts? The difficulties we face when making decisions based on theories and arguments proposed by experts and specialists is the subject of Chapter 12.

Throughout this book's treatment of all of these topics, a strong underlying purpose of *Critical Reasoning* is to provide procedures for determining what is reasonable to believe. When presented with an argument or theory, one might take it as an occasion for a contest, an occasion for defending prior beliefs and defeating anything that contradicts them, or as an opportunity to determine whether past beliefs are inadequate and should be modified. Our basis for urging the latter course is the proposition that there is more to be gained by building a more reasonable set of beliefs than by winning contests when disagreements occur.

EXERCISE 1.2

A Beginning Step: Identifying Main Points and Supporting Points

A. Putting an argument that you hear or read into your own words is an important step in critical reasoning. We will be discussing how to do this in detail throughout the book, but as a start, for each passage (a) write what you take to be the author's main claim and (b) list any reasons the author offers to support this claim. Set aside, for the moment, your own position on the issues raised, and try to capture the author's position as best you can. It is often useful to simplify a passage, eliminating what is inessential and simplifying cumbersome statements.

1. America cannot allow widespread outsourcing of jobs to other countries because it needs to narrow the gap between the very wealthy and the rest of us. In the last few decades, the difference between the wealthiest 20 percent and the poorer classes has expanded drastically. If the differential becomes too great, American democracy is at risk. We can only hope to reverse this dangerous state of affairs if we keep jobs in this country that pay wages adequate for workers to support their families and not allow widespread outsourcing.
2. People are dying all over the United States as victims of drugs. These victims often have their lives destroyed, if not by drugs themselves, then by a disease such as AIDS that often comes with drug use. But of course, drug users are not the only victims. The drug trade brings with it the violence we see in cities all over North America. Gangs supported by drug money bring terror to the streets in both the United States and Mexico. But political systems are also victims: The truly incredible amount of money available to drug kingpins inevitably leads to corruption among the police and in the government. The fabric of the country is in danger. The scourge of drugs remains one of the greatest security problems our country will face over the next decade.
3. The abortion issue seems to be in the news practically every week. There are rallies and political speeches. Various candidates are jockeying for political advantage by embracing one side or the other on this controversial issue. Abortion raises some fundamental issues that bring into conflict our very conception of humanity and our ideals of liberty. In spite of the importance of the topic, abortion should not be made the central issue in political campaigns. Candidates for public office differ in a variety of ways, some of which are more important to the fate of the country than abortion policy is. If we do not adequately deal with problems such as medical coverage and crime, both our ideals of humanity and our liberty will be threatened. There should be no "litmus test," no single criterion, in judging people for public service in our complex and increasingly vulnerable world.
4. Our fear of terrorism is prompting proposals that are simply unfeasible. We should not be wasting our efforts on increased border security, for the reason that effectively sealing our borders against entry by terrorists is an impossible task. Even if we make major entry points more secure, we simply cannot deploy enough

personnel to secure our thousands of miles of borders. Our limited resources would be better spent on hunting down known terrorists and increasing surveillance on terrorist organizations. Admittedly, this strategy doesn't guarantee success in the war on terror, but no strategy that we are actually willing to finance and carry out would guarantee success.

5. Review your notes from a lecture that you heard recently. In your own words, briefly state the most important points and any main supporting points.

B. The following passages are typical of opinion pieces found in a newspaper. For each one, consider what is the main claim and identify any supporting reasons. Pay particular attention to title of each passage. Write down the main claim or claims and the supporting reasons in your own words.

1.

Letter to the Editor

Grandkids Will Pay One Way Or The Other

I'm convinced by all the scientific evidence that the world faces global warming and that one cause is all the greenhouse gases we are sending into the atmosphere. The question now is what to do about it. All the options will be expensive, and much of the cost will be passed on to future generations. Some say we can't burden our grandchildren with these costs. I say that since they will get the benefit, they should bear some of the cost. If we do nothing, we will be passing on even more expensive problems such as rising sea levels and destructive storms. We should act now.

Edwin Showalter

2.

Letter to the Editor

Hunker Down and Cut Our Losses

I am responding to a letter by Edwin Showalter that appeared last week. I don't dispute the evidence of global warming, but I do dispute Showalter's argument about what should be done. I've read that without drastic action the world temperatures could increase up to 6 or 7 degrees, which would cause radical change in climate and destruction of cities along shorelines. But it is just unrealistic to think that we could get the worldwide cooperation we need to significantly change the warming trend. Since this is so unlikely, it would be better to channel our resources into limiting the damage as much as we can. We could restrict building along shorelines and prepare for long-term relocation of coastal buildings and roads.

Rose Aleano

3.

OP ED: *Saving the Future*

American greatness in the 20th century, the so-called American Century, rests on the unglamorous foundation of infrastructure: the sewers and water distribution systems that made it healthy to live in large cities, the systems of roads and bridges, especially the interstate highways that made rapid transportation of goods nationwide possible, the dams, and the electrical grid that links individual homes and business to sources of energy.

Much of this infrastructure is over 50 years old and some more than 100. As the recent I-35W bridge collapse in Minneapolis shows, design problems and lack of maintenance are threatening life and limb. Recent calls to limit the federal deficit and curtail spending at the state level, even to cut taxes, will make it impossible to maintain and replace these essential, but often ignored elements of our way of life.

In the mid 20th century we were investing as much as 15% of the gross domestic product in building and maintaining infrastructure. China and India now surpass us. Furthermore, if predications about global warming are even a little correct, the extremes of weather, the increased threat of drought, and the expected rise in ocean levels will put our already deteriorating infrastructure in even greater peril.

If we don't act boldly and make the requisite investments, even at the cost of higher taxes or greater deficit, we are very likely to follow the lead of ancient Rome, built on a superior foundation of roads, water pipes, and sewers, but destroyed when this infrastructure was no longer maintained.

C. Read both of the following editorials. For each one, write out what you take the main claim to be. Some candidates are listed below, but you need not limit yourself to these choices. Next, state in your own words one or two points from the editorial that support the main claim.

Some candidates for the main claim of the editorial *Gay, Straight: What's the Deal?*:

a. Gay marriage is morally wrong.
b. Gay marriage will undermine the family.
c. Gay marriage will threaten special rights given to heterosexual married couples.
d. Heterosexual married couples should not get special rights.
e. Neither heterosexual married couples nor gay married couples should get special rights.
f. Gay marriage is morally right.

Some candidates for the main point of the editorial *Truth about 'Assistance'*:

a. Many people who want assisted suicide are not terminally ill.
b. Assisted suicide would lead to helping people die who are depressed and might later want to live.

c. Advocates of assisted suicide are trying to mislead us.
d. Assisted suicide should not be made legal.
e. Assisted suicide is morally wrong.

1.

Gay, Straight: What's the Deal?[3]

The U.S. Senate has blocked the proposed constitutional amendment that would ban gay marriage. In doing this, the senators have earned my gratitude—though for reasons not directly related to gay rights. Rather, the move will spare us all some of the repetitive back-and-forth that has characterized this debate. It has gotten boring, and both sides of the argument irritate me. About 82 million unmarried American adults will know of what I speak.

Gay advocates always note the thousand-plus federal rights and benefits that are available to married heterosexuals and not to committed same-sex couples. The guardians of traditional values then counter that marriage has always been a man-and-woman thing—letting gay couples in on the deal would harm whatever is left of the American family.

What really rankles me, though, is "the deal" itself. That hit home in a news story around the time that Massachusetts started recognizing gay marriages. The day after a lesbian couple wed, the women filed a medical-malpractice lawsuit. One of them suffered from advanced breast cancer which, the suit claimed, a doctor had failed to detect. The other wanted to collect for "loss of consortium." In other words, the doctor's alleged negligence was depriving her of the love and companionship of a mate, and she wanted monetary compensation for her pain.

You can't read this without thinking about similar hurts being felt all the time in non-marital relationships. People develop intense connections with old friends, neighbors and grandmothers. Why can't they sue for loss of companionship also?

Quickie marriages get more legal respect than friendships lasting decades. An hour after Britney Spears gets hooked to her next husband, the federal government will shower her with all sorts of rights and benefits not available to the man who has spent eight years caring for a mother with Alzheimer's.

So here is the point: The push toward gay marriage doesn't threaten hetero marriages as much as it threatens "the deal." It puts light on the illogic behind handing a variety of goodies to certain people because some civil authority issued them marriage certificates.

There is a potent political issue here, which could complicate matters for candidates. They must do more than just choose between advocates of gay rights and those of so-called traditional values. They must consider the lot of single Americans, who could cause a ruckus if they ever woke up.

So much attention is paid to married couples that most of the public—including single people themselves—thinks of unmarried adults as a marginal minority. Actually, they account for half of America's grownups. Households headed by single people are now the majority in 13 states and 113 congressional districts.

These districts are wildly diverse. Some include the poorest black inner cities, while

[3]Froma Harrop, *Seattle Times*, July 20, 2004. Reprinted by permission of Froma Harrop and Creators Syndicate, Inc.

others are wealthy and mostly white. In the nation's richest congressional district—located on Manhattan's East Side—more than 70 percent of the households are headed by unmarried adults.

Government should have no interest in a citizen's marital status. It certainly has no business sending a bigger tax bill to cohabiting sisters than to a man-and-wife team reporting the same income and deductions as the sisters.

Marriage is a fine institution and a very important stabilizing force for the raising of children. Some purists will argue that even child tax credits are a kind of social engineering. Using the tax code to help people pay for child expenses seems OK to me. But giving tax breaks to Larry King and his seventh wife—and in the name of helping children—is outrageous.

Of course, stereotypes underpin these unfair policies. Married couples are seen as the moral backbone of America. Singles, on the other hand, are regarded as questionable citizens and possibly misfits. In truth, single America includes everything from 21-year-old serial daters and bachelor playboys to widowed grandfathers and divorced parents. And whose business is it, anyway?

Perhaps the diversity of the group helps explain why unmarried adults haven't made common cause. They should, and when they do, the whole conversation will change. The real issue will no longer be whether gays should get in on the same marriage deal as heterosexuals, but why the deal exists in the first place.

2.

Truth about 'Assistance'[4]

There are many good reasons respected groups oppose suicide. Here are some of them.

By Wesley J. Smith

To paraphrase the old musical classic, assisted-suicide advocates are great pretenders.

They promise that it will be restricted "as a last resort" to mentally competent, terminally ill people. They argue that the killing will be facilitated only by supercareful Marcus Welby clones. They promise that the entire practice will be strictly controlled and, above all, compassionate.

Balderdash. Let's open our eyes to the truth.

► Assisted suicide is not about terminal illness.

Jack Kevorkian epitomizes what actual assisted-suicide practice would look like. Approximately 20% of his subjects (his term) have been terminally ill. The largest category of people he has helped to die were disabled. Three had no physical illness on autopsy.

That's not all.

The 9th Circuit Court of Appeals decision, now before the Supreme Court, specifically held that the disabled "will, along with non-impaired individuals, be beneficiaries" of legalized assisted suicide.

[4]Wesley J. Smith, *USA TODAY*, January 9, 1997. Reprinted with permission of the author. Wesley J. Smith is an attorney for the International Anti-Euthanasia Task Force and author of the book, *Forced Exit*.

Moreover, the court ruled that "a decision by a duly appointed surrogate decision maker is, for all legal purposes, the decision of the patient himself." This means that if upheld, it would allow the permissible, nonvoluntary killing of those who are legally incompetent, which could include Alzheimer's patients, mentally retarded people and, perhaps, children.

▶ It is not about compassion.

Studies show that suicidal people who are dying or disabled are no different from those who want to die because of, say, a lost business or divorce. Almost all are clinically depressed.

We will interfere with the jilted lover's "right to die," by force if necessary. Yet we are supposed to allow doctors to assist the suicides of persons with multiple sclerosis or cancer when next week or next month they might regain the desire to live.

That isn't compassion; it is the ultimate in abandonment.

▶ Follow the money:

Headlines announce almost daily the pressure that for-profit HMOs place on doctors to reduce the cost of health care.

Plug legalized assisted suicide, which is far cheaper than long-term care, into the HMO equation.

Imagine "choosing" assisted suicide because your HMO denied you adequate access to specialists in pain control or appropriate treatment for depression. It could happen.

Or think how you would feel if an HMO doctor recommended suicide as the best "treatment" for your spouse, and you knew that the doctor could be fired or lose bonus income for providing your beloved with too much care but would be financially untouched for assisting in his or her suicide.

These are just a few of the many reasons the American Medical Association, the Hospice Nurses Association and the Clinton administration, among many diverse others, have filed briefs in the Supreme Court against legalizing assisted suicide.

It's time to stop pretending, open our eyes, and see assisted suicide for what it really would be: a moral and ethical catastrophe.

CHAPTER 2

The Anatomy of Arguments: Identifying Premises and Conclusions

When someone gives reasons to support a claim, that person is offering an *argument*. We refer to the reasons given to support a claim as the *premises* of an argument. The claim that is being supported is the *conclusion*. You encounter arguments in your reading and in your conversations with others, and you commonly offer arguments to support your own beliefs. When you are presented with an argument, you are faced with the opportunity to decide whether the reasons given are good enough to warrant incorporating the conclusion that is being advanced into your own set of beliefs. To make this decision wisely, you need to clearly understand the argument and then evaluate it.

The main focus of this and several of the following chapters is a kind of argument called *deductive*. But before we begin our study of deductive arguments, we should provide a broader view of arguments, including nondeductive arguments. Since an argument gives reasons (one or more) in support of a claim, both of the following examples would surely count as arguments. In each of them, at least one reason is given to support a claim.

Sample 1

Deductive Argument

Eliminating plea bargaining would overwhelm the court system with criminal trials. If it would do this, then plea bargaining should not be eliminated. Therefore, plea bargaining should not be eliminated.

Sample 2

Informally Stated Argument

Any practice that could help cure disease while not causing harm should be continued. So using embryonic stem cells in research should be continued.

Although these samples each give one or more reasons in support of a claim, there are important differences between them. Sample 1 has a form or structure that makes the conclusion follow necessarily from the premises. That is, if the premises are true, then the conclusion must be true. This is an example of a *deductive argument*.

If an argument doesn't already have a structure that makes the conclusion follow from the premises, we could try to restate it so that it does have such a structure. For example, we could treat Sample 2 as being a fragment of a longer, more complete, deductive argument.

Example 2.1 ***Sample 2 Restated as a Complete Deductive Argument***

Any practice that could help cure diseases while not causing harm should be continued. ***Using embryonic stem cells in research could help cure diseases while not causing harm.*** *So using embryonic stem cells in research should be continued.*

When we add the second (boldfaced) sentence to Sample 2, we are restating it in a way that makes the conclusion—*using embryonic stem cells in research should be continued*—follow necessarily from the premises. Some might claim that the second sentence is already *implicit* in the original example. If this is taken to mean that anyone who asserts the original argument must "have in mind" the unstated premise *using embryonic stem cells in research could help cure diseases while not causing harm*, then we are not committed to this view—we aren't guessing what the arguer has in mind. Rather, when we add this premise to create a complete deductive argument, we are trying to make it easier to decide whether to accept the argument's conclusion. By adding the unstated premise, we can see all of the statements we would have to judge as acceptable or unacceptable in order to decide whether this argument compels us to accept its conclusion. The premises of a deductive argument are like a checklist: Is it reasonable to believe that any practice that could help cure diseases while not causing harm should be continued? Is it reasonable to believe that using fetal cells in research could cure diseases while not causing harm? If there are no reasonable grounds for rejecting either of these claims, then I am driven to the conclusion that using embryonic stem cells in research should be continued.

For the next several chapters, our general approach will be to interpret arguments as deductive. If they are not stated as complete deductive arguments, we will try to restate them so that they are. Later chapters will study certain kinds of arguments that, for purposes of evaluation, might be best interpreted as nondeductive. If an argument is *nondeductive*, its conclusion doesn't necessarily follow from its premises. If the argument is successful, its premises provide *some support* for the conclusion; but even if the premises are true, the conclusion could be false.

The following samples could all be taken as nondeductive.

Some Types of Nondeductive Arguments

Sample 3

Inductive Argument

The rate of violent crime fell last year in a sample of fifty U.S. cities and towns, so it is likely that the rate fell in the nation as a whole.

Sample 4

Argument from Analogy

The universe has an order and precision similar to a clock's. Since the clock had a maker, the universe probably had a maker.

Sample 5

Convergent Argument

Legalizing physician-assisted suicide would lead to (1) helping disabled people die who are not terminally ill, (2) helping people die who are depressed and might later want to live, and (3) helping people die in order merely to save on medical expenses. These are all reasons against legalizing physician-assisted suicide.

Sample 3 is typical of a type of argument called *inductive*. Its premise describes a characteristic found in a sample (fifty U.S. cities and towns). The conclusion asserts that it is *likely* this same characteristic—a decline in the rate of violent crime—is true of a larger population (the nation as a whole). The fact that this conclusion asserts only a probability is what makes this kind of argument nondeductive. Sample 4 is called an *argument from analogy*. It argues that two things are alike in certain respects, so they are probably alike in some further respect. As with the previous example, the conclusion—that the universe had a maker—is asserted as probable only, not as necessarily following from the premise, so this, too, is best interpreted as a *nondeductive* argument.

Sample 5 gives three reasons against legalizing physician-assisted suicide. These reasons could be presented as having *some weight*, even if it doesn't follow necessarily that physician-assisted suicide should be illegal. The argument might be taken as leaving open the possibility that considerations in favor of legalization outweigh considerations against it.

Of course, Sample 5 could also be interpreted as a deductive argument that is not completely stated. It could be taken as having the implicit premise that if legalizing physician-assisted suicide would have these three results, then it should be kept illegal. The conclusion that physician-assisted suicide should be kept illegal would then follow necessarily. In the next several chapters, we will interpret arguments such as Sample 5 as deductive, but in Chapter 9 we will introduce an alternative way of viewing them; that is, as a kind of nondeductive argument sometimes called *convergent*.

All five samples, then, constitute *arguments* in the broad sense that they give one or more reasons (premises) in support of a conclusion. Chapters 8 and 9 will provide techniques for understanding and evaluating nondeductive arguments.

We now turn to the task of identifying premises and conclusions of deductive arguments.

THE KEY TO IDENTIFICATION: SEEING WHAT IS SUPPORTED BY WHAT

To understand deductive arguments fully, you first need to learn to identify their parts—the *premises* and the *conclusion*. This will ultimately help you to evaluate arguments better. As in medicine you must learn the anatomy of an animal before you can systematically diagnose its ills and improve its health.

We will begin our investigation of premises and conclusions by looking at short, simplified passages that contain arguments. For example, a reader of the editorial on gun control reprinted later in this chapter might restate one of its arguments in this way:

Example 2.2 *If gun control laws worked, then the states with the toughest gun-control laws would have the lowest crime rates. But they don't have the lowest crime rates. Therefore, gun control laws don't work.*

The first two statements support the third. They provide reasons for believing that gun control laws don't work, so each one individually is a premise of the argument. The conclusion is the statement that the premises are supposed to support: Gun control laws don't work.

Consider a second example. Suppose someone who doesn't know much about biology argues as follows:

Example 2.3 *Whales are not mammals, since no fish are mammals, and whales are fish.*

In this argument the premises and the conclusion are not given in separate sentences, but we can nevertheless distinguish what is supported from that which is offered as support. The first clause, *whales are not mammals*, is meant to be supported by the two clauses that follow: *no fish are mammals* and *whales are fish*. The latter two statements are the premises, and the first statement, *whales are not mammals,* is the conclusion. This conclusion happens to be false, but it is nevertheless the conclusion of the argument—a faulty argument, in this case.

Two cautions are in order: (1) Some people misconstrue the conclusion as a mere summary of the premises. The conclusion of an argument does not, however, simply restate the sentences in a passage. (2) Others tend to think of the conclusion as the most important point in the passage. Often it is, but it need not be. The conclusion can be singled out because it stands in a special relationship to the other statements—that is, it is supposed to be supported by the other statements. To find the conclusion in a passage, we must see which statement is supposed to be supported by the others.

Clues to Identifying Argument Parts: Indicator Words

Sometimes the person offering an argument provides clues that identify the premises and conclusion. Consider the following pessimistic argument about gun control:

Example 2.4 *Either we ban all handguns or homicide rates will remain high. We will not ban all handguns. We can conclude that homicide rates will remain high.*

In this case the speaker tells us which statement is the conclusion of the argument by using the phrase "We can conclude that . . . " We call expressions that serve this purpose *conclusion indicators*. Numerous expressions can fill this role, including the following:

Conclusion Indicators

so
thus
therefore
hence
we can conclude that
consequently

There are also expressions that help identify premises. Among the most common of these are:

Premise Indicators[1]

since
for
because
for the reason that

The statement that immediately follows a conclusion indicator is the conclusion; that following a premise indicator is a premise. This will seem natural when you consider that premises are reasons given in support of the conclusion, and all the premise indicators mean roughly "for the reason that."

Additional indicators typically come between premises and conclusions:

Premise–Conclusion Indicators

(premise)	. . . shows that . . .	(conclusion)
"	. . . indicates that . . .	"
"	. . . proves that . . .	"
"	. . . entails that . . .	"
"	. . . implies that . . .	"
"	. . . establishes that . . .	"
"	. . . allows us to infer that . . .	"
"	. . . gives us reasons for believing that . . .	"

[1]These words are not always used as premise indicators. For example, *since* can also be used to indicate order in time, as in the statement "Since (that is, in the time since) Joe went to medical school, he has established a practice in the field of AIDS treatment."

Or, alternatively, they can come between conclusions and premises:

Conclusion–Premise Indicators

(conclusion)	. . . is shown by . . .	(premise)
"	. . . is indicated by . . .	"
"	. . . is proven by . . .	"
"	. . . is entailed by . . .	"
"	. . . is implied by . . .	"
"	. . . is established by . . .	"

Marking the Parts of Arguments

The distinction between the premises and conclusion in an argument can be marked more formally in several ways. We can graphically set them apart by putting the argument into a *standard form*. To do this, we list the premises, numbering each statement separately. Then we draw a horizontal line to separate the premises from the conclusion. The conclusion is stated below the line. Traditionally, conclusions are indicated by a sign consisting of three dots (∴) or by the word "therefore." The argument in Example 2.4 would be written in standard form as

Example 2.5

(1) Either we ban all handguns or homicide rates will remain high.

(2) We will not ban all handguns.

∴ Homicide rates will remain high.

Note that we leave out premise and conclusion indicators, as well as words that connect the premises, such as *and* or *but*.[2] These words become unnecessary because our manner of displaying the argument already indicates which statements are premises, how many there are, and which statement is asserted as the conclusion.

For simple arguments written out in detail, a second, abbreviated version of the process of putting an argument in standard form is to circle the parts of a passage that contain premises and the conclusion and mark the premises with the symbols P1, P2, and so on, and the conclusion with C. Take a look at Example 2.6.

Example 2.6

P1
Since (whales and dolphins are mammals) and
(mammals need to breathe air,) P2
(whales and dolphins need to breathe air.) C

[2]If the word *and* occurs within a premise rather than between premises, it should not be omitted.

Notice that the premises and the conclusion must be complete statements. In Example 2.7, the fragment "If we ought to have a sustainable health care system" alone can't serve as a premise because it is not a complete statement. Notice as well that this argument contains three premises as well as a conclusion.

Example 2.7

P1 *If we ought to have a sustainable health care system, then we need to contain costs.*

P2 *If we need to contain costs, then we ought to limit heroic measures to save the life of the very elderly. We ought to have a sustainable* P3 *health care system. Therefore, we ought to restrict health care*

C *for the very elderly.*

Theoretically, there is no limit to the number of premises an argument can contain. However, most arguments in ordinary discourse contain only a few premises.

EXERCISE 2.1 **Techniques for Marking the Parts of Arguments**

Try these techniques in the following exercises. Put Exercises 1 and 2 into *standard form*; for Exercises 3–16, *circle and label* the premises and conclusions.

1. Any friend of mine deserves my respect. Ed is a friend of mine. Therefore, Ed deserves my respect.

(In standard form:)

(1)

(2) ______________________________

∴

2. Abortion raises serious moral questions because abortion involves the taking of a human life, and anything that involves the taking of a human life raises serious moral questions.

(In standard form:)

(1)

(2) ______________________________

∴

(*Circle and label* the premises and conclusion in the following exercises.)

3. If your mind were organized, your desk would be organized. Your desk isn't organized. It follows that your mind isn't organized.

4. If a child has formed a strong bond with the family that adopted her, then the biological parents should not reclaim her. Natalie has formed a strong bond with the family that adopted her. Hence, her biological parents should not reclaim her.
5. An activity pays if the people who engage in it come out ahead economically more often than not. The people who engage in many crimes come out ahead economically more often than not. It follows that many crimes pay.
6. Technologies aimed at evading political censorship will change global politics. This is because such technologies will subvert repressive regimes, and anything that subverts repressive regimes will change global politics.
7. It is wrong for society to kill a murderer. This follows for the reason that if a murderer is wrong in killing his victim, then society is also wrong in killing the murderer. And a murderer is wrong in killing his victim.
8. All pornography should be banned. This allows us to infer that *National Geographic* magazine should be banned, because anything that contains pictures of naked adults and children is pornographic, and *National Geographic* contains pictures of naked adults and children.
9. If belief based on faith is belief without evidence, then belief based on faith is never justified. Belief based on faith is belief without evidence. We can conclude that belief based on faith is never justified.
10. Any area of study that contributes to the field of medicine should be well supported. Therefore, biology should be well supported, since it contributes to the field of medicine.
11. If privatizing schools would leave poorer, more-difficult-to-educate students at a disadvantage, then privatizing schools will only worsen the problems of inner cities. It follows that privatizing schools will worsen the problems of inner cities since privatizing would leave poorer, more-difficult-to-educate students at a disadvantage.
12. If you have an irresponsible mate, then either you should avoid having a child or you should prepare yourself for the difficulties of single parenting. Hence, you should avoid having a child since you do have an irresponsible mate, and you don't want to prepare yourself for the difficulties of single parenting.

It might seem more difficult to identify premises and conclusions in passages with long, complex sentences. Actually, the task is still fairly simple if you can locate the indicator words that divide an argument into its parts, as in the following exercises.

13. Capital punishment should be abolished. This is so because a nonwhite murderer whose victim is white is much more likely to be executed than a white murderer whose victim is either white or nonwhite. If that is the case, then either this kind of discrimination should be eliminated, or the death penalty should be abolished. Unfortunately, this kind of discrimination cannot be eliminated.
14. If capital punishment deters potential murderers, then if it is not inflicted, some innocent person will be murdered. It is better for a murderer to be executed than for an innocent person to be murdered. Thus, if capital punishment deters potential murderers, then it should be inflicted.

15. Since judges shouldn't be influenced by campaign contributors, we can conclude that they should not be chosen by election. This is because if judges are chosen by election, then they will be influenced by campaign contributors.
16. If Americans reject congressional candidates who propose to rein in spending on Medicare and farm subsidies, then either we will suffer from a growing deficit or we will need to raise taxes. The public won't tolerate raising taxes, and Americans will reject candidates who propose to rein in spending on Medicare and farm subsidies. It follows that we will suffer from a growing deficit.

WHAT TO DO WHEN THERE ARE NO INDICATOR WORDS: THE PRINCIPLE OF CHARITABLE INTERPRETATION

Indicator words explicitly mark the intended role of statements in an argument. But authors often omit indicator words on the assumption that it is obvious which of their statements are offered as support and which statement is being supported. When there are no indicator words, and it is questionable what an argument's premises or conclusion are, you should employ what might be called the *Principle of Charitable Interpretation:*

> **Principle of Charitable Interpretation:** When more than one interpretation of an argument is possible, the argument should be interpreted so that the premises provide the strongest support for the conclusion.

This principle is in keeping with the rationale for critical reasoning offered in Chapter 1. The object is not to make your opponent's argument look as weak as possible, but to decide what is most reasonable to believe. It is to this end that arguments under consideration should be given the strongest possible interpretation.

One way to identify the premises and conclusion is to try each statement of an argument in the role of conclusion, with the remaining statements acting as premises. Whichever statement is best supported by the other statements should be taken as the conclusion. Consider the following argument:

Example 2.8 *You should have come to the meeting. You promised Alicia you would come. If you promise to do something, you should do it.*

It can be seen fairly readily that the first statement is better supported by the remainder of the argument than either of the other two. If we put the argument into standard form, alternating each statement in the role of conclusion, we can see more easily that this reading is the best. Although this lengthy process is seldom necessary in actually interpreting an argument, it might be helpful in this case to go through it to show how the plausibility of the different alternatives varies.

Putting the argument into standard form with the first sentence as the conclusion gives us

Interpretation 1

(1) If you promise to do something, you should do it.

(2) You promised Alicia you would come.

∴ You should have come to the meeting.

This interpretation of the passage is best because if the premises are true, the conclusion must also be true. And, as will be explained in succeeding chapters, this is precisely the relationship of support between premises and conclusion that is one requirement for a good deductive argument. By considering what each statement means, you can see that the premises adequately support the conclusion. The first premise states that if you satisfy a certain condition (making a promise), then you have an obligation (keeping the promise). The second premise adds that you did satisfy the condition of promising something (that is, to come to the meeting). If these premises are true, then the conclusion—*you should have come to the meeting*—must be true.

In contrast, the supposed premises in the other readings do not adequately support their supposed conclusions. The premises could be true without the conclusion being true.

Interpretation 2

(1) You should have come to the meeting.

(2) You promised Alicia you would come.

∴ If you promise to do something, you should do it.

It could be true that you should have come to the meeting, and that you promised Alicia, but these facts do nothing to support the more general conclusion that if you promise to do something, you should do it.

Interpretation 3

(1) You should have come to the meeting.

(2) If you promise to do something, you should do it.

∴ You promised Alicia you would come.

The claims that you should have come, and that if you promise something, you should do it, do not support the claim that you promised Alicia you would come. It could be that you should have come (you would have had the chance to meet some interesting people), and that you should keep your promises; but it could at the same time be false that you promised Alicia you would come.

Again, in actual practice, the context in which you find a passage limits the number of possible interpretations that can reasonably be made. The formulation of the Principle of Charitable Interpretation given here should be taken as preliminary and subject to this qualification.

EXERCISE 2.2

Using the Principle of Charitable Interpretation to Identify Premises and Conclusions in Arguments Without Explicit Indicator Words

Identify the premises and the conclusion in each of the following arguments. Interpret each argument so that the premises give the best support for the conclusion. As we have indicated, arguments do not ordinarily occur in such simplified form, with every statement in a passage serving as either a premise or a conclusion. We are presenting these stylized passages to sharpen your skills at identifying argument parts.

1. If you buy a fur coat, then you are supporting the fur industry. If you are supporting the fur industry, then you are encouraging cruel treatment of animals. If you buy a fur coat, you are encouraging cruel treatment of animals.
2. Either the government should protect children from abuse and neglect by their parents, or it should reinstitute orphanages. The government will not protect children from abuse and neglect by their parents. The government should reinstitute orphanages.
3. Every person should avoid keeping loaded guns around the house. All those who have the capacity to kill should avoid keeping loaded guns around the house. Every person has the capacity to kill.
4. You will dread growing older. If you take too much pride in your physical appearance, you will dread growing older. You take too much pride in your physical appearance.
5. Anyone who is overly ambitious will alienate her friends. Sheila is overly ambitious. Sheila will alienate her friends.
6. If you respected my opinion, you would seek my advice. You don't seek my advice. You don't respect my opinion.
7. Either the United States will effectively curtail illegal border crossings, or it should effectively discourage employers from hiring illegal immigrants. The U.S. will not curtail illegal border crossings. It follows that the U.S. should effectively discourage employers from hiring illegal immigrants.
8. All judges must sometimes be interpreters of the law. All interpreters of the law are judicial activists. All judges must sometimes be judicial activists.
9. Any anti-gun law gives advantage to lawbreakers. Anything that gives an advantage to lawbreakers makes law-abiders less safe. Any anti-gun law makes law-abiders less safe.
10. The ban on selling hypodermic needles should be lifted. If we want to combat AIDS, then we must prevent drug users from sharing dirty needles. If we must prevent the sharing of dirty needles, then the ban on selling needles should be lifted. And obviously, we do want to combat AIDS.

11. If capital punishment deterred murder better than life imprisonment, then states with capital punishment would have lower murder rates than states with life imprisonment only. States with capital punishment do not have lower murder rates than states with life imprisonment only. Capital punishment does not deter murder better than life imprisonment.
12. Couples should be discouraged from marrying young. Marriage requires a great adjustment. If marriage requires a great adjustment and the young find such adjustment difficult, they should be discouraged from marrying. The young find adjustment to the demands of marriage difficult.

PATTERNS OF ARGUMENT

The Principle of Charitable Interpretation asks us to interpret an argument so that the statements we take as premises best support the statement we take as the conclusion.[3] We have assumed that you are already able to see, in the simplest cases, which statement is best supported by the remaining statements. But to become clearer about this relationship of support, consider two ways of interpreting the following argument:

Example 2.9 *If my car is out of fuel, it won't start. My car won't start. My car is out of fuel.*

Interpretation 1

(1) If my car is out of fuel, it won't start.

(2) My car is out of fuel.

∴ My car won't start.

Interpretation 2

(1) If my car is out of fuel, it won't start.

(2) My car won't start.

∴ My car is out of fuel.

In interpretation 2, the conclusion does not follow from the premises. There are other reasons a car might not start than that it is out of fuel: perhaps the ignition system has failed. Even if the first premise is true and the car does not start, it does not follow that it is without fuel. Now contrast this to interpretation 1. If it is true that the absence of fuel prevents starting, then it is unavoidable that if you are out of fuel, the car will not start. We can't find a situation

---

[3]Again, when you apply this principle, you are limited by what can plausibly be interpreted as the intent of the passage.

for interpretation 1 (such as the ignition problem for interpretation 2) that would make the premises true but the conclusion false.

You could try to reason through to the best interpretation in this way each time you encounter a passage without indicator words and are unsure of what to pick as premises and what as the conclusion. But it is helpful to note that the two interpretations that were just considered are instances of argument patterns that you will encounter again and again; every time you see an instance of the pattern in interpretation 1, the conclusion *does* follow from the premises, whereas for the pattern in interpretation 2, the conclusion *doesn't* follow.

A pattern involves the repetition of elements. In interpretation 1, the two statements are repeated: *My car is out of fuel* and *It (my car) won't start.* It is customary to represent these elements by letters.[4] The pattern in interpretation 1 might be represented as:

(1) If A, then B.
(2) A.
____
∴ *B.*

MODUS PONENS or AFFIRMING THE ANTECEDENT

This pattern is so common that it has been given a name: *modus ponens*.[5] The faulty pattern in interpretation 2 might be represented as:

(1) If A, then B.
(2) B.
____
∴ *A.*

AFFIRMING THE CONSEQUENT (Faulty)

Even though this is a faulty pattern, it is common enough that it also has acquired a name. It is known as the *fallacy of affirming the consequent* (because the second premise *affirms* the "then . . . " part,—that is, the *consequent* of the first premise).

The point of the foregoing discussion is that if a passage could be fit into either of the two patterns, the Principle of Charitable Interpretation would dictate fitting into the *modus ponens* pattern, because with this interpretation the premises provide the best support for the conclusion.

---

[4]In the example we use the letters *A* and *B*, but you could use other letters—for example, *F*—to remind us of the statement involving *Fuel* and *S* to remind us of a statement containing *Start*.

[5]Notice that what remains after the repeated elements are marked by the letters *A* and *B* is the expression "if . . . then." This expression along with "or" and "and" are called *logical connectives*—they connect two statements. Special symbols are sometimes used to represent them: the arrow, →, for "if . . . then"; the ampersand, &, for ". . . and . . ."; the *vel*, ∨, for "or." This way of showing form is discussed at greater length in Chapter 5, which covers a more formal approach to deductive arguments. We could represent *modus ponens* as:

(1) A→B.
(2) A.
____
∴ *B.*

A related but different pair of interpretations can be given for the argument: *If you respected my opinion, you would seek my advice. You don't seek my advice. You don't respect my opinion.* Here are two ways of identifying the premises and conclusion:

Interpretation 1

(1) If you respected my opinion, you would seek my advice.

(2) You don't seek my advice.

∴ You don't respect my opinion.

Interpretation 2

(1) If you respected my opinion, you would seek my advice.

(2) You don't respect my opinion.

∴ You don't seek my advice.

In interpretation 1, the conclusion does follow from the premises. The first premise states that *if you respected my opinion, then you would seek my advice.* Suppose, as the second premise states, you don't seek my advice. Now in order to make both these premises true, we are compelled to say that you don't respect my opinion. If we tried to claim both that the first premise is true and that you do respect my opinion, then we would be forced to say that you would seek my advice. But this would make the second premise false. In other words, the only possible way to make both premises true is to make the conclusion true also. This pattern of argument is called *modus tollens* and is represented as:[6]

(1) If A, then B.

(2) Not B.

∴ Not A.

MODUS TOLLENS or
DENYING THE CONSEQUENT

In interpretation 2, the conclusion *doesn't follow from the premises.* It very well could be that *if you did respect my opinion, you would seek my advice.* (Suppose you need information badly and will go to any source you consider reliable.) It also could be that you don't respect my opinion; maybe you have heard that I have given faulty advice more often than not. But it doesn't follow that you won't seek my advice. You might do so just to flatter me and keep me

---

[6]In addition to the symbols →, &, and ∨ (for "if . . . then," "and," and "or," the symbol ¬ or just a dash, – , is often used for "It is not the case that . . .". Unlike the first three symbols, which come between two statements, ¬ stands in front of a single sentence. Using this symbol, we can represent *modus tollens* in this way:

(1) A→B.
(2) ¬ B.

∴ ¬ A.

as a friend. That is, there might be more than one reason for a given consequent. It is perfectly possible for the premises of this argument to be true without the conclusion being true. Arguments of this pattern are often persuasive, even though they shouldn't be. The pattern, called *denying the antecedent,* looks like this:

(1) If A, then B.

(2) Not A.

∴ Not B.

DENYING THE ANTECEDENT *(Faulty)*

Although there are numerous argument patterns besides *modus ponens* and *modus tollens* whose premises guarantee the truth of their conclusions, there are a few that occur so frequently that they are worth learning at the outset. The following chart displays seven common argument patterns, including *modus ponens* and *modus tollens*. Any argument that fits one of these patterns will satisfy the criterion that if the premises are true, the conclusion must be true. Therefore, any plausible reading of a passage that fits one of these patterns would be supported by the Principle of Charitable Interpretation.

Some Common Successful Argument Patterns

Statement-Based Patterns

Argument Pattern	**Examples**
i. Modus Ponens	
(1) If A, then B.	*(1) If I lie, then I'll be sorry.*
(2) A.	*(2) I'll lie.*
∴ B.	*∴ I'll be sorry.*
ii. Disjunctive Argument	
(1) Either A or B.	*(1) Either I should exercise or I should diet.*
(2) Not A.	*(2) I should not exercise.*
∴ B.	*∴ I should diet.*
iii. Modus Tollens	
(1) If A, then B.	*(1) If you study, then you learn.*
(2) Not B.	*(2) You didn't learn.*
∴ Not A.	*∴ You didn't study.*

iv. Hypothetical Argument

(1) If A, then B.	*(1) If I pay now, then I'll save.*
(2) If B, then C.	*(2) If I'll save, then I'll have money later.*
∴ If A, then C.	*∴ If I pay now, then I'll have money later.*

v. Chain Argument

(1) A.	*(1) The whole group is coming.*
(2) If A, then B.	*(2) If the whole group is coming, then we'll need more refreshments.*
(3) If B, then C.	*(3) If we'll need more refreshments, then we'll have to go to the store again.*
∴ C.	*∴ We'll have to go to the store again.*

Predicate-Based Patterns

vi. Predicate Instantiation

(1) All P1s are P2s.	*(1) All good teachers are sensitive to the needs of students.*
(2) m is a P1.	*(2) Jones is a good teacher.*
∴ m is a P2.	*∴ Jones is sensitive to the needs of students.*

vii. Universal Syllogism

(1) All P1s are P2s.	*(1) All good teachers treat students with respect.*
(2) All P2s are P3s.	*(2) All who treat students with respect listen to students.*
∴ All P1s are P3s.	*∴ All good teachers listen to students.*

The capital letters *A*, *B*, and *C* in patterns i–v stand for whole *statements*; we call this type of argument pattern *statement-based*. In patterns vi and vii, the terms *P1*, *P2*, and *P3* stand for parts of statements, such as "good teacher," which refer to classes of objects. The lowercase letter *m* in pattern vi stands for a name or description of a particular person or thing. These names or descriptions can be seen as subjects that fit with a *predicate* such as "is a good teacher" to form a whole statement: "Jones is a good teacher." We will call the argument patterns vi and vii *predicate-based*. This chart provides only a sample of commonly found successful patterns. We discuss what makes them successful and how to determine whether a prospective pattern represents a *valid deductive* argument form in Chapter 4.

By becoming familiar with these patterns, you should get a feel for the kind of relationship between premises and conclusions you are looking for when you apply the Principle of Charitable Interpretation. Chapters 4 and 5 discuss argument patterns in greater detail, explaining some of the ways we determine whether an argument pattern is successful.

EXERCISE 2.3

Using Argument Patterns to Identify Premises and Conclusions in Arguments Without Explicit Indicator Words

Each of the exercises in this section fits one of the patterns identified on the preceding pages or a combination of them. Several tips will help you to identify these patterns in written arguments. First, the order of the premises makes no difference:

(1) If B, then C.

(2) A.

(3) If A, then B.

∴ C.

exhibits the same pattern for our purposes as

(1) A.

(2) If A, then B.

(3) If B, then C.

∴ C.

Second, in an *either–or* type sentence, order does not make any difference (though it does in an *if–then* type sentence):

(1) Either B or A.

(2) Not A.

∴ B.

exhibits the same pattern as

(1) Either A or B.

(2) Not A.

∴ B.

Third, arguments can fit these patterns even if some key words are missing. For example, *if–then* sentences often occur without the *then*, as in: "If you lend me ten dollars, I'll love you forever." They may even have the *if* part at the end of the sentence, as in: "I'll bring the food, if you'll bring the wine." *Either–or* type sentences may occur without the *either* stated: "I'll have coffee or tea." And the word *all* may be replaced by other expressions such as *every* or *any*, as in: "Every person needs a friend."

In the process of identifying premises and a conclusion, other features of a passage may provide further clues. First, since the conclusion is often the main point in an argumentative passage, look carefully at readings that treat the beginning or the final sentences as the conclusion. Second, the conclusion of an argument is seldom longer and more complex than the premises. For example, we should be suspicious of a reading in which the conclusion is an *if–then* sentence but the premises are not.

As we have indicated, arguments do not ordinarily occur in such simplified form. We are presenting these "unnatural" passages to sharpen your skill at identifying premises, conclusions, and argument patterns.

A. Go back to Exercise 2.2 and use the argument patterns to identify premises and conclusions. Note any arguments you interpreted incorrectly before you learned the argument patterns.

B. Identify the premises and conclusion, as well as the argument pattern, for each of the following:

   1. John is bound to sharpen his argumentative skills. He is studying critical reasoning, and anyone who studies critical reasoning is bound to sharpen his argumentative skills.
   2. If your relationship with your spouse were based on fair exchanges, then it would be stable. It is not stable. Your relationship with your spouse is not based on fair exchanges.
   3. If Paul can find the strength to resist Sheila's advances, then he will be able to salvage some measure of self-respect. He will find this strength. He will salvage some self-respect.
   4. Anyone who deceives other people is guilty of a form of coercion. Anyone who deceives others is manipulating their choices. Anyone who manipulates the choices of others is guilty of a form of coercion.
   5. Your car doesn't have fuel. If it had fuel, it would have kept running. It didn't keep running.
   6. Alvin has not fulfilled the graduation requirements. If he has fulfilled the graduation requirements, then he is eligible for graduation. Alvin is not eligible for graduation.
   7. Any armed intervention should be entered only as a last resort. Any armed intervention has many innocent victims. Any activity that has many innocent victims should be entered only as a last resort.
   8. Students will not become more interested in learning for its own sake. Universities will become more vocationally oriented. Either students will become more interested in learning for its own sake or universities will become more vocationally oriented.

9. If a human being is created at the moment of conception, then abortion always kills a human being. If abortion always kills a human being, then it is never justified. If a human being is created at the moment of conception, then abortion is never justified.
10. Casual sex is justifiable in some cases. If some people can't find a partner who is willing to enter a serious relationship, casual sex is their only alternative to abstinence. Some people can't find a partner who is willing to enter a serious relationship. If casual sex is the only alternative to abstinence for some people, then casual sex is justifiable in some cases.
11. Roberta will eventually become desensitized to violence. Everyone who watches a lot of violent films eventually becomes desensitized to violence. Roberta watches a lot of violent films.

C. The following arguments don't exactly fit any of the seven patterns listed on the chart in this chapter. Try to determine their patterns. Identify the premises and conclusion and formulate the (new) patterns.

1. True conservatives resist spending for social programs. Our senator doesn't resist spending for social programs. Our senator is not a true conservative.
2. We shouldn't abolish capital punishment. If we do, prisons will become more crowded. If prisons become more crowded, then we will have to build more prisons. We don't want to build more prisons.
3. Some judges have been subjected to corrupting influences. Anyone who has practiced law has been subjected to corrupting influences. Some judges have practiced law.
4. If we really want to provide universal health care, then we must either ration some medical procedures or deploy more resources toward health care than our society can afford. We really want to provide universal health care. We must not deploy more resources toward health care than our society can afford. We must ration some medical procedures.
5. Either you should take control of your own life or trust the advice of a mentor. If you trust the advice of a mentor, then you stand the risk of being used to fulfill the mentor's own dreams. You should not take that risk. You should take control of your own life.

IDENTIFYING PREMISES AND CONCLUSIONS IN LONGER PASSAGES

So far, we have presented short passages consisting entirely of premises and conclusions. In such cases, the task of identifying the argument parts is simplified—we know that one of the statements is the conclusion and the remaining ones are premises. If we don't immediately see which statement is the conclusion, we can go through a process of elimination, trying each statement in that role and asking how well the remaining statements serve as support.

In longer passages, identifying premises and conclusions is more difficult and more a matter of interpretation. Even if the main purpose of a passage is to present an argument, most of the statements in it are usually neither premises nor conclusions. The passage displayed below is an adaptation of an opinion piece opposing restrictions on gun ownership. It contains several paragraphs

Only the Law-abiding Will Submit to Restrictions, thereby Making Crime Easier

(Excerpt from opinion piece by Andre Marrou, 1992 Libertarian Party Presidential nominee, with statements added in brackets to make the argument more explicit. The unmodified op-ed piece is found as an exercise at the end of Chapter 3.)

First Argument

If anti-gun laws worked, then New York and Washington, with the toughest anti-gun laws, would have the lowest crime rates. But they have the *highest*. [So anti-gun laws don't work.]

Conversely, crime rates plummeted up to 90% after certain cities and states—like Orlando, Fla., and Kennesaw, Ga.—allowed law-abiding citizens to carry concealed handguns.

Second Argument

The reason should be obvious: law-abiding citizens know and obey the law. Criminals don't care what the law is and won't obey it. So who benefits when gun ownership and use are restricted? The criminals, because decent folks are disarmed by the law... [If so, then these laws make it]... easier for criminals to prey upon them. [And if that is the case, then criminals benefit.]

Registering guns and licensing gun owners won't reduce crime any more than registering cars and licensing drivers now reduce traffic accidents—which is to say, hardly at all. With millions of highly restrictive laws, still about 44,000 Americans yearly die in traffic accidents, while about 15,000 are shot to death. Since there are fewer cars than guns, cars are clearly more dangerous than guns. Should we outlaw cars?

Like cars, guns are dangerous tools. So are kitchen knives (ask John Bobbitt) and chain saws; should we register or outlaw them, or license their use? Just because something is dangerous—say climbing mountains or riding bulls—doesn't mean we should restrict its use or test and license its practitioners.

Guns are tools, not evil instruments capable of their own malevolence. A gun simply amplifies its user's power. In a rapist's hands, a gun is bad; in a law-abiding woman's hand, it's good. New York and Washington have proved that guns cannot be kept from criminal hands; shouldn't we let decent people arm themselves without licensing? Ultimately, "gun control" is not about guns. It's about control. Beware.

from the original with the addition of several sentences that make the arguments in the passage more explicit. As you will see in Chapter 3, it is extremely rare for a prose passage to present an argument with all the premises and the conclusion explicitly stated. By adding implicit premises and conclusions in the passage below, we have made it an unnatural phrased argumentative passage. However, it still illustrates several features that must be dealt with in order to identify premises and conclusions in more typical prose passages. It contains sentences that are not part of any argument, so we must read for argumentative structure: Which sentences play a role of providing support or being supported? We can't simply go through the passage statement by statement and decide, for each one, whether it is a premise or whether it is a conclusion; some are neither. Also, most of the statements that serve as premises or conclusions must be restated in order to fit into a pattern. As we read a passage, we need to think of possible patterns that premises and conclusions might fit into. We can then put statements into our own words so that they fit patterns such as the ones presented in this chapter. Also, as is often the case, this passage presents more than one argument, so it is necessary to see where one argument ends and where another begins.

Paragraphs 1 and 3 can be interpreted as presenting fully developed arguments when the bracketed material is included. In paragraph 1, the conclusion—anti-gun laws don't work—is indicated by the word "so," and the previous two statements can be seen as supporting this conclusion. Presenting these premises as they are stated in the passage, we have:

Rough interpretation of first argument

(1) If anti-gun laws worked, then New York and Washington, with the toughest anti-gun laws, would have the lowest crime rates.

(2) They have the highest crime rates.

∴ Anti-gun laws don't work.

If we look for a way to express this argument so that it fits one of our patterns, we can see that *modus tollens* lends itself.

Argument pattern

(1) If A, then B.

(2) Not B.

∴ Not A.

We can adjust the wording of the argument in order to fit this pattern precisely.

Paraphrased version of first argument

(1) If anti-gun laws worked, then New York and Washington would have the lowest crime rates.

(2) New York and Washington don't have the lowest crime rates.

∴ Anti-gun laws don't work.

In paragraph 3, the question "So who benefits when gun ownership and use is restricted?" is answered with: "Criminals." Since this is followed by the premise indicator "because," we can interpret the following three statements as premises supporting the conclusion *Criminals benefit from restrictions on gun ownership and use.*

Rough interpretation of second argument

(1) Decent folks are disarmed by the law.

(2) If decent folks are disarmed by the law, then these laws make it easier for criminals to prey on decent folks.

(3) If these laws make it easier for criminals to prey on decent folks, then criminals benefit from anti-gun laws.

∴ Criminals benefit from restrictions on gun ownership and use.

This argument already comes very close to fitting the **chain argument** pattern:

Argument pattern

(1) A.

(2) If A, then B.

(3) If B, then C.

∴ C.

We can refine this interpretation by clarifying the phrase "the law" and by adjusting the wording of the third premise to match that of the conclusion.

Paraphrased version of second argument

(1) Decent folks are disarmed by restrictions on gun ownership and use.

(2) If (1), then restrictions on gun ownership and use make it easier for criminals to prey on decent folks.

(3) If these restrictions make it easier for criminals to prey on decent folks, then criminals benefit from restrictions on gun ownership and use.

∴ Criminals benefit from restrictions on gun ownership and use.

The material in succeeding chapters will help you in interpreting longer passages. Use of indicator words as well as recognition of argument patterns will help you in carrying out this task. Passages found in editorials and other real-world contexts contain a variety of statements that are not essential (strictly speaking) to the presentation of an argument. They contain illustrations and references to sources, as well as repetitions. Furthermore, as we will discuss in the next chapter, most of these passages do not explicitly contain all the elements needed to reconstruct an argument in standard form. The task of reconstruction is not purely mechanical. You have to be prepared to discard many (in some cases most) of the statements in a passage to tease out an argument. The last part of the passage we have been discussing, for instance, can be interpreted as containing an additional argument about licensing guns that is not fully explicit.

EXERCISE 2.4 Reconstructing Explicit Arguments in Longer Passages

Restate in standard form what you take to be the main argument put forth in the following passages. If you can, make the argument fit a pattern so that the conclusion follows from the premises. This may involve putting the premises and conclusion into your own words. You may need to rewrite your interpretation several times before it will fit into a concise pattern. (After you have worked on this individually, you might want to work with a group of other students, combining some of your insights to produce a better interpretation.)

1.

Guns and Free Discourse

The Second Amendment guarantee to bear arms is no less clear than the First Amendment guarantee of free expression. Gun control advocates overlook this similarity. Often the same person supports gun control but opposes censorship of controversial "art." But if gun control is constitutional, then it is also constitutional to restrict artistic expression.

The courts have consistently ruled that the Constitution assures adults freedom of expression. Even though some might be offended, it is not enough that people find a work distasteful. Our Constitution guarantees the right to produce and view it. So even though contemporary society suffers from too many guns, gun possession is similarly assured by our Constitution.

2.

Networks Don't Get Connection[7] (Excerpt from column by Cal Thomas *Seattle Post-Intelligencer,* May 14, 1992)

ABC Television broadcast a special "Men, Sex and Rape,"... full of "pretension to virtue." . . . First Amendment absolutists have resisted every attempt to control the huge levels of effluent [from TV] that have turned our society into a toxic waste dump. . . . One does not have to be a social scientist to see a connection between increased incidents of rape, and other acts of violence against women, and the way women are treated in the popular media. . . . If rape is a terrible crime, and it is, and if there is a connection between pornography and the cultural permission it gives those already predisposed to perform these acts on women, then the government has an obligation and duty to control its proliferation.

[7]The full, unmodified version of the editorial is given as an exercise at the end of Chapter 4.

3.

Gender Tests May Not Be Worth Risk of Misuse (Excerpt from column by Ellen Goodman, with statements added in brackets for clarification in this exercise)[8]

The woman beside me pats her rounded stomach and rolls her eyes to the ceiling, exclaiming, "Is she ever active today!" The "she" in this action won't be born until March. But my pregnant companion already knows the gender of this gestation.

I have grown accustomed to the attachment of a pronoun to a fetus by now. Most women I know of her age and anxiety level have had "the test" and gotten the results.

Over the past two decades, through amniocentesis and then CVS and sonograms, a generation of parents has received a prenatal exam, a genetic checkup on their offspring. They have all been given new information and sometimes new, unhappy choices. . . .

But this test may increase the possibility of abortion for sex selection by those who regard gender—the wrong gender—as a genetic flaw. . . .

It is the rare person who defends it on the grounds of population control or pure parental choice. It is a rarer American who chooses it. Indeed, the only countries in which sex selection occurs in discernible numbers have been those such as India or Korea where daughters have long been unwanted. It is almost always female fetuses that are aborted.

But gender testing and the capacity for gender choosing—before and after conception—is an ethical issue in this country, too. This is the first, but hardly the last time, that the new technology will be available to produce designer babies. Today, genetic testing is valued in America because it leads to the diagnosis of diseases that cause pain and death and disability. Eventually it may lead to their cure. But in the future, we also are likely to have access to much more information about genes than we need medically. We may be able to identify the gene for height, hair color, eye color, perhaps even athletic ability or intelligence. [America's fascination with technology suggests that we will not be able to resist the temptation to use this technology for sex selection.

If gender testing and gender choosing are permitted to become widely and easily available, then we must be able to resist using it.] . . . At the moment, the moral consensus against sex selection is holding. . . . But in the longer run, the rest of us may be called upon to ask whether our curiosity about gender is worth the risk that others will misuse that information. [Consequently, programs of gender testing and choosing should not be permitted to become more broadly accessible.] It may be wiser to learn if the baby is a "he" or a "she" the old-fashioned way.

---

[8]The full editorial is presented as an exercise in Chapter 11.

CHAPTER 3

Understanding Arguments Through Reconstruction

Many of the examples considered in Chapter 2 sound contrived because we don't usually hear or read arguments spelled out in such painful detail. Ordinary communication often assumes that the audience will be able to fill in the missing details. If you were discussing gender discrimination with a friend, for example, he might argue this:

Example 3.1 *I don't care what you say; if it's wrong to discriminate against a woman on the basis of her gender, then it is equally wrong to discriminate against a man on the basis of his.*

In this passage, there is no explicit conclusion, and a premise needed to complete the argument is missing.[1] In everyday discourse, arguments are often presented with implicit (that is, unstated) premises, and even implicit conclusions. In this chapter, we explain how the argument fragments that we commonly hear and read can be reconstructed so that their entire content, including implicit premises or conclusions, is explicitly displayed. In many situations such a full reconstruction is unnecessary. However, when you encounter complicated passages or seek to criticize an argument, it is often helpful to create such reconstructions. Once you have worked

[1]The argument omits the premise that it is wrong to discriminate against a woman on the basis of her gender and the conclusion that it is wrong to discriminate against a man on the basis of his gender.

through some reconstruction exercises, you should find it easier to recognize what has been left implicit in fragmentary arguments, such as the one stated in Example 3.1, even when you do not actually restate or rewrite the argument in reconstructed form. You are then in a better position to evaluate the assumptions or presuppositions behind the argument.

UNDERSTANDING ARGUMENTS BY IDENTIFYING IMPLICIT CONCLUSIONS

The least complicated case of reconstruction is one in which premises are supplied, with the audience left to "draw its own conclusion." In such circumstances the person offering the argument expects the context to make the conclusion clear. Suppose we hear a radio disc jockey giving this radio spot:

Example 3.2 *The smoother the sound, the better the station. The music is smoother at WARM radio.*

The obvious conclusion here is that station WARM is better. In many cases like this, where only the conclusion is missing, the argument seems to point directly to the implicit conclusion.

Unfortunately, it isn't always so simple. Sometimes you might be in doubt about whether the conclusion of an argument is actually missing. In such a circumstance the technique of considering alternative readings, which was discussed in Chapter 2, might help. Consider the following example:

Example 3.3 *If most American voters recognize that Social Security must be saved, then the government will ultimately act. But everyone with friends or relatives who will eventually depend on Social Security recognizes that Social Security must be saved. And most American voters have friends or relatives who will eventually depend on Social Security.*

This passage has something to do with government response to Social Security costs. It does not, however, give many hints about its conclusion. To many readers, it will be intuitively clear that the unstated conclusion is that the government will ultimately act. But what if we didn't see this? How could we proceed? We might begin by treating each of the three statements as the conclusion of the argument.

Reconstruction 1

(1) If most American voters recognize that Social Security must be saved, then the government will ultimately act.

(2) Everyone with friends or relatives who will eventually depend on Social Security recognizes that Social Security must be saved.

∴ Most American voters have friends or relatives who will eventually depend on Social Security.

Reconstruction 2

(1) If most American voters recognize that Social Security must be saved, then the government will ultimately act.

(2) Most American voters have friends or relatives who will eventually depend on Social Security.

∴ Everyone with friends or relatives who will eventually depend on Social Security recognizes that Social Security must be saved.

Reconstruction 3

(1) Everyone with friends or relatives who will eventually depend on Social Security recognizes that Social Security must be saved.

(2) Most American voters have friends or relatives who will eventually depend on Social Security.

∴ If most American voters recognize that Social Security must be saved, then the government will ultimately act.

Think about the meaning of the premises and conclusion in each case. *Does the conclusion follow from the premises?* In Reconstruction 1, for instance, the premises offer no reason for believing that "most American voters have friends or relatives who will eventually depend on Social Security." Although this statement might follow from the premises in some *other* argument, the premises supplied here are irrelevant. In each of the other two interpretations, the premises also fail to give reasons that adequately support the conclusion. Such a mechanical process of developing alternative readings for an argument might seem overly cumbersome, but working through it a few times will help you begin to get a feel for argument structure and to sharpen your sense of whether a conclusion has been explicitly stated or left implicit. Because in this case we have found that the conclusion is not explicitly stated, our next step is to formulate the implicit conclusion. To discover the hidden conclusion that the premises support, you will sometimes find it useful to list the premises.

Reconstruction 4

(1) If most American voters recognize that Social Security must be saved, then the government will ultimately act.

(2) Everyone with friends or relatives who will eventually depend on Social Security recognizes that Social Security must be saved.

(3) Most American voters have friends or relatives who will eventually depend on Social Security.

∴ ???

Think about what statement these premises jointly support and how they are linked. The second and third premises together support the statement that most American voters recognize that Social Security must be saved. This taken with the first premise supports the conclusion of the entire argument: "The government will act."

Reconstruction 4 illustrates two important features of a good reconstruction for arguments with missing elements. First, it strives, *other things being equal,*[2] to interpret the argument in such a way that *the conclusion does indeed follow from the premises*. In this reading the conclusion follows from the premises, whereas in each of the other three readings, the supposed conclusion *does not* follow from the premises. Further, it is difficult to find acceptable implicit premises that could be used to support these "conclusions." Secondly, the argument *uses all stated premises*. Notice the way Reconstruction 4 uses all three premises to support the conclusion and then compare this reading with the following reconstruction, which makes some of the premises contained in the passage unnecessary:

Reconstruction 5

(1) *If most American voters recognize that Social Security must be saved, then the government will ultimately act.*

(implicit) (2) *If the government acts, then the reputation of the Congress will be enhanced.*

(implicit) ∴ *If most American voters recognize that Social Security must be saved, then the reputation of the Congress will be enhanced.*

Reconstruction 5 does not use all the available material in the passage. It picks out one element as a premise, disregards the rest, and reaches a conclusion that is not even hinted at in the passage. Of course, in order to do so, an implicit premise also needs to be added. In Chapter 2 we encouraged applying the Principle of Charitable Interpretation, but attributing an argument that is not even suggested by the text is not providing an *interpretation* that is charitable, even if the argument is a good one.

UNDERSTANDING ARGUMENTS BY IDENTIFYING IMPLICIT PREMISES

More common than the argument with an implicit conclusion is the argument that presents a conclusion and some of the premises needed to support it, but leaves out one or more statements necessary to guarantee the truth of the conclusion. These missing premises are sometimes referred to as *assumptions* or *presuppositions* of the argument.[3] Consider this example:

Example 3.4 *A law that would reduce the blood alcohol limit for driving is a bad idea, because anything that would put ordinary social drinkers in jail is a bad idea.*

---

[2]Other things are *not* equal if the passage actually suggests a reading in which the conclusion does not follow from the premises.

[3]We might distinguish between an assumption and a presupposition this way: Calling the missing premise an *assumption* interprets it as a position that is likely held but not stated by the arguer, whereas to call it a *presupposition* allows that the author of the argument may be unaware that this premise is required.

The indicator word *because* flags the second statement in this sentence as a premise and the first as the conclusion. In standard form we have:

Reconstruction 1 (partial)

(1) Anything that would put ordinary social drinkers in jail is a bad idea.

∴ A law that would reduce the blood alcohol limit for driving is a bad idea.

What is missing in this argument is the assumption that links the stated premise to the conclusion. As the argument is now written, it is assumed that a law that would reduce the blood alcohol limit for driving would put ordinary social drinkers in jail, an assumption that might well be doubted. This assumption is made explicit in the following version of the argument, which is easier to understand and to criticize.

Reconstruction 2 (implicit)

(1) Anything that would put ordinary social drinkers in jail is a bad idea.

(2) A law that would reduce the blood alcohol limit for driving would put ordinary social drinkers in jail.

∴ A law that would reduce the blood alcohol limit for driving is a bad idea.

Sometimes the missing premise is an assumption about the definition of a term in the argument. For example:

Example 3.5

Abortion involves intentionally taking the life of an innocent person, so abortion is murder.

What is missing here is a statement that characterizes *intentionally taking the life of an innocent person* as *murder.* Once this definitional assumption is made explicit, it is apparent that the conclusion follows from the premises. The implicit premise in itself is not very controversial, although the argument might provoke debate.[4] Indeed, if you have a choice in adding implicit elements to an argument reconstruction, *the more plausible, less questionable statements should be selected.* In the argument in Example 3.5, for instance, the conclusion would still follow if we added a premise stating that the taking of a human life constituted murder, irrespective of whether it was done intentionally or involved an innocent person. But in the context of the passage, which includes the words *intentionally* and *innocent,* such a reading would not be charitable.

Although the Principle of Charitable Interpretation enjoins us to add the most reasonable implicit premises or conclusions that can be plausibly attributed to the author, given what is stated in the passage, it need not be one that *we*

---

[4]The explicit premise would probably be the focus of concern because it is true only if we consider the fetus to be a full-fledged person. If we do not, then it is false to say that abortion involves taking the life of an innocent *person.*

believe is true. In fact, one of the advantages of reconstructing an argument is that we sometimes expose a hidden premise that is controversial, as in Example 3.6:

Example 3.6 *Stealing is wrong. Using a friend's car without asking is taking property without permission. So using a friend's car without asking is wrong.*

The implicit premise needed to reconstruct this passage can be stated: *Taking property without permission is (always) stealing.* This premise is, at best, doubtful. Special circumstances, such as an emergency or the absence of any intention to keep the car, suggest that sometimes taking property without asking permission is not an act of stealing.

Reconstruction

(1) Stealing is wrong.

(2) Using a friend's car without asking is taking property without permission.

(implicit) *(3) Taking property without permission is stealing.*

∴ Using a friend's car without asking is wrong.

ADDING BOTH CONCLUSION AND PREMISES

There are also cases in which both the conclusion and some of the premises are missing. In such cases the best way to begin is to supply what appears to be the intended conclusion, and then to consider the premises needed as plausible assumptions to support it. In making this reconstruction, it is helpful to pay close attention to the context, as you can see in the following example:

Example 3.7 *Those who fear the future have misled us. If Americans will mobilize the forces that have made them great, then they will ultimately weather the problem of global economic competitiveness and develop effective new products and manufacturing techniques to meet the challenge.*

The editorial comment *those who fear the future have misled us* indicates that the author would assert a conclusion that is not one of fear. The second clause of the next sentence—*they will ultimately weather the problem of global economic competitiveness*—offers hope, suggesting that this is the author's intended conclusion. This first step in reconstruction yields:

Reconstruction 1

(1) If Americans will mobilize the forces that have made them great, then they will ultimately weather the problem of global economic competitiveness and develop effective new products and manufacturing techniques to meet the challenge.

(implicit) *∴ Americans will ultimately weather the problem of global economic competitiveness and develop effective new products and manufacturing techniques to meet the challenge.*

What is left unstated in this formulation is the assumption that Americans will indeed mobilize the forces that have made them great. The Principle of Charitable Interpretation directs us to understand the argument in this more fully developed way.

Reconstruction 2

(1) *If Americans will mobilize the forces that have made them great, then they will ultimately weather the problem of global economic competitiveness and develop effective new products and manufacturing techniques to meet the challenge.*

(implicit) (2) *Americans will mobilize the forces that have made them great.*

(implicit) ∴ *Americans will ultimately weather the problem of global economic competitiveness and develop effective new products and manufacturing techniques to meet the challenge.*

The implicit premise—Premise 2—is the most controversial part of the argument. Only when it is made explicit can we criticize the contention effectively.

Guidelines and Warnings about Adding Implicit Premises and Conclusions

Our discussion of the Principle of Charitable Interpretation in Chapter 2 suggests guidelines for reconstructing arguments with missing elements. The following general rules apply when there is no *explicit* evidence to the contrary.[5]

Guidelines for Reconstruction

Within the limits of faithfulness to the text, the reconstructed argument should:

1. Arrive at a conclusion that follows from the premises.
2. Avoid false or highly questionable premises.
3. Include all premises that are explicitly stated or strongly suggested. (These often need to be paraphrased in ways that make the entire argument fit into a pattern.)
4. Include implicit premises that bring out underlying assumptions or presuppositions in a way that promotes critical discussion.

We followed these guidelines in our reconstructions in the previous sections, but our comments relied on a general understanding of the passages and a feel for the structure of arguments. To follow all the guidelines at once,

[5]Often, in "real-life" passages that contain arguments, much of the material serves other purposes than directly presenting the argument. Not every sentence corresponds to a premise or a conclusion; indeed, most do not. Hence, a good reconstruction *excludes all irrelevant material.* Nevertheless, some of the material—such as illustrations or even the title—can give us useful hints about the missing premise or conclusion.

you must balance content and structure. An argument must be complete, but a statement or assumption cannot be included as part of the argument if it isn't connected to the other premises in such a way that leads to the conclusion. Achieving this balance is, to some extent, an art. It requires practice. We try to avoid obviously false or highly questionable premises, but sometimes this can't be avoided if the conclusion is to follow. Sometimes our insights into arguments fail us initially, particularly when passages are complicated. Fortunately, there is a more mechanical process that can help in some cases. It takes advantage of the search for structure we described in Chapter 2.

To apply guideline 1, a useful first step is to determine the structure of the argument as best we can. If we can see the argument as an instance of a successful argument pattern, we can get a better picture of what is needed to make the conclusion follow from the premises. Suppose we read the following selection from an essay in a magazine:

Example 3.8

Television programming has become segregated: There are separate programs for and about blacks, whites, and Hispanics, with little overlap. The NAACP blames the networks for this situation, but the fault lies more with us than with the studios. Programming decisions are based on viewing habits and marketing. If segregated television continues to be aired, then we the public are choosing to watch it.[6]

In this passage, the *if–then* structure of the last sentence can be recognized as occurring in some of the argument patterns discussed in Chapter 2. But this sentence ("If segregated television continues to be aired, then we the public are choosing to watch it.") needs to be connected with the rest of the passage. The first sentence suggests that the author would assert the "if " part of the *if–then* sentence to be true. The claim that although the NAACP blames segregated television on the studios, "the fault lies more with us than with the studios" suggests that the passage is presenting reasons why we, the public, deserve most of the blame for segregated television. If we put these elements together, we have the partial reconstruction:

Reconstruction (partial)

(1) Segregated television continues to be aired.

(2) If segregated television continues to be aired, then the public is choosing to watch it.

∴ The public deserves most of the blame for segregated television.

This reconstruction has the structure

(1) A.

(2) If A, then B.

∴ C.

[6]Adapted from Tamar Jacoby, "Adjust Your Sets," *The New Republic*, January 24, 2000.

which we can recognize as needing the additional premise *If B, then C* to complete the pattern of the chain argument.

(1) A.

(2) If A, then B.

(3) If B, then C.

∴ C.

This allows us to complete the reconstruction of the argument.

Full Reconstruction

(1) Segregated television continues to be aired.

(2) If segregated television continues to be aired, then the public is choosing to watch it.

(3) If the public is choosing to watch it, then the public deserves most of the blame for segregated television.

∴ The public deserves most of the blame for segregated television.

These steps in using patterns to help reconstruct arguments are summarized in the procedural steps presented in the box below. These procedures are a supplement to the *Guidelines for Reconstruction* on page 51. They call for stating the premises and the conclusion of an argument in such a way that makes the conclusion follow from the premises, and these procedures provide help in doing this. This recommendation provides only general criteria for evaluating alternative reconstructions. It cannot be followed blindly. For some arguments or argument fragments, there is no way *faithful to the text* that allows us to reconstruct them so that the conclusion follows from the premises.

Procedure for Making an Argument fit a Pattern

1. Look for structuring words or word pairs like *if . . . then, either . . . or, not, all,* or *every;* look as well for statements or parts of statements that are repeated.
2. Write out the partial pattern for the portion of the argument that is stated.
3. Determine what the complete pattern should be.
4. From the part of the pattern that is missing, determine what statements are missing. It is often useful to paraphrase the more explicit parts of the argument in order to make it and any implicit parts all fit into a pattern.

Notice that there is an *overly easy* way of adding a premise to complete any argument. It should be used only as a last resort. Let's use the following example of a partially reconstructed argument:

Example 3.9

(1) No one who wants fame can be trusted.

(2) Edward is a journalist.

∴ Edward can't be trusted.

It is always possible to write an *if–then* premise that connects the premises already stated with the conclusion. Using this procedure, we can complete Example 3.9 in this manner:

Easy Way of Completing Example 3.9 (implicit)

(1) No one who wants fame can be trusted.

(2) Edward is a journalist.

(3) If no one who wants fame can be trusted and Edward is a journalist, then Edward can't be trusted.

∴ Edward can't be trusted.

Using the easy way, we have made Premises 1 and 2 into the "if " part of our added premise, and the conclusion into the "then" part. However, there is an alternative way of completing Example 3.9 that adheres more closely to guideline 4 from the list on page 51.

Preferred Way of Completing Example 3.9 (implicit)

(1) No one who wants fame can be trusted.

(2) Edward is a journalist.

(3) All journalists want fame.

∴ Edward can't be trusted.

This latter formulation is better because it states more specifically what is presupposed in the argument presented in Example 3.9. If you were to criticize the argument, the preferred reconstruction would direct you to scrutinize the claim that all journalists want fame. With the easy *if–then* reconstruction, you can see only that the argument presupposes some connection between the stated premises and the conclusion, but it is not clear what this connection is. You can just as easily question whether the conclusion of the argument follows from the premises as you can whether the implicit *if–then* premise is true. For this reason, the "easy" reconstruction violates guideline 4 because it does *not* bring out underlying presuppositions in a way that promotes critical discussion.

Picking out an *interesting, not overly easy,* implicit premise was relatively straightforward for the partially reconstructed argument in Example 3.9. But deciding what implicit premise to add in reconstruction in less stylized contexts can be a greater problem. If Example 3.9 were an argument embedded in a passage that focused on TV news becoming more like sensationalist "tabloid" journalism, we might have added this to Premise 2 and modified the implicit Premise 3 to take this into account:

(modified) *(2′) Edward is a "tabloid" journalist.*

(implicit) *(3′) All "tabloid" journalists want fame.*

Alternatively, if the argument were embedded in a context that discussed the cutthroat competition in the market in which Edward worked, then another version of the implicit premises would be appropriate:

(modified) *(2″) Edward is a journalist in a cutthroat market.*

(implicit) *(3″) All journalists in a cutthroat market want fame.*

Notice that implicit Premise 3 makes the boldest claim. It applies to "all journalists." The other two—3′ and 3″—make less-bold statements about all journalists of a certain type or journalists working in a certain kind of market. These qualifications might make one version of a prospective implicit premise more defensible than another. If, however, the passage gives no hint about such a more qualified version, then you are not required by the guidelines to supply it. At a certain point, the burden of clearly stating the argument falls on its author.

There is *no simple formula* for selecting which version of an implicit premise to include. Sometimes elements of the passage will suggest which version is more appropriate. Other times you will need to rely on the Principle of Charitable Interpretation and pick the version that seems most acceptable from among those that can be plausibly attributed to the author.

EXERCISE 3.1

Recognizing Argument Patterns and Adding Implicit Premises, Conclusions, or Both

This exercise should help prepare you to identify premises and conclusions that are left unstated. It will give you practice in learning to apply the procedure for making an argument fit a pattern (p. 53) as well as the Guidelines for Reconstruction (p. 51). When it is not immediately obvious what premise or conclusion has been left unstated, identifying the pattern of the argument can be helpful.

Part A below asks you to fill in the blanks and indicate the pattern for a series of incomplete arguments such as this one:

Sample:

Suppose you are trying to identify the missing premise in this argument:

(1) If Dan lied, then he kept the money for himself.

(2) [ ].

∴ Dan didn't lie.

As indicated in the box on page 53, to identify the pattern of an argument, look for words or word pairs like *if . . . then, either . . . or,* or *not,* and look for statements or parts of statements that are repeated in the argument. If we substitute *A* for *Dan lied* and *B* for *he [Dan] kept the money for himself,* we can represent the argument with the following "partial" pattern:

(1) If A, then B.

(2) [ ].

∴ Not A.

Now compare this partial pattern to the list of complete patterns in Chapter 2. Our partial pattern is a fragment of the following complete pattern:

(1) If A, then B.

(2) Not B.

∴ Not A.

The implicit premise, then, is *Not B.* To put this into an English sentence, you have to find what *B* stands for in Premise 1 and then deny that sentence. In this case, Premise 2 is *Dan did not keep the money for himself.* You could insert this in the sample above.

Write patterns here.

Go through steps 1–4 in the Procedure for Making an Argument Fit a Pattern (see the box on p. 53) for the following problems. We have helped you by filling in key words in some of the missing premises and conclusions.

A 1. (1) *If the Netwizard desktop computer runs VideoMaker software, then it can meet my computing needs.*

(2) [ ].

∴ The Netwizard desktop computer can meet my computing needs.

2. (1) *Either [ ]*
or I should buy the Hacker laptop.
(2) *I shouldn't buy the Netwizard desktop computer.*

∴ *I should buy the Hacker laptop.*

3. (1) *If the Hacker laptop does not run VideoMaker software, then I can't create DVDs and video for the web.*
(2) *If [ ],*
then [ ].

∴ *If the Hacker laptop does not run VideoMaker, then it doesn't meet my needs.*

4. (1) *If David can afford a new 60-inch high-definition plasma TV,*
then [ ].
(2) *David can't afford to pay off his credit card debts.*

∴ *David can't afford a new 60-inch high-definition plasma TV.*

5. (1) *Either [ ] or [ ].*
(2) *I shouldn't buy a Econoplasma high-definition TV.*

∴ *I should buy a Primeoview high-definition TV.*

6. (1) *If the Hacker laptop has only 3 Gigs of RAM,*
then [ ].
(2) *If it can't run VideoMaster software, then I shouldn't buy it.*
(3) *[ ].*

∴ *I shouldn't buy it.*

7.[7] (1) *All Primeoview high-definition plasma TVs are products guaranteed for three years.*
(2) *All [ ] are [ ].*

∴ *All Primeoview high-definition plasma TVs are products that give you a lot of protection against faulty engineering and workmanship.*

---

[7]Fill the slots in Exercises 7 and 8 with words that apply to classes of objects (for example, "high-definition plasma TVs") or that designate a particular object belonging to a class (for example, "my new 60-inch high-definition plasma TV"). Do not insert a complete sentence into the slots for these exercises.

8. *(1) Any addition to my TV entertainment system is an extravagance.*

(2) [ ] is [ ].

∴ A new 60-inch high-definition plasma TV is an extravagance.

The following exhibit more complicated patterns, not listed in Chapter 2. Can you figure out the patterns they exhibit?

9. *(1) If the Netwizard desktop computer can run VideoMaster software, and it is cheaper than the Hacker laptop, then I should buy it.*

(2) [ ].

(3) [ ].

∴ I should buy the Netwizard desktop computer.

10. *(1) Either I'll spend my tax refund on a new 60-inch high-definition plasma TV, or I'll repair my car (but not both).*

(2) If I do not repair my car, then I risk a serious accident.

(3) [ ].

∴ I won't spend my tax refund on a new 60-inch high-definition plasma TV.

11. *(1) Either I should buy more books or a smartphone.*

(2) If this money was given to me for my education, then I should not buy a smartphone.

(3) [ ].

∴ I should buy more books.

B. Put the following arguments into standard form. Add implicit premises and conclusions. Leave out any editorial comments. For problems 1–11, indicate the argument pattern, using letters to represent repeated elements.

1. You promised to be here at 8:00. If you promised to be here at 8:00, then you should have arrived at 8:00.
2. I should either study more or prepare to accept failure. I should study more.
3. If you tell lies frequently, then you must remember not only what you have done but also what you said you have done. Therefore, if you tell lies frequently, your memory becomes burdened.

4. Harold should be sensitive to other people because any teacher should be sensitive to other people.
5. American universities are eroding their public support. Any social institution that spends beyond the willingness of the public to pay is eroding its public support.
6. If being affectionate were the only important virtue, then Maurice would be a saint. So being affectionate is obviously not the only important virtue.
7. We will face substantial energy shortages by the year 2020 because there are not enough alternative fuel facilities under construction. *(Note:* Sometimes there is no alternative to adding the easy linking premise: *"If Premise 1, then conclusion.")*
8. Many baby boomers are reaching retirement age. But if that is so, then many new, younger workers will be hired. It follows that, before long, businesses will become more energetic.
9. Every successful politician has to compromise his principles occasionally. Everyone who has to compromise his principles occasionally loses integrity.
10. The number of unmarried adults in the United States is continuing to increase. If there is an increase in people unsupported by close personal bonds, there will be an increase in alcoholism and suicide. So there will be an increase in alcoholism and suicide.
11. The current generation in their 20s has a chance at avoiding impoverishment if the baby boom generation and those over sixty limit the deficit. If the older generation really accepts its responsibility for the future, it will limit the deficit. The generation in power is now beginning to realize its obligation to posterity, so the conclusion is clear.

Passages 12–17 do not fit into the common patterns of argument we have considered previously. Reconstruct them in standard form.

12. The higher the interest rates, the better the bank. The interest rates at CASH National Bank are the highest in town.
13. Apparently you don't take mood-altering prescription drugs since everyone who takes mood-altering prescription drugs is happy.
14. Either I should spend my tax refund on paying off my debts or I should buy books for this term. But if I don't buy books, I'll risk failing my courses. So I shouldn't spend the refund on paying off my debts.
15. It looks like Bruce will get a promotion. Alice has a great new job in Minneapolis. If so, she'll be moving, and that will create an opening for either Bruce or Frank.
16. Every human action is determined by laws of nature. But for a person to deserve praise or blame, it is necessary for the person to have been able to act differently than he or she in fact did act. So no person deserves praise or blame.

17. The industrialized nations will resolve the environmental crises that are looming in the near future if these nations mobilize all the technological resources at their disposal. If political incentives are sufficiently high, then the mobilization of resources will occur. Public awareness about global warming, greenhouse gases, and oil spills is growing rapidly. If so, political incentives are sufficiently high. The conclusion is clear.

In the following passages much of what is stated is either not part of the argument or must be restated to make the structure of the argument clear. There may be more than one acceptable reconstruction.

18. As we all know, the American public is reluctant to try any new approach to education that might erode support for public schools. But the problems of education in inner cities have become so critical that there is little to lose. Either we give the voucher system and charter schools a fair trial, or we abandon the potential of the children of inner cities to become educated.
19. If a bad social environment causes people to become criminals, then everyone from a bad social environment would be a criminal. But for every criminal who comes from a bad social environment, there are thousands who hold jobs.
20. We have before us the question of rights for gays and lesbians—a question which I hope disturbs you as much as it does me. My friends, I am as much concerned about other people as anyone. But I am opposed to these so-called rights. The reason is that if the United States passed rights for gays and lesbians, then the United States would support what is unnatural. But the United States should never support what is unnatural.

C. Use the Guidelines for Reconstruction to determine which, if any, of the reconstructions provided are adequate for the passages given. Indicate why you reject the reconstructions you do. If you find all of them faulty, supply one yourself.

1. Either we should permanently cut taxes, or we should use this opportunity to preserve Social Security and Medicare. If we cut taxes now, we will be unable to fund these programs when the need inevitably arises. The conclusion is clear.

Reconstructions

a. *(1) Either we should permanently cut taxes, or we should use this opportunity to preserve Social Security and Medicare.*

(2) We shouldn't preserve Social Security and Medicare.

∴ *We should permanently cut taxes.*

b. (1) *Either we should permanently cut taxes, or we should use this opportunity to preserve Social Security and Medicare.*

(2) *If we permanently cut taxes now, we will be unable to fund Social Security and Medicare when the need inevitably arises.*

(3) *We should not be unable to fund Social Security and Medicare when the need inevitably arises.*

∴ *We should use this opportunity to preserve Social Security and Medicare.*

c. (1) *We should preserve Social Security and Medicare.*

(2) *We have an obligation to those who paid into Social Security, and it would be inhumane to leave our citizens without Medicare.*

∴ *We shouldn't permanently cut taxes.*

2. I don't care what you say: If it's wrong to discriminate against a woman on the basis of her gender, then it is equally wrong to discriminate against a man on the basis of his. Permitting combat roles in the military for men only is unjust.

Reconstructions

a. (1) *If gender discrimination is wrong, then combat roles for men only are unjust.*

(2) *Combat roles for men only are unjust.*

∴ *Gender discrimination is wrong.*

b. (1) *If it is wrong to discriminate against a woman on the basis of her gender, then it is equally wrong to discriminate against a man on the basis of his.*

(2) *Combat roles for men only discriminate against a man on the basis of his gender.*

∴ *Combat roles for men only are unjust.*

c. (1) *If gender discrimination against women is wrong, then it is unjust to discriminate against a man on the basis of his gender.*

(2) *Gender discrimination against women is wrong.*

∴ *Combat roles for men only are unjust.*

3. Since Mervin has devoted himself to becoming a famous journalist, you should be careful what you tell him.

Reconstructions

a. (1) *If Mervin has devoted himself to becoming a famous journalist, you should be careful what you tell him.*

(2) *Mervin has devoted himself to becoming a famous journalist.*

∴ *You should be careful what you tell Mervin.*

b. (1) *If Mervin has devoted himself to becoming a famous journalist, all people should be careful what they tell him.*

(2) *Mervin has devoted himself to becoming a famous journalist.*

∴ *All people should be careful what they tell Mervin.*

c. (1) *Everyone should be careful what they tell anybody who wants to become a famous journalist.*

(2) *Mervin has devoted himself to becoming a famous journalist.*

∴ *Everyone should be careful what they tell Mervin.*

4. An early-stage fetus doesn't have the capacity for sentience and cognition that would qualify it as a human person. It follows that abortion at an early stage of pregnancy can sometimes be justified.

a. (1) *An early-stage fetus doesn't have the capacity for sentience and cognition that would qualify it as a human person.*

(2) *If an early-stage fetus doesn't have the capacity for sentience and cognition that would qualify it as a human person, then abortion at an early stage of pregnancy can sometimes be justified.*

∴ *Abortion at an early stage of pregnancy can sometimes be justified.*

b. (1) *Abortion at an early stage of pregnancy can sometimes be justified.*

(2) *If abortion at an early stage of pregnancy can sometimes be justified, then an early-stage fetus doesn't have the capacity for sentience and cognition that would qualify it as a human person.*

∴ *An early-stage fetus doesn't have the capacity for sentience and cognition that would qualify it as a human person.*

c. (1) *An early-stage fetus lacks the capacity for sentience and cognition that would qualify it as a human person.*

(2) *Ending the life of something that doesn't qualify as a human person can sometimes be justified.*

(3) *If an early-stage fetus lacks the capacity for sentience and cognition that would qualify it as a human person, and ending the life of something that doesn't qualify it as a human person can sometimes be justified, then abortion at an early stage of pregnancy can sometimes be justified.*

∴ *Abortion at an early stage of pregnancy can often be justified.*

MOVING TO REAL-WORLD DISCOURSE

In real-world prose passages that contain arguments, it is often surprisingly difficult to determine exactly what claim an author is trying to make and how that claim is supported. We briefly alluded to this problem in Chapter 2. You might find it difficult, for instance, to identify the conclusion in the midst of all the other statements in a passage. Furthermore, the distinction between explicit and implicit premises and conclusions is not always sharp. A premise or conclusion can be strongly suggested but not stated precisely. You will seldom be able to copy a series of sentences from a passage and say, "These are the premises and the conclusion." More often than not, it is necessary to paraphrase statements in a way that clarifies their meaning and also makes the structure of the whole argument apparent.

To that end, we propose a method of successive approximation that is aimed at interpreting arguments that occur in prose passages. The method involves first formulating a simplified rough approximation of the argument. This first approximation will often oversimplify what was intended, but it provides a foundation for developing a more detailed second approximation that represent the premises and conclusion more accurately while still retaining a structure of argument such that the conclusion follows from the premises.

Consider the excerpt from a newspaper op-ed piece entitled "Job Programs and Other Bromides," which appears on the next page.

We should begin by surveying the passage as a whole and noting the context. The passage comments on different government approaches to combating poverty that had been attempted in the years preceding the publication of this piece. The title, in referring to job programs and other programs as "bromides," suggests that such programs are ineffective. The passage itself expresses criticisms of government anti-poverty programs that have been offered either by the political left ("Great Society" programs) or the right ("Reagan era" programs). At the end of the passage, the author suggests a third alternative—a "more authoritative social policy in which the needy are told how to live."

Example 3.10

Urban social programs can produce results, often enough to justify their costs. But none has shown a large impact on poverty. None can emancipate poor individuals and families from the personal problems of early pregnancy, crime and social failure that shackle them. . . . Choice or privatization can often improve the effectiveness of programs, but "empowerment" as a basis for anti-poverty policy tends to presume exactly what is questionable—the poor can be competent managers of their own lives. If poor adults behaved rationally they would seldom be poor for long in the first place. Opportunity is more available than the will to seize it. . . . The effect of racial bias is mainly to limit the quality of jobs blacks can get, not to deny them employment. . . . Without a "smoking gun," America cannot cure poverty with traditional reformism of either the left or right. Merely to expand government spending on the poor, or to cut it back does not motivate the entrenched poor to take available jobs. That is why neither the Great Society nor the Reagan era succeeded in overcoming poverty. Instead the nation needs a more authoritative social policy in which the needy are told how to live instead of merely being subsidized.[8]

Simplifying and Paraphrasing

Rather than trying to fit all or most of the sentences of a passage such as this into the role of premise or conclusion, it is often better to begin by putting a simplified version of the argument into your own words in a way that captures the basic structure of the argument. The author lays out three alternatives for combating poverty: the approach of the political left, which he describes as "expanding government spending on the poor"; the approach of the political right, described as "choice or privatization"; and the author's own proposal, an approach in which the needy are told how to live. He eliminates the first two and advances the third. An argument structure that emerges from this view of the passage is an expanded version of the disjunctive argument pattern with three rather than two alternatives:

First Approximation

(1) Either A or B or C.

(2) Not A.

(3) Not B.

∴ C.

[8]Lawrence M. Mead. "Job Programs and Other Bromides", *New York Times* Op-Ed page, 19 May 1992, A 19. Reprinted with permission of the author.

Recognizing this, we can state the argument in a simplified, paraphrased form as follows:

(1) Either poverty should be combated by the programs of the liberals, by the programs of the conservatives, or by programs that tell the poor how to live.

(2) Poverty can't be combated by the programs of the liberals.

(3) Poverty can't be combated by the programs of the conservatives.

∴ Poverty can be cured by programs that tell the poor how to live.

In reviewing the passage itself and this first formulation of the argument contained in it, we can see that there is one main element that this approximation leaves out. The author doesn't simply reject the anti-poverty programs of liberals and conservatives out of hand. He gives a reason that they fail, which is put in various ways: that urban social programs can't free the poor from "personal problems of early pregnancy, crime and social failure"; that the empowerment programs of the right presume incorrectly that poor people can manage their own lives; that spending money on the poor doesn't motivate them to take available jobs. It is this element of changing the way the poor manage their lives that his own alternative is intended to address, and which he sees the other two alternatives as leaving out. Furthermore, we could convey more explicitly the two alternatives that are being rejected rather than simply referring to them as programs of liberals and conservatives. The passage is not very helpful in characterizing the programs of the left, but it does characterize them as expanding spending on the poor. The references to choice, privatization, and jobs, in connection with programs proposed by the right, suggest that these are programs that encourage the poor to enter jobs and businesses.

We can address these shortcomings in a second approximation of the argument.

Second Approximation

(1) Either poverty should be combated by programs that expand spending on the poor, by programs that encourage the poor to enter jobs and businesses, or by programs that tell the poor how to live.

(2) The poor cannot manage their own lives.

(3) If the poor can't manage their own lives, then poverty can't be combated by expanding spending on the poor.

(4) If the poor can't manage their own lives, then poverty can't be combated by encouraging the poor to enter jobs and businesses.

∴ Poverty should be combated by programs that tell the poor how to live.

If we studied the entire op-ed piece from which this passage is excerpted, we might be able to make further refinements in our reconstruction of this argument.

Finding an Argument in a Sea of Words

When we are faced with a passage that contains much nonargument prose, a strategy that often works is to determine first what the conclusion is, either by locating a statement that expresses the main claim that is supported by the passage or by putting this claim in your own words. Next, find some statement or statements that seem to support the conclusion most directly (this might require some paraphrasing), and then add whatever implicit premises are necessary. As you do this, keep the argument patterns in mind.

We can apply this method to the following passage:

Example 3.11

Well, I insist—and I here follow von Hildebrand—that we parents, we married people, in no way believe sex is dirty, but we believe it is private and intimate. Therefore, it cannot endure being publicized the way mathematics or even the way health is publicized. It is quite tactful for you to go to a party and talk about your tonsils. It is not tactful—not acceptable—for you to go to a party and talk about how your wife makes love to you, not because you think it is dirty, my friends, but because you think it is intimate.[9]

We can paraphrase what is essential here in a much simpler way:

Conclusion

Sex should not be publicized.

Now we need to look through the passage to see what is offered as direct support for this conclusion. It is crucial to avoid simply listing all the sentences in the passage as though they were premises. Boil the passage down until it can be fit into a structured argument such as those represented by the patterns in Chapters 2 and 4. In the first two lines, the author claims that she does not believe that sex is dirty. We can ignore this material for the purpose of reconstructing the argument, since we want to locate what she *does* believe in support of her conclusion. The second line presents a likely candidate, which we can write as a premise: *It (sex) is private and intimate*. So far, then, we have:

Partial Reconstruction of Example 3.11

(1) Sex is private and intimate.

∴ Sex should not be publicized.

Look at the remainder of the passage. It presents an example of something that may be publicized and claims again (in different words) that sex should not be publicized. None of this adds to the argument. What we need to get from the premise to the conclusion is a *general rule*. With a little thought you can see that the premise the passage leaves implicit is: Whatever is private and intimate should not be publicized. Adding this, we have this reconstruction.

---

[9]Quotation cited in Gloria Lentz, *Raping Our Children: The Sex Education Scandal* (New Rochelle, NY: Arlington House, 1972), 76.

Full Reconstruction of Example 3.11 (implicit)

(1) Sex is private and intimate.

(2) Whatever is private and intimate should not be publicized.

∴ Sex should not be publicized.

This reconstruction is a fair approximation that fits an argument pattern and captures the main reasoning of the passage. Given the context of the argument, a more detailed reconstruction might take as the conclusion of the argument that sex education classes should not be taught in the public schools.

For the purpose of reconstructing arguments, first approximations need not be written out in full. You may find it easier to penetrate the prose if you mark up the passage to indicate the central concepts (this might also involve noting whether the same concept is presented in different words). You can eliminate excess by simply crossing out irrelevant elements. And you can focus on argument pattern by circling words that provide logical structure such as *if . . . then, either . . . or, not, all,* and any indicator words. You can label any stated premises and conclusions. We have done this for the following passage, which offers a view of contemporary American culture.

Example 3.12

American culture is undergoing a change that will significantly affect the U.S. economy. Anticipated energy shortages, a concern for the environment, and a general disgust with the excesses that led to the mortgage crisis have led to a cultural mindset that idealizes living well on a small scale. Lavish personal spending on clothing and cars is in many quarters ridiculed rather than admired.

Premise 1 suggested in several ways

The McMansion that was so recently and widely coveted is being passed over for the well-designed house of smaller scale. If (as is likely) this downsizing continues, then there are two possibilities for the U.S. economy. First, there might be stabilization at a lower level of activity and growth than in recent decades that were characterized by plentiful energy and near-boundless demand for personal goods. Either that or U.S. economic expansion will be driven not by the retail and housing sectors but by innovation in areas such as energy conservation and technology, as well as in participation in the economies of developing nations such as China and India. But considering the availability of investment capital and the likelihood of investment opportunities in these other areas, we can rule out the alternative of low-growth stabilization of the U.S. economy. We are led, therefore, to the second alternative.

Premise 2 as an if–then statement suggested

Consequent of Premise 2 suggested

Premise 3 suggested

Consequent of Premise 4 suggested

Conclusion indicated

Once the passage has been analyzed in this way, it is easier to write out a sketch of the argument. This sketch might use just sentence fragments to display the main links. It is important to keep these elements relatively simple in the first stage of reconstruction so that you can easily understand the general "drift" of the argument.

Example 3.13

ARGUMENT SKETCH OF THE PASSAGE ABOUT AMERICAN CULTURE

(1) Americans are downsizing.

(2) If downsizing, then either lower economic activity or expansion in areas other than retail and housing.

(3) Available capital and opportunities in other areas.

(4) If 3, then not low growth.

∴ Expansion in areas other than retail and housing

An argument sketch such as this might be seen as a preliminary step in the method of successive approximation. The next step would be a reconstruction of this version of the argument, using complete sentences, which could then be further refined.

The reconstructions of Examples 3.11 and 3.12 illustrate how passages often demand extensive paraphrase and interpretation. In reconstructing an argument, as in paraphrasing single sentences, we have two conditions to meet: (1) the reconstruction should capture the apparent meaning of the original and (2) the reconstruction should provide more clarity. For any given argument, these guidelines can be satisfied by a number of different acceptable reconstructions.

Reconstructing Arguments with Subordinate Conclusions

Many passages contain several interrelated arguments. A reconstruction of such a passage may be presented in two different ways: (1) as several distinct arguments or (2) as a composite, continuous argument in which some statements are both a subordinate (or intermediate) conclusion and a premise.

Example 3.14

(S1) A social policy that permits technological eavesdropping on the nation's own citizens without probable cause will inevitably lead to greater violations of the rights of the person. (S2) Such a consequence will undermine the mutual respect for the humanity of fellow citizens upon which democratic society is based. (S3) Any policy that destroys social bonds in this way threatens the society that engages in it. (S4) Hence a social policy permitting unwarranted eavesdropping on citizens threatens democratic society.

This passage can be reconstructed in two ways.

Reconstruction 1 (Two Separate Arguments)

FIRST ARGUMENT

(from S1) *(P1)* *A social policy permitting unwarranted technological eavesdropping on citizens will inevitably lead to greater violations of the rights of the person.*

(rewrite of S2)	*(P2)*	*A social policy that leads to greater violations of the rights of the person will undermine the mutual respect for the humanity of fellow citizens upon which democratic society is based.*
(implicit subordinate conclusion)	*(C1) ∴*	*A social policy permitting unwarranted technological eavesdropping on citizens will undermine the mutual respect for the humanity of fellow citizens upon which democratic society is based.*

SECOND ARGUMENT

Conclusion (C1 = from First Argument)	*(P3)*	*A social policy permitting unwarranted technological eavesdropping will undermine the mutual respect for the humanity of fellow citizens upon which democratic society is based.*
(rewrite of S3)	*(P4)*	*Any policy that undermines the mutual respect for the humanity of fellow citizens upon which democratic society is based threatens the democratic society that practices it.*
(rewrite of S4)	*(C2) ∴*	*A social policy permitting unwarranted technological eavesdropping on citizens will inevitably threaten the democratic society that practices it.*

Reconstruction 2 (as a Continuous Argument)

Subordinate Conclusion	*(P1)*	*A social policy permitting unwarranted technological eavesdropping on citizens will inevitably lead to greater violations of the rights of the person.*
	(P2)	*A social policy that leads to greater violations of the rights of the person will undermine the mutual respect for the humanity of fellow citizens upon which democratic society is based.*
	(P3)	*A social policy permitting unwarranted technological eavesdropping will undermine the mutual respect for the humanity of fellow citizens upon which democratic society is based.*
	(P4)	*Any policy that undermines the mutual respect for the humanity of fellow citizens upon which democratic society is based threatens the democratic society that practices it.*
Main Conclusion	*(C) ∴*	*A social policy permitting unwarranted eavesdropping on citizens will inevitably threaten the democratic society that practices it.*

Whenever we strive to simplify or rewrite what someone else has produced, we run the risk of distorting what that writer said. The method of first approximation is a crude instrument designed to make rough cuts. Once we have discovered the basic structure, we can go back and paraphrase the argument more sensitively, thus capturing some of the subtleties we might have previously ignored. It is too easy for us to be lost in a sea of words when we face a complex passage. Simplification, paraphrase, and argument sketches are ways of finding our way through it.

EXERCISE 3.2

Putting All This into Practice

A. Reconstruct the arguments contained in the following passages. Simplify or paraphrase whenever possible. Add implicit conclusions or premises, or both, as needed. Most of the arguments can be reconstructed in several different ways.

1. We can't restore democracy to Haiti. We can't restore democracy when it never existed.[10]
2. I recognize, as do Roman Catholics generally, the great potential for human therapeutics in stem cell research. I do not oppose stem cell research per se if the cells are obtained from sources such as adult humans, miscarriages, or placental blood. What is morally unsustainable is the harvesting of stem cells by either of two currently proposed methods: (1) the creation and destruction of human embryos at the blastocyst stage by removal of the inner cell mass or (2) the harvesting of primordial germ cells from aborted fetuses. Both cases involve complicity in the direct interruption of a human life, which Roman Catholics believe has a moral claim to protection from the first moments of conception. In both cases, a living member of the human species is intentionally terminated.[11]
3. Well, I insist—and I here follow von Hildebrand—that we parents, we married people, in no way believe sex is dirty, but we believe it is private and intimate. Therefore, it cannot endure being publicized the way mathematics or even the way health is publicized. It is quite tactful for you to go to a party and talk about your tonsils. It is not tactful—not acceptable—for you to go to a party and talk about how your wife makes love to you, not because you think it is dirty, my friends, but because you think it is intimate.[12] **(Go beyond the analysis given in the text. Treat this as an argument against sex education classes in the schools.)**

---

[10]CBS Sunday Evening News, July 17, 1994.

[11]From Testimony of Edmund D. Pellegrino, M.D., before the National Bioethics Advisory Commission, published in *Ethical Issues in Human Stem Cell Research, Vol. III, Religious Perspectives,* Rockville, MD: June 2000.

[12]Cited in Gloria Lentz, *Raping Our Children: The Sex Education Scandal* (New Rochelle, NY: Arlington House, 1972), 76.

4. There is a continuity of development from the moment of conception on. There are constant changes in the foetal condition; the foetus is constantly acquiring new structures and characteristics, but there is no one stage which is radically different from any other. Since that is so, there is no one stage in the process of foetal development, after the moment of conception, which could plausibly be picked out as the moment at which the foetus becomes a living human being. The moment of conception is, however, different in this respect. It marks the beginning of this continuous process of development and introduces something new which is radically discontinuous with what has come before it. Therefore, the moment of conception, and only it, is a plausible candidate for being that moment at which the foetus becomes a living human being.[13] **(Hint: Try using the implicit premise that either the fetus becomes human at the moment of conception or it becomes human at some moment thereafter.)**
5. African-Americans have been subject to centuries of racism. Today, some blame the victims for the problems of our country. Don't they know that most African-Americans are hardworking, good citizens? . . . That important parts of American culture—from music to language to literature to fashion—have been created by African-Americans. I insist: All collective judgments are wrong. Only racists make them. And racism is stupid, just as it is ugly. Its aim is to destroy, to pervert, to distort innocence in human beings and their quest for human equality.[14]
6. A. L. T. Allen has been thinking about inner-city crime and violence and family deterioration. She's read the politicians, the sociologists and the pundits. And she thinks everybody has it wrong. ". . . The emphasis has been on the African-American male"—as the missing father and as the perpetrator and victim of violence. Says Allen: "It occurs to me that perhaps we are focusing on the wrong group. Our efforts should be aimed at reaching not the males, but the females. . . As long as women tolerate this behavior in men, it will continue. As long as women continue to have relationships with, and continue to bear the children of, men who do not marry them, men will continue to be absent fathers.[15]
7. If reporters want to get at the truth, they cannot continue to act as if only one side in this debate [over passive smoking] has an ax to grind. They need to be just as skeptical about the EPA and the Coalition on

---

[13]Baruch Brody, "On the Humanity of the Foetus," *Abortion: Pro and Con*, ed. Robert Perkins (Cambridge, MA: Shenkman, 1974), 70–71.

[14]Elie Wiesel, "Have You Learned the Most Important Lesson of All?" *Parade Magazine*, May 24, 1992, 5. Elie Wiesel is a Nobel Peace Prize recipient.

[15]William Raspberry, "Hope for a Decent Society May Lie with Young Women," *The Oregonian*, November 30, 1993, B5. William Raspberry is a syndicated columnist for the *Washington Post*.

Smoking or Health as they are about Philip Morris. . . . Writing in *Toxicologic Pathology,* Yale epidemiologist Alvan Feinstein cautioned his fellow scientists against automatically believing everything the "good guys" say and rejecting everything the "bad guys" say. His message applies to journalists as well as scientists: "If public health and epidemiology want to avoid becoming a branch of politics rather than science, the key issues are methods and process, not the 'goodness' of the goals or investigators. In science more than law, the 'bad guy' . . . should always have the right to state his case, and a well stated case has the right to be heard, regardless of who pays for it."[16]

8. So how should we react when the Philip Morris and R. J. Reynolds tobacco companies embark on an advertising campaign to convince us that secondhand smoke is harmless? . . . Who's telling the truth? Put the question to a simple test: who benefits and how? The tobacco giants have demonstrated that their paramount interest is protecting their $45 billion industry, and that the addiction, disease and premature death caused by cigarettes are not factors that concern them.[17]
9. Books and magazines that use a vocabulary that deludes women into thinking themselves rebels and outlaws, on the cusp of some new freedom, misperceive our basic situation. A defect in the early thinking of the women's movement was a tendency to liberate women not for life but for life in the counterculture; when that life was over, many women found themselves in limbo. . . . If we wish to be firm-voiced and progressive about meeting our primary needs, we should not point our heads in the direction of the wrong revolution. Vague definitions such as sister, rebel and outlaw may be handy for magazines in search of a vast circulation, but are of no use to thinking adults. Sexual liberation without economic security grants women merely the right to stay marginal. Women must cease being conned into substituting fantasy sexual revolutions for political pressure or real reforms that would give us true equality.[18]
10. The trouble with health care in America, says Muriel Gillick, a geriatrics expert at Harvard Medical School, is that people want to believe that "there is always a fix." She argues that the way Medicare is organized encourages too many interventions toward the end of life that may extend the patient's lifespan only slightly, if at all, and can cause

---

[16]Jacob Sullum, "Passive Reporting on Passive Smoke," *Forbes MediaCritic*. From the last of a four-part series of advertisements titled "How to Spot Flaws in Secondhand Smoke Stories."
[17]Gerald Alfers, *Olympian* (Olympia, WA), July 18, 1994, A7. Gerald Alfers is a board member and former president of the American Lung Association of Washington. His column was in response to the advertisement from which the previous passage was taken.
[18]Barbara Probst Solomon, "This Take-a-Lover Chatter Overlooks the Bottom Line," *International Herald Tribune*, July 10, 1992, 7.

unnecessary suffering. It would often be better, she thinks, not to try so hard to eke out a few more hours or weeks but to concentrate on quality of life.[19]

B. The following selections each contain arguments. Use the techniques of reconstruction discussed in this chapter to reconstruct one or two of the more important and interesting ones.

1. *Lecture Fragment*

Lecture Fragment on Plea Bargaining

Plea bargaining (agreeing to plead guilty in exchange for a reduced sentence) generates problems. Innocent defendants who can't afford bail may plead guilty just to avoid jail time waiting for trial. The process makes no presumption of innocence. Guilt is not determined in an adversarial process, it is negotiated. It makes work easier for prosecutors, defense attorneys, and judges, but it sometimes results in dangerous offenders receiving less jail time than they otherwise would. {first argument}

Given these problems, some have suggested that plea bargaining be eliminated. But this might create an even worse problem. Ninety percent of defendants plead guilty, and most of those do plea-bargain. Suppose plea bargaining were eliminated and the percentage of guilty pleas dropped to 80 percent. This would double the number of criminal trials, placing a staggering burden on the criminal justice system. The practice of plea bargaining should be continued if eliminating it might have this disastrous result. {second argument}

The experience of Alaska, however, calls this fear into question. Alaska has virtually done away with plea bargaining. There was some increase in the number of trials, but not as much as expected. In the year before elimination of plea bargaining, there were seventy-two felony trials in Fairbanks. In the year after, there were ninety. This is only a 25 percent increase.

Why was the increase so small? The explanation of why defendants plead guilty could be because most of them are factually guilty, and they don't have a viable legal argument for their defense (i.e., they are legally guilty as well); so they believe it is unlikely that they would win in a trial. If this is the case, then, as Alaska's experience indicates, while it may be difficult to eliminate plea bargaining, it is not impossible.

(Note: There are several arguments in this lecture fragment. After formulating your reconstructions, compare them to those made on page 10. Remember that the reconstruction of arguments from longer passages allows for some degree of individual interpretation.)

[19] "A world of Methuselahs: The benefits, and the costs, of living longer," *The Economists*, June 27–July 3, 2009, 9.

2.

Reply to "License users of guns, just like drivers of cars" Opposing view: Only the law-abiding will submit to such restrictions, thereby making crime easier.[20]

By Andre Marrou, 1992 Libertarian Party presidential nominee

If anti-gun laws worked, then New York and Washington, with the toughest anti-gun laws, would have the lowest crime rates. But they have the *highest*.

Conversely, crime rates plummeted up to 90% after certain cities and states—like Orlando, Fla., and Kennesaw, Ga.—allowed law-abiding citizens to carry concealed handguns.

The reason should be obvious: law-abiding citizens know and obey the law. Criminals don't care what the law is and won't obey it. So who benefits when gun ownership and use are restricted? The criminals, because decent folks are disarmed by the law, making it easier for criminals to prey upon them.

Registering guns and licensing gun owners won't reduce crime any more than registering cars and licensing drivers now reduces traffic accidents—which is to say, hardly at all. With millions of highly restrictive laws, still about 44,000 Americans yearly die in traffic accidents while about 15,000 are shot to death. Since there are fewer cars than guns, cars are clearly more dangerous than guns. Should we outlaw cars?

Like cars, guns are dangerous tools. So are kitchen knives (ask John Bobbitt) and chain saws; should we register or outlaw them, or license their use? Just because something is dangerous—say climbing mountains or riding bulls—doesn't mean we should restrict its use or test and license its practitioners.

Guns are tools, not evil instruments capable of their own malevolence. A gun simply amplifies its user's power. In a rapist's hands, a gun is bad; in a law-abiding woman's hand, it's good. New York and Washington have proved that guns cannot be kept from criminal hands; shouldn't we let decent people arm themselves without licensing?

Ultimately, "gun control" is not about guns. It's about control. Beware.

---

[20]The January 1, 1994 issue of *USAToday* contained an editorial titled "License users of guns, just like drivers of cars," which presented the position of the editorial staff. It defended the position that "as a matter of public safety and accountability, the states should require that all gun users be licensed." The André Marrou selection above presents an opposing argument.

3.

The First Amendment Unworthily Used[21]

A lawyer for the Brooklyn Museum of Art misappropriated a revered American concept in a hearing stemming from the museum's controversial art exhibit.

The lawyer was protesting an order by New York City Mayor Rudolph Giuliani to deny the museum $7.2 million in city financing in retaliation for its showing of the exhibit, which included a portrait of the Virgin Mary partly composed of elephant feces and surrounded by pornographic cutouts. Catholic groups have called the portrait offensive.

Denial of the museum funds, the lawyer said, is a First Amendment catastrophe. He likened it to a book burning, the destruction of free expression. The First Amendment prohibits Congress from abridging the freedom of speech.

Certainly Giuliani's fund-withholding tactic leaves plenty of room for criticism. As has been said before in this space, the ideal relationship between the government and the arts is a hands-off policy, even if the government is paying part of the bill. Otherwise, the result is to have elected officials or bureaucrats deciding what is or isn't art, an assignment that they are rarely qualified to carry out.

Of course, the arts professionals to whom the responsibility is delegated also have a responsibility to exercise judgment. More than once in recent years, people in such a position have seemed to let their judgment be guided mostly by considerations of what would shock and offend—stuff that, as has been noted in some cases, would constitute a hate crime if it were smeared on the wall of a church or synagogue instead of being hung in a museum.

Giuliani is entitled to criticize the exhibit. But the directors of the museum were hired to exercise judgment. Just because the mayor disagrees with their judgment is insufficient cause to nuke their funding for the year. His are the actions of a man who has lost perspective.

The same is true of the lawyer. The city has suppressed nothing. No paintings have been banned or burned. No one has been barred by law from seeing the exhibit.

Indeed, it is widely predicted that the controversy has raised the potential market price of items in the display, some of which may be put up for sale when the run at the Brooklyn is finished.

The only question involved here is whether offensive art has an unquestioned entitlement to public subsidy. To make that a first Amendment question is a misrepresentation. The owner of the art is free to display it around the country and to assume he will have the backing of the courts if the government tries to stop him.

---

[21]Copyright 1999 by the *Omaha World-Herald*. Reprinted with permission.

CHAPTER 4

Evaluating Arguments: Some Basic Questions

This chapter will focus on two questions we must ask when we evaluate an argument:

1. Does the conclusion follow from the premises?
2. Should the premises be accepted as true?

If the conclusion does follow and the premises are true, then we call an argument *sound*. Corresponding to these two criteria of soundness are two ways of criticizing an argument: showing that the conclusion does not follow, and showing that the premises are doubtful.

Criteria for Soundness	*Corresponding Criticisms*
1. Conclusion follows from premises	1. Show that conclusion doesn't follow from the premises
2. Premises are true	2. Show that premises are doubtful

Before we explore these two features that we look for in a good argument and the corresponding criticisms we can make of bad arguments, it will be helpful to explain the difference between them. Obviously, Examples 4.1 and 4.2 are both faulty arguments, but what is wrong with 4.1 is wholly different from what is wrong with 4.2.

Example 4.1

(1) If HIV/AIDS is harmless, then we need not take precautions against it.

(2) HIV/AIDS is harmless. ← **Conclusion follows but premise 2 is false**

∴ We need not take precautions against HIV/AIDS.

Example 4.2

(1) Any disease that threatens many lives is worth our concern.

(2) Mumps is worth our concern.

∴ Mumps is a disease that threatens many lives. ← **Premises are true but conclusion does not follow**

When we say that the conclusion does not follow from the premises, as in Example 4.2, we are saying that something is wrong with the form or pattern of the argument. On the other hand, when we say that a premise is not acceptable, as in Example 4.1, it is the content, not the pattern of the argument, that we are criticizing.

Think of an argument as like a building, with the premises being the foundation, the conclusion being the house that it supports, and the form or pattern of the argument being the design of the building. The design could be a perfectly good one, but if the foundation is made of weak material the house could collapse. Similarly, an argument could fit a correct pattern, but if the premises are false, the conclusion could be false as well. On the other hand, the foundation could be perfectly strong, but if the design is faulty, the house might collapse in this case too because of this poor design. Analogously, an argument could have true premises but an incorrect pattern, in which case the conclusion could be false. Example 4.1 is like a building with a good design but a faulty foundation. The pattern is *modus ponens*, from our list of common successful patterns, but the second premise—*HIV/AIDS is harmless*—is obviously false. Example 4.2 is like a building with a strong foundation (true premises) but a bad design.

Pattern of Example 4.2 (Faulty Argument)

(1) All P_1's are P_2's.

(2) m is a P_2.

∴ m is a P_1.

The following section will explain some ways of showing that for any argument with this pattern, the conclusion does not follow from the premises.

In contrast to Examples 4.1 and 4.2, Example 4.3 both exhibits one of the common successful patterns from our list and in addition has true premises. Logicians call this property *soundness:* having true premises and a conclusion that follows from them (a good foundation and a good structural fit).

Example 4.3

(1) Any disease that threatens many lives is worth our concern.

(2) HIV/AIDS threatens many lives.

∴ HIV/AIDS is worth our concern.

Sound argument
True premises
conclusion follows

Again, an argument's conclusion follows from its premises because of the form, or pattern, of the argument. The technical term for this property of having a correct pattern so that the conclusion does indeed follow is *validity*. Validity plus true premises constitutes soundness.

In the following section, we will discuss in greater detail what it means for the conclusion to follow from the premises and offer some techniques for showing that the conclusion does not follow. This topic of how to determine the validity or invalidity of an argument is treated more formally in Chapter 5.

WHEN DOES THE CONCLUSION FOLLOW FROM THE PREMISES?

In Chapter 2 we presented a chart of seven argument patterns. A portion of this chart is repeated below. We claimed that, for any argument that fits one of these patterns, its conclusion follows from its premise.

Some Common Successful Argument Patterns

i. Modus Ponens

(1) If A, then B.
(2) A.
∴ B.

ii. Disjunctive Argument

(1) Either A or B.
(2) Not A.
∴ B.

iii. Modus Tollens

(1) If A, then B.
(2) Not B.
∴ Not A.

iv. Hypothetical Argument

(1) If A, then B.
(2) If B, then C.
∴ If A, then C.

v. Chain Argument

(1) A.
(2) If A, then B.
(3) If B, then C.
∴ C.

vi. Predicate Instantiation

(1) All P_1*'s are* P_2*'s.*
(2) m is a P_1*.*
∴ m is a P_2*.*

vii. Universal Syllogism

(1) All P_1*'s are* P_2*'s.*
(2) All P_2*'s are* P_3*'s.*
∴ All P_1*'s are* P_3*'s.*

What do we mean when we say that the conclusion of an argument follows from its premises? A less metaphorical way of putting it is that if the premises are true, then the conclusion must necessarily be true. In other words, it is impossible for the premises to be true and the conclusion false. We will try to make this clearer by contrasting several of the successful patterns from the chart with unsuccessful ones—patterns that would permit the possibility that the premises could be true but the conclusion false. At the same time, we will illustrate two techniques of showing that a conclusion doesn't follow from the premises. Two sentence-based patterns from the chart, *modus ponens* and *modus tollens,* were contrasted to unsuccessful patterns in Chapter 2. Here we will examine the predicate-based patterns.

Example 4.4

Universal Syllogism	**Contrasting Unsuccessful Pattern**
(1) All P_1's are P_2's.	*(1) All P_1's are P_2's.*
(2) All P_2's are P_3's.	*(2) All P_2's are P_3's.*
∴ All P1's are P3's.	*∴ All P3's are P1's.*

For any argument that fits the pattern on the left, if the premises are true, then the conclusion must be true. An argument could fit the pattern on the right, however, and have true premises and a false conclusion. Here is an example of each kind of argument.

Example 4.5

Argument 4.5A	***Argument 4.5B (Faulty)***
(1) All good teachers treat students with respect.	*(1) All good teachers treat students with respect.*
(2) All who treat students with respect listen to what students say.	*(2) All who treat students with respect listen to what students say.*
∴ All good teachers listen to what students say.	*∴ All who listen to what students say are good teachers.*

When we say that the conclusion of Argument 4.5A follows from its premises (that is, that the argument is valid), we are making a universal claim about all arguments that fit this same pattern. We are saying that the pattern is such that it will always take us from true premises to a true conclusion. Make up any argument you like. As long as the premises are true and they fit the pattern

(1) All P_1's are P_2's.
(2) All P_2's are P_3's.

then the conclusion, *All* P_1's are P_3's, will be true also. For example, it is true that *all cats are mammals* and that *all mammals are animals*. Since these premises fit the stated pattern, it follows that *all cats are animals*.

How do we evaluate whether an argument's conclusion follows from the premises? Our list of successful argument patterns provides a method for *some* cases. As we indicated in Chapter 2, any argument fitting these patterns is valid; that is, the premises follow from the conclusion. But what should a practitioner of critical reasoning do if the argument in question does not fit one of these patterns? The techniques of formal logic allow us to assess the validity of the arguments more broadly—we discuss some of them in Chapter 5—but there are also two informal techniques that can be used for showing invalidity: finding a counterexample, and explaining how the premises could be true and the conclusion false.

The Counterexample Method of Showing that an Argument's Conclusion Does Not Follow Since the claim that an argument's conclusion follows from its premises is universal (it applies to all cases having the same pattern), we can identify one way of showing that an argument's conclusion does not follow—that is, give a counterexample to this general claim.[1] The general claim (which is implicit any time we advance an argument) is: *All arguments that fit this same pattern and have true premises will have a true conclusion.* A counterexample to this claim, then, is an argument that *fits the same pattern*, has (obviously) *true premises*, and has an (obviously) *false conclusion.*

Suppose someone actually advanced Argument 4.5B:

(1) All good teachers treat students with respect.

(2) All who treat students with respect listen to what students say.

∴ All who listen to what students say are good teachers.

The person who advances this argument, in believing that the conclusion follows from the premises, is implicitly committed to the belief that if any other argument fits this same pattern, its conclusion will also follow from its premises. To give a counterexample, then, we could say: "That's just like arguing: 'All cats are mammals, and all mammals are animals, so all animals are cats'!" This argument fits the same pattern as Argument B and the premises are obviously true, but the conclusion is obviously false.

---

[1]The counterexample method of showing that an argument pattern is invalid should not be confused with the counterexample method of showing that a universal premise is false. The latter will be explained on pages 91–92.

Method 1: Find a Counterexample

In order to show that the conclusion of an argument **does not follow** from the premises, you should:

1) determine the pattern of the argument you wish to criticize, and
2) make up a new argument, with
   a) the same pattern,
   b) obviously true premises, and
   c) an obviously false conclusion.

We say "obviously true" premise and "obviously false" conclusion because you want to make it as clear as possible to the arguer (and to yourself) that the pattern in question can take you from true premises to a false conclusion. It is a good idea to use simple, familiar objects and relationships in your counterexample, as we did in the argument about cats, mammals, and animals.

This counterexample method is the main one we recommend for criticizing the structure of arguments in ordinary discourse. Even this simple method requires an audience willing to listen patiently and thoughtfully to understand your point. More sophisticated techniques might not be readily understood except by those already schooled in logic. For a general audience, you might have even avoided referring to arguments with correct patterns as *valid,* because this technical logician's term could be misleading. Since many people would think of a valid argument as completely successful, not just formally correct, it would be confusing to them to hear an argument referred to as valid if it had obviously false premises.

The other predicate-based pattern on our list can also be contrasted to a similar but unsuccessful version:

Example 4.6

Predicate Instantiation	Contrasting Unsuccessful Pattern
(1) All P_1's are P_2's.	(1) All P_1's are P_2's.
(2) m is a P_1.	(2) m is a P_2.
$\therefore m$ is a P_2.	$\therefore m$ is a P_1.

Because Argument 4.7A, below, fits the successful pattern, its conclusion follows from its premises, while for Argument 4.7B (which fits the unsuccessful pattern), the conclusion does not follow.

Example 4.7

Argument 4.7A	*Argument 4.7B (Faulty)*
(1) All good athletes are well coordinated.	*(1) All good athletes are well coordinated.*
(2) Maria is a good athlete.	*(2) Maria is well coordinated.*
∴ Maria is well coordinated.	*∴ Maria is a good athlete.*

Because of its successful pattern, it is impossible for the premises of Argument A to be true and its conclusion to be false. This is not to say that the argument's premises or its conclusion are in fact true—Maria could be a terrible athlete and poorly coordinated. But as long as the premises *are true,* the conclusion will be true also. Furthermore, for any other argument that fits this pattern, if it has true premises, it will also have a true conclusion. In this section, we do not discuss techniques for showing that an argument has a successful pattern (this is done in Chapter 5), but a few moments of thought should assure you that the pattern of Argument 4.7A will always take you from true premises to a true conclusion. The first premise asserts that one class of things is contained in a second class of things. The second premise locates a certain individual in the first class. Now if this first class is contained in the second class of things, the individual (Maria in this case) can't be in the first class without being in the second class. What the argument asserts is true no matter what classes and what individuals we are discussing. A second example of this successful pattern would be:

Argument with Same Pattern as Argument 4.7A

(1) All U.S. presidents have been U.S. citizens.

(2) George W. Bush has been a U.S. president.

∴ George W. Bush has been a U.S. citizen.

Using these same familiar relationships, we can construct a counterexample to show that the conclusion of Argument 4.7B does not follow from its premises:

Counter-example to Argument 4.7B

(1) All U.S. presidents have been U.S. citizens.

(2) I have been a U.S. citizen.

∴ I have been a U.S. president.

Since this argument has true premises and a false conclusion and fits the same pattern as Argument 4.7B, the pattern of Argument 4.7B is not successful; its conclusion does not follow from its premises.

A Second Method of Showing that an Argument's Conclusion Does Not Follow Although this counterexample method is often the easiest way to show that a conclusion doesn't follow, a second method is sometimes easier yet: We can simply explain how it would be possible for the premises of an argument to be true but the conclusion false. This doesn't involve making up a new argument, just discussing the argument at hand. Again, we can use Argument 4.7B as an example:

Argument 4.7B Repeated

(1) All good athletes are well coordinated.

(2) Maria is well coordinated.

∴ Maria is a good athlete.

The following passage describes a possible situation in which the premises of Argument 4.7B are true and the conclusion is false:

> *Suppose it is true that all good athletes are well coordinated and that Maria has excellent coordination. But suppose also that Maria is extremely slow, in bad physical condition, and has never practiced any athletic endeavors.*

Here we have a situation in which the premises of Argument 4.7B would be true but the conclusion is false. But what it means for the conclusion of an argument to follow from the premises is that it is impossible for the premises to be true and the conclusion false. Hence, we have shown that the conclusion of Argument 4.7B does not follow from the premises.

Method 2: Describe an Invalidating Possible Situation

In order to show that the conclusion of an argument does not follow from the premises, you should:

> Describe a possible situation in which the premises are obviously true and the conclusion is obviously false.

Consider the following argument:

Example 4.8

Argument to Be Evaluated

(1) If alcohol consumption is declining, then drunken driving is declining.

(2) If drunken driving is declining, then the auto accident rate is declining.

(3) The auto accident rate is declining.

∴ Alcohol consumption is declining.

This argument has the pattern:[2]

(1) If A, then B.

(2) If B, then C.

(3) C.

∴ A.

We can see this is an invalid argument by using either of the two methods described above. By method 1, we can construct a counterexample.

Example 4.9 *Counterexample*

(1) If the White House is in Cleveland, then it is in Ohio.

(2) If the White House is in Ohio, then it is in the United States.

(3) The White House is in the United States.

∴ The White House is in Cleveland.

All three of the premises are true. If any building is in Cleveland, then it is in Ohio. If a building is in Ohio, then it is in the United States. Finally, the White House is in the United States. But of course, it is in Washington, D.C., not in Cleveland, Ohio. This counterexample shows that the original argument does not reflect a valid argument form.

Method 2 leads us to describe a situation in which the argument to be evaluated has true premises and a false conclusion. Suppose that highways are improved or the proportion of young male drivers declines. Each of these could produce a decrease in the accident rate, even though the amount of alcohol consumption does not decline. In such a case all the premises could be true and the conclusion false.

Both these methods focus on showing that it is possible for all the premises to be true and the conclusion false. When a deductive argument is valid, it is *impossible* for this to occur. This logical impossibility is due to the form or pattern of the argument. We discuss logical impossibility at greater length in Chapter 5. For now, a few physical analogies should help introduce the concept.

> An argument is valid just in case there is no possible situation in which all of its premises are true and its conclusion is false.

---

[2]This should not be mistaken for the valid argument form

(1) If A, then B.

(2) If B, then C.

(3) A.

∴ C.

which is a variant of pattern (v) on our chart.

Depicting Validity An analogy with physical impossibility is useful in clarifying the concept of validity for statement-based arguments. It illustrates a connection between structure (in this case, physical structure) and possibility. As shown below, we can model the valid chain argument by representing Premises 1 and 2 as an arrangement of blocks or dominoes set up close to each other. If the first (A) is pushed, the second (B) falls, and then the last (C) falls. In this model, it is impossible to push A without C falling, given how the blocks are related to each other. The same is true for the logical links created by the if–then statements. If A is true, then C must be as well.

Valid Argument Pattern

(1) If A, then B.

(2) If B, then C.

(3) A.

∴ C.

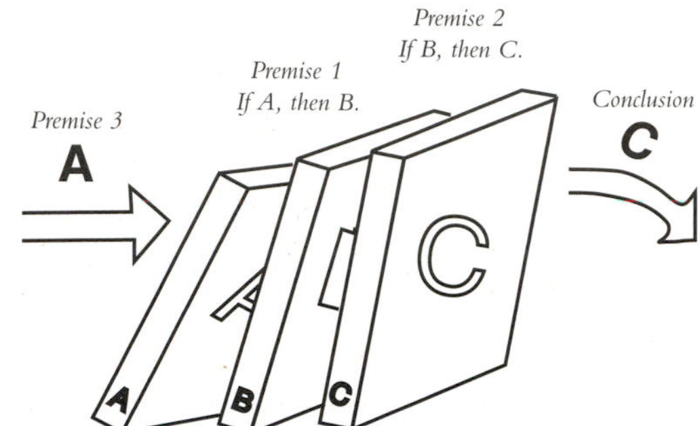

Contrast this relation with that of the invalid argument in Example 4.9:

Invalid Argument Pattern

(1) If A, then B.

(2) If B, then C.

(3) C.

∴ A.

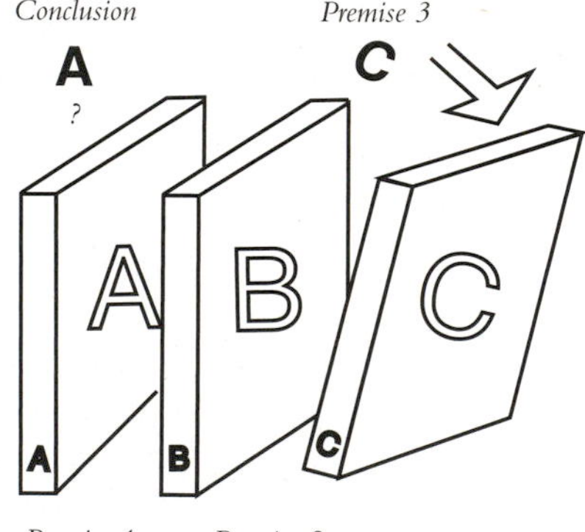

In this case, pushing block *C* doesn't force *A* to fall, even though *A* is next to *B* and *B* is next to *C*. Similarly, as the application of the two methods shows, it is logically possible for the premises to be true and the conclusion false.

The analogy with falling blocks is not meant as a method for testing validity. Another way of depicting validity is also a method of testing validity for some arguments. Simple examples of predicate-based arguments can be represented using Venn diagrams.[3] Consider the following valid "predicate-based" argument from Argument 4.7A.

---

[3]Named after British logician John Venn (1834–1923), who developed this method of presenting relationships.

Argument 4.7A	***Pattern: Predicate Instantiation***
(1) All good athletes are well coordinated.	*(1) All P1's are P2's*
(2) Maria is a good athlete.	*(2) m is a P1.*
∴ Maria is well coordinated.	*∴ m is a P2.*

Unlike statement-based arguments, which depend on the relationship of statements joined by connecting words such as *if–then* and *either–or*, predicate-based arguments depend on the internal structure of statements. We can illustrate the structure of a statement like *All good athletes are well coordinated*—which exhibits the pattern "All P_1's are P_2's"—using the following Venn diagram:

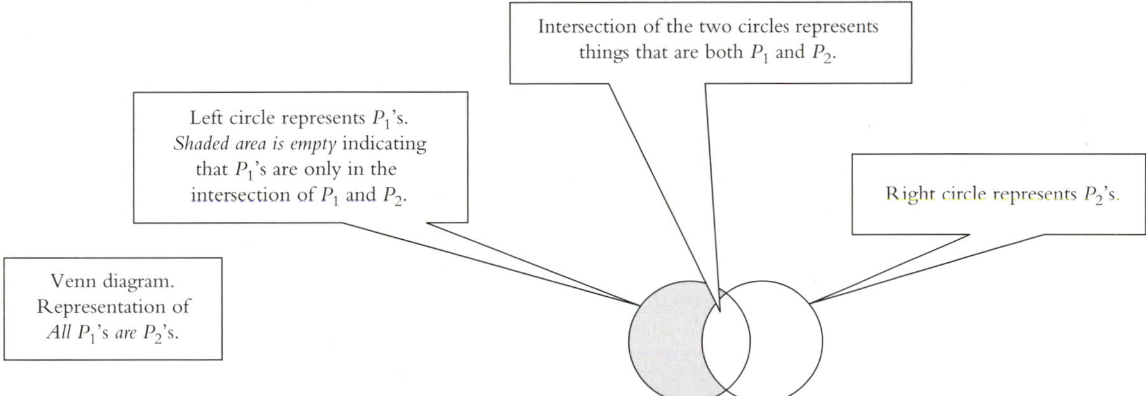
Intersection of the two circles represents things that are both P_1 and P_2.
Left circle represents P_1's. *Shaded area is empty* indicating that P_1's are only in the intersection of P_1 and P_2.
Right circle represents P_2's.
Venn diagram. Representation of *All P_1's are P_2's.*

The left-hand circle represents the class of P_1's (in this case, good athletes), and the right-hand circle represents the class of P_2's (in this case, the well coordinated). By shading the part of the P_1's circle that doesn't overlap the P_2's circle, we are indicating that this part of the circle is *empty*—that all P_1's are P_2's. Now if we place an *m* in the unshaded part of the P_1's circle, indicating that *m* is a P_1 (in our argument, Maria is a good athlete), we see that *m must* lie within the P_2's circle, which is our conclusion—*m* is a P_2 (Maria is well coordinated) according to pattern (vi) for Predicate Instantiation.

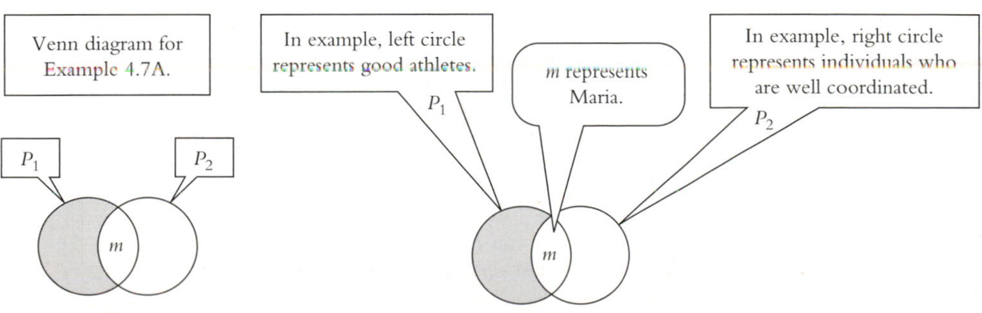
Venn diagram for Example 4.7A.
P_1
P_2
m
In example, left circle represents good athletes.
P_1
m represents Maria.
In example, right circle represents individuals who are well coordinated.
P_2
m

This diagram shows that the argument is valid by showing that the only possible situation that makes the premises true also makes the conclusion true. If it is true that all P_1's are P_2's (*All good athletes are well coordinated*), then we must represent the portion of the P_1 circle that is outside the P_2 circle as being empty—it is an impossible situation for premise 1 to be true and for some P_1 to not be a P_2. If premise 2 is also true, then we are compelled to put *m* (Maria) in the unshaded part of the P_1 circle. We can't represent her as being outside the P_1 circle since Premise 2 says she is a P_1. The only place left to put her is in the part of the P_1 circle that is also inside the P_2 circle. But now we see that by representing the premises in the only way possible, we have already represented the conclusion: *m* is a P_2. It is impossible to put *m* outside the P_2 circle without making at least one of the premises false. This shows that the argument is valid.

These ways of making the conclusion false also make a premise false. There is no possible way of making both the premises true without making the conclusion true.

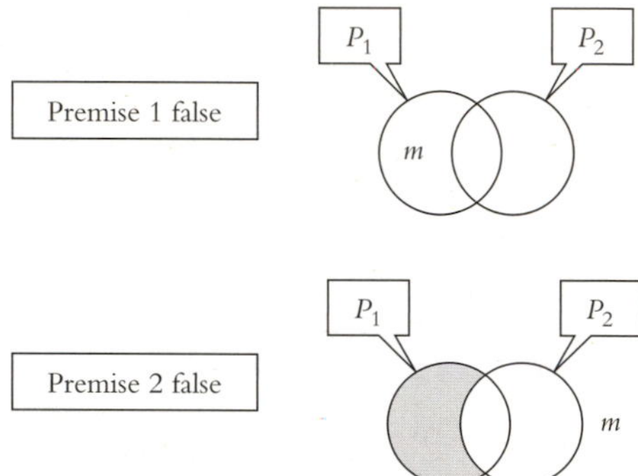

By contrast consider the invalid argument from Example 4.7B.

Argument 4.7B	*Faulty Argument Pattern*
(1) All good athletes are well coordinated.	*(1) All* P_1*'s are* P_2*'s*
(2) Maria is a good athlete.	*(2) m is a* P_2.
∴ *Maria is well coordinated.*	∴ *m is a* P_1.

We can represent a possible counterexample using the same circles and shading as before for the first premise, but this time we are not assured of the truth of the conclusion. As shown below, one possible way in which the second premise could be true is represented by the *m?* in the P_2 circle (indicating that Maria is well coordinated). In this case, the conclusion is false because *m* is not in the P_1 class (i.e., Maria is not a good athlete).[4]

[4]Of course, *m* could also be in the intersection of P_1 and P_2 as represented by the question mark, but it *need not be*. If an argument is valid, then there is no possibility that the premises are all true and the conclusion is false. This Venn diagram depicts just such a situation, so the argument is invalid. Chapter 5 contains further discussion of Venn diagrams as a method of testing the validity of simple predicate-based argument patterns.

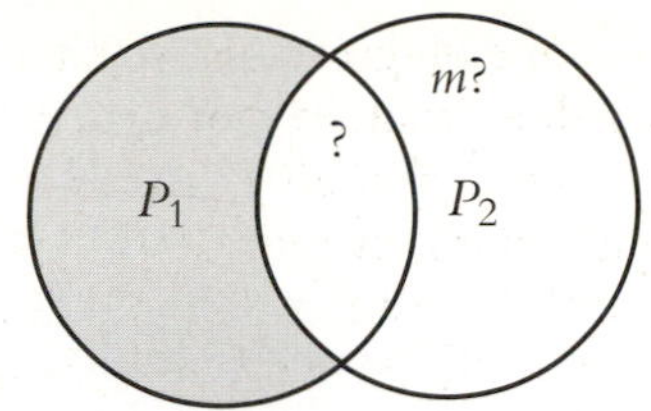

How Often Do We Need to Show that an Argument's Conclusion Doesn't Follow? It is actually rare in everyday discourse to encounter an argument whose conclusion *clearly* doesn't follow from its premises. This is partly because it is rare for all the premises and the conclusion of an argument to be explicitly stated. If we make a charitable interpretation of what has been said or written, we can almost always reconstruct an argument so that its conclusion follows. However, it is still important to understand the concept of validity and to be able to explain to yourself why the conclusions of some arguments don't follow from the premises. In fact, whenever you reconstruct an argument with missing parts, you must think about correct structure as you attempt to make the argument fit a successful pattern. We might say that the criterion that the conclusion must follow from the premises is used primarily in *self-evaluating* your reconstruction of an argument rather than in expressing a criticism of someone else's argument.

Notice that this section gives you some techniques for showing that an argument's conclusion *doesn't* follow, but no techniques for showing that a conclusion *does* follow. As we have said, in most cases when you reconstruct an argument you will either make it follow one of the seven successful patterns or a pattern that is such a simple variation or combination of these patterns that you can readily see that it is successful. Another reason is that the techniques for showing that a conclusion does follow require considerable explanation and some introduction of formal symbols, as we indicate in Chapter 5.

EXERCISE 4.1

Showing Invalidity

Show that each of the following arguments is invalid (that is, the conclusion doesn't follow from the premises). Use either the counterexample method or the possible situation method. Explain what you are doing clearly enough that an intelligent general audience would understand the point you are making.

1. Anyone who lives with a smoker has an above-average risk of heart disease. Sarah doesn't live with a smoker. So Sarah doesn't have an above-average risk of heart disease.
2. If federal government oversight is lax, then financial institutions take excessive risk. Financial institutions did take excessive risk. So federal government oversight was lax.
3. If dinner guests are coming, then we need more food. If we need more food, then we need to go to the store. Dinner guests aren't coming. Therefore, we don't need to go to the store.

4. No great singer has a weak voice. Abby is not a great singer. It follows that Abby has a weak voice.
5. If the American people feel economically secure, then they will press for tax cuts. The American people don't feel economically secure. So they won't press for tax cuts.
6. All doctors have studied medicine. Paul is not a doctor. Therefore, Paul has not studied medicine.
7. All compassionate people are honest people. This is so because all good friends are compassionate people, and all good friends are honest people.
8. Nanotechnology is the business opportunity of the future. This is so because stocks in technology will be strong. If nanotechnology is the business opportunity of the future, then it will attract more investment. If it will attract more investment, then stocks in technology will be strong.
9. Anyone who is good at science is good at math. Anyone who is good at math is intelligent. So, anyone who is intelligent is good at science.
10. Either we will ration health care, or we will spend too much on health care. We will ration health care. So we won't spend too much on health care. (**Hint:** To call this argument invalid is to take the word "or" in the inclusive sense of "either A or B or both." A counterexample would need to be an argument of the same pattern that clearly used or in this inclusive sense.)

WHEN SHOULD THE PREMISES BE ACCEPTED AS TRUE?

As we have seen, an argument's conclusion can follow from its premises, even though some or all of the premises are false.

Example 4.10

(1) If an effective cure for HIV/AIDS is available, the world community should provide it to all who need it but can't afford it.

(2) An effective cure for HIV/AIDS is available.

∴ *The world community should provide it to all who need it but can't afford it.*

Unfortunately, although this argument is valid (that is, its conclusion follows), the second premise is false. (At least, we take it to be false at the time of the writing of this book.) Because the second premise is false, the argument is not sound; it doesn't justify our belief in the conclusion.

In general, the question of whether an argument's conclusion follows can be answered with greater certainty than the question of whether its premises are true. As we have noted, logicians have developed techniques that can tell us whether an argument is correctly structured, even when we are dealing with much more complex arguments than those illustrated on our list of patterns. By contrast, there is no general method of determining whether premises are true or false.

Most of the arguments we encounter in our everyday lives have premises whose truth or falsity cannot be determined with certainty. Consider our *judgment* that the argument about an HIV/AIDS cure (Example 4.10) is *unsound* because the premise An *effective cure for HIV/AIDS is available* is false.[5] We are not as certain about this judgment of falsity as we would be if an argument contained statements from arithmetic. We can only give reasons why it is highly unlikely that an HIV/AIDS cure is available. For example, we can point out that this would be such important news that we surely would have heard about it, and that it would be difficult to suppress news of the discovery of an HIV/AIDS cure.

We use reasons such as these to justify our *judgment* that the premise *A cure for HIV/AIDS is available* is false even though we are not absolutely certain that it is false. We also use comparable reasons for making judgments that some premises of arguments are true. Sometimes we are relatively certain about premises because of clear, direct observations we have made (for example, that a friend has acted aggressively) or because we have evidence from many independent sources (for instance, that the U.S. deficit has increased). But at other times, we must decide whether to accept the premises of an argument when we are not all that certain of their truth or falsity.

Most of the examples and exercises in the remainder of the book are not ones in which you will be led to a clear, definite decision: "This argument is sound." You will sometimes be able to determine with absolute certainty that an argument is *unsound* because it is *invalid*—that is, the conclusion doesn't follow. But typically, you will be reconstructing the arguments you read in a way that makes them valid. Then the question remains of whether you should accept the premises as true. Answering this will be an exercise in using the background information and beliefs you already possess to give reasons for or against accepting premises.

Even though there is no general methodology for determining whether premises should be accepted as true, there are techniques that can be quite successful for criticizing certain broad categories of premises. Some of these are described in the following section.

Tips on Casting Doubt on Premises Since any kind of statement can serve as a premise in an argument, the question of how to cast doubt on premises is obviously too broad to be dealt with here in detail. How can you cast doubt on any statement? We have to assume that this is the sort of thing you already know how to do. We can, however, provide some techniques for attacking certain kinds of premises, as well as advice concerning which kinds of premises can be criticized most easily and fruitfully. The techniques we introduce in this section are: (1) giving counterexamples to premises that generalize; (2) breaking the connection in *if–then* premises; and (3) scrutinizing further implications of premises.

Presenting Counterexamples to Universal Generalizations Perhaps the most straightforward criticism of a premise is a counterexample to a universal

---

[5]There is no cure and a preventative vaccine has not been developed, although there are promising treatments that can improve the chances for a long and relatively healthy life, at least for those who can afford them.

generalization.[6] If a premise claims that *All* P_1*'s are* P_2*'s*, or that *No* P_1*'s are* P_2*'s—All lying is wrong; No sea animals are mammals*—try to think of a clear counterexample (lying to save an innocent person's life; whales or seals). Some universal generalizations are true, but many can be shown to be false by pointing out that something is clearly a P_1 but is clearly not a P_2. Or, if the claim is that *No* P_1*'s are* P_2*'s*, point to something that is *clearly* a P_1 and is clearly also a P_2. When we say "clearly," we mean that it should be uncontroversial to your audience that your counterexample really is a counterexample. Some additional examples will show why this is important.

Suppose someone is arguing that all abortion should be illegal, and this person uses the premise *All killing of human beings is wrong*. You want to present as a counterexample something that is clearly a case of killing but that is clearly not wrong. To state that executing a murderer is not wrong would not be as effective for most audiences as to use the counterexample of killing another person in self-defense. This is because capital punishment is a controversial issue, and your audience might believe that executing a murderer is wrong. Then you would be sidetracked into debating this second issue. It is much less likely that your audience would believe that killing in self-defense is wrong, particularly if you described a situation in which killing the assailant was the only alternative to being killed. Obviously, the worst kind of attempted counterexample in this context would be to claim that killing a fetus is not wrong, since the issue being discussed is abortion and the arguer, presumably, believes that killing a fetus is wrong.

Consider the universal generalization *Any practice that is harmful should be illegal*. Contrast the clear counterexamples below to the controversial or "borderline" counterexamples. Neglecting to exercise and eating many doughnuts are practices that are somewhat harmful to health, but surely they should not be illegal. The borderline cases are more controversial. Hang gliding and Russian roulette are clearly harmful, but some would claim that they should be illegal as well.

Any practice that is harmful should be illegal.

Good Counterexample	*Controversial, Borderline Counterexample*
Neglecting to exercise	Hang gliding
Eating many doughnuts	Russian roulette

[6]A universal statement applies to every case (in the "universe" under discussion). In this case it says that everything has a characteristic *(All* P_1*'s are* P_2*'s)* or everything does not have the characteristic *(No* P_1*'s are* P_2*'s)*.

Breaking *if–then* Connections A second broad category of premise that can be challenged in a fairly straightforward way is an *if–then* premise, which claims a connection between two things. If the premise is of this type, try to think of ways the first thing could occur without the second occurring. For example, consider the premise *If birthrates continue to increase, then the world will become overcrowded.* What if death rates increase more rapidly than birthrates? What if people start colonizing other planets? In both cases, the first condition could occur—birthrate could continue to increase—without the second occurring—overcrowding of the world.

This kind of criticism is weaker than a clear counterexample to a universal generalization. Raising the possibility that the "if" part won't be followed by the "then" part doesn't show that the premise is false, just that it is less than certain. The more likely the event that would break the *if–then* connection, the less likely the premise.

Pointing Out Doubtful Implications A third kind of criticism can be attempted against any premise. That is, every premise has *further* implications—statements that *would* be true if the premise in question were true. Try to think of such implications, particularly ones that are highly doubtful. For example, someone might use as a premise the claim that punishment does not deter crime. This implies that if there were no punishment, there would still be no more crime than there is now. Do you believe this? For example, would you personally still refrain from stealing to the same extent that you do now, even if you knew you wouldn't be punished? Would you still pay your income taxes?

Some Ways to Cast Doubt on Premises

1. Presenting a counterexample for a universal generalization
2. Finding a clear case in which the antecedent is true and the consequent false for an *if–then* premise
3. For any premise, pointing out further implications that are doubtful

In general, after you have determined whether an argument's conclusion follows from its premises, you will want to survey the premises to decide where to begin your evaluation. As a general strategy, we suggest initially directing your attention to premises that can be discussed on the basis of generally shared background information. This is certainly preferable to quibbling over matters that require research and documentation that can't actually be carried out on the occasion of the discussion. Then, if you determine that your appraisal of the argument really hinges on specific facts that need to be researched, you can do the necessary investigation.

Much of the material in the following chapters will help you criticize more specialized kinds of premises. Chapter 6, on fallacies, will identify some specific kinds of premises that are typically doubtful. Chapter 7 will help you evaluate definition-like premises. Premises that make statistical generalizations based on observational data will be scrutinized in Chapter 8. Sometimes, elements of scientific theories are used as premises. Techniques for evaluating such premises are discussed in Chapter 10.

EXERCISE 4.2

Casting Doubt on Premises

Each of the following statements might occur as a premise in an argument. (Indeed, some of them are used as premises in the arguments in Exercise 4.4.) For each statement, think about what you might say to persuade someone that the claim being made is not true—or at least that it is doubtful. If you need more information about a topic, do a little research, either by consulting a source or by talking with someone you consider knowledgeable about the subject. Then put your ideas into writing, formulating a short paragraph casting doubt on each statement. Keep in mind the tips for casting doubt on universal claims and on *if–then* claims. If you find yourself initially inclined to agree with a statement, try to imagine what an intelligent critic on the other side of the issue might say to cast doubt on it.

1. If capital punishment is completely abolished, then the homicide rate will increase rapidly.
2. People shouldn't make promises unless they are certain they can keep them.
3. Any activity that makes people aggressive should be discouraged.
4. If the fetus is connected to a pregnant woman's body, then it is part of the woman's body.
5. Any activity that poses a risk to the health of bystanders violates their rights.
6. If two people aren't compatible, then they can't live together.
7. No person should pay taxes to support parts of government that that person doesn't use.
8. If abortion continues to be legal, then respect for life will decline.
9. If Asian and European countries continue to score much higher on international science and math exams, then the United States should adopt their educational methods.
10. All material that arouses lewd desires is pornographic.
11. Any practice that could help cure disease without causing harm should be continued.
12. If gay marriage is allowed in any form, then family life in America will be threatened.

SAMPLE APPRAISALS: EXAMPLES OF TECHNIQUES OF CRITICISM

As we have learned in the previous sections, an argument can be criticized by (1) showing that the conclusion doesn't follow, or (2) showing that one or more premises should not be accepted as true. It is best to determine first whether the conclusion follows. In the process of making this determination, you will typically try adding one or more implicit premises to make the conclusion follow. Having done this, you will have a complete list of the premises you can challenge as you move to the second criticism. If it turns out that there is no plausible way of making the argument valid, then you need not waste your time evaluating the premises, since the faulty pattern will make the argument unsound even if the premises are true. This sequence of criticism is illustrated in the sample appraisal of the arguments in Examples 4.11 and 4.12, as well as in some additional comments on the relation between the two types of criticism.

Example 4.11

(1) John has withheld information.

(2) Withholding information is lying.

(3) Anyone who has lied has done something wrong.

∴ John has done something wrong.

Example 4.12

(1) It is wrong for any person to kill another person.

(2) If the state executes a murderer, then the state is killing a person.

∴ It is wrong for the state to execute a murderer.

The initial question concerning either argument, then, is whether the conclusion follows from the premises. Even though the argument in Example 4.11 doesn't exactly fit one of our seven patterns, we can see fairly readily that it is valid. The first two premises—*John withheld information* and *Withholding information is lying*—amount to the claim that *John has lied.* If we put this together with Premise 3, we have an argument of the same type as pattern (vi) or Predicate Instantiation, in our list:

(1) All P_1's are P_2's.

(2) m is a P_1.

∴ m is a P_2.

That is,

(1) All who have lied have done something wrong.

(2) John has lied.

∴ John has done something wrong.

So the conclusion *does* follow. To admit this is not to admit that the premises are true; but if they are true, then the conclusion must be true as well.

In the second argument (Example 4.12), however, there is no such relation between premises and conclusion. Even if it is wrong for any person to kill another person, and granting that the state, by executing a murderer, is killing a person, it doesn't follow that it is wrong for the state to execute a murderer because the state is not a person. There may be special considerations that justify killing by the state. So the second argument can be criticized as invalid.

The second kind of criticism (casting doubt on premises) can be raised against either argument. But before we discuss specific criticisms of premises, we should make some general points about the relation between the two kinds of criticisms. First, as we can see in Example 4.11, if the conclusion of an argument follows, then the only means of criticism left is an attack on the premises. If you decide that there are adequate grounds for believing the premises, then you should be compelled by these reasons to believe the conclusion. If it is impossible for the premises to be true and the conclusion false, and you believe the premises, then it is irrational not to believe the conclusion. Second, if an argument is invalid, then it is not necessary to criticize the premises. You can point out that it does not matter whether the premises are true or not—even if they are true, the conclusion still does not follow.

There is a fairly obvious move, however, that might be made in defense of an argument that has been called invalid: this is to claim that there are implicit premises that, if added, will make the argument valid. In the case of Example 4.12,

Example 4.12 Repeated

(1) It is wrong for any person to kill another person.

(2) If the state executes a murderer, then the state is killing a person.

∴ It is wrong for the state to execute a murderer.

it might be claimed that the argument should be expanded by the addition of an implicit premise.

Example 4.12 with Implicit Premise Added (implicit)

(1) It is wrong for any person to kill another person.

(2) If the state executes a murderer, then the state is killing a person.

(3) Everything that is wrong for a person to do is wrong for the state to do.

∴ It is wrong for the state to execute a murderer.

Your criticism will be more effective if you show that you are aware that the conclusion of an argument can be made to follow by adding premises. (This point was made in Chapter 3.) Often, the premise or premises left unstated are precisely the ones that, if made explicit, can be seen to be doubtful. A good procedure, then, is to point out first that the argument, as stated, is invalid. Second, you can raise the possibility of adding premises yourself. You might formulate the premise or premises that would make the argument valid, then discuss whether these premises are deserving of belief. In our expanded version of Example 4.12, the added premise says that *Everything that is wrong for a person to do is wrong for the state to do*. To cast doubt on this premise, you can point out that if it were true, then not only would the state be wrong in executing murderers, the state would also be wrong in imprisoning any offenders, levying taxes, or generally carrying out any of the functions of government that are beyond the just power of any individual citizen.

We can now return to criticizing the premises in Example 4.11. They were:

1. *John has withheld information.*
2. *Withholding information is lying.*
3. *Anyone who has lied has done something wrong.*

Premise 3 can be criticized by giving counterexamples to this generalization. It is doubtful, for example, that someone who has lied to prevent great harm to another has done something wrong.

Premise 2 asserts a conceptual relationship between withholding information and lying. We discuss the criticism of claims such as these at some length in Chapter 7. The arguer in this case is guilty of stipulating a meaning of *lying* that is not ordinarily assumed by people who use this word, then proceeding in the argument with this misleading definition.

Premise 1 is the kind of claim that might be evaluated on the basis of direct observation or reports of direct observation. Suppose John has been accused of selling his house without telling the buyer that the basement walls leak. Maybe you or someone else actually heard John say that the basement walls leak. Or, in the absence of such direct evidence, the premise could be supported by a further argument that we would then have to evaluate. For example, the buyer of the house could argue that all the junk John piled up against the water-stained wall was a deliberate attempt to hide its condition.

Even if there is direct observational evidence for Premise 1, however, this doesn't settle the matter with absolute certainty.[7] We sometimes make mistakes about what we see and hear. And studies of "eyewitness testimony" in connection with criminal justice research have clearly indicated that our memory for what we have supposedly seen can be notoriously inaccurate especially in emotionally charged situations.

Philosophers and logicians have been trying at least from the time of Descartes (1596–1650) to establish unassailable foundations for all our reasoning. Unfortunately, efforts by philosophers to find a list of unassailably true premises with the same kind of certainty and precision that logicians have achieved in establishing the validity of argument patterns have been unproductive if not misguided. Still, we are sometimes justified in *accepting* premises as true, even if we lack absolute certainty. If the arguments in which these premises occur also follow correct patterns (that is, they are valid), then we are justified in accepting these arguments as *sound.*

One of the main points of this chapter that we emphasized in our sample appraisals is the need to evaluate two separate features in arguments. We must be aware of each and not get confused. First there is the structure or pattern—the

---

[7]But expecting "absolute certainty" is a high standard indeed. Such criticism of Premise 1 would be stronger if we offered some specific reason for doubting eyewitness testimony in this particular case.

way the premises and conclusion fit together. When the argument has a correct pattern, we say that *the conclusion follows from the premises*, or to use the more technical term of the logician, the argument is *valid*. Second, there is the content of the premises—broadly, what they say about the world. When we evaluate the premises we decide whether to accept them as *true*. When an argument satisfies both these criteria—when it is *valid* and *all the premises are true*—then it is a *sound argument*. We are then justified in accepting its conclusion.

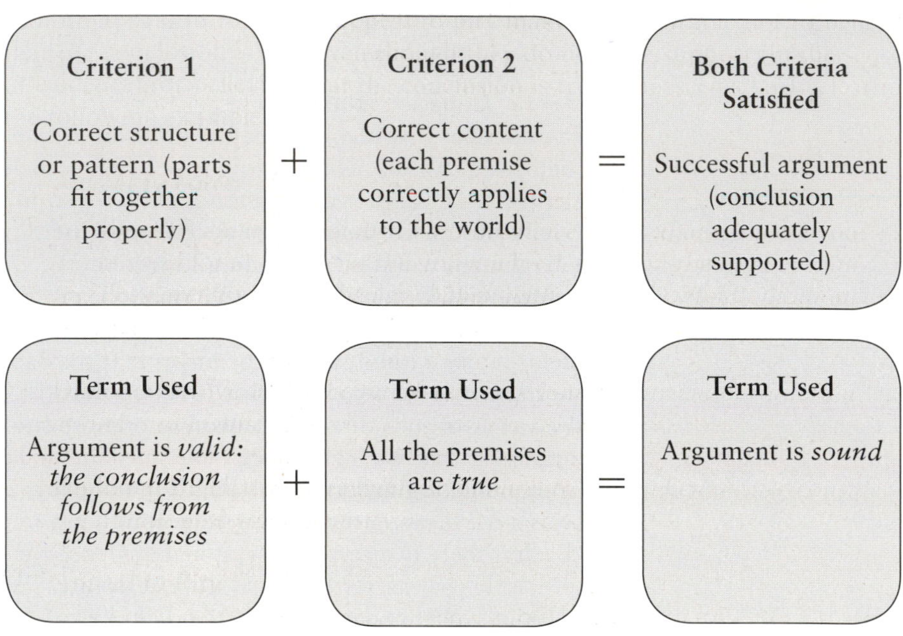

Criterion 1
Correct structure or pattern (parts fit together properly)
+
Criterion 2
Correct content (each premise correctly applies to the world)
=
Both Criteria Satisfied
Successful argument (conclusion adequately supported)
Term Used
Argument is valid: the conclusion follows from the premises
+
Term Used
All the premises are true
=
Term Used
Argument is sound

EXERCISE 4.3

Distinguishing the Validity of an Argument (That Is, Whether the Conclusion Follows) from the Truth of Its Premises

A. For each argument,state

(i) whether or not the conclusion follows, and if so
(ii) whether or not the premises are true.

1. *(1) Every U.S. president has been a faithful husband.*

   (2) Franklin Roosevelt was a U.S. president.

   ∴ Franklin Roosevelt was a faithful husband.

2. *(1) Every U.S. president is a U.S. citizen.*

   (2) I am not the U.S. president.

   ∴ I am not a U.S. citizen.

3. *(1) If I pay my taxes on time, the Internal Revenue Service will be satisfied.*

   (2) I won't pay my taxes on time.

   ∴ The IRS won't be satisfied.

4. *(1) All dogs are mammals.*

   (2) All mammals are animals.

   ∴ All dogs are animals.

B. Write in standard form an example (of your own creation) of each of the following:

1. An argument that is valid but obviously unsound.
2. An argument that is obviously sound, given common knowledge.
3. An argument that is invalid and has at least one false premise.
4. An argument that is invalid but has true premises and a true conclusion.

C. One aspect of the terminology we have introduced may be confusing. In ordinary speech, we occasionally refer to individual statements as "valid," as in "The speaker made a valid point." In these cases, *valid* means "acceptable" or "true." As logicians use the term , however, it is only *arguments* that are valid or invalid. Validity does not apply to individual statements. Likewise, only arguments are sound or unsound. On the other hand, only individual *statements* are true or false. It is inappropriate to call an argument true or false.

1. Which of the following statements make sensible use of the terms?

   a. The argument you just gave is true.
   b. Your premises are unsound.
   c. Your conclusion is false.
   d. Your statement is true.
   e. Your statement is invalid.
   f. You are arguing from true premises to an invalid conclusion.

2. Which of these statements are consistent—that is, for which of them can the two parts both be true together?

   a. Your argument is sound, but not valid.
   b. Your argument is valid, but your conclusion is false.
   c. Your argument is valid, but not sound.
   d. Your argument is sound, but your conclusion is false.

SOME SPECIAL CASES: ARGUMENTS THAT WE SHOULD OR SHOULD NOT DO SOMETHING

Think of how frequently our discussions focus on whether we should or should not do something. Should we ban smoking in public places? Should potential parents be informed of the gender of their baby-to-be? Should guns be more tightly restricted? Should capital punishment be abolished? These are typical of the issues discussed in newspaper editorials and public forums. Conversations among individuals focus more commonly on personal issues, but even then, the question is often what someone should do.

Because this question is so common, reconstructions of arguments will often take the form of premises that give reasons for or against doing something and a conclusion stating what we should or should not do. We discuss here how these arguments can be treated as roughly fitting certain common patterns from our list, but with certain qualifications.

We Shouldn't Do *A*, Because *A* Will Result in *B* Consider a reconstruction of an argument from the editorial on gun control that appeared in Chapters 2 and 3:

Example 4.13 (implicit)

(1) If gun ownership is restricted, then it is easier for criminals to prey on decent folks.

(2) It should not be easier for criminals to prey on decent folks.

∴ Gun ownership should not be restricted.

You will see this general kind of argument again and again.

Pattern in Example 4.13[8]

(1) If A, then B.

(2) B shouldn't happen.

∴ A shouldn't happen (or alternatively, we shouldn't do A).

Because this kind of argument is so common, it is important to decide whether it can be taken as following a valid pattern. In particular, should we take it as following something like *modus tollens:*

Modus Tollens Pattern

(1) If A, then B.

(2) Not B.

∴ Not A.

The argument pattern in Example 4.14 is similar to *modus tollens* in some respects (but not all). Like *modus tollens*, the pattern of the argument above can be contrasted to a kind of argument that is clearly not valid:

---

[8]The "pattern" is roughly stated for simplicity. A closer approximation would be: *if A, then B*, it shouldn't be brought about that *B*. Therefore, it shouldn't be brought about that *A*. If premise *A* stands for a statement such as "gun ownership is restricted," in the conclusion, *Not A* stands for something like "that gun ownership is restricted shouldn't happen" or "we shouldn't bring it about that gun ownership is restricted."

Example 4.14

Fallacy of Affirming the Consequent	*Fallacious Should-Argument Pattern*
(1) If A, then B.	*(1) If A, then B.*
(2) B .	*(2) B should happen.*
∴ A .	*∴ A should happen.*

The conclusion doesn't follow, because (for one thing) there could be other, better ways to make *B* happen. Consider the similarity between the following two instances of these invalid patterns:

Example 4.15

Fallacy of Affirming the Consequent	*Fallacious Should-Argument Pattern*
(1) If you're a dog, then you have feet.	*(1) If we restrict the highway speed limit to 5 mph, then we would reduce highway deaths.*
(2) You have feet.	*(2) We should reduce highway deaths.*
∴ You're a dog.	*∴ We should restrict the speed limit to 5 mph.*

The conclusions don't follow because there are other better, more convenient ways to save lives, and you could have feet by virtue of being something other than a dog.

Although there is a similarity in contrast between these invalid patterns and the patterns in question, there are also differences between *modus tollens* and the pattern in Example 4.13. Both begin by saying that if *A* happens, then *B* happens; however, *modus tollens* proceeds to say that *B doesn't* happen, not that it *shouldn't.* Given the premises of *modus tollens,* the conclusion has to follow. Suppose it's really true that *If I study, then I learn,* and that *I haven't learned.* It follows necessarily that *I must not have studied.* Compare this to the argument that *If gun ownership is restricted, then it will be easier for criminals to prey on decent folks,* and *It shouldn't be easier for criminals to prey on decent folks.* Does it follow with the same kind of necessity that *Gun ownership shouldn't be restricted?*

The answer to this question depends on how we interpret *shouldn't* in the second premise. There are two options: a weak interpretation and a strong interpretation. According to the weak interpretation to say that it shouldn't be easier for criminals to prey on decent folks means only that it is undesirable or unwanted for this to happen. But this leaves open the possibility that there are other, good consequences of restricting gun ownership that might outweigh this admittedly undesirable consequence. The increase in criminals preying on decent folks could be slight, but the increase in accidental deaths due to lack of restriction on firearms could be great. We could then accept that it is undesirable to make it easier for criminals to prey on decent folks, but still conclude that we should restrict gun ownership.

We could, however, interpret *shouldn't* to mean something stronger, such as, "All things considered, this must not be allowed to happen." If it were true in this sense that it *shouldn't* be easier for criminals to prey on decent folks, and true also that restricting gun ownership would have this result, then the conclusion would follow that we should leave gun ownership unrestricted. Keep in mind, though, that this stronger version of the premise would be much more difficult to accept. You would need to consider *all* the likely consequences of restricting gun ownership and of not restricting it, and then decide that the likely increase in criminals preying on the innocent would be an overriding consideration.

The lesson to be learned from the analysis of this kind of argument is to be cautious. If the argument is interpreted in the weak sense of "shouldn't" as in Example 4.16, then the conclusion doesn't follow.

Example 4.16

(1) If A, then B.

(2) B is an undesirable or bad outcome.

∴ We shouldn't do A.

If the argument is taken in the strong sense as in Example 4.17 the conclusion follows but the second premise will be harder to accept and need additional support.

Example 4.17

(1) If A, then B.

(2) B must not be allowed to happen under any circumstance.

∴ We shouldn't do A.

> ***Two Senses of B Shouldn't Happen***
>
> Weak sense: *B* is an undesirable outcome.
>
> Strong Sense: *B* should not be allowed to happen under any circumstances.

A slight variation of this same kind of argument is:

Example 4.18

(1) If we don't do A, then B.

(2) B shouldn't happen.

∴ We should do A.

An instance would be: If we don't restrict gun ownership, then homicide rates will increase. Homicide rates shouldn't increase, therefore we should restrict gun ownership. This argument also is valid only if the second premise is taken in the strong sense, not the weak sense of "it would be undesirable for homicide rates to increase." Again, we must be cautious about accepting this kind of argument.

We Should Do *A*, Because *A* Will Result in *B* Another kind of argument urges us to do something, not to avoid some unacceptable result but to bring about something good. For example,

Example 4.19

Governments should impose limits on greenhouse gas emissions because global warming will be slowed.

How should we interpret an argument of this kind? One way *not* to interpret it is by adding an implicit premise to produce the following:

Interpretation of Example 4.19 as a Faulty Argument (implicit)

(1) If governments impose limits on greenhouse gas emissions, then global warming will be slowed.

(2) Global warming should be slowed.

∴ Governments should impose limits on greenhouse gas emissions.

This interpretation commits the same fallacy as the argument about saving lives by restricting the speed limit (Example 4.15). The conclusion doesn't follow because there might be other, better ways to bring about the same result. Government-imposed limits on greenhouse gas emissions might not be the only way of slowing global warming. Raising energy costs or promoting life style changes in developed countries might have the same effect.

What, then, is an alternative? We could interpret the argument along the lines of modus ponens.

Better Interpretation (implicit)

(1) Government-imposed limits on greenhouse gas emissions will slow global warming.[9]

(2) If (1), then governments should impose limits on greenhouse gas emissions.

∴ Governments should impose limits on greenhouse gas emissions.

---

[9]This premise might occur in a prose passage as an *if–then* sentence: *If government imposes limits on greenhouse gas emissions, then global warming will be slowed.*

Alternatively, we could make the implicit premise more general:

Alternative Interpretation (implicit)

(1) Government-imposed limits on greenhouse gas emissions will slow global warming.

(2) Governments should carry out any action that would slow global warming.

∴ Governments should impose limits on greenhouse gas emissions.

Even with these improved interpretations, the arguments must be evaluated with caution. The fact that an action will have *one* good result won't always justify carrying it out. The positive result of government-imposed limits on greenhouse gas emissions must be weighed against possible negative results (such as slowing the progress of developing nations). Exercise set 4.4 at the end of this chapter includes a number of arguments with conclusions that we should or should not do something. Keep the discussion from this section in mind as you reconstruct and evaluate them.

The Context of Arguments Containing "Should" We have pointed out a significant potential weakness in arguments that we should or shouldn't do *A*, because *A* will result in *B*. That is, the harm or benefit associated with *B* could be outweighed by other consequences of doing *A*. However, arguments of this form are sometimes put forth in a context of prior debate or discussion that has already identified *B* as a crucial factor in deciding whether to do *A*. Other pros and cons of doing *A* might have already been determined to balance out roughly equally, and *B* is now seen as providing a tipping point. For example, knowledge of international relations might be seen as a tipping point in an argument for a particular vice-presidential running mate among candidates who have been judged roughly equal in other respects. In another forum on another issue, *B* might have already been determined to be a deal-breaker by a majority of decision makers. In many forums on proposed global warming legislation, for example, the significant impact on economic growth or the potential to add significantly to the budget deficit, might be taken as deal-breaking considerations. Unless we wish to call the entire prior discussion into question, attention to context would obviously affect our evaluation of arguments such as these.

In discussing the evaluation of arguments that we should or shouldn't do something, we have emphasized the importance of weighing pro- and counter-considerations. In doing this, we don't mean to imply that decision-making always boils down to weighing harms and benefits of consequences. If we included ethical decision making under such a procedure, we would be committing ourselves without argument to a particular kind of ethical theory (sometimes called "consequentialist," one version of which is known as "utilitarianism")[10]. We would be excluding from consideration alternative

---

[10]Roughly speaking, utilitarianism requires us, when choosing among alternative actions, to perform the one that would produce the greatest balance of benefits over harms for all who are affected by our action.

ethical theories that base decision-making on principles that sometimes must be followed regardless of harmful consequences and regardless of the benefits of alternative actions. Using this approach, one might argue that we should not do *A* because it would result in deceiving others, or that it would be unfair. If the counter-argument were raised that we would enjoy considerable benefits from doing *A*, this consideration would be seen as irrelevant. The only counter-consideration that might be seen as relevant would be an ethical principle of greater weight that we would be breaking if we did not do *A*. An example might be lying in order to save someone's life. In the context of ethical decision making, the kinds of pro- and counter-considerations that are relevant in evaluating an argument that we should or shouldn't do *A* would sometimes be determined by one's choice of an ethical theory.[11]

If an argument that we should or shouldn't do *A* is to be judged by the weight of pro- and counter-considerations, a case can be made that it should not be reconstructed as a deductive argument to begin with. In Chapter 2, we introduced a kind of nondeductive argument called a convergent argument, which bases its conclusion on independent pro-considerations. We provide an expanded discussion of this kind of argument in Chapter 9 and present some advantages of a convergent reconstruction over a deductive reconstruction.

THE RATIONALE FOR USING THESE CRITICAL TECHNIQUES

The procedure we have recommended for understanding and criticizing arguments is fairly simple: boil a passage down to its stated premises and conclusion (rephrasing if necessary); add any unstated premises or conclusion; and determine whether the conclusion follows and whether the premises should be accepted.[12]

Now we raise the question: Why use this procedure? We can give a partial answer at this time by contrasting our procedure to what is probably the most common way of criticizing an argument: simply to attack the conclusion. This approach is in line with the activity of mere disagreement that we contrasted to critical reasoning in Chapter 1. The problem with this approach is that it does not help us in progressing toward a better-justified set of beliefs.

The point of interpreting your opponent's position as an *argument* is that then you can make progress toward determining whether one of you should change your position. You can ask whether the reasons (premises) given for the conclusion are ones that you have grounds for believing, or grounds for doubting. And you can ask if the conclusion follows from these reasons (premises).

Let us illustrate this point. Suppose someone offers the following argument.

[11]In practice, the underlying ethical theory may be presupposed without being explicitly included in the argument. In which case, it would appear as an implicit premise in an argument reconstruction.

[12]An elaboration of this procedure will be presented in Chapter 11.

Example 4.20

(1) Killing is wrong.

(2) Capital punishment is killing.

∴ *Capital punishment is wrong.*

The least fruitful way of replying would be: "No, capital punishment is not wrong." To stubbornly adhere to this, without regard for the argument that has been presented, is to miss the point of argument and criticism. You have been given reasons for believing that capital punishment is wrong. If you agree with the statements given as reasons, and if the conclusion follows from these reasons, then you should change your mind and agree to the conclusion. If you can show that your opponent should *not* believe the statements given as reasons, or that the conclusion does *not* follow, then your opponent should give up this argument. You could then press your opponent: "Was this the only reason you had for believing your conclusion? Let's look at any other arguments you might have made. Let's look at some arguments against believing that capital punishment is wrong. Perhaps there is an argument on one side or the other that we find conclusive."

Admittedly, there are cases in which it would be appropriate to deny the conclusion of someone's argument. Suppose that someone is presenting an argument that it will not rain today because of the combination of barometric pressure, temperature, and humidity. Just as the person is finishing the argument, you look out the window and see the rain coming down. Of course, it is perfectly appropriate to say, "I don't know where your argument went wrong, but we can see that your conclusion is false."

Still, this is an exceptional case. Usually, we make an argument when our conclusion is one that someone might doubt and we do not have a direct means of determining if it is true. That is why we must look for premises to support our conclusion. And in this standard sort of case, it is not appropriate simply to deny the conclusion.

The same considerations apply when you are defending your own position. It is not enough merely to assert unsupported statements. You should build your argument on the firm foundation of true premises interconnected in a valid argument form.

EXERCISE 4.4 Criticizing Arguments

A. Write a paragraph or two criticizing each of the following arguments. First, set out the argument. (You might find it useful to sketch a version of the argument in standard form on a piece of scratch paper to help you determine its structure and whether it has any missing premises.) Second, indicate whether the conclusion follows. Third, see if you can cast doubt on any of the premises. (When you do this, don't just make a general statement aimed at discrediting several premises at once; instead, tackle the premises specifically, one at a time, clearly identifying which premise you are attacking.) Fourth, consider relevant reformations and whether they can be criticized.

1. Football should be discouraged, for the reason that football makes people aggressive, and any activity that makes people aggressive should be discouraged.
2. The United States is not really democratic, since if it were democratic, each person's opinion would have a significant effect on government.
3. If the government's antiviolence policies are effective, then youth violence will begin to decline. Youth violence is beginning to decline. So the government's antiviolence policies are effective.
4. If you should not be blamed for what your ancestors did, then neither can you take pride in their deeds. It would follow that you are not entitled to take pride in what your ancestors accomplished.
5. If the average couple has more than two children, the population will rise drastically. But we should prevent the population from rising drastically. So we should prevent any couple from having more than two children.
6. If the universe was created, then there was a time at which it did not exist. If there was a time at which it did not exist, then there was a time at which nothing was converted into something. But this is impossible. So the universe was not created.
7. We shouldn't allow doctors to determine the gender of a fetus whenever parents request it. This is so because if we allow such testing, then some parents will abort a fetus simply because of its gender.
8. People have the right to do whatever they want to with their own bodies. Therefore, a pregnant woman has the right to have the fetus aborted if she wants to.
9. All tax increases are unjustified at this time. But since user fees to get into national parks are not taxes, increasing them is justified.
10. No one should get married. This is so because getting married involves promising to live with a person for the rest of one's life. But no one can safely predict that he or she will remain compatible with some other person for life.
11. People should pay taxes to support only parts of government they use. It stands to reason that people without children shouldn't be required to pay for schools.

B. Read each of the following selections and reconstruct what you take to be the main argument. (This is to some degree a matter of interpretation.) Write out the argument in standard form so that it follows a valid pattern. Then write a few paragraphs evaluating the premises.

1.

Global Warming: Confusing Moral and Practical Arguments[13]

David Friedman, December 22, 2006

Concerning Global Warming More Generally

I should add that I am taking no position here on the other usual questions about global warming. I do not know if it is happening, although it seems likely enough. I do not know if, if it is happening, it is due to human action, although that again seems a plausible enough guess. And it is not all clear to me that, if it happens, it will be a bad thing, let alone a catastrophe.

The crucial fact for me is that the more persuasive predictions of bad effects are well into the future; at one point the estimate was a sea level rise of half a meter to a meter over the next century. In my view, the next century is sufficiently uncertain so that it makes little sense to take expensive precautions against risks that far off. By the time the risk arrives, if it arrives, we may have already wiped ourselves out in some other way. If we have not wiped ourselves out, our lives may have changed in a way that eliminates or even reverses the problem; commuting via virtual reality produces little CO_2. If we are still around and the problem is still around, we are likely to have a level of technology and wealth that will make possible a range of solutions well beyond what we are currently considering.

All of these are reasons why I think a persuasive case for doing something about global warming requires evidence, not yet available, of serious negative effects in the fairly near future. But that conclusion does not depend on whether whatever is happening to the climate is or is not our fault.

2.

The West cannot survive if we continue to avert our eyes from the obvious[14]

By Kathleen Parker

In the wake of last week's foiled terrorist plot to blow up 10 U.S. jetliners flying between Britain and the United States, sensible people are reconsidering our government's stubborn opposition to profiling.

Among the sensible elsewhere are officials of the British Department for Transport, who are proposing ethnic profiling as a means of more effectively identifying potential terrorists. The predictable chorus of opposition has chimed in on cue.

The Muslim Council of Britain has warned the government to think "very carefully," saying that including "behavioral

[13]Selection from http://daviddfriedman.blogspot.com/2006/12/global-warming-confusing-moral-and.html. Reprinted with permission of the author.

[14]From *Jewish World Review*, August 16. 2006. http://www.JewishWorldReview.com. Reprinted by permission.

pattern recognition" in passenger profiling would lead to discrimination. A spokesman for the council said, "Before some kind of religious profiling is introduced, a case has to be made." Challenge accepted.

Most terrorist acts of the past several decades have been perpetrated by Muslim men between the ages of 17 and 40. A complete list would fill this space, but following is a partial Islamic terrorist resume:

> *Eleven Israeli athletes murdered at the Munich Olympics (1972); U.S. Marine barracks blown up in Beirut (1983), Achille Lauro cruise ship hijacked and elderly, disabled American passenger killed (1985); TWA Flight 847 hijacked (1985); Pan Am Flight 103 bombed (1988); World Trade Center bombed (1993); U.S. embassies bombed in Kenya and Tanzania (1998); USS Cole bombed (2000); Sept. 11, 2001; Madrid and London train bombings (2004 and 2005).*

Yet we are torn. Profiling seems both un-American and dangerous in an era of slippery slopes. The paranoid leap is that detention camps are just around the bend. Thus, instead of deciding to closely scrutinize airline passengers who fit the description of a likely perpetrator—based not on bigotry, but on evidence, history and common sense—we frisk the elderly and confiscate toddlers' sippy cups.

Critics of profiling insist that focusing on one group will distract us from other possible terrorists—presumably all those Baptist grandmothers recently converted to Islam. They also invariably point to Timothy McVeigh, our own homegrown terrorist who blew up a federal office building in Oklahoma City. As if one white-bred misfit—or the occasional Caucasian Muslim—cancels out 35 years of Middle Eastern terrorists invoking Muhammad.

For a nation that laments its lapse in dot-connecting before 9/11, we are curiously blind when it comes to dealing honestly with certain people of a certain sort. Profiling isn't aimed at demonizing Muslims; it's aimed at saving lives, including Muslims.

We learned from investigators of the foiled London-based plot that Muslims played a key role in busting the conspirators, for which the world is grateful. But the idea that profiling young males of Asian or Middle Eastern descent now would alienate those who heretofore had been helpful, as some have argued, presumes that Muslims have no interest in self-preservation.

Or that they're all so belligerently ethnocentric that they'll cease cooperating if airport security officials suddenly start behaving competently.

Identifying potential terrorists is complicated by their sheer numbers in places like Britain, where between 16,000 and 18,000 Muslims are suspected to be Islamic extremists, according to Britain's MI5 counterterrorism unit. How do you track 15,000 people? You don't.

But we can focus energies and resources where plausible, including at airports where profilers are invited to be polite and discreet. And we can listen to sensible Muslims like Abdel Rahman al-Rashed, general manager of the al-Arabiya news channel, who wrote in the Arab News two years ago what our own officials struggle to say:

"It is a certain fact that not all Muslims are terrorists, but it is equally certain, and exceptionally painful, that almost all terrorists are Muslims. . . . We cannot clear our names unless we own up to the shameful fact that terrorism has become an Islamic enterprise; an almost exclusive monopoly, implemented by Muslim men and women."

And the West cannot survive if we continue to avert our eyes from the obvious. On the legal questions, profiling has at least one notable defender—John Banzhaf, the George Washington University public interest law professor best known for taking on tobacco and fast food.

Banzhaf argues that racial profiling is constitutional if done in accordance with U.S. Supreme Court guidelines that ethnicity not be the sole criteria. Other considerations for potential hijackers might be age, gender, behavior or clothing. He also notes that courts have upheld using race/ethnicity to further "compelling state interest," as in considering race for college admissions.

"Obviously, the government's interest in protecting the lives of thousands of citizens from a major terrorist attack is at least as 'compelling' as a better college education," he says.

For the past several years, Banzhaf has been a pain in the neck to the tobacco and fast food industries. Let's hope he proves equally troublesome to the terrorists among us.

3.

Networks Don't Get Connection[15]

by Cal Thomas

ABC Television broadcast a special "Men, Sex and Rape," last week that was, as New York Times reviewer Walter Goodman noted, full of "pretension to virtue."

After the obligatory tabloid-television approach featuring "swelling breasts and buttocks, mostly amid the sands of Palm Beach," as Goodman summarized it, the program attempted to move to the brain for some serious discussion of a troubling subject. The approach had the moral impact of going to confession after a long-planned orgy.

First Amendment absolutists have resisted every attempt to control the huge levels of effluent that have turned our society into a toxic waste dump. Then they create programs like the one broadcast on ABC in which they wring their hands and decry what they have helped to create. It would be like the tobacco industry criticizing the growing number of lung-cancer deaths.

Women are being raped in record numbers—as many as 1,871 per day if one rape—victims rights group is accurate.

One does not have to be a social scientist to see a connection between increased incidents of rape, and other acts of violence against women, and the way women are treated in the popular media. One quick look at MTV offers a sample of the diet on which many young people feed at an early age.

A new Michael Jackson video called "In the Closet" features Michael and a woman thrusting their pelvises at each other. Michael sings, "there's something about you, baby, that makes me want to give it to you."

This video is followed immediately by another called "Baby's Got Back," in which women are shaking their behinds at the camera, various fruits and vegetables shaped like body parts are shown, and the rapper says he like women's buttocks and feels like "sticking it" to them.

[15]Op-Ed, *Seattle Post-Intelligencer*, 14 May, 1992. Reprinted with permission of Tribune Media Services.

Pornography is worse, of course, but this stuff is what might be called the beginners' material for the raping of the young American mind.

Andrea Dworkin, the feminist writer who has crusaded for tougher anti-pornography laws, wrote a profound letter to The New York Times last week in which she told of her own sexual abuse. She believes rape is linked to the tolerance and promotion of pornography and sexual images that give cultural permission for men to treat women as objects, not fellow human beings.

To the purists who will not tolerate any controls on "speech" or pictures, Dworkin wrote: "Freedom looks different when you are the one it is being practiced on. Those sexy expletives are the hate words he uses on you while he is using you." Dworkin added that men "act out pornography. They have acted it out on me." She correctly indicated men who hide behind the First Amendment so they can traffic for profit in women's misery. "They eroticize inequality in a way that materially promotes rape, battery, maiming and bondage; they make a product they know dehumanizes, degrades and exploits women; they hurt women to make the pornography, and then consumers use the pornography in assaults both verbal and physical."

For networks (or movie and magazine publishers) to claim that there is no connection, or that they are not responsible if there is a connection, between pictures and words and the brutalizing of women is a lie. Do they tell their advertisers there is no connection between consumer behavior and images of soap, cars and beer? Not if they want to sell ad space and commercial time. For advertisers, they make the opposite claim.

Chris O'Sullivan, a social psychologist who is writing a book on group sexual assault on college campuses, sees a link between sex crimes and visual images. In a letter to The New York Times, he wrote: "There is a higher level of aggression, sexual and nonsexual, among those who most often expose themselves to depictions of sexual and nonsexual violence than among those who do not."

Were such a connection established, or even likely, in any other field, government would quickly move to do something about it. Kentucky Republican Sen. Mitch McConnell is trying to take a small step towards clearing up the mainstream of some of this filth in his bill that would compensate victims of sexual assault who could link the assault to pornography. Most of the media establishment has written editorials and lobbied against the bill.

Yet, it is a bill and an idea deserving of support. Women deserve as such protection against rape as it is possible for society to offer. As Dworkin wrote: "A photograph shields rape and torture for profit. In defending pornography, as if it were speech, liberals defend the new slavers. The only fiction in pornography is the smile on the woman's face."

If rape is a terrible crime, and it is, and if there is a connection between pornography and the cultural permission it gives those already predisposed to perform these acts on women, then the government has an obligation and duty to control its proliferation. The McConnell bill is a good place to start.

CHAPTER 5 (OPTIONAL)

When Does the Conclusion Follow? A More Formal Approach to Validity

The informal discussion of validity found at the beginning of Chapter 4 described the structural relationship between the premises and conclusion in a valid argument. It tried to capture the sense of logical necessity in which, if an argument is valid and its premises are true, it is necessary for the conclusion to be true. This same relationship between premises and conclusion that makes an argument valid can also be defined in terms of logical impossibility: An argument is valid if and only if it is logically impossible for all the premises to be true and the conclusion false.

The illustrations given in Chapter 4 appealed to your informal sense of necessity or impossibility. Logicians (philosophers interested in the validity of arguments) have devised a variety of more formal techniques for illustrating the concept of *logical necessity* and the related concept of *logical impossibility,* which in turn are ways of systematically illustrating the concept of validity. Further, these methods provide us with useful techniques for testing whether an argument is valid.

The method used by logicians is formal in the sense that it abstracts the form or pattern of an argument from its verbal content. This is seen as an appropriate move because validity is a feature of the structure of an argument independent of its particular content. More generally: An argument is valid if and only if all arguments of the same form are such that it is logically impossible for all the premises to be true and the conclusion false.

In an effort to characterize the form of arguments, logicians have introduced standard ways of presenting an argument. We have taken some steps in this direction in our chart of Some Common Successful Argument Patterns. For example, we gave the form of *modus ponens* as

Example 5.1

(1) If A, then B.

(2) A.

$\therefore$ *B.*

In this example, the capital letters A and B are used to stand for statements in an argument.[1] We have also numbered the premises, drawn a line, and used the symbol $\therefore$ meaning "therefore," to indicate that we have an argument with premises and a conclusion.

Logicians commonly go even further in their use of symbols. Whereas we have continued to use fragments of English such as "If . . . then . . . " and "Either . . . or . . . " to display more complex, logical features of statements, logicians typically illustrate form by using special symbols roughly (but only *roughly*) the equivalent to the English language terms we have employed. So, for example, the following table gives these symbols for some common "logical words" that apply to whole statements. These logical words are often called *logical connectives*; most *connect* two or more statements.

Symbol	***Name***	***Example***	***Rough English Equivalent***
$\neg$	Negation	$\neg A$	It is not the case that *A*
&	Conjunction	$A \& B$	*A* and *B*
$\vee$	Disjunction	$A \vee B$	Either *A* or *B* (or both)[2]
$\rightarrow$	Conditional	$A \rightarrow B$	If *A*, then *B*
$\leftrightarrow$	Biconditional	$A \leftrightarrow B$	*A* if and only if *B*

---

[1]We use the term *statement* rather than *sentence* because the same sentence (for example, "It flew") can be used to make different statements on different occasions depending on the reference of the pronoun. Further, different sentences can be used to make the same statement (for instance, "It flew," and "The plane flew").

[2]This use of $\vee$ to include the case when both are true is called the *inclusive use of or* as opposed to the *exclusive or*, which excludes this case.

Using these symbols we could illustrate some of the standard statement-based argument forms as follows:

Modus Ponens	***Modus Tollens***	***Disjunctive Argument***	***Hypothetical Argument***
(1) $A \rightarrow B$	(1) $A \rightarrow B$	(1) $A \vee B$	(1) $A \rightarrow B$
(2) A	(2) $\neg B$	(2) $\neg A$	(2) $B \rightarrow C$
$\therefore B$	$\therefore \neg A$	$\therefore B$	$\therefore A \rightarrow C$

These symbols can be used to present a variety of more complicated arguments. For instance:

(1) $A \rightarrow B$
(2) $C \rightarrow D$
(3) $(B \& D) \rightarrow E$
(4) A
(5) C

$\therefore E$

(1) $A \rightarrow B$
(2) $C \rightarrow D$
(3) $A \vee C$
(4) $\neg B$

$\therefore D$

EXERCISE 5.1

Formalizing

A. Assign letters to each *simple* statement given below and use our connective symbols to translate the more complex statements built out of them into our formalism using letters and symbols as described in the previous section.

1. The United States will continue to delay significant steps to reduce greenhouse gas emissions.
2. If the United States will continue to delay significant steps to reduce greenhouse gas emissions, then global warming will produce irreversible degradation of the environment.
3. If the United States will continue to delay significant steps to reduce greenhouse gas emissions, then the United States will face frequent, massive destruction from violent weather.
4. Either the United States will not continue to delay significant steps to reduce greenhouse gas emissions, or it will face frequent massive destruction from violent weather.
5. If the United States will continue to delay significant steps to reduce greenhouse gas emissions, then either we must be willing to pay vast sums to repair destruction from violent weather or we must be prepared to live with the damage.

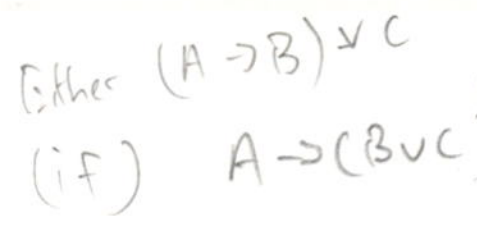

6. The United States will continue to delay significant steps to reduce greenhouse gas emissions, and vast sums will be needed to repair destruction from violent weather.

7. If the United States will continue to delay significant steps to reduce greenhouse gas emissions, and vast sums will be needed to repair destruction from violent weather, then the U.S. deficit will be vastly increased or U.S. taxes will be drastically raised.
8. If the U.S. deficit will not be vastly increased and U.S taxes will be not be drastically raised, then the United States will not continue to delay significant steps to reduce greenhouse gas emissions. **(Hint: Use parentheses to group elements together. For instance, "Both *A* and *B*," can be grouped (*A* & *B*).)**

B. The following statements have less obvious translations into our formalism.

1. It is not the case that stiff penalties for drug crimes will not continue.
2. Prisons are crowded now, but this will not be a problem if drug arrests decrease. **(Hint: *But* can typically be translated like "and.")**
3. Stiff penalties for drug crimes will continue unless political sentiments in the United States change. **(Hint: *Unless* can often be translated like "or.")**
4. The prison population will subside only if stiff penalties for drug crimes will not continue. **(Hint: *A only if B* can often be translated like "If *A*, then *B*.")**
5. Neither will the prison population subside nor will stiff penalties for crimes be reduced. **(Hint: *Neither A nor B* can be translated like "It is not the case that either *A* or *B*" and also like "It is not the case that *A*, and it is not the case that *B*." As we will see in the next section, the latter two statements in a sense say the same thing.)**

C. 1. Translate the arguments in Exercise 3.1, A1–5 into our formalism. Be sure to indicate which letter stands for which statement.
2. Translate the various reconstructions found in Exercise 3.1, Cl (a, b, c), C2a, and C3a into our formalism. Be sure to indicate which letter stands for which statement.

D. Translate the following arguments into our formalism:

1. *(1) Either prisons will remain crowded or vast sums will be spent on new prisons.*

   (2) If vast sums are spent on new prisons, then taxes will remain high.

   (3) Taxes will not remain high.

   ∴ Prisons will remain crowded.

2. *(1) If the HIV/AIDS epidemic continues unabated, then there will be an increased burden on already-strained worldwide health care systems.*

   (2) If there will be an increased burden on already-strained, worldwide health care systems, then there will be increased pressure for world governments to provide money to save the health care system.

(3) If there will be increased pressure for world governments to provide money to save already-strained, worldwide health care systems, then economic growth will be significantly limited especially in the developing world.

∴ If the HIV/AIDS epidemic continues unabated, economic growth will be significantly limited especially in the developing world.

3. *(1) The United States will ensure long-term prosperity only if it devotes more of its wealth to long-term economic development.*

   (2) It will devote more of its wealth to long-term economic development only if the government changes its antitrust laws to allow much greater cooperation among competing companies.

   (3) The United States will not change its antitrust laws unless American consumers become willing to pay much more for their consumer goods.

   (4) American consumers will not become willing to pay much more for their consumer goods.

   ∴ The United States will not ensure long-term prosperity.

4. *(1) A widespread spiritual awakening will occur in the United States by the year 2020 if and only if personal success becomes measured by the quality of a person's character, not the size of his wallet.*

   (2) Personal success will continue to be measured by the size of his wallet unless American education concerns itself with issues of ethics and morality.

   (3) America will continue to be able to exclude religious instruction from the classroom only if American education does not concern itself with issues of ethics and morality.

   ∴ America will continue to exclude religious instruction from the classroom only if a widespread spiritual awakening will not occur in the United States by the year 2020.

STATEMENTS CONTAINING LOGICAL CONNECTIVES: WHEN ARE THEY TRUE? WHEN ARE THEY FALSE?

To evaluate whether an argument is valid, it is necessary to consider the situations in which the statements that make it up are true or false. When a simple statement is represented by a single letter—for instance, *A*—only two possible situations exist: either *A* is true or *A* is false. We can represent these alternatives as follows:

A
T
F

Given these two possible situations, we can determine the truth value of the slightly more complicated statement we obtain by negating *A*. In the situation in which *A* is true, the negation of *A* ("It is not the case that *A* . . .") is false, and when *A* is false, the negation of *A* is true. We can represent these alternatives as:

A	¬ *A*
T	F
F	T

We can extend this way of evaluating the truth statements to embrace compound statements created when we connect two simpler statements to form a conjunction, disjunction, conditional, or biconditional. To represent the possible situations when we have two statements linked by one of the logical connectives, first we have to display the joint possibilities. If we have two statements, when the first is true, the second can be either true or false, and when the first is false, the second can again be either true or false. This gives us four possibilities: (1) both are true; (2) the first is true and the second false; (3) the first is false and the second true; or (4) both are false.

A	*B*
T	T
T	F
F	T
F	T

This allows us to define the various logical connectives. A conjunction (for example, *A* & *B*) is true if both elements are true (for instance, both *A* and *B*). It is false otherwise.

This can be displayed graphically as

Possible Situations		***Truth Value of Compound Statement***
A	*B*	*A* & *B*
T	T	T
T	F	F
F	T	F
F	F	F

A disjunction (for instance, *A* ∨ *B*) is true if one element or the other or both are true (for example, *A* is true or *B* is true or both are true). It is false otherwise. This captures the *inclusive* sense of *or* that includes the case in which both disjuncts are true.

Possible Situations		*Truth Value of Compound Statement*
A	*B*	$A \vee B$
T	T	T
T	F	T
F	T	T
F	F	F

A conditional is true if either the first element is false or the second element is true. It is false only if the first element is true and the second false.

Possible Situations		*Truth Value of Compound Statement*
A	*B*	$A \rightarrow B$
T	T	T
T	F	F
F	T	T
F	F	T

A biconditional is true if both elements are true together or false together. It is false if they have different truth values.

Possible Situations		*Truth Value of Compound Statement*
A	*B*	$A \leftrightarrow B$
T	T	T
T	F	F
F	T	F
F	F	T

The definition of the logical connective & is closely related to our informal understanding of the connective *and*. But you should not assume, even in this case, that the formal, logical connective is a perfect translation of the everyday term. Consider the two statements:

A: The student took the exam.

B: The student looked at the answers.

The statement *A* & *B* has the same truth value as the statement *B* & *A* although you might well distinguish the first from the second:

The student took the exam and the student looked at the answers.

The student looked at the answers and the student took the exam.

Sometimes *and* means "and then" in English. The connective & does not capture the meaning "and then." Similarly, when a parent says, "You can have either cookies or cake," it is usually meant in the "exclusive" sense that the child can have one or the other but not both. If we translated this statement as $A \vee B$, we are treating it as involving not this exclusive sense but the inclusive sense of *or* that allows for both to be true. To represent the strictly exclusive sense we would need a more complicated expression:

$$((A \vee B) \;\&\; \neg (A \;\&\; B))$$[3]

The conditional "→" provides an even rougher translation of the English analogue "If . . . then . . . " Suppose we have the statement *If I lie, then I'll be sorry.* It seems reasonable enough to call this premise true if I do lie and I am sorry. And it is surely reasonable to call it false if I do lie and I am not sorry (rows 1 and 2 in the display table for the conditional). But why call it true if I don't lie but I'm still sorry, or if I don't lie and I am not sorry (rows 3 and 4 in the table)?

According to the definition of the conditional we have given, some statements in the formal language will be interpreted as true even though in our natural language we would ordinarily consider them to be false.[4] As long as the "if" part of the conditional is false, the whole conditional statement will be interpreted as true. To preserve the simplicity of our method of relating the truth of the elements in a compound sentence to the truth of the whole so that the truth of the whole is *a function* of just the truth value of the parts, we accept some slack in our translation of the *if–then* statement. We take *If I lie, then I'll be sorry* to assert nothing more than *It won't be the case that I'll lie and not be sorry.* That is, the only situation in which we say that *If A, then B* is false is when *A* is true and *B* is false. Suppose I said, *If you pay me ten dollars, then I'll juggle fourteen eggs.* I might insist that my statement wasn't false if you don't pay me and I don't juggle. And if you don't pay but I juggle the fourteen eggs anyway, then you certainly can't complain that I lied. But if you do pay me and I don't juggle, then my statement clearly wasn't true.

In the examples given above, we examined compound statements consisting of a logical symbol and one or two statement letters. But the definitions for the symbols apply even when they link more complicated expressions. For example, all the following expressions are also negations:

$$\neg (A \;\&\; B)$$
$$\neg (\neg A \rightarrow B)$$
$$\neg ((A \;\&\; B) \vee (C \leftrightarrow D))$$

---

[3]The truth table for "exclusive or" (*xor*) is

A	*B*	*A xor B*
T	T	F
T	F	T
F	T	T
F	F	F

[4]For example, assume that I won't snap my fingers. The most natural interpretation in this contrary-to-fact condition treats as true the statement, "If I snap my fingers, then I will hear a sound," and as false the statement, "If I snap my fingers, then I will turn into a bird," even though both are true in this counterfactual situation according to the definition of "→."

As in the instance of simple negations, the truth value of the whole compound depends on the truth of the statement it contains. So, ¬ (*A* & *B*) is true if (*A* & *B*) is false, and ¬ (*A* & *B*) is false if (*A* & *B*) is true. Since the symbols can link complex elements, not just simple statements, we can display the various compound statements in a more general way: We represent one element of a compound (no matter how complex) with a square (□) and another with a triangle (Δ). The following display lists the possible situations in which generalized compounds involving the logical symbols are true or false.

Possible Situations		*Negation*
Row	□	¬ □
1	T	F
2	F	T

Possible Situations			*Conjunction*	*Disjunction*	*Conditional*	*Biconditional*
Row	□	Δ	□ & Δ	□ ∨ Δ	□ → Δ	□ ↔ Δ
1	T	T	T	T	T	T
2	T	F	F	T	F	F
3	F	T	F	T	T	F
4	F	F	F	F	T	T

We can use these generalized definitions to evaluate complex statements. For example, consider ¬(*A* & *B*). It is a denial that contains a conjunction as a part. To evaluate the truth of the whole denial, we need to determine the truth of the contained conjunction. Suppose that the simple statement *A* is T(rue) and *B* is F(alse). In this situation (row 2 of the definition), the conjunction is F(alse). We have now evaluated the contained conjunction; we know that it is false. But the overall statement is a negation of this conjunction. If we look in row 2 of the definition for negation, we see that, if the contained element is F(alse), the whole negation is T(rue). So in the situation in which *A* is T(rue) and *B* is F(alse), ¬ (*A* & *B*) is T(rue). We can represent these steps diagrammatically as follows:

Example 5.2

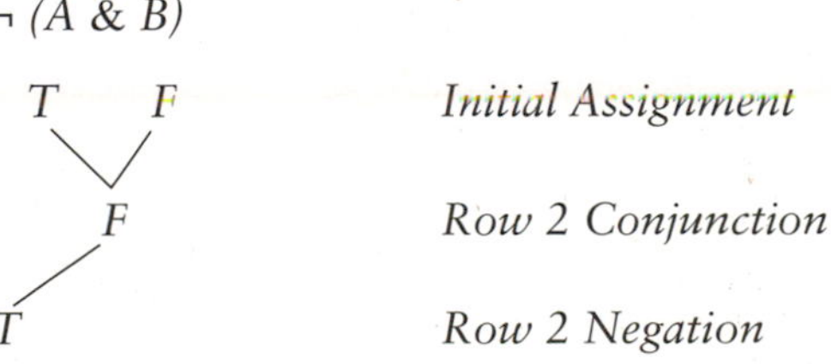

A similar technique will help us evaluate the compound ¬ (¬ *A* → *B*), where *A* is T(rue) and *B* is F(alse).

Example 5.3 $\neg(\neg A \rightarrow B)$

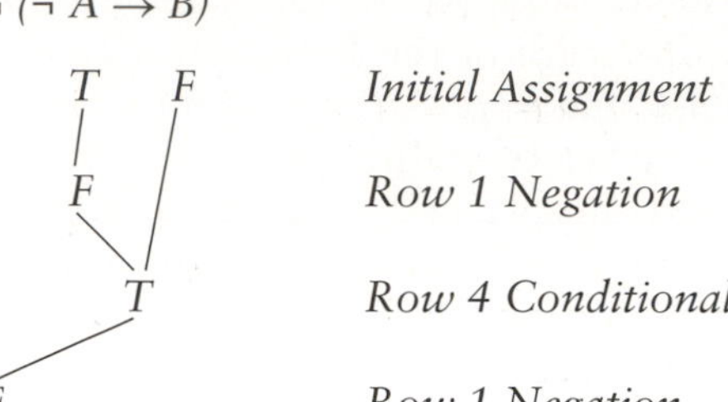

Finally, consider the following assignment and evaluation:

Example 5.4 $\neg((A \,\&\, B) \vee (C \leftrightarrow D))$

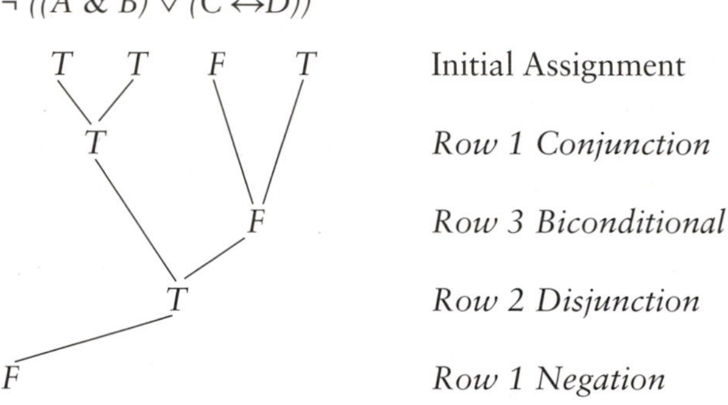

EXERCISE 5.2

Evaluating Statements

A. Assume the following initial assignment of truth values to the statements: *A* is T(rue), *B* is F(alse). Use the techniques of evaluation listed above to determine the truth value of the following compound statements. Be sure to list the appropriate row and connective to justify each step in the evaluation diagram.

1. $A \rightarrow \neg B$
2. $\neg B \rightarrow A$
3. $\neg(A \,\&\, \neg B)$
4. $\neg A \vee \neg B$
5. $\neg(A \leftrightarrow B)$

B. Evaluate the compound statements in step 1, but with the initial assignment *A* is F(alse), *B* is F(alse).

C. Assume the following initial assignment of truth values to the statements: *A* is F(alse), *B* is T(rue), *C* is T(rue), *D* is F(alse). Create evaluation diagrams for the following compound statements. (You don't need to list a justification for each step, but you should note to yourself how the definitions apply to each move you make.)

1. $A \rightarrow (B \vee C)$
2. $(A \,\&\, B) \rightarrow C$

3. $(A \vee B) \rightarrow (C \,\&\, D)$
4. $A \rightarrow (B \rightarrow C)$
5. $(\neg A \rightarrow B) \vee (\neg D \rightarrow C)$
6. $(A \leftrightarrow B) \vee (\neg C \leftrightarrow D)$
7. $\neg ((A \vee \neg B) \,\&\, C)$
8. $\neg (\neg (\neg A \rightarrow B) \vee \neg (\neg C \leftrightarrow \neg D))$

TRUTH TABLES AS A TEST FOR VALIDITY

The technique of displaying the possible situations that make individual statements true or false can be extended to formulate a test for the validity of arguments: the *truth table test*. Such a table lists the truth or falsity of *all* the statements in an argument for all possible situations. A truth table can be used to assess whether an argument is valid—that is, to determine whether there is a possible situation that makes all the premises and the conclusion false. If we find such a counterexample, then the argument is invalid. If there is no such counterexample, then the argument is valid. Consider the argument and formalization below.

Example 5.5

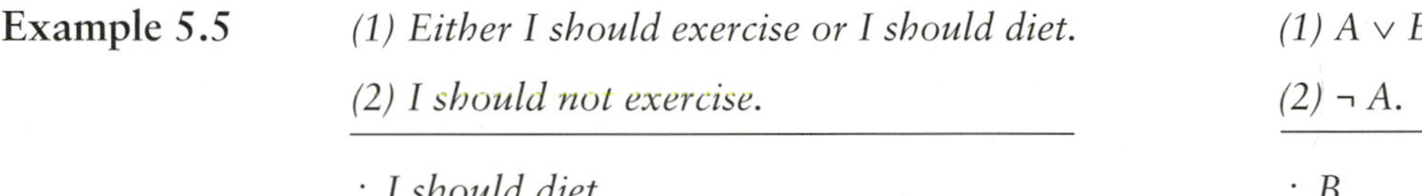

(1) Either I should exercise or I should diet.	*(1) A* $\vee$ *B.*
(2) I should not exercise.	*(2)* $\neg$ *A.*
$\therefore$ *I should diet.*	$\therefore$ *B.*

This argument involves only two simple statements. We can construct a table that lists the four possible situations—that is, initial assignments of truth or falsity to these two statements—much as we did in our definition of the connectives in the previous section. The truth table for the argument adds an evaluation for each of the statements in the argument (Premises 1 and 2 and the conclusion) for each of these four possible initial situations.

Initial Assignments			*Evaluation of Statements for These Assignments*		
Possible Situations			*Premises*		*Conclusion*
	A	B	$A \vee B$	$\neg A$	*B (Repeated)*
1	T	T	T	F	T
2	T	F	T	F	F
3	F	T	T	T	T
4	F	F	F	T	F
			Disjunction	Negation	

Each row represents a possible situation. As in our previous discussion, the first line, for example, is a situation in which A is true and B is true; the second line is a situation in which A is true and B is false. The premise and conclusion columns evaluate the various statements in each of these possible situations.

The column under "$A \vee B$" indicates the truth or falsity of this disjunction for each possible situation listed at the left. The column under "$\neg A$" gives the negation of A in each situation. Since A is T(rue) in the first two situations and F(alse) in the second two, its negation will be the opposite—F(alse) in the first two rows, T(rue) in the second two. Finally, in this simple example, the conclusion is itself a simple statement, so we merely repeat the initial assignment of B in each of the four situations.

Because a truth table displays all possible initial assignments of truth values to simple statements contained in an argument and allows comparison of all premises with the conclusion, we can use it as a test of *validity* for arguments. You will recall that an argument is *valid* if it is *impossible* for all the premises to be *true and* the conclusion *false*. We can apply this account to arguments by asking whether there is a possible initial assignment of truth values to simple statements such that all the premises are T(rue) and the conclusion is F(alse). If there is no such counterexample, then the argument is *valid*.

In Example 5.5, there are only four possible situations, and we can examine each possibility in turn. In the first situation—row 1 where both A and B are T(rue)—the premise $A \vee B$ is T(rue) but premise $\neg A$ is F(alse). Since not all the premises are T(rue), this could not be a possible case in which all the premises are true and the conclusion is false.

Similarly, in row 2 where A is T(rue) and B is F(alse), again $\neg A$ is F(alse), so not all the premises are true. In row 3 where A is F(alse) and B is T(rue), however, the premise $A \vee B$ and the premise $\neg A$ are both T(rue), but in this possible case, the conclusion B is also T(rue). So here again, we satisfy the requirements for validity. Finally, in row 4 with the initial assignment of F(alse) to both A and B, we have the premise $A \vee B$ is F(alse); hence not all premises are true, so again examination shows that we don't have a possible situation in which all the premises are true and the conclusion is false.

We have examined all possible situations (that is, all possible initial assignments of truth or falsity, T or F, to the simple statements that make up the argument). We have found no counterexample in which all the premises are true and the conclusion is false. (Alternatively, we could say that in every case in which the conclusion is false, at least one of the premises is false.) When this occurs, we declare the argument to be *valid*.[5]

Notice that, given this account of *validity*, the only cases that could show that the argument was not valid are those in which all premises are true. If one or more premises is false for a given possible situation—that is, for a row in the truth table—then it makes no difference whether the conclusion is true or false on that line, because it could not be a case in which all the premises are true and the conclusion *is false*. So, to use the truth table method as a test of

[5]To be more precise, the argument is *deductively valid*. Note as well that an argument might fail this test and still be deductively valid. As we will see below, some deductively valid arguments have a form that cannot be completely represented in terms of statement letters, negation, conjunction, disjunction, conditional, and biconditional.

validity, you need only construct the table and examine the rows in which all the premises are true. The argument is valid if, for each such case, the conclusion is also true.[6] If we find even one line in which all premises are true and the conclusion *is false,* we have found a counterexample (to the claim that the argument is valid).

Consider the following *invalid* argument and its formalization:

Example 5.6

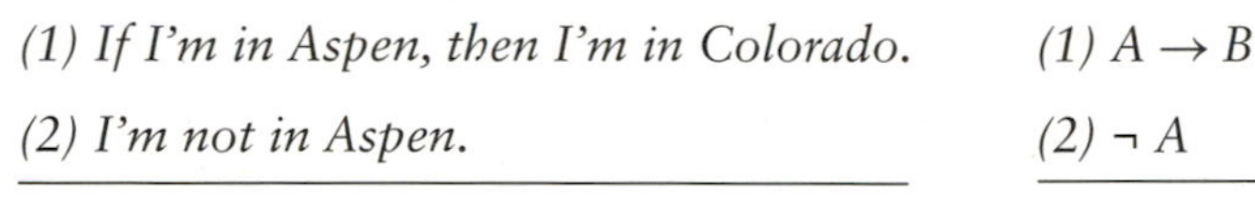

(1) If I'm in Aspen, then I'm in Colorado. — (1) $A \rightarrow B$

(2) I'm not in Aspen. — (2) $\neg A$

∴ I'm not in Colorado. — $\therefore \neg B$

We can construct the following truth table:

	Initial Assignments		*Premises*		*Conclusion*
	A	B	$A \rightarrow B$	$\neg A$	$\neg B$
1	T	T	T	F	F
2	T	F	F	F	T
3	F	T	T	T	F
4	F	F	T	T	T

Counterexample: situation where all the premises are true but the conclusion is false. (row 3)

Counterexample: A Situation Where All the Premises Are True but the Conclusion Is False Given this truth table, the only rows that we need to examine to apply the test for validity are rows 3 and 4. These are the only possible situations in which all the premises are true. In this example, row 3, where A is false and B is true, has all premises true, but the conclusion, $\neg B$, is false. So here we have an instance in which there is a possible initial assignment of truth values to the simple statements such that, given the definitions of the *logical connectives* involved, the premise statements are both true but the conclusion is false. Thus the structure of the argument (as given by the logical connectives) does not guarantee that if the premises are all true the conclusion is also. It makes no difference that row 4 has both premises true and the conclusion also true. Even an invalid argument can have all true premises and a true conclusion in some situations, as in row 4 of this example. But this argument form does not guarantee that this happens, as row 3 shows. In a valid argument, situations such as that in row 3 do not occur; truth of premises guarantees truth of the conclusion.

[6] In the strange case in which there are no rows where all the premises are true, we say that the premises are *inconsistent* (that is, there is no possible case in which they are jointly true). However, arguments with such an inconsistent set of premises are said to be *valid* because there will be no case in which all the premises are true and the conclusion is false simply as a consequence of there being no case in which all the premises are true.

The truth table method can be extended to arguments that contain more than two simple statements. With each additional statement letter, we double the number of rows in our truth table:

one letter	2 rows
two letters	4 rows
three letters	8 rows
four letters	16 rows
and so on.	

The test for validity can easily be extended to such arguments. Consider an argument of the following form:

Example 5.7 *(1)* $A \rightarrow B$

(2) $B \rightarrow C$

(3) $\neg C$

$\therefore \neg A$

The argument generates this truth table:[7]

	Initial Assignments			*Premises*			*Conclusion*
	A	B	C	$A \rightarrow B$	$B \rightarrow C$	$\neg C$	$\neg A$
1	T	T	T	T	T	F	F
2	T	T	F	T	F	T	F
3	T	F	T	F	T	F	F
4	T	F	F	F	T	T	F
5	F	T	T	T	T	F	T
6	F	T	F	T	F	T	T
7	F	F	T	T	T	F	T
8	F	F	F	T	T	T	T

All premises true but conclusion also true

The truth table method illustrated here provides a useful way of testing an argument whose validity depends on the logical structure generated by negation, conjunction, disjunction, the conditional, and the biconditional as long as only a few simple statements are involved. It becomes ungainly if we have more than four or five different simple statements. For this reason,

[7]Note that a simple way of getting the eight possible cases is to repeat the four possibilities for the two letters *B* and *C*. We have these four situations when *A* is true and again when *A* is false. If we had a four-letter argument, we could generate the sixteen possible situations by including the eight we have in this example, when this fourth statement is true and again when it is false, giving us the requisite sixteen lines for a table with four simple statements. Each time we add a letter, we double the number of rows needed in the truth table.

more general proof techniques are used in such cases. We will give you the flavor of these methods in another section of this chapter. Nevertheless, many commonly encountered arguments can be formalized and tested for validity using simple truth table methods. As we will see in the next section, however, some arguments that fail the truth table test can still be considered *valid*. To show their validity we need to look at logical structure in a more fine-grained way. Logical form, as we have considered it so far, consists of rather coarse relations between statements. We have simple statements, and compound statements built up of them. Consider the following argument:

Example 5.8

(1) All pigs are beings having a four-chambered heart.

(2) Mike is a pig.

∴ Mike is a being having a four-chambered heart.

If we try to represent this argument using the methods discussed so far, we would have to assign a single, separate statement letter to each premise and the conclusion. It would have the form

(1) A

(2) B

∴ C

and the truth table

	Initial Assignments			*Premises*		*Conclusion*
	A	*B*	*C*	*A*	*B*	*C*
1	T	T	T	T	T	T
2	T	T	F	T	T	F
3	T	F	T	T	F	T
4	T	F	F	T	F	F
5	F	T	T	F	T	T
6	F	T	F	F	T	F
7	F	F	T	F	F	T
8	F	F	F	F	F	F

Conterexample: both premises are true but the conclusion is false.

As indicated by row 2, it is possible for an argument of this form to have both premises true and the conclusion false. This is just what we would expect. There need not be any logical relation between the three separate sentences. Nevertheless, there is another way of representing logical form that, so to speak, goes inside the simple statements to represent their internal structure. We have already seen this structure in our list of successful argument patterns. Example 5.8 is an instance of Predicate Instantiation, pattern (vi).

(1) All P_1's are P_2's.

(2) m is a P_1.

∴ m is a P_2.

We will discuss techniques appropriate to arguments such as these in the next section.

EXERCISE 5.3

Truth Tables

A. Complete the truth tables for the two *if–then* argument patterns from our chart listed below. Note that when three separate statements (*A*, *B*, *C*) are used to construct the premises and conclusion, there are eight possible situations represented by combinations of truth and falsity of these statements. Use the same interpretation of *if–then* as we used in the example above—that is, a statement of this form will be taken to be false only when the "if" part is true and the "then" part is false.

1.

Initial Assignments		*Premises*		*Conclusion*
A	B	$A \rightarrow B$	$\neg B$	$\neg A$
T	T			
T	F			
F	T			
F	F			

2.

Initial Assignments			*Premises*			*Conclusion*
A	B	C	$A \rightarrow B$	$B \rightarrow C$	A	C
T	T	T				
T	T	F				
T	F	T				
T	F	F				
F	T	T				
F	T	F				
F	F	T				
F	F	F				

B. Complete the following truth tables for invalid argument patterns. Note which rows indicate a case in which the premises are all true but the conclusion is false.

1.

Initial Assignments		*Premises*		*Conclusion*
A	*B*	$\neg A \to B$	*A*	*B*
T	T			
T	F			
F	T			
F	F			

2.

Initial Assignments			*Premises*			*Conclusion*
A	*B*	*C*	$A \to B$	$B \to C$	$\neg A$	*C*
T	T	T				
T	T	F				
T	F	T				
T	F	F				
F	T	T				
F	T	F				
F	F	T				
F	F	F				

C. Create truth tables for determining whether the following argument patterns are valid.

1. *(1) If A, then not B.*
   (2) B.
   ∴ Not A.

2. *(1) If A, then not B.*
   (2) Not B.
   ∴ Not A.

3. *(1) If A, then B.*
   ∴ If B, then A.

4. *(1) If A, then B.*
   ∴ If not B, then not A.

5. *(1) Either A or B.*
   ∴ If not A, then B.

6. *(1) Either A or B.*
   ∴ If not B, then A.

7. *(1) Either A or B.*
   (2) If B, then C.
   ∴ *If not A, then C.*

8. *(1) If not A then B.*
   (2) If C, then B.
   ∴ *If not A, then C.*

9. *(1) If A, then not B.*
   (2) Either not B or C.
   (3) A.
   ∴ *C.*

10. *(1) If A, then not B.*
    (2) Either C or B.
    (3) A.
    ∴ *C.*

11. *(1) If A and B, then C.*
    (2) A and B.
    ∴ *C.*

12. *(1) If A and B, then C.*
    (2) A and not B.
    ∴ *C.*

13. *(1) A if and only if B.*
    (2) If B, then C.
    (3) Not C.
    ∴ *A.*

14. *(1) (Not A) or B.*
    (2) (Not B) or C.
    (3) Not C.
    ∴ *Not A.*

REPRESENTING STRUCTURES WITHIN STATEMENTS: PREDICATES AND QUANTIFIERS

In previous sections we explored the way the concept of *validity* could be made precise for arguments that could be formalized in terms of statement letters, and logical connectives. Our aim in this section is to look more closely at logical form by examining arguments whose validity depend on structure within statements. We have represented statements such as *Mike is a pig* as having the structure *m is a* P_1. We could represent it even more simply as *Pm,* where the letter *P* stands for the predicate "is a pig," which is combined with the letter *m*, which stands for "Mike," to form a complete statement. Similarly, if we represent *Mike is a being having a four-chambered heart* by *Hm, H* stands for the predicate and *m* for the name that is the subject of the statement.

The aspect of logical form that generates validity depends on more than the simple relationship between a named individual and some characteristic represented by a letter standing for a predicate. In particular, these arguments depend on logical words such as *all, no,* or *some,* which indicate the "quantity" of individuals having the characteristic. For this reason, we will refer to words such as these as *quantifiers*. In a later section, we will also use this expression to refer to symbols that can take the place of these words. In this section, we will represent statements such as *All pigs are beings having a four-chambered heart* as having the structure *All A's are B's*.[8]

Testing Validity of Arguments Containing Quantifiers

Although the straightforward methods of the truth table do not extend to arguments containing quantifiers, simple forms of these arguments can be checked using another tool. Consider the valid predicate-based argument patterns (vi) and (vii) from the chart Some Common Successful Argument Patterns given in Chapters 2 and 4.

Example 5.9

vi. ***Predicate Instantiation***

(1) All A's are B's.

(2) m is an A. *(or Am)*

∴ m is a B. *(or Bm)*

vii. ***Universal Syllogism***

(1) All A's are B's.

(2) All B's are C's.

∴ All A's are C's.

As we showed in Chapter 4, we can capture the structure of a statement such as *All A's are B's* using a Venn diagram. The shading indicates that this part of the *A* circle is empty. No *A*'s lie in this part of the circle. The only place where an instance of *A* can lie is in the overlap between the *A* circle and the *B* circle. In other words, *all A's are also B's*.

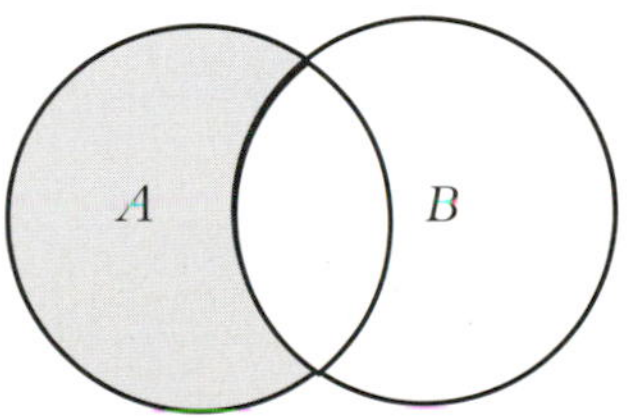

Placing an *m* inside the nonshaded portion of *A* indicates that some instance, *m*, is an *A*. This represents the second premise of the Predicate Instantiation argument. By inspection we can see that this instance *must* also be a *B*, which is the conclusion of the argument.

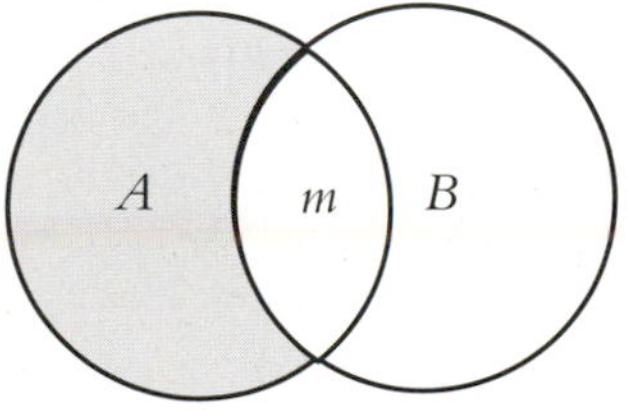

[8]We will use letters without subscripts, *All A's are B's*, in place of *All* P_1*'s are* P_2*'s*, in this chapter to indicate predicates. When translating, we will pick letters from the English sentence to remind us which elements of our formalism correspond to what part of the sentences they represent.

We can extend this method of representation to pattern (vii), Universal Syllogism. We represent *All A's are B's* as before, but we can add a third, overlapping circle to indicate the class of C's.

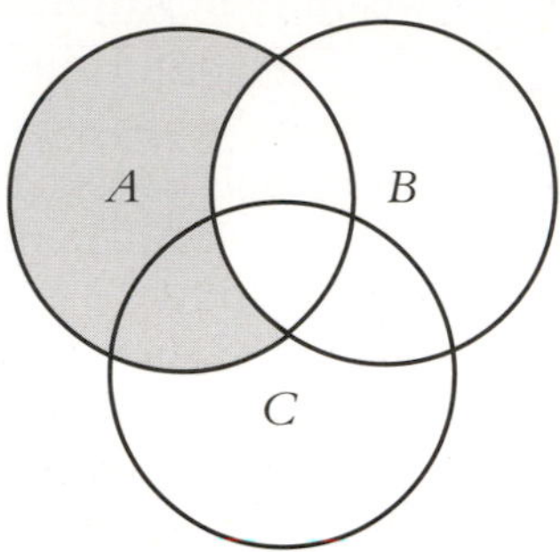

We shade a portion of the *B* circle, representing *All B's are C's,* and we see that our conclusion follows—*All A's are C's* (the only nonshaded or white area in *A* is also in *C*).

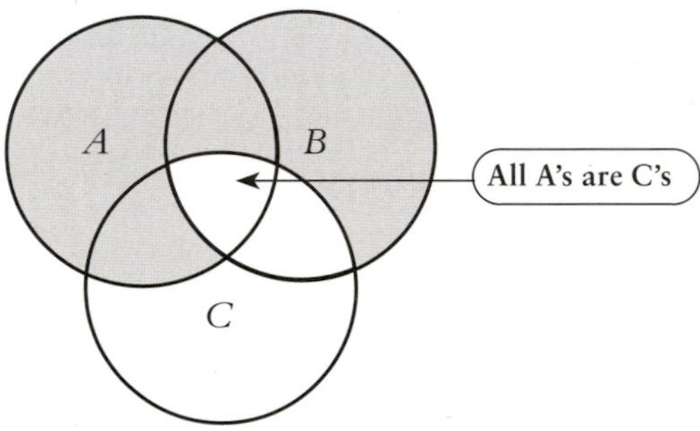

Contrast these cases to two invalid argument patterns and their corresponding Venn diagrams.

Example 5.10 *Venn Diagram for Invalid Argument Patterns*

(i) *Argument Pattern*

Invalid

(1) All A's are B's.

(2) All A's are C's.

∴ All B's are C's.

Venn Diagram

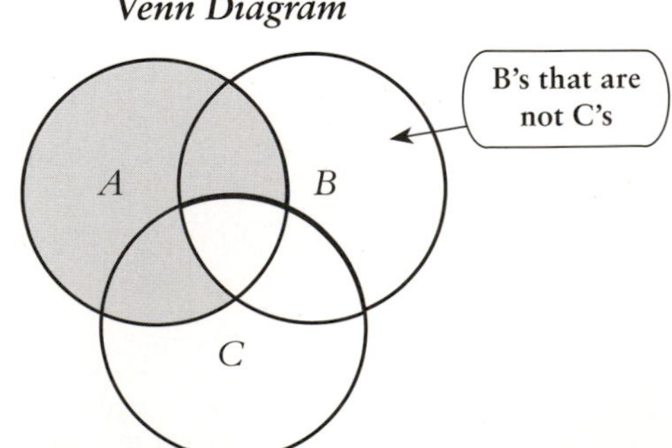

(ii) ***Argument Pattern*** ***Venn Diagram***

Invalid

(1) All A's are B's.

(2) m is a B.

∴ m is an A.

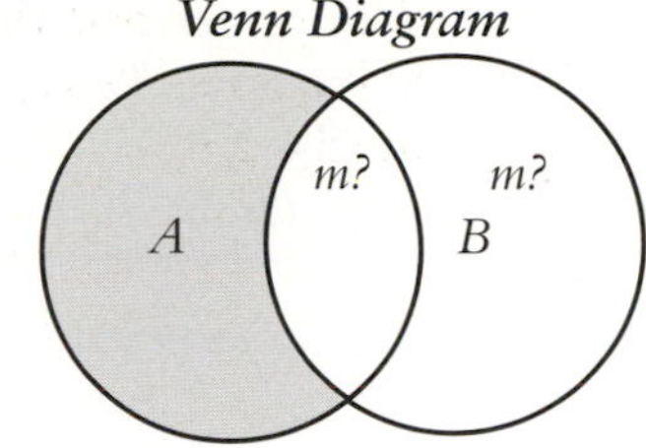

Again we can look for a counterexample. We construct the Venn diagrams to make the premises true. We can then ask whether the conclusion must be true. If it is possible for the conclusion to be false, then the argument is not valid. The possibility of objects that are *B* but not *C* as indicated by the upper unshaded portion of the Venn diagram in Example 5.10(i) shows that its conclusion can be false according to the Venn diagram even though the premises are all true. It serves as a counterexample. No valid argument can admit this possibility so this one must be *invalid*. Similarly the possibility that the named object *m* might be in the right-hand portion of the Venn diagram (ii) serves as a counterexample that demonstrates that this argument is invalid as well.

The method can be extended to testing related arguments using the "logical" word *no* and related terms. For instance, *No clinically tested substance is a cure for AIDS,* which exhibits the pattern *No T's are C's,* is represented by the Venn diagram that darkens the overlap in the circles.

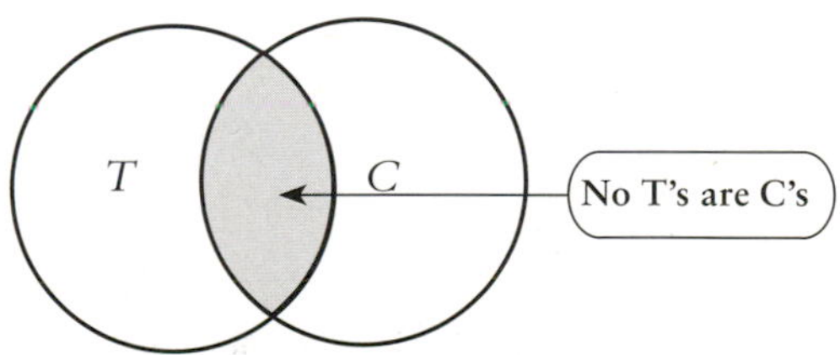

Notice that this is the same Venn diagram you would use for statements of the form *All T's are not C's*. Indeed, we can easily combine Venn diagrams for many statements containing *no* and *not* with those containing *all*.

Example 5.11 (i) ***Argument Pattern*** ***Venn Diagram***

Valid

(1) No A's are B's.

(2) All C's are B's.

∴ No C's are A's.

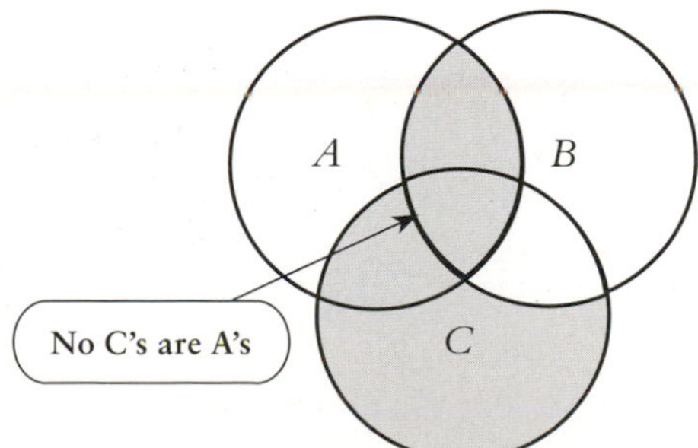

(ii) ***Argument Pattern***

Valid

(1) No A's are B's.

(2) m is an A.

∴ m is not a B.

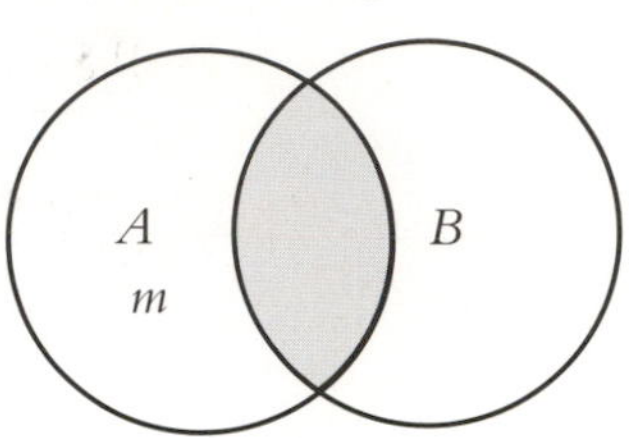

Finally, we can expand the method of representation we used for statements about some named individual to the more general case in which we are talking about some unnamed individual in statements such as *Some savings and loan presidents are not honest* in Example 5.12.

Example 5.12

(1) All people worthy of respect are honest.	*All W's are H's.*
(2) Some savings and loan presidents are not honest.	*Some S's are not H's.*
∴ Some savings and loan presidents are not worthy of respect.	*∴ Some S's are not W's.*

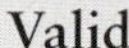

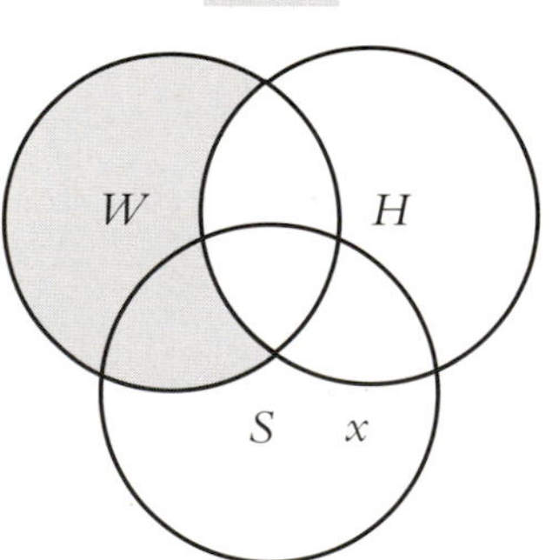

In Example 5.12 the second premise assures us that there is at least one entity—call it *x*—that is in the *S* circle but not in the *H* circle. But as we can directly see, this means that there is at least one individual in the *S* circle that is not in the *W* circle. So we can see that it is impossible for both the premises to be true and the conclusion to be false. By contrast, in Example 5.13 the two premises can be true, as indicated by the *x* in the intersection and the letter *s* in the right circle as well as outside either circle. We don't know whether it is inside or outside the right circle from the information supplied in Premise 2. But we aren't assured that the named individual is *not* in the right circle. Hence, it is possible for the premises to be true without the conclusion being true. This provides a counterexample that indicates the argument is invalid.

Example 5.13

(1) Some journalists are intelligent.	*(1) Some J's are I's.*
(2) Stephen Hawking is not a journalist.	*(2) s is not a J. (or ¬ Js)*
∴ Stephen Hawking is not intelligent.	*∴ s is not an I. (or ¬ Is)*

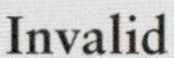

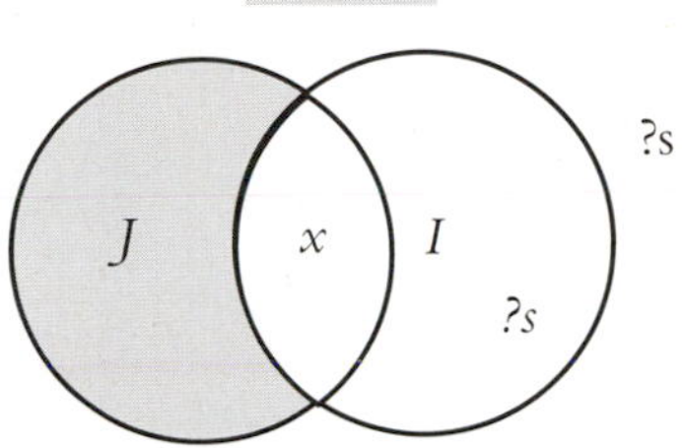

(Optional) A More Formal Way of Representing Statements with Quantifiers

We have extended our formalism by using terms like *Pm* for the statement *Mike is a pig* and ¬ *Js* for *Stephen Hawking is not a journalist.* We *can* extend it to quantifiers as well. A statement such as *All pigs are beings having a four-chambered heart,* which we represented as having the structure *All* P_1*'s are* P_2*'s,* can be reformulated as *For all things, if it is a pig, then it is a being having a four-chambered heart.* This allows us to introduce the symbol (*x*) as meaning "*For all things.*" With this symbolism we can then represent the structure within the sentence

All pigs are beings having a four-chambered heart.

as

$(x)\ (Px \rightarrow Hx).$

Given this formalism, we can represent the argument given in Example 5.8 as

Example 5.14

(1) All pigs are beings having a four-chambered heart.	*(1)* $(x)\ (Px \rightarrow Hx)$
(2) Mike is a pig.	*(2) Pm*
∴ Mike is a being having a four-chambered heart.	*∴ Hm*

Similarly, we can represent the more complicated argument using this formalism:

Example 5.15

(1) All pigs are mammals.	*(1)* $(x)\ (Px \rightarrow Mx)$
(2) Every mammal is a being having a four-chambered heart.	*(2)* $(x)\ (Mx \rightarrow Hx)$
∴ All pigs are beings having a four-chambered heart.	∴ $(x)\ (Px \rightarrow Hx)$

Thus far, the formalism using the quantifier *(x)* helps us capture the logical structure of statements containing logical words such as *all* and *every.* We can also use it to represent statements such as *No clinically tested substance is a cure for AIDS.* We can see the appropriate way to use this symbol if we realize that this statement can be rewritten as *For all things, if it is a clinically tested substance, then it is not a cure for AIDS.* So the sentence can be formalized as $(x)\ (Tx \rightarrow \neg\ Cx)$, where *Tx* stands for *It is a clinically tested substance* and *Cx* stands for *It is not a cure for AIDS.* This suggests the following formalization:

Example 5.16

(1) No clinically tested substance is a cure for AIDS.	$(1)\ (x)(Tx \rightarrow \neg\ Cx)$
(2) AZT is a clinically tested substance.	$(2)\ Ta$
∴ AZT is not a cure for AIDS.	$\therefore \neg\ Ca$

Finally, we can use another symbol to represent one more logical word important in representing argument structure. Consider the statements *Some politicians are corrupt* and *Some politicians are not corrupt.* There is no translation into statements involving *all* or *no.* We need a separate symbol $(\exists x)$ meaning *There exists at least one thing that . . .* so that *Some politicians are corrupt*—that is, "There exists at least one thing that is a politician and corrupt"—can be represented as $(\exists x)(Px\ \&\ \neg\ Cx)$ and *Some politicians are not corrupt* can be represented as $(\exists x)(Px\ \&\ \neg\ Cx)$.[9] With this symbolism in hand, we can translate arguments as follows:

Example 5.17

(1) All people worthy of respect are honest.	$(1)\ (x)(Wx \rightarrow Hx)$
(2) Some politicians are not honest.	$(2)\ (\exists x)(Px\ \&\ \neg\ Hx)$
∴ Some politicians are not worthy of respect.	$\therefore (\exists x)(Px\ \&\ \neg\ Wx)$

EXERCISE 5.4

Venn Diagrams

Give an example in English of an argument having each of the following patterns. Construct Venn diagrams to test for the validity of the patterns. If you studied the optional last section of this chapter, translate each argument into our formalism using quantifiers.

---

[9]The quantifier *(x)*, sometimes written $(\forall x)$, is called the *universal* quantifier—it applies, to all or every item in our universe of interpretation. The quantifier $(\exists x)$ is called the *existential* quantifier—it asserts the existence of some (at least one) entity in the universe having a certain characteristic.

A. 1. *(1) All A's are B's.*
(2) All C's are B's.
∴ All A's are C's.

2. *(1) All A's are B's.*
(2) m is not a B.
∴ m is not an A.

3. *(1) All A's are B's.*
(2) All B's are C's.
(3) m is an A.
∴ m is a C.

4. *(1) All A's are B's.*
(2) All B's are C's.
(3) m is a C.
∴ m is an A.

5. *(1) All A's are B's.*
(2) All C's are B's.
(3) m is not an A.
∴ m is not a C.

6. *(1) All A's are B's.*
(2) All C's are B's.
(3) m is not a B.
∴ m is not an A and m is not a C.

B. 1. *(1) No A's are B's.*
(2) All C's are B's.
∴ No A's are C's.

2. *(1) No A's are B's.*
(2) No C's are B's.
∴ No A's are C's.

3. *(1) No A's are B's.*
(2) No B's are C's
∴ No A's are C's.

4 *(1) No A's are B's.*
(2) m is a B.
∴ m is not an A.

5. *(1) No A's are B's.*
(2) All C's are Bs.
(3) m is a C.
∴ m is not an A.

6. *(1) No A's are B's.*
(2) All B's are C's.
(3) m is a C.
∴ m is not an A.

C. 1. *(1) All A's are B's.*
(2) Some C's are A's.
∴ Some C's are B's.

2. *(1) All A's are B's.*
(2) Some C's are B's.
∴ Some C's are A's.

3. *(1) All A's are B's.*
(2) Some C's are not A's.
∴ Some C's are not B's.

4. *(1) Some A's are B's.*
(2) Some C's are B's.
∴ Some A's are C's.

5. *(1) No A's are B's.*
(2) Some C's are A's.
∴ Some C's are not B's.

6. *(1) No A's are B's.*
(2) All B's are C's.
∴ Some C's are not A's.

A GLIMPSE AT NATURAL DEDUCTION

Although truth tables and Venn diagrams serve to characterize *validity* for a variety of simple arguments encountered in everyday deductive reasoning, they are cumbersome techniques to use when arguments become complex. To handle these more complex cases, logicians have formulated a variety of systems of rules, which, if followed, allow us to say the conclusion follows from the premises. These systems of rules can themselves be shown to be justified.

The oldest of these systems of rules was given initial impetus by Aristotle in the fourth century B.C. His rules concerned the *syllogism,* a simple three-predicate argument of the type we examined in the previous section. The rules of the syllogism allow us to determine which of the combinations produce valid arguments. More recently, a variety of "natural deduction" systems have been developed that are roughly based on rules that human reasoners might *naturally* follow. One such rule might be a generalized form of *modus ponens.* Let us call a chain of reasoning in accordance with a set of rules for natural deduction a *proof.*

Modus Ponens Rule

In a proof, if □ is justified and □ → Δ is justified, then Δ is justified.[10]

This rule would allow us to carry out the following proof, which consists of a series of lines that begins with a set of premises (above the line) followed by a series of "conclusions" that follow from the premises. Each line is *justified* either as a *premise* or *as following from previous lines according to a rule of deduction.*

Example 5.18

	JUSTIFICATION
(1) A & B	*premise*
(2) (A & B) → (C ∨ D)	*premise*
(3) (C ∨ D) → E	*premise*
(4) E → F	*premise*
∴ (5) (C ∨ D)	*(1)(2) modus ponens*[11]
∴ (6) E	*(5)(3) modus ponens*
∴ (7) F	*(6)(4) modus ponens*

[10]The symbols □ and Δ stand for any statement in our formal language no matter how complex.
[11]In this illustration, the numbers indicate the line numbers of statements previously given in the proof from which the current line follows in accordance with listed rules. We have only introduced one such rule, *modus ponens.*

We might add other rules. For example, we might have a conjunction rule that allowed us to join two separate lines and get a conjunction.

Conjunction Rule

In a proof, if □ is justified and Δ is justified, then □ & Δ is justified.

This allows simple *proofs* such as

Example 5.19

	JUSTIFICATION
(1) A	*premise*
(2) B	*premise*
∴ *(3) A & B*	*(1)(2) conjunction*

as well as more complicated proofs:

Example 5.20

	JUSTIFICATION
(1) A	*premise*
(2) B	*premise*
(3) $(A \& B) \rightarrow C$	*premise*
(4) D	*premise*
(5) $(C \& D) \rightarrow E$	*premise*
∴ *(6) A & B*	*(1)(2) conjunction*
∴ *(7) C*	*(6)(3) modus ponens*
∴ *(8) C & D*	*(7)(4) conjunction*
∴ *(9) E*	*(8)(5) modus ponens*

Natural deduction systems come in a number of varieties, differing in the particular rules they take as most basic. Furthermore, the two simple rules we have introduced deal only with whole statements. Additional rules might be used to handle quantifiers. For instance, we could have a rule allowing us to go from the negation of a universally quantified statement to an existentially quantified statement.

Quantifier Interchange Rule

In a proof, if ¬ (*x*) □ is justified, then (∃*x*) ¬ □ is justified.

This could be used in the following proof:

Example 5.21

	JUSTIFICATION
(1) $(x)\, Px$	*premise*
(2) $(x)\, Px \rightarrow \neg (x)Qx$	*premise*
(3) $(\exists x) \neg Qx \rightarrow (\exists x) \neg Rx$	*premise*
∴ *(4)* $\neg (x)Qx$	*(1)(2) modus ponens*
∴ *(5)* $(\exists x) \neg Qx$	*(4) quantifier interchange*
∴ *(6)* $(\exists x) \neg Rx$	*(5)(3) modus ponens*

A full set of rules for natural deduction is beyond the scope of this chapter. Many of the details are especially relevant only to those interested in logic or mathematics. But you should note that, even in everyday contexts, loose types of proofs are given to establish that a conclusion is actually supported by premises.

Example 5.22 *Given political realities, taxes aren't going to be raised significantly in the near future. So an extensive medical care plan will be delayed. Consequently, many Americans will be left without medical insurance.*

We can represent the three sentences in this passage as follows:

T: Taxes aren't going to be raised significantly in the near future.
P: An extensive medical care plan will be delayed.
M: Many Americans will be left without medical insurance.

The proof is:

Example 5.23

	JUSTIFICATION
(1) T	*premise*
(2) $T \rightarrow P$	*premise (implicit)*
(3) $P \rightarrow M$	*premise (implicit)*
$\therefore$ (4) P	*(1)(2) modus ponens*
$\therefore$ (5) M	*(4)(3) modus ponens*

Notice that both of the conclusions, including the subordinate conclusion in line 4, are explicitly mentioned in the passage. What are left out are the obvious conditions 2 and 3. It is useful in interpreting arguments to keep in mind that some of the intermediate steps employed in reaching a final conclusion are often included to guide the reader or listener from premises to ultimate conclusion. The *modus ponens* (or chain) rule is used in *direct* proofs to spin out the implications of a set of premises. Another more *indirect* tactic is sometimes employed. Instead of trying to directly establish a conclusion, it is sometimes more effective to examine its denial. If this denial leads to an unacceptable (absurd) result, then the original statement can be embraced. This method of indirect proof is sometimes called *reductio ad absurdum*, or just *reductio*.

Rule of Indirect Proof *(reductio ad absurdum)*

In a proof, if adding □ to a set of justified assertions leads to a contradiction (Δ & $\neg$ Δ), then $\neg$ □ is justified.

Example 5.24 *It can't be that our perceptions represent things as they really are. I perceive this stick in water as bent. I perceive this stick out of water as not bent. Suppose that things really are as we perceive them. Then the same stick would be both bent and not bent.*

We can represent the simple statements in this passage as follows.

W: I perceive this stick in water as bent.
O: I perceive this stick out of water as not bent.
R: Things really are as we perceive them.
B: This stick is bent.

The proof is:

Example 5.25

	JUSTIFICATION
(1) W	*premise*
(2) O	*premise*
(3) $R \rightarrow (W \rightarrow B)$	*premise (implicit)*
(4) $R \rightarrow (O \rightarrow \neg B)$	*premise (implicit)*
(5) R	ASSUMPTION
(6) $W \rightarrow B$	(3)(5) *modus ponens*
(7) $O \rightarrow \neg B$	(4)(5) *modus ponens*
(8) B	(1)(6) *modus ponens*
(9) $\neg B$	(2)(7) *modus ponens*
(10) $B \,\&\, \neg B$	(8)(9) *conjunction*
(11) $\neg R$	(5)(10) *indirect proof (reductio)*

Here again, the comments in the passage present elements in the proof rather than a straightforward statement of premises. Recognizing this as a fairly common strategy might help you reconstruct the arguments of others and shape or edit your own arguments.

We have only touched on the issues that would be raised in a full-fledged presentation of a natural deduction system. Such a presentation would provide a systematic account of deductive validity that can handle all of the argument types we have considered in this chapter, as well as more that we have not explored.

CHAPTER 6

Fallacies: Bad Arguments That Tend to Persuade

A *fallacy* is a bad argument that tends to persuade us even though it is faulty. In this chapter we look at twelve common fallacies. We examine why each is a bad argument and also why it nevertheless tends to persuade us. All except one are bad arguments either because they have a false premise or because the conclusion doesn't follow from the premises. They are persuasive for a variety of reasons. We focus on persuasiveness that involves distraction, that takes advantage of resemblance to good arguments, or that exploits a confusion of emotion with reason.

PERSUASIVENESS: LEGITIMATE AND ILLEGITIMATE

Fallacies tend to persuade us, but so do good arguments. Before we look at how fallacies persuade us in *illegitimate* ways, we should try to understand by contrast the *legitimate* ways in which good arguments persuade us. To be persuasive, a good argument must go beyond merely presenting true premises and a conclusion that follows; a fully successful argument must also have premises that an audience will understand and believe and a structure that enables the audience to see that the conclusion follows. It does no good to present true premises if the audience can't understand them or won't believe them. Nor does it do any good to present an argument whose structure is so complicated that the audience can't see that the conclusion follows. Being convincing to an audience, in this legitimate sense of making the audience realize that the conclusion follows from premises that the audience accepts, can be added to the criteria for a fully successful deductive argument.

By contrast, if an argument is illegitimately persuasive, then it inclines an audience to accept its conclusion for reasons unrelated to its deserving belief.[1] Recognizing why these arguments are tempting but fallacious provides both a basis for criticism and a means of explaining to people who commit the fallacy why they might have thought they were offering a good argument when they were not.

TYPES OF PERSUASIVE FALLACIES

There are three primary ways an argument can incline an audience to accept its conclusion for reasons unrelated to its deserving belief. First, an argument can trick you by distracting your attention away from the weak point of the argument, just as a sleight-of-hand artist or magician distracts you so you don't see the false move. Second, an argument can appear to be sound because of a counterfeit resemblance to an argument that really is sound. This is also a trick that a magician uses: substituting props or dummies for the real thing. Third, an argument can persuade you by confusing emotion with reason. We will describe three *distraction* fallacies, four *resemblance* fallacies, three *emotion* fallacies, and two fallacies that persuade by means of a combination of emotion and resemblance.

DISTRACTION FALLACIES: FALSE DILEMMA, SLIPPERY SLOPE, STRAW MAN

False Dilemma This fallacy is a bad argument because it has a false premise: It presents an *either–or* choice when in fact there are more alternatives. It tends to persuade through the technique of distraction. Here is an example of this fallacy:

Example 6.1 *Either we legalize drugs, or we keep building new prisons and filling them with drug offenders.*

[1]We will not call a bad argument a fallacy merely because it happens to persuade some unwary person. There must be a common tendency for the argument to be of a kind that persuades people, even though they should not be persuaded.

The implicit premise, obviously, is that we should not keep building new prisons and filling them with drug offenders. This type of argument is typical of a false dilemma. *The arguer claims that there are two alternatives and that one is unacceptable, so we should choose the other. But in fact, there are more alternatives than the two stated.* We are distracted by how undesirable, or preposterous, one of the alternatives is, and we tend not to ask whether these are the *only* two alternatives. In Example 6.1, there are other alternatives. We could substitute fines or community service for prison time. We could reduce the amount of prison time that is mandated for some or all drug offenses. We could substitute house arrest with drug testing for prison sentences. It *may* be that certain drugs should be legalized, but if this is true, it is not because the only alternative is building new prisons and filling them with drug offenders.

The false dilemma fallacy actually has a valid pattern:

(1) Either A or B.

(2) Not A.

∴ B.

But if it is really a *false* dilemma argument, then it is unsound because the premise *Either A or B* is not true. Examples 6.2 through 6.4 are also examples of false dilemma. Notice that one premise and the conclusion are often left implicit. Sometimes a false dilemma is stated in the form: *If we don't choose alternative A, then we will be left with the (undesirable) outcome of alternative B.*

Example 6.2 *If we don't give people the death penalty, they will get off with a few years in prison and then parole. So we should not abolish the death penalty.*

Example 6.3 *Either we allow abortion or we force children to be raised by parents who don't want them.*

And then there is the motto from the Vietnam War era, used by opponents of war protesters:

Example 6.4 *America: Love it or leave it.*

Notice how easy it is to be distracted from the issue of whether these are the only alternatives.

The element of distraction might not be universally present in false dilemma arguments. We sometimes accept an *either–or* premise that ignores other alternatives that we should consider, simply because we like to have our choices simplified. When someone asks us which of two good restaurants we'd like to go to, or which of two good movies we'd like to see, there is obviously no attempt to make one of the choices look bad in order to distract our attention from other possible choices. If there are other choices that should be considered, it would be unreasonable to focus only on the two that are presented. But if a quick decision needs to be made, it might actually be reasonable to narrow the field and not spend time considering all possible choices. It might be the reasonableness of simplifying our choices in these quick-decision situations that prevents us from seeking out other alternatives, even when we should.

Slippery Slope Sometimes we object to something on the grounds that *if* it is done, *then* something else will happen or is likely to happen as a result, and *if* so, *then* something else, and then something else, right down the "slippery slope" to a situation that is clearly undesirable. This may be a good argument or it may be a fallacy depending on whether it has acceptable premises. When it is a fallacy, one of the *if–then* premises will be doubtful. Typically, we don't see that it is doubtful because our attention is drawn away from the weak premise toward the bottom of the slope. For example:

Example 6.5 *Now they make us register handguns, then pretty soon it will be all guns. If that happens, then they'll be in a position to take our guns away. We'll be set up for a police state.*

As with false dilemma, our attention is distracted by the thought of how horrible the situation is that threatens us (according to the argument). We do not attend to the question of whether all the steps down the slippery slope are really connected. If it is doubtful that all the steps are connected, as in Example 6.5, then an argument of this sort is fallacious. Another example of the slippery slope fallacy is:

Example 6.6 *We must keep the classics of European thought at the core of our college curriculum. If we continue to move our curriculum in a multicultural direction, quality will be sacrificed in the name of diversity. Pretty soon we'll be treating pop music and pulp fiction as serious art.*

In Example 6.5, the conclusion of the argument is made explicit in the first sentence. When it is not, as in Example 6.6, the implicit conclusion is usually that the first step on the slope should not be taken.

Straw Man The straw man fallacy is more complicated than false dilemma or slippery slope, but it too relies on the technique of distraction. *Straw man consists of making your own position appear strong by making the opposing position appear weaker than it actually is.* If the entire argument were presented in detail, we could identify two premises that are false: (1) the premise that inaccurately describes the opponent's position and (2) the (implicit) premise that you must either support this untenable position or support the position taken by the speaker. (Typically there are other alternatives.) You might think of this fallacy as a combination of misrepresenting another person's views and the false dilemma of choosing either this (weakened) position or the speaker's position. The absurdity of the opposing position is what distracts us. Some examples are:

Example 6.7 *Our senator opposes an agreement to limit carbon emissions. He must think that climate change poses absolutely no serious threat.*

Example 6.8 *We should keep Social Security as it is. Senator Belnap claims we should divert funds into private accounts for investment in stocks. He must believe that the stock market will always rise and never fall.*

In Example 6.7 our attention is drawn to how weak the senator's argument is for not limiting emissions, and there is a tendency to move directly to the conclusion that an agreement to limit emissions should be passed. Similarly, in Example 6.8 our attention goes to the weakness of the argument for changing Social Security. We don't stop to think that some arguments for changing the system are tougher to knock down. If you are really trying to test a position you hold, you should build the *strongest* case you can in opposition to it, not the weakest.

Here is another example of the straw man fallacy:

Example 6.9 *We need to maintain a health care program that provides for the needs of the poor. Those who oppose this idea think that the private sector will take care of the needs of the poor. But this has not been the case in the past and will not be in the future.*

Many opponents of expanded publicly funded health care don't base their position on this argument. The fact that *this* particular argument against an expanded health care program can be easily refuted is irrelevant to whether we should in fact have such a program.

Keep in mind that the person who commits the straw man fallacy cites *someone else's* argument. False dilemma is a broader category of fallacy. The choices in a false dilemma are not limited to points of view; they could be actions to take, objects to select, and so on. Also, straw man fallacies not only present a false *either–or* premise; in addition, they misrepresent the opposing view. Consider how Example 6.10 commits the more specific fallacy of straw man, while Example 6.11 is a false dilemma but not a straw man fallacy.

Example 6.10 ***Straw man:*** *We should ban all guns. Those who oppose a ban on guns don't think very many crimes involve guns, but statistics prove otherwise.* (Arguer makes the argument look strong by citing an opposing argument that is obviously weak.)

Example 6.11 ***False dilemma:*** *Either we ban all guns or we let crime run amok.* (Arguer claims there are only two alternatives; one is unacceptable.)

EXERCISE 6.1 Identifying Distraction Fallacies

A. We have discussed three fallacies that use the sleight-of-hand tactic of distraction. You can solidify what you have learned by identifying the fallacies in the following passages and by writing a brief explanation of why each fallacy might be persuasive. There may be more than one fallacy in some passages.

Sample: *I'm in favor of legalized gambling. There are those who oppose it, but they apparently think that anything that's fun is sinful.*

Fallacy: Straw man. There are much stronger reasons for opposing legalized gambling than that anything fun is sinful. Many opponents claim that legalized gambling disproportionately draws money from those who can least afford it and results in ruined lives. We are distracted by the weakness of the opposition as it is stated, which might lead us to agree with legalizing gambling.

1. If you're not going to save *a lot* of money on fuel, then you might as well not waste the effort. Putting weather stripping around your doors doesn't save you that much.
2. In the early stages the compulsive gambler doesn't behave differently from the casual gambler. He plays a little poker on Friday night; he bets on the Sunday football games. Slowly, he begins to bet more. Winning becomes the high point of his week. A loss means several days of depression. Finally, he runs out of his own money and is forced to get it any way he can. He begs, borrows, and ultimately steals. Beware! That first flip of the coin can spell disaster.
3. You're either part of the solution or part of the problem.
4. I oppose the development of the Alaska oil fields. Those who support it base their case on the fantasy that such development poses absolutely no risk to the environment.
5. Those who support the practice of prayer in the classroom must believe that there is no constitutional provision for separation of church and state. But such a separation is clearly provided for. Prayer in the classroom cannot be tolerated.

6.

The Two Paths[2]

What Will the Girl Become?

---

[2]B. G. Jefferis and J. L. Nichols, *Light on Dark Corners: A Complete Sexual Science and Guide to Purity* (New York: In Text Press, 1928), 43. Used by permission.

7.

8. Now is no time to restrict embryonic stem cell research. Either we move vigorously ahead without restrictions, or we might as well abandon this field and let millions suffer from diabetes and Parkinson's disease.

---

[3]B. G. Jefferis and J. L. Nichols, *Light on Dark Corners: A Complete Sexual Science and Guide to Purity* (New York: In Text Press, 1928), 41. Used by permission.

9. I believe we can win the war against terrorism. My opponent thinks we can't win this war. He must believe there is no effective strategy for waging the war and that we will lose.

B. **Creating examples of fallacies.** Write one example (of your own creation) of each of the following fallacies: false dilemma, slippery slope, straw man.

RESEMBLANCE FALLACIES: AFFIRMING THE CONSEQUENT, DENYING THE ANTECEDENT, EQUIVOCATION, AND BEGGING THE QUESTION

The second kind of trick the sleight-of-hand artist uses is to substitute props and dummies for the objects they resemble. Certain fallacies can trick you in the same way; they can seem like good arguments because they resemble good arguments. The first two fallacies are sometimes called *formal fallacies* because they have an incorrect *form* or pattern. Arguments of this kind are bad because they are invalid. Their premises might be true, but this is not enough to make an argument sound.

Affirming the Consequent, and Denying the Antecedent *Affirming the consequent and denying the antecedent* resemble two of the most common valid argument patterns—*modus ponens (or affirming the antecedent)* and *modus tollens* (or *denying the consequent*). We introduced both the valid and fallacious forms in Chapter 2 and mentioned them again in Chapter 4. We can display these patterns as follows. (Remember, in an *if–then* sentence, the "if" part is the antecedent and the "then" part is the consequent.)

Example 6.12

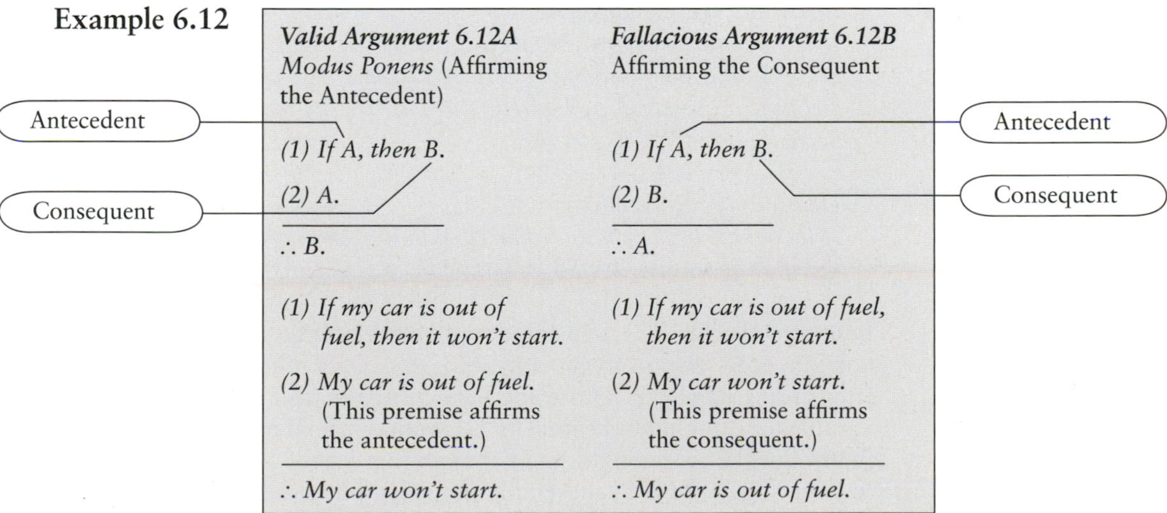

Valid Argument 6.12A *Modus Ponens* (Affirming the Antecedent)	*Fallacious Argument 6.12B* Affirming the Consequent
(1) If A, then B.	*(1) If A, then B.*
(2) A.	*(2) B.*
∴ B.	*∴ A.*
(1) If my car is out of fuel, then it won't start.	*(1) If my car is out of fuel, then it won't start.*
(2) My car is out of fuel. (This premise affirms the antecedent.)	*(2) My car won't start.* (This premise affirms the consequent.)
∴ My car won't start.	*∴ My car is out of fuel.*

Example 6.13

Valid Argument 6.13A *Modus Tollens* (Denying the Consequent)	*Fallacious Argument 6.13B* Denying the Antecedent
(1) If A, then B.	*(1) If A, then B.*
(2) Not B.	*(2) Not A.*
∴ Not A.	*∴ Not B.*
(1) If you respected her opinion, then you would seek her advice.	*(1) If you respected her opinion, then you would seek her advice.*
(2) You won't seek her advice. (This premise *denies* the consequent.)	*(2) You don't respect her opinion.* (This premise denies the antecedent.)
∴ You don't respect her opinion.	*∴ You won't seek her advice.*

The fallacious arguments (Examples 6.12B and 6.13B in the right-hand columns)—affirming the consequent and denying the antecedent—are bad arguments because their patterns are invalid. Even if the premises are true, the conclusions could be false. My car could fail to start but not be out of fuel (for example, if the battery was dead). It could be true that I don't respect her opinion, but I could seek her advice anyway (for instance, to flatter her).

Here are some additional examples:

Example 6.14

Affirming the Consequent
If Homeland Security does its job well, then there will be no catastrophic attacks on the United States during its watch. There have been no catastrophic attacks on the United States during its watch. So Homeland Security has done its job well.

Example 6.15

Denying the Antecedent
If he denies that he knows her, then he's been cheating on me. He admitted that he knows her. So he hasn't been cheating on me.

These are fallacies. The Department of Homeland Security could have done a poor job, even though there have been no catastrophic attacks on the United States during its watch. This could have been a matter of luck. And the man in Example 6.17 could be cheating on his woman friend even though he didn't get caught. But the reasoning is good enough that it will often get by. Why is this? We have suggested that these fallacies resemble valid arguments. But which valid arguments? Surely we don't transpose the second premise and the conclusion of Example 6.16, changing it into the following *modus ponens* argument:

Example 6.16 *If Homeland Security has done its job well, then there will be no catastrophic attacks on the United States during its watch. Homeland Security has done its job well. Therefore there have been no catastrophic attacks on the United States during its watch.*

We are more likely to confuse the first premise of Example 6.14, *If Homeland Security has done its job well, then there will be no catastrophic attacks on the United States during its watch*, with *If there are no catastrophic attacks on the United States during its watch, then Homeland Security has done its job well.* This would make Example 6.16 a valid argument. Perhaps we tend to confuse *If A, then B* with *If B, then A* because if *B* follows from *A*, it is fairly common for *A* to follow from B also. (If there's smoke, there's fire; if there's fire, there's smoke. If someone flips the switch, the lights come on; if the lights are on, someone flipped the switch.)

Thus, we might be fooled by Example 6.15 because we might confuse *If he denies that he knows her, then he's been cheating on me* with *If he's been cheating on me, then he will deny that he knows her.* This confusion *does* seem likely. And this change in the first premise would make Example 6.15 a valid argument.

In general, then, the fallacies of affirming the consequent and denying the antecedent can be persuasive because we tend to confuse *If A, then B* with *If B, then A,* and once we make this change, these fallacious forms become valid. When you identify these fallacies in Exercise 6.2, see if this account is not plausible.

Equivocation When a word or an expression shifts meaning from one premise to another, it commits the fallacy of *equivocation.* We introduce this fallacy briefly in this chapter and will discuss it at greater length in Chapter 7, along with other issues concerning the way arguments are affected by differences in meaning. The related fallacy of *misleading definition* will also be discussed in Chapter 7.

Here is an example of equivocation:

Example 6.17 *You are perfectly willing to believe in miracles such as a person landing on the moon. If this is so, you shouldn't be so skeptical of the miracles described in the Bible.*

In the first occurrence, *miracle* means something that is amazing, that you wouldn't have thought could be done. But in the second occurrence, *miracle* means something that defies the laws of nature. The fact that the first kind of miracle occurred doesn't make it more likely that the second kind occurred.

Example 6.18 might commit the fallacy of equivocation if it shifts the meaning of the term *small.*

Example 6.18 *In these times of scarce resources, people who drive small cars are to be commended. McGruder drives a small car. So McGruder is to be commended.*

A sense of "small car" that would make the first premise true would be "light car with a small engine." Perhaps McGruder's car has a small wheel base, but is a gas-guzzler.

Here is a subtler example:

Example 6.19 *The law says that insane people should not be punished. Anyone who murders must be insane. So murderers should be treated in mental wards, not punished.*

The sense of *insane* that makes the first premise true concerns a person knowing right from wrong. The sense of *insane* that might make the second premise true concerns a person being abnormally cruel (which still could allow that the person knows that cruelty is wrong).

An equivocation is a bad argument because it can't have both a valid pattern and true premises. If the meanings of its terms are kept the same, one of the premises is false (as we have just seen); if, on the other hand, the meaning is allowed to shift, the argument is invalid. We can see this more clearly in the insanity argument if we simplify it to make the pattern apparent:

Example 6.19 Argument in Standard Form

(1) All murderers are insane people.

(2) All insane people shouldn't be punished.

∴ All murderers shouldn't be punished.

If *insane* is made to keep the same meaning, one of its premises is false, but it has a valid pattern:

Pattern If No Equivocation

(1) All P_1's are P_2's.

(2) All P_2's are P_3's.

∴ All P_1's are P_3's.

Valid

If *insane* shifts meaning from one premise to the next, then it no longer has the valid pattern above. With the meaning shifting, the argument could be stated like this:

Example 6.19 with Equivocation

(1) All murderers are ***abnormally cruel*** *people.*

(2) All ***legally insane*** *people shouldn't be punished.*

∴ All murderers shouldn't be punished.

This argument has the invalid pattern:

(1) All P_1's are P_2's.

(2) All P_3's are P_4's.

Invalid

∴ All P_1's are P_4's.

Why can arguments like these be persuasive? Like the other counterfeit fallacies, they *closely resemble* good arguments. Typically, an argument that commits the fallacy of equivocation would be valid *if it were not for the shift in meaning*. (In Example 6.19, for example, it would follow that murderers should not be punished.) Furthermore, all the premises can be made true by the shift in meaning (and sometimes the shift in meaning is barely noticeable). So if you lose track of the fact that the meaning has shifted, an argument that commits this fallacy seems sound.

Begging the Question We stated at the beginning of this chapter that all but one of the fallacies we discuss are bad arguments because they either have invalid argument patterns or they have a false premise. Begging the question is the fallacy that could both have a valid pattern and have true premises. Why, then, do we call it a fallacy? Consider this example:

Example 6.20 *Whatever is less dense than water will float, because such objects won't sink in water.*

The premise of this argument happens to be true. The conclusion follows from the premise in the trivial sense that it simply restates the premise in different words. If we rephrase the argument, it simply says: Whatever is less dense than water will float. Therefore, whatever is less dense than water will float. The argument has the pattern:

"Trivial" Pattern of Argument That Begs the Question

(1) A

∴ A

Technically, this pattern satisfies the definition of validity. If the premise is true, the conclusion must be true. Still, it is a bad argument because the premise does not give a *reason* for believing the conclusion. This is why the name "begging the question" is appropriate. When someone asks, "Why should I be honest?" that person is asking you to present an argument. If instead of doing this you say "Because you shouldn't be dishonest," you are *missing* the question at issue *(begging* the question).[4]

---

[4]Recently, the expression "begging the question" has been commonly misused to mean "raising the question." A television commentator, for example, might respond to the news that Congress has passed an expensive health care bill by saying, "This begs the question of how we will pay for it." In order to avoid confusion with the claim that Congress has committed a fallacy of circularity (begging the question in the sense that we have just explained), it would be clearer to say, "This raises the question of how we should pay for it."

The fallacy is fairly obvious in an argument as short as the one in Example 6.22, but in a longer, more complicated argument, you might not see that the conclusion is just a restatement of one of the premises. Consider, for example, the following exchange:

Example 6.21

> **Realtor:** *If you're choosing between the house our competitors have listed and this one, you ought to buy this one. You'd make more money on it.*
>
> **Customer:** *Why would I make more money on it?*
>
> **Realtor:** *Well, you said you planned to sell in five years. You have to consider real appreciation, not just how many dollars you pay and how much you sell for. That means figuring in the rate of inflation. I would estimate that at the rate houses like this appreciate, taking account of fees, taxes, and so on, in five years you'd come out with a greater net profit on this house than on the other one.*

All the realtor really has said is that you'd make more money on this one because you'd make more money on this one.

In any valid argument, fallacious or not, the conclusion is, in a sense, contained in the premises. Taken together, the premises guarantee the truth of the conclusion. But remember that the object of presenting an argument is to make the conclusion more reasonable to believe. To accomplish this, you must use premises that, individually, will be taken to be more certain than the conclusion. *If a premise is either a restatement of the conclusion or a statement that will be equally doubtful on grounds similar to those which make the conclusion doubtful, then the argument doesn't make any progress toward supporting the conclusion and is guilty of begging the question.*

The following example begs the question even though the conclusion does not simply restate a premise:

Example 6.22

> *The Bible says God exists, and everything the Bible says is true since God wrote it. Therefore God exists.*

Anyone who doubted the conclusion—God exists—would have the same reason for doubting the premise that God wrote the Bible.

Review: Fallacies of Distraction and Resemblance

A fallacy is a kind of argument that tends to persuade, even though it is a bad argument. So far, we have explained two ways a fallacy can be persuasive: by *distraction* (taking your attention away from the weak point of the argument) and by *resemblance* to a good argument. We have described seven of the most common fallacies that use these tricks. They are listed again below. It is important to see that what makes them persuasive is different from what makes them unsuccessful arguments. The distraction fallacies are bad arguments because they each have a false premise. The first three resemblance fallacies are bad arguments because they have invalid patterns. The last one—begging the question—has a pattern that is technically valid (*A, therefore A*), but an argument of this type fails to give a reason for believing its conclusion. As you read through the list, try to state a general definition of each fallacy. If you have difficulty, refer back to the appropriate section.

Distraction Fallacies

1. *False dilemma.* Either we legalize drugs or we keep building new prisons and filling them with drug offenders.
2. *Slippery slope.* Now, it's register handguns. Next, it will be all guns. Then they'll ban guns, and we'll be set up for a police state.
3. *Straw man.* We should keep Social Security as it is. Senator Belnap claims we should divert funds into private accounts for investment in stocks. He must believe that the stock market will always rise and never fall.

Resemblance Fallacies

1. *Affirming the consequent.* If the economy is improving, stock prices will rise. Stock prices are rising. So the economy is improving.
2. *Denying the antecedent.* If she loves you, she'll marry you. She doesn't love you. So she won't marry you.
3. *Equivocation.* Insane people shouldn't be punished. Someone who commits murder must be insane. So murderers should not be punished.
4. *Begging the question.* The Bible says God exists. Everything in the Bible is true, since God wrote it. So God does exist.

EXERCISE 6.2

Identifying Distraction and Resemblance Fallacies

A. The following are all fallacies from the *resemblance* category (which includes affirming the consequent, denying the antecedent, equivocation, and begging the question). Identify the fallacy in each selection and discuss briefly why it might be persuasive.

1. If everybody benefited from the present education system, then there would be no reason to change it drastically. But not everybody is helped by current teaching methods. So we should radically overhaul the way kids are educated.
2. Callous though it sounds, I do not believe we have an obligation to redistribute wealth to the less fortunate. The reason that I believe this

is that what a person earns is rightfully his or hers. No one else has a claim to it.

3. They say that nice guys finish last. So let's finish last to show that we're nice guys. (**Hint: Write the first premise as an *if–then* statement.**)
4. It won't be dangerous to ride with Gary, because he hasn't been drinking. If he had been drinking, it would be dangerous.
5. The senator's denial of wrongdoing is hardly credible, since it is obvious that the senator was not telling the truth.
6. If Alvin really loved Alice, then he would have given up his evil ways. He does seem to have reformed—he's even quit hanging out in pool halls and doing drugs. He must really love Alice.
7. Ending affirmative action in college admissions is a bad idea. If this strategy had good results in California and Texas, then it would be wise to try it in other states. But it didn't have good results in California and Texas.
8. To the editor: Five million illegal aliens in this country is more than a crime. It's an invasion. Why not just put the military in place to use lethal force to stop this invasion? (From the *Omaha World-Herald,* 1999.)

B. *Creating examples of fallacies.* Write one example (of your own creation) of each of the following fallacies: affirming the consequent, denying the antecedent, equivocation, begging the question.

C. *Identifying fallacies—comprehensive review.* The following is a collection of fallacies from both the *distraction* and the *resemblance* categories. The fallacies may include instances of false dilemma, slippery slope, straw man, affirming the consequent, denying the antecedent, equivocation, and begging the question. Identify the fallacy in each selection and discuss briefly why it might be persuasive.

1.

FUNKY WINKERBEAN
Tom Batiuk
STUDENT CURRICULUM GUIDE
PHILOSOPHY I - (Prerequisite - five hours of sitting around doing nothing)
Philosophy I is where you learn how the great thinkers of the past view man's existence, such as Descartes who said, "I think, therefore I am."
It turns out he was right because he stopped thinking a while back, and now he no longer is!

© 1980 Field Enterprises, Inc. Courtesy of Field Newspaper Syndicate.

2. If you can't lick them, join them.
3. According to my theory, men who had doting mothers will seek women who are independent and not overly affectionate. This is a reaction to having been smothered by their mothers' affection. Now if my theory is correct, Ed would be attracted to someone like Carla. Ed *is* attracted to Carla. So I would say that my theory is correct.

4. If a society encourages freedom of thought and expression, then creativity will flourish. New theories will replace old ones; traditions will be challenged; inventiveness will reign. The eighteenth century was perhaps the period of American history when creativity flourished most, showing the degree to which free thought was encouraged during that period.
5. Should you be hip or smart?[5]
6. Most students go to college to improve their job prospects. But the fact is that many areas of study—particularly the liberal arts—don't strike students as preparing them for a vocation. They fail to see that living a life enriched by ideas *is* a kind of vocation. So when they quit college to get a job they are making a big mistake.
7. If I continue to live in the dorm, the noise will make me nervous and irritable. I'll worry all the time about not getting my studying done. I'm honestly afraid that I'd have to start seeing a psychiatrist about these problems. I'd have to borrow the money for the psychiatrist from my parents. And if I flunk out of school I wouldn't be able to get a good job to pay them back. The alternative is to move into a nice apartment complex near campus. It's pretty expensive, but actually it might save money in the long run.
8. So the thing to do when working on a motorcycle, as in any other task, is to cultivate the peace of mind that does not separate one's self from one's surroundings. When that is done successfully, then everything else follows naturally. Peace of mind produces right values, right values produce right thoughts. Right thoughts produce right actions and right actions produce work that will be a material reflection for others to see of the serenity at the center of it all.[6] (**Hint: This might be interpreted as committing one of the fallacies "in reverse."**)

Note: What seems to be a fallacy might not be one. Some additional arguments that might or might not commit fallacies are presented at the end of the chapter.

EMOTION AND REASON IN ARGUMENT

In the first part of this chapter, we discussed fallacies that can be persuasive because of the sleight-of-hand tricks they play. In this part, we discuss a source of persuasiveness that is quite different: confusing emotion with reason. We identify three prominent fallacies that draw their persuasiveness from this source. Then, to complete our discussion of fallacies, we identify two fallacies that rely on a combination of sleight of hand and emotional manipulation in order to persuade, and which can be extremely effective as a result.

---

[5]*Esquire Magazine,* September 1994.

[6]Robert M. Pirsig, *Zen and the Art of Motorcycle Maintenance: An Inquiry into Values* (New York: Bantam Books, 1974), 290.

Before examining the illegitimate use of emotion in argument, note that there are many cases in which it is appropriate for an argument to appeal to emotion. We may become clearer about what is involved in fallacious appeals to emotion if we contrast these cases to legitimate ones.

Suppose a friend tries to convince you to wear a helmet when you ride your motorcycle. The friend describes some severe head injuries received by other riders who didn't wear helmets. You are reminded of how miserable your friends and parents would be if you suffered such an injury. And the friend points out that if you wear a helmet you are much less likely to be seriously injured. Your friend has certainly appealed to emotion, but was that appeal illegitimate? It would hardly seem so. When you are considering an action that will affect you or other people for good or for ill, one kind of consideration that is often relevant is just *how* well or *how* badly you or others will be affected.[7] If certain consequences of your actions have only limited probability of occurring, or will occur far into the future, or will be removed from your sight, then you tend to ignore them. You need to be reminded graphically of them—have them brought before your consciousness as though they were immediate.

Consider a different example. Suppose that you are deciding whether to give political support to a government policy that might make ethnic war in some part of the world more probable. If a friend reminds you of the horrors of modern warfare and all its innocent victims, this appeals to emotions but is certainly legitimate.

The *amount of weight* that should be given to such an appeal, however, is open to question. The possible bad consequences could be pictured so graphically that you would lose sight of any potential benefits of the policy in question—benefits that should be weighed against possible risks. Suppose the policy involves making a strong response to the aggression of a group preaching "ethnic cleansing." Perhaps the reaction in question is not so strong as to *significantly* raise the probability that the conflict will spread. Perhaps a weaker reaction would have some chance of leading to war also, because it would encourage future aggression. All these considerations must be weighed; they must not be neglected. An appeal that arouses emotion, even if it is relevant to the issue, runs the risk of leaving a one-sided impression because of the way such an appeal can command your attention. The point remains, nevertheless, that an emotional appeal can be a legitimate kind of appeal, as we have seen from our two examples.

When Is an Emotional Appeal Illegitimate?

Let us contrast the cases we have just described to one in which the appeal to emotion is *not* legitimate. Suppose you are deciding which of two candidates is better qualified for office. You discuss the choice with your parents and they

[7]We say that how well or badly you or others will be affected is *often* relevant, because in some cases the good or bad effects of an action on a person could plausibly be seen as morally *irrelevant*. For example, the inconvenience of keeping a promise, at least on some moral theories, is irrelevant to whether one should keep the promise.

get upset about the candidate you are favoring. They support the other candidate and claim that you are being disloyal. You decide their candidate isn't so bad after all.

If the question to be decided is which candidate is better qualified, then the appeal to loyalty is an illegitimate appeal to emotion.[8] There is a difference between this example and the earlier examples in this chapter. In the earlier examples, the question was whether a certain act should be done: Should you wear a helmet? Should you support a certain foreign policy? These actions might have certain consequences—injury, death—and considering these consequences arouses emotions. But these consequences *must* be considered to determine whether the actions in question should be taken. In the candidate example, however, the question of whether your choice will upset your parents is *not* relevant to whether your candidate is better qualified. The fact that your parents want you to be loyal might give you a *motive* for believing that their candidate is better. But this consideration does not provide support, in the sense of evidence, for the belief that their candidate is better qualified. Does the candidate in question have good judgment? Would the candidate's programs succeed? Is the person honest? These are the relevant kinds of considerations that would determine the candidate's qualifications.

We must be careful here to make a certain distinction. If you are considering whether to state your political preference in front of your parents, or even whether to act on the basis of your preference when you go to vote, then the question of loyalty *might* be considered relevant. This question of how to act is a question of ethics. Should you let family loyalty override your own political principles? You may feel that one of these factors clearly outweighs the other. For example, you may feel that it is much more important to maintain your own integrity by voting according to your conscience than to remain loyal to your family. But although this factor of loyalty might be outweighed when it comes to voting, it is totally irrelevant when it comes to deciding which candidate is better qualified. When you are deciding how to act, all motives are in a sense relevant. But when you are deciding what to believe, these motives are not relevant. The fact that it would be more comfortable for you to believe that your parents' candidate is better qualified gives you a *motive* for holding that belief, but it does *not* provide evidence that the belief is true.

We will call fallacies that provide a motive for belief rather than supporting reasons *emotion* fallacies. Three fallacies within this category deserve discussion. Two of them are commonly recognized and have acquired names: *appeal to force* and *appeal to pity*. The other, although commonly used, is not as commonly identified and is referred to by different names at different times. We call it *prejudicial language*.

---

[8]We are not, at this point, identifying the particular fallacy being committed here. We are still in the process of characterizing a general category of fallacies. Depending on how your parents stated their argument, they could be committing any one or more of the fallacies to be discussed later: *appeal to force, appeal to pity,* or *prejudicial language*.

Emotion Fallacies: Appeal to Force and Appeal to Pity, Prejudicial Language

Appeal to Force and Appeal to Pity *Appeal to force and appeal to pity* can best be explained together because they have an important similarity. *When people get you to agree to something because they will be hurt if you don't agree, this is an appeal to pity. If people get you to agree because they will hurt you if you don't agree, this is an appeal to force.*[9] In both cases, the factor that makes the argument persuasive is motive for belief in place of support. That is, both appeal to force and appeal to pity make it undesirable not to believe that the conclusion is true even though they do not give support (in the sense of evidence) for believing that the conclusion is true. This seems fairly clear in the following examples.

Appeal to Force

Example 6.23 *So you're an environmentalist. I'd think twice about that if I were you. There are a lot of people in this town who depend on the lumber industry. They aren't going to be very happy with you if they find out about your views on preserving forests.*

Example 6.24 **Diplomat A:** *We think the interference of your country in our internal affairs is unjustified.*

Diplomat B: *That is a very unwise opinion to hold when we are considering a trade embargo against you.*

Appeal to Pity

Example 6.25 *I am qualified for the job. I have a little experience in the area, and I've been out of work for two months so I really need the money.*

Example 6.26 *Your mother and I devoted years of our lives raising you to believe in the Christian religion. Don't you know how it hurts us for you to abandon those beliefs now?*

In each of these examples, it is not that a certain belief is made desirable, but rather that it would be harmful (either to yourself or others) to *not* hold a certain belief—that environmentalism is a bad policy, that a political action was justified, and so on. It might seem unlikely that you would be fooled into *believing* these things; rather, you might just *say* you believed them to avoid certain undesirable consequences. If this were the case, you really couldn't be accused of committing a fallacy; you might be doing a very reasonable thing. The problem is, we often end up convincing ourselves that we really do believe the position we publicly state. Perhaps we convince ourselves because

---

[9]Notice that although this fallacy is called *appeal to force*, the harm threatened need not be physical harm.

we don't like to admit that we didn't stand up for the truth. Let's look at two other examples in a little more detail.

Appeal to Pity

Example 6.27 *A friend asks you to write a letter of recommendation for him, but he is not really qualified for the job. You write the letter saying he is qualified, because you know it will hurt his feelings if you don't.* ***(And you end up convincing yourself that he really was qualified.)***

Appeal to Force

Example 6.28 *You are asked to evaluate the performance of your supervisor at work. She has done a very poor job, but you give her a high evaluation because she has made it clear that she can make it tough on you if you don't.* ***(And you end up saying to yourself, "I didn't really lie. The supervisor did a pretty good job.")***

Two issues must be kept separate in situations like these. One is whether you should state something to avoid harm to others or to yourself, even though the statement is probably not true. This is a moral question, not a question of logic. In some circumstances, you might believe that a greater moral end outweighs the obligation to be truthful. The second issue is whether you should believe such a statement if you do make it. This *is* a matter of logic, and the answer is no. To do so would be to commit a fallacy. It is important to see that these two issues are often confused. The desirability of a conclusion and the evidence for it (the motive and the support) seem to operate as competing forces; either one can be strong enough to produce belief, even though they are totally different. If you think about the plausibility of Examples 6.29 and 6.30, about the discomfort people feel in acknowledging that they have lied, and about the uncanny ability of people to tailor their beliefs to make themselves comfortable, then you will probably agree that appeals to force and to pity *can* be persuasive.

Why are appeal to pity and appeal to force bad arguments? Do they all contain false premises, or do their conclusions not follow from their premises? Looking at some simplified models of this kind of argument will help us understand what is going wrong.

Appeal to Force—Model 1

(1) If you appear to believe X, you will be harmed.

(2) You don't want to be harmed.

∴ You should not believe X.

In this interpretation, the conclusion doesn't follow. Even if you accepted the premises, it doesn't follow that you shouldn't believe X, just that you shouldn't *appear* to believe X. That is, you shouldn't let the arguer know that you believe X. You could still decide what to believe on the basis of what you think is true.

Appeal to Force—Model 2

(1) If you believe X, you will be harmed.

(2) You don't want to be harmed.

∴ You should not believe X.

In this interpretation, the first premise will be questionable for the same reason that the conclusion doesn't follow from the premises in Model 1. You could believe X but avoid being harmed by not letting on that you believe X.

Perhaps neither of these first two models raises the moral issue that makes appeal to force troubling. Let's represent the argument as it might occur to the person receiving the threat of force.

Model That Raises the Moral Issue

(1) Either I appear to believe X or I will be harmed.

(2) I don't want to be harmed.

(3) I don't want to appear to believe X and not really believe it. (That is, I shouldn't pretend to believe what I don't.)

∴ I should appear to believe X and really believe it.

This person is in a difficult position. She could give up Premise 2 and face the harm, go ahead and pretend (giving up the moral principle in Premise 3), or somehow make herself believe something without evidence. (We can assume that if there were evidence for X there would be no need for the threat of force.) It may not be possible for her to directly make herself believe something in the absence of evidence, but perhaps she could indirectly manipulate herself into believing X by turning her attention away from counterevidence and focusing on considerations that make X likely. The moral issue is whether she should allow the potential discomfort of pretending to believe something while not really believing it to outweigh her respect for the truth. If not, then the conclusion—that she *should* appear to believe X and really believe it—doesn't follow from the premises.

Until now, we have spoken loosely of a fallacy being committed, without specifying whether it is committed by the person offering the argument or by the one accepting it. In this last instance, it seems reasonable to say that *both* parties are committing a fallacy. However, as stated before, if someone makes a statement to avoid personal harm or harm to others but does not believe it, then the person is not committing a fallacy of appeal to force or pity but is using deceit as a tactic in a difficult situation.

Prejudicial Language An argument can also provide a motive for belief without providing support for belief by using *prejudicial language*. Consider these examples:

Example 6.29 *I hope you aren't going to say that you support the backward philosophy of emphasizing basic skills in primary and secondary education. I tend to take the progressive view that there are many things at least as important for students to learn as reading, writing, and arithmetic.*

Example 6.30 *Chris outgrew the naive view of human beings as mechanistic, robot-like creatures and came to the more sophisticated view of human beings as autonomous and possessing a will.*

Identifying a position using such words as *backward* or *naive* provides a motive for rejecting the position, and using such words as *progressive* and *sophisticated* provides a motive for adopting a position, all without giving any evidence either for the arguer's position or against an opponent's position. There is an element of trickery or distraction here, since in each example two issues are falsely presented as one: (1) Do you support teaching basic skills? (2) Is such a philosophy backward? and (1) Did Chris give up a mechanistic view of humankind? (2) Is such a view naive? But the main persuasive factor is motive in place of support. You would often not separate the two issues and argue each one through, because the prejudicial language causes you to either endorse or reject the position in question before any discussion can get started.

Should we say that to use prejudicial language is to advance a poor argument? In an example like "I hope you're not going to say that you support the backward philosophy of emphasizing basic skills in primary and secondary education," reasons are not *explicitly* given for a conclusion. Yet it is strongly suggested that basic skills should not be emphasized because this is a backward philosophy. Calling this approach "backward" implies more than that it is no longer popular; the implication is that it is less effective than current approaches. The issue of whether the suggested argument is a fallacy depends on whether this implication is true.

To sum up, then, prejudicial language is used to advance a bad argument when the prejudicial expression makes a false implication. By contrast, a statement such as "I hope you don't condone a careless attitude toward the dangerous disease, AIDS," doesn't involve a fallacy because it makes no false implication.

EXERCISE 6.3 Identifying Emotion Fallacies

Identify instances of the fallacies of appeal to force, appeal to pity, and prejudicial language that occur in the following passages. Note that prejudicial language can be used in combination with other fallacies.

1. How can you call my serve "out" when it's that close and I'm behind five games to one?
2. Politicians should keep in mind, when they are deciding whether abortion is right or wrong, that we pro-lifers have big families who grow up to be part of the voting public. Pro-abortionists tend to have no families at all.
3. You've been contradicting everything I say. The point I'm making is an obvious one. Government-supported universal health care would ruin the quality of medical practice.

4. I've poured my soul into the task of writing this novel. I've worked on it late at night after spending the day on my regular job. I've endured rejections, gone through revisions, and at last it's published. What do you think about it?
5. Senator Adamson has been critical of every policy this administration has proposed. Perhaps we should make the senator's ideological errors clear by emphasizing that we can arrange income tax audits for government officials.
6. You say we need to expand Head Start programs? There you go again, thinking we can solve problems by throwing money at them.
7. I think you've been judging your secretary's performance too harshly. Just remember when you write her performance evaluation and send it to me, that I write your evaluation.
8. More tax "incentives" for the ultra-rich? When are you going to grow out of that outdated, Reaganite, "trickle-down" mentality?

Emotion and Resemblance Combined: Appeal to Authority and Attacking the Person

These two fallacies—and particularly *attacking the person*—are probably the most common and most persuasive fallacies. They often draw from *two* sources of persuasiveness: These fallacies appeal to emotion by using your disapproval of a person to turn you against a point of view or by using your admiration for a person to turn you in favor. At the same time, these two fallacies resemble good arguments. There are many legitimate cases of appealing to the expertise of authorities or of attacking the credibility of someone making a claim. The fallacious cases of appeal to authority or attacking the person borrow some persuasiveness from these legitimate cases.

Appeal to Authority and Attacking the Person We often doubt a statement because there is something wrong with the person who makes it, or give additional credit to a statement because a famous or highly admirable person makes it. Sometimes it is legitimate to do this, but more often, these moves constitute a fallacy.

Appeal to Authority

Example 6.31 *A majority of doctors think that the morals of our young people have declined.*

Example 6.32 *Bruce Springsteen supports him. He's probably the best candidate.*

Attacking the Person

Example 6.33 *Our former mayor favored legalizing prostitution. But he was the most corrupt mayor we ever had. There's no way we should legalize it.*

Example 6.34 *Most of the men who say war is wrong are cowards.*

Although doctors may be much admired and knowledgeable in the field of medicine, there is no reason to believe they are experts in the field of morality. A similar criticism can be made of the argument concerning the choice of a candidate. The question of whether prostitution should be legalized is independent of the question of the character of its supporters; and the question of whether war is wrong is independent of the question of the courage of its opponents.

As we will see, it is sometimes legitimate to appeal to an authority. The fact that an expert makes a claim about something that truly lies within that person's area of expertise is a reason in favor of believing it. Also, pointing out correctly that someone is prone to lie can be a good reason against believing what this person says. Appealing to authority is a fallacy when a person really isn't an authority in the area in question. Attacking the person is a fallacy when the person gives reasons for his or her point of view—reasons that can be judged independently of the person's character or motives. In such cases, what makes an appeal to authority or an attack on the person a bad argument is that the premises are *irrelevant* to the conclusion. Even if I am a physician, and I say that morals have declined, it doesn't follow that morals really have declined. Even if I am a coward, that is irrelevant to whether I am correct about war being wrong.[10]

But since these criticisms seem fairly easy to make, the same question should be asked of these fallacies as was asked of the previous fallacies: Why do they tend to persuade? The answer is they can rely on both emotion and also resemblance to sound arguments, but in subtle ways.

How Both of These Fallacies Appeal to Emotion If you like a person, this is a motive for agreeing with the person. You treat agreeing with someone as a way of honoring that individual. Similarly, if you don't like a person, this is a motive for disagreeing with the person. For example, liking a singer such as Bruce Springsteen might make you inclined to agree with his choice of political candidates. And the idea that someone is a coward might make you less inclined to honor him by agreeing with his view on war.

But there is a further dimension to be explored here. Recall our discussion in Chapter 1 of the way in which an exchange of views can become a contest, rather than an occasion to determine what is reasonable to believe. It is in part a victory to discredit the other person's point of view, and a defeat to be discredited. When a disagreement becomes a contest, discrediting your opponent is on a continuum with insulting and physically attacking. A *person* is engaged in a contest, not just a point of view. Looked at in this way, the fallacy of *attacking the person* gains effectiveness because it identifies a person as a common enemy—someone it would be satisfying to defeat—and it associates a certain point of view with this enemy. This approach helps create a motive for the person hearing the argument to attack the enemy's point of view as a way of doing battle with another individual. And by contrast, associating a point of

---

[10]The arguments in question could be made valid by adding implicit premises, but such premises would be wildly implausible.

view with someone who is generally admired makes one less inclined to attack the view because to do so would be to take this person on as an opponent.

How a Fallacious Appeal to Authority Resembles a Good Argument It is often legitimate to defend a statement by appeal to authority. Because of this, even when an appeal to authority is fallacious, it draws some persuasiveness from its similarity to legitimate cases.

It is certainly not a fallacy to say you should take a particular medicine because a doctor prescribed it. Since we don't have time to become experts in every field, it often makes sense to trust someone (within limits) who has proof of expertise in a certain field. Unfortunately, a "halo" effect seems to apply to statements that lie outside an expert's area of knowledge.

This is particularly the case if some relationship is believed to exist between the area in which the person *is* an expert, and the area in which he or she is offering an opinion. As a result, we have examples such as:

Example 6.35 *Astronaut Willard has been to outer space and believes there is a God.*

Example 6.36 *Judge Wong believes that most murderers are really mentally ill.*

Sponsors are probably shrewd to have actors who play doctors on television endorse pain relievers and other medicines. After all, thousands of people wrote to fictional television doctor Marcus Welby, M.D., for medical advice.[11]

In between the cases in which appeal to authority is clearly legitimate and cases in which it is clearly fallacious, there are many cases that are difficult to decide. If someone has the title "physicist" and supports nuclear power, how much more weight should his opinion carry than the opinion of an ordinary citizen who has done some reading on the subject? If someone teaches economics, what additional weight should be given to her views on how to combat inflation? We examine this troublesome issue in Chapter 12.

How a Fallacious Attack on a Person Resembles a Good Argument It is also legitimate in some cases to criticize a statement by attacking the person who makes it. This similarity to legitimate arguments lends persuasiveness to *attacking the person,* even when such an attack is fallacious. To see why attacking the person is sometimes legitimate, let us consider the example of a witness in a court of law. Suppose that Thompson says he saw Smith take a woman's purse. If we have no reason to believe that Thompson wants to deceive us, then we will take his statement as evidence (at least partial evidence) that Smith did take the purse. But if we hear testimony that Thompson hates Smith or has often lied before, then these attacks on the person will justifiably discredit his testimony by showing an ulterior motive.

[11]Jerry Mander, *In the Absence of the Sacred* (San Francisco: Sierra Books, 1991), 88.

It is legitimate to attack Thompson's statement by attacking his credibility because our initial faith in his statement was based on the fact that Thompson had been in a position to see what went on, had presented his statement, and had no apparent reason to lie. But in other cases it is *not* legitimate to attack the person making a claim. Suppose someone is offering an argument—premises in support of a conclusion. In such cases it is legitimate to attack either her premises or the validity of her argument, but attacking the person making the argument is irrelevant.[12] Still, because attacking the person is relevant in the courtroom testimony kind of case, it can *seem* relevant in this latter case also.

Perhaps we can clarify the distinction between a legitimate attack on a person and an illegitimate one by applying it to more examples. Contrast the attack made by the supervisor against the manager with that made by the father against the daughter in these examples:

Example 6.37

Manager: *Charles shouldn't get the promotion. I worked with him two years ago and he never did his share.*

Supervisor: *I doubt that you can judge him impartially. You've been hostile toward him ever since that woman chose to marry him instead of you.*

Example 6.38

Daughter: *I don't believe that God exists. If there were such a being, then it would not allow all the suffering we see in the world.*

Father: *You've just turned against religion because you think it isn't fashionable. None of those so-called intellectuals you hang out with believe in it.*

In Example 6.37, the supervisor's attack on the manager is relevant. The manager expects his testimony about Charles's work record to be taken as evidence by itself that Charles doesn't deserve the promotion. But the credibility of this testimony is damaged by the information about the manager's attitude toward Charles. Example 6.38 is different in that the daughter is not simply expecting her father to believe her testimony against God's existence. She is giving a reason, the strength of which can be judged independently of an assessment of the daughter's character or circumstances. Her father's attack on her is irrelevant.

It is not always easy to judge how much weight to give to an attack on a person's credibility. Even with the example of the manager, although it is *relevant* to point out his hostility toward Charles, does it follow that his testimony should be discounted completely? A judgment must be made of *how biased* the manager is and *how able* and inclined he is to overcome bias in making claims about other people. These judgments, although they lack precision, are

[12]If she is simply expecting you to take her word that her premises are true, an attack on the person might still be relevant. But if she is drawing from information that is generally accessible to anyone, an attack on the person is not legitimate.

not impossible to make. Often, corroboration from other sources helps determine a person's credibility.

In analyzing legitimate and fallacious cases of attacking the person, we have sought to do two things. First, we have tried to show that there are legitimate cases; this fact accounts, in part, for why fallacious cases tend to be convincing. (This is in addition to the more obvious appeal to emotion in place of reason.) Second, we have sought to show how you can distinguish, if you are careful, between the legitimate and fallacious cases of attacking the person.

Variations of the Fallacy of Attacking the Person Certain common variations of this fallacy have been given separate names. Think about the differences among the following examples:

Example 6.39 *Discipline is important in education. Rousseau opposed discipline, but he was a pervert.*

Example 6.40 *Senator Spohn says we've been too hasty in closing our military bases. But she's got a base in her home state that she's trying to save.*

Example 6.41 *You're telling me I should drink less? You haven't been sober in a year.*

Whereas Example 6.39 is a straightforward attack on a person's character (calling Rousseau a pervert), Example 6.40 attacks a person's credibility by suggesting that she has something to gain by getting people to agree with her. These two variations are occasionally referred to by their Latin names, *ad hominem abusive* and *ad hominem circumstantial,* respectively. (*Attacking the person,* in general, is often referred to by the Latin name *ad hominem.*) Example 6.41 points out that a person has the same fault that the person is accusing someone else of having. This is called *tu quoque* (Latin for "you, too"). Of the three variations, *ad hominem abusive* relies most heavily on emotion for its persuasiveness; *ad hominem circumstantial* draws its persuasiveness primarily from its similarity to legitimate attacks on credibility; and *tu quoque* moves a discussion from the arena of critical reasoning to that of a personal conflict.

A NOTE ON TERMINOLOGY

Some of the terms we have used in this chapter are terms that are commonly used, while others are terms we invented. The idea of categorizing fallacies by their source of persuasiveness—*distraction, resemblance, emotion,* and *emotion and resemblance combined* is our own. A more common (but in our view less useful) division is into formal and informal fallacies, with such fallacies as *affirming the consequent* and *denying the antecedent* included under "formal," and most of the remaining ones included under "informal." All the names for individual fallacies are fairly commonly used, except for *prejudicial language*. Fallacies in which language creates prejudice *against* a certain view are commonly called *poisoning the well*. We used a broader category name so that we could include cases of prejudice *in favor of* a view.

People often use Latin names for fallacies. We noted these for the variations of *attacking the person (ad hominem abusive, circumstantial,* and *tu quoque).* Some other commonly used Latin names are *petitio principii* ("petitioning the premises") for *begging the question, ad baculum* ("to the stick") for *appeal to force,* and *ad misericordiam* ("to misery") for *appeal to pity.* Another commonly used Latin term is *non sequitur.* Calling an argument a *non sequitur* means literally that the conclusion *does not follow*—that is, the argument is invalid. More specifically, this term is often used to apply to an argument whose conclusion is wildly different from anything suggested by the premises.

REVIEW: FALLACIES OF DISTRACTION, RESEMBLANCE, EMOTION, AND EMOTION AND RESEMBLANCE COMBINED

It might be helpful to review the twelve fallacies identified and discussed in these chapters. They are arranged in categories below, with an example of each.

Distraction

1. *False dilemma.* The arguer claims there are only two alternatives and one is unacceptable, so we should choose the other. But in reality, there are more alternatives than the two stated.
   Example: Either we legalize drugs or we keep filling prisons with drug offenders.
2. *Slippery slope.* The arguer says we shouldn't do P because P probably leads to Q, which probably leads to R, and so forth down the "slippery slope" to a final consequence that is clearly undesirable. But some of these steps are implausible.
   Example: Now they want us to register handguns. Next it will be all guns. Then they'll ban guns, and we'll be set up for a police state.
3. *Straw man.* The arguer makes a position appear strong solely by making the opposing position appear weaker than it really is. The arguer puts a weak argument in an opponent's mouth when stronger arguments are available.
   Example: We need a health care program that provides for the needs of the poor. Those who oppose this idea think that the private sector will provide for the poor. But this has not been the case in the past and will not be the case in the future.

Resemblance

1. *Affirming the consequent.* Any argument that has the following invalid pattern:
   (1) If A, then B.
   (2) B.
   ―――――――――
   ∴ A.
   Example: If the economy is improving, stock prices will rise. Stock prices are rising, so the economy is improving.
2. *Denying the antecedent.* Any argument that has the following invalid pattern:
   (1) If A, then B.
   (2) Not A.
   ―――――――――
   ∴ Not B.
   Example: If she loves you, she'll marry you. She doesn't love you. So she won't marry you.
3. *Equivocation.* An argument in which an expression shifts its meaning from one premise to another, making the pattern invalid.
   Example: Insane people shouldn't be punished. Someone who commits a murder must be insane. So murderers should not be punished.
4. *Begging the question.* An argument resting on a premise that is either a restatement of the conclusion or that would be doubted for the same reasons that the conclusion would be doubted.
   Example: The Bible says God exists. Everything in the Bible is true, since God wrote it. So God does exist.

Emotion

1. *Appeal to force.* The arguer tries to get you to agree by indicating that *you* will be harmed if you don't agree.
   Example: If you want to keep working here, you should reconsider your criticisms of company policy.
2. *Appeal to pity.* The arguer tries to get you to agree by indicating that *she* or *he* will be harmed if you don't agree.
   Example: I *am* qualified—I have some experience and I really need the money.
3. *Prejudicial language.* The arguer uses language that biases you in favor of a position or against an opponent's position without giving evidence for or against the position.
   Example: Would you be so naive as to doubt the generally accepted fact that the finest painters were French?

Emotion and Resemblance Combined

1. *Appeal to authority.* Appealing to someone whose expertise is not relevant to the issue at hand, or appealing to someone who is famous or admired, but not an expert on the issue at hand. (*Note:* We have just described *fallacious* appeals to authority. There are also *legitimate* appeals to authority—appeals to people who really are experts in the appropriate areas.)
   Example of fallacious appeal: A majority of doctors think that the morality of young people has declined.
2. *Attacking the person.* Arguing that a person's point of view should be doubted because the person has bad traits of character or because the person has something to gain by being believed. (*Note:* There are legitimate as well as fallacious cases of attacking the person. See text above.)
   Example of fallacious attack: Most of the people who want drugs legalized are closet users.

EXERCISE 6.4

A Comprehensive Review of Fallacies

A. Write an example (of your own creation) of each of the following fallacies: appeal to force, appeal to pity, prejudicial language, attacking the person, appeal to authority.

B. The following passages contain fallacies from all the categories we have discussed. For each passage, identify the fallacy or fallacies. Many of the passages contain more than one fallacy.

   1. Is gun control legislation justified? Yes. The argument by those who oppose it seems to be that it is a great inconvenience to register guns. But this inconvenience is incidental when you consider the stakes. Either we pass an even stronger gun control bill or we can watch the violence in our cities continue. Gun control cannot be seen as unconstitutional in these modern times, for the reason that the so-called right to bear arms is completely out of date.
   2. If U.S. antiterrorist policies are effective, then there will be fewer terrorist attacks on Americans. There have been fewer attacks. So the antiterrorist policies have been effective.
   3. As warden, I don't think your complaints about how this penitentiary is run are well founded. The parole board is not likely to look favorably on the attitude you have been taking. You seem to think that inmates are entitled to dictate the policies of this institution. To me, this is not consistent with the purposes for which you are here. If inmates are made to feel that they have done wrong, they have a chance of becoming reformed. With your proposals, they would

not be made to feel they had done wrong. So they wouldn't have a chance of being reformed.

4. Rudi says that the government should provide more jobs for people. He should know. He couldn't get a job on his own if he had to. I had to look for months before I found work. My family even ran low on food. It was humiliating to plead with employers for a job. But I stuck it out and found work, and people like Rudi can do the same.
5. Those animal rights weirdos have really gone around the bend. Now they're saying no one should wear a fur coat. They won't be happy until we're all eating bean sprouts and wearing sackcloth. To them, a weasel is a dog is a human. Everything's the same.
6. There is no need for schools to make a conscious effort to select multicultural materials, since every author's viewpoint is unique. Any curriculum that includes several authors will provide diverse viewpoints, and any curriculum that reflects diverse viewpoints will have the effect of a multicultural curriculum.
7.

Commissioners in Developers' Pockets
Editorial: *The Daily Herald*

The County Commissioners want to destroy the country. They are in the pockets of the big land developers. The rezoning decision of last week just proves it. Once multiunit dwellings are permitted in neighborhoods with single-family dwellings, then the sense of community that now exists will be lost. Before you know it we will have strip development as far as the eye can see. Fast-food places will be squeezed between discount stores. If we resist the developers now, then our community will be saved. The voters will remember how the commissioners voted during the next election.

Cynthia Drew
1212 N.W. Breadbasket
City

8. Two congressional committees have issued scathing reports which condemn about every aspect of the cancer insurance industry and the product it offers to the public. One committee recommended that the sale of cancer insurance to the elderly be banned by federal law. . . . Statements in the report of the committees, as quoted in news stories, are too ridiculous to be taken seriously, although a lot of congressmen apparently are not laughing. Neither should the public be laughing because the thrust of this blatant effort to destroy a private business is a new warning that bureaucratic wrath and bureaucratic thirst for power threatens our very freedom of choice and individual preference . . . and isn't it a bit frivolous to have congressional

committees, which will BUY just about anything ($660 billion worth a year and climbing), advising the public on how to spend $25 to $75 a year?[13]

EXERCISE 6.5

Fallacious or Not?

It is debatable whether any or all of the following passages commit fallacies. Write a brief discussion of each passage, explaining why you think a fallacy is or is not being committed. You may wish to refer back to the relevant sections of the text for help in your deliberations.

1. The decision of whether to convict this man is more than academic. We are talking about sending a flesh-and-blood human being like you and me into a cage. He is a man with a family—his family is surely innocent of any offense. And yet they will suffer too because of the absence of a breadwinner. These are some of the consequences you will bring about if you decide to convict.
2. I believe the economic issue is the important one in this election. I don't know that much about economics myself, but my mother-in-law teaches economics and my uncle has run a large business for years. I've talked it over with them, and I think that the Republican candidate would probably do a better job of guiding the country's economic policies.
3. You can't claim that you have a *right* to free childcare, for the reason that neither I nor anyone else has an *obligation* to provide it. What have we done to create such an obligation? You might think that I am merely assuming what I am trying to prove. But by getting you to look at the matter from my point of view I hope you will be less inclined to claim that something you simply desire is your *right*.
4. The company was responsible for sending Bert into the chamber without properly checking for poisonous gases. Clearly, Bert has suffered substantial nerve damage that confines him to his home and makes it difficult for him to carry out even the most mundane activities such as feeding himself. The action of the company has caused him great physical pain and psychological suffering. He deserves compensation.
5. Here you are quoting Franklin on the subject of how one should live his life. But what kind of a life did Franklin himself live? I've read that he was a very difficult man, prone to depression, hard to please, impatient with those around him. When you judge a man's philosophy you have to see how it worked for him.
6. Tina has never had a teddy bear. A mother's love. A doll to cuddle. Tina knows nothing of these things. But she does know fear, rejection, and hunger. For just $15 a month, you can help save a child like Tina. Through our "adoption" program you can help provide a child with a better diet, clothes, medical attention, school. And even a toy or two.

[13]Millard Grimes, advertisement for American Family Life Assurance Company, originally published in the Columbus, Georgia, *Sunday Ledger-Enquirer*.

But don't wait. There are so many. And somewhere, right now, a child is dying from starvation and neglect.[14]

7. If you look at a map you'll see that the outline of South America closely parallels that of Africa. This and other similarities between the coast of North America and Europe justify the theory that these continents were at one time part of one supercontinent and have subsequently moved apart. If the geological theory of plate tectonics is correct, then we would expect just such movement.
8. The ease with which the 9/11 terrorists entered the United States illustrates the dilemma we face regarding our borders. We must either tighten border security to the point at which virtually all unauthorized immigrants are screened out, or we will live with an unacceptably high risk of another major terrorist attack.

[14]Adapted from an advertisement for Children, Inc. in Time Magazine, December 12, 1979, 12, with permission of the advertiser.

CHAPTER 7

"That Depends on What You Mean by . . ."

In Chapter 4, we distinguished two tasks that must be carried out in the evaluation of arguments: (1) determining whether the conclusion follows from the premises and (2) determining whether the premises should be accepted. Until now, we have assumed that the words that make up our arguments are reasonably clear in their meaning. This assumption simplifies the tasks we just mentioned. As we see in this chapter, when we look at arguments whose words and phrases are unclear in their meaning, it becomes more difficult to judge whether a conclusion follows and whether to accept premises.

Often, the question of how to judge an argument seems to depend on the meaning of a word or phrase.

Example 7.1 *Jane is emotionally disturbed, and emotionally disturbed people shouldn't be allowed to own guns. So Jane shouldn't be allowed to own guns.*

Example 7.2 *Frank is not a war veteran since he fought only in Vietnam, and the conflict in Vietnam was not a war.*

Example 7.3 *The YourFriends.com website contains images of people in sexually provocative poses. Since such images contribute to lewd desires, it follows that the YourFriends.com website is pornographic.*

You can almost hear the quick replies: "That depends on what you mean by *emotionally disturbed*," "That depends on what you mean by *war*," "That depends on what you mean by *pornographic*." But if the discussion proceeds at all, it is likely to get confused. Suppose the arguer in Example 7.1 indicates what she meant by *emotionally disturbed*, and according to her definition, Jane is emotionally disturbed. Does this save her argument? Or suppose the arguer in Example 7.2 supports his premise that "Vietnam was not a war" by insisting that a conflict is not a war unless one country officially declares war on another. Should we then accept the conclusion? Suppose the listener in Example 7.3 disagrees with the arguer's assumptions about the meaning of the word *pornographic*. Is there a way to proceed?

If there is a disagreement about meaning in any of these cases, someone will probably claim, "Now we're just arguing semantics, so there's no use in continuing." What do people mean by "just arguing semantics"? Are they making a worthwhile point? Is it true that there is no use in continuing? Can the issue of meaning be decided? How? By using a dictionary?

In an attempt to sort out and answer these questions, we note that situations in which problems with meaning arise are not all of the same kind. We distinguish three different situations in which considerations of meaning might affect our appraisal of an argument.

First, there might be a shift in meaning from one premise to the next, so that the argument's pattern is made invalid. Depending on the circumstances, this might be true of Example 7.1. The meaning of *emotionally disturbed* might shift from one premise to the next.

Second, the premises of an argument might support the conclusion only if an expression is given a special meaning. Unless this is pointed out, the argument's conclusion can be misleading. This criticism could be made about Example 7.2. The conclusion "Frank is not a war veteran" could be misleading.

Third, an argument might contain a premise that rests on a claim about the meaning of an expression. To evaluate the argument, we will need to decide whether to accept this claim about meaning. Example 7.3 could be interpreted as having the implicit premise "Material that arouses lewd desires is pornographic." And this claim could be thought to express something about the meaning of *pornographic*. How do we tell whether a claim like this should be accepted? In the remainder of this chapter we will explore each of these problems in turn.

UNCLEAR EXPRESSIONS IN THE PREMISES: LOOKING FOR SHIFTS IN MEANING

When an expression whose meaning is unclear is used in more than one premise, its meaning might shift from one premise to the next. If this happens, the usual result is that the conclusion does not follow from the premises. This kind of mistake is called *equivocation.* This fallacy was introduced briefly in Chapter 6. We now discuss it in greater detail.

Let's return to Example 7.1, focusing on the expression *emotionally disturbed,* which occurs in both premises.

Example 7.1 ***in Standard Form***

(1) Jane is ***emotionally disturbed.***

(2) ***Emotionally disturbed*** *people shouldn't be allowed to own guns.*

∴ Jane shouldn't be allowed to own guns.

It might be thought that the arguer can protect the argument from criticism by saying what she means by *emotionally disturbed*. Or, if the arguer is not present, perhaps we could help the argument by suggesting a definition that makes at least one of the premises true. Suppose the arguer is present and she says, "I mean by *emotionally disturbed* anyone who would score outside the normal range of the Minnesota Multiphasic Personality Inventory Version 2 (MMPI-2) test, and Jane would score outside the normal range of the relevant scales."

This definition saves the truth of the first premise, but it raises doubts about the second. As long as we vaguely suppose the expression *emotionally disturbed* to apply to people with certain severe disturbances such as paranoid delusions, it is easy to accept the claim that they shouldn't be allowed to own guns. But if we accept the stipulation that *emotionally disturbed* means "anyone who would score outside the normal range on the MMPI-2," then the second premise becomes doubtful. This is particularly apparent when we realize that the MMPI-2 has a masculinity–femininity scale according to which women who reject traditional sex roles tend to have high scores that could put them outside the normal range. It is implausible to maintain that such a rejection of roles alone is relevant to whether people should own guns. The problem is not that the second premise remains vague, but that it is probably false if *emotionally disturbed* is stipulated to mean "anyone who would score outside the normal range on the MMPI-2."

The lesson from this example is important, and it can be applied in many instances of criticism. When an expression is used in more than one premise, it must have the same meaning in all premises (unless the structure of the argument does not depend on these terms having the same meaning).[1] When the

---

[1]We have to add this qualification to handle special cases such as those involving two distinct meanings for a single word. Take, for example, the argument: "Don't build your bank near the bank of the river, it floods over its banks regularly, and your bank would be open to substantial damage." This argument is *not* faulty even though there is a (harmless) shift between the two meanings of *bank*.

meaning shifts in structurally relevant ways, the pattern of the argument is destroyed, and the conclusion does not follow from the premises. If *emotionally disturbed* kept the same meaning throughout the argument, the argument would have a pattern in which the conclusion follows:

(1) Jane is a P_1.

(2) All P_1's are P_2's.

∴ Jane is a P_2.

But if emotionally disturbed shifts its meaning, then the pattern becomes one in which the conclusion does not follow:

(1) Jane is a P_1.

(2) All P_3's are P_2's.

∴ Jane is a P_2.

As a second example of equivocation, consider the following reconstruction of an argument from Exercise 4.4. We'll focus on the expression *significant effect.*

Example 7.4

(1) If the United States were democratic, each citizen's opinion would have a ***significant effect*** *on government.*

(2) Each citizen's opinion does not have a ***significant effect*** *on government.*

∴ The United States is not really democratic.

Significant effect could mean many things, but let's try to interpret it in a way that makes both the premises of this argument plausible. In Premise 2, having a "significant effect" might be taken to mean having the government do what each person wants it to do. It is certainly true that each person's opinion doesn't have this kind of effect. But if we interpret *significant effect* in this same way in Premise 1, then that premise becomes completely implausible. If we refused to call the United States a democracy unless the government did what each individual wanted, then we are requiring something that is impossible. On the other hand, we could make Premise 1 plausible by interpreting *significant effect* in a more modest way, requiring only that citizens be allowed to vote and have their vote counted. But then Premise 2 becomes false.

The question is whether there is some interpretation of *significant effect* that makes both these premises true, and this is beginning to appear doubtful. Unless there is such an interpretation, Example 7.4 involves equivocation.

The way we dealt with Examples 7.1 and 7.4 suggests a three-step procedure for judging whether an argument is guilty of equivocation:

Three-Step Procedure for Judging Equivocation

1. Locate any unclear expressions that occur in more than one premise.
2. Determine what the expression must mean to make one of the premises true.
3. Determine whether the other premise(s) can be made true without changing the meaning of the unclear expression.

THE POSSIBILITY OF MISLEADING DEFINITION

A slightly different problem can arise when an unclear expression occurs both in a premise and in the conclusion, and a different critical approach is required. The way the expression is used in the premise can give it a special meaning. If we interpret the expression as having its ordinary meaning in the conclusion, then the conclusion is misleading. Suppose it is argued that:

Example 7.5

(1) The average height of women in the United States is five-feet-five inches.

(2) Any woman over the average height for women in the United States is tall.

(3) Bianca is five-feet-five and one-half inches tall.

∴ Bianca is tall.

This problem is not one of equivocation. The meaning of *tall* need not shift in order to make both Premise 2 and the conclusion true. The problem is that the definition of *tall* that would make Premise 2 true is not a definition that would ordinarily be assumed if we heard someone referred to as "tall." So if the arguer proceeded, on the basis of this argument, to go around preparing people to meet a tall woman when they meet Bianca, these people would be misled.

A fruitful way of criticizing this kind of argument is to point out to those presenting it that they should simply substitute their stipulated definition for the unclear term in the conclusion. We could suggest, "If all you mean by *tall* is 'above the average height for women in the United States,' then why not simply say Bianca is slightly above average height?"

The same critical approach could be used with Example 7.2:

Example 7.2 *in Standard Form*

(1) Frank fought only in Vietnam.

(2) The conflict in Vietnam was not a war.

∴ Frank is not a war veteran.

To keep the meaning of war from shifting, we must take it to mean "declared war." But it would be misleading to make this assumption and at other times, without explaining the stipulation, to claim that Frank is not a war veteran. If the arguer were required, however, to substitute the stipulated definition and say, "Frank didn't serve in a declared war," then the claim would lose its misleading effect.

KINDS OF UNCLARITY: VAGUENESS AND AMBIGUITY

So far in this chapter, we have referred broadly to "unclear meaning." Two kinds of unclarity are commonly distinguished: vagueness and ambiguity.

Vagueness *Emotionally disturbed,* as used in Example 7.1 concerning who should own guns, is a typical vague expression. Where do you draw the line between people who are emotionally disturbed and people who are not? *Tall,* as it is used in Example 7.5 concerning the height of women in the United States, is another vague expression. There is no definite boundary between people who are tall and those who are not. There is a range of height, and we would not hesitate to call people at the high end of the range tall, but it is somewhat arbitrary where to draw the line between those who are tall and those who aren't. *When there is no definite boundary (as in these cases) between the objects an expression applies to and those to which it does not, the expression is vague.*

It is no particular fault of an argument that it uses vague language. Most of the expressions we use could be called vague to some degree. As we can see from the examples in this chapter, a problem can arise when an argument uses the same vague expression in more than one premise. Then the question is whether it is used *consistently.* That is, does the vague expression apply to one portion of a range of objects in one premise, but to another portion of the range in the other premise?

In Example 7.4, concerning whether the United States is a democracy, the expression *significant effect* is vague. We can imagine a range of effects that citizens could have on government, from the most slight (voting for a losing proposition) to more significant (deciding what is to be law). The problem with Example 7.4 is that, to be plausible, one premise must be taken to use *significant effect* in a way that refers to less weighty effects within this range, while the other premise refers to more weighty effects. There is no answer to—and in this case no point in answering—the question, What does *significant effect* really mean? The question is whether *significant effect* can mean the *same* thing throughout the argument.

If a vague expression is used in a premise and a conclusion, it might be used consistently but still be misleading. As we saw in Example 7.2 concerning whether Frank is a war veteran, *war* is vague enough that it could be used to apply to declared wars exclusively. But it is misleading not to stipulate this when asserting the conclusion.

Ambiguity A second kind of lack of clarity is *ambiguity. An ambiguous expression has more than one meaning.* The word *dream,* for example, can mean either something hoped for or a sequence of images occurring during

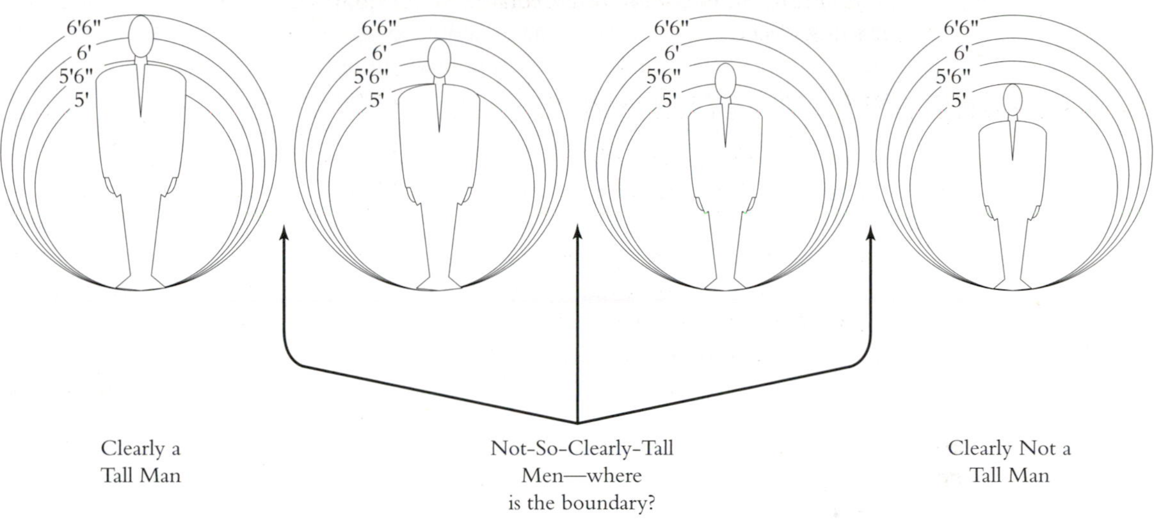
Vagueness: Indistinct Borders for Meaning
6'6"
6'
5'6"
5'
Clearly a Tall Man
Not-So-Clearly-Tall Men—where is the boundary?
Clearly Not a Tall Man

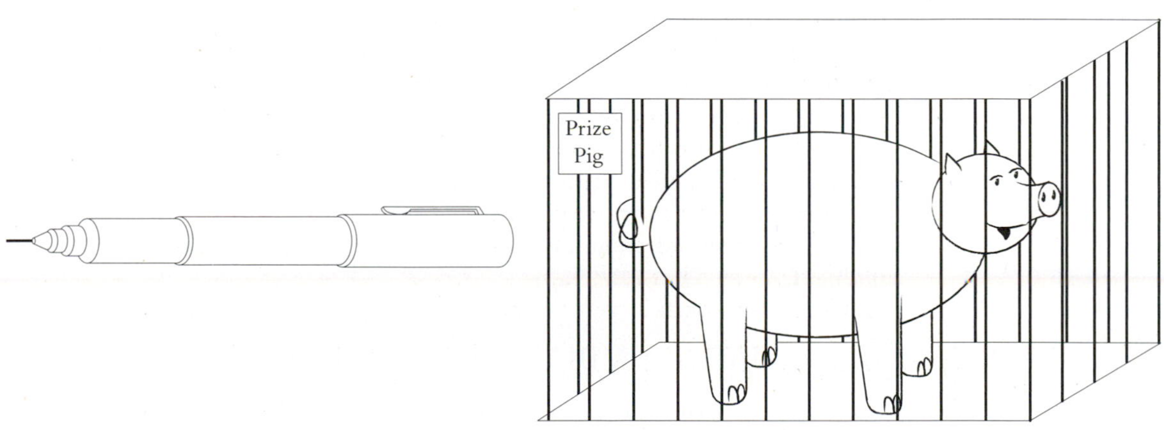
Ambiguity: Two or More Distinct Meanings
Prize Pig
Pen: an implement for writing in ink
Pen: an enclosure

sleep. An expression can be ambiguous without being vague. Both meanings of *dream* are fairly precise. Or an ambiguous expression can be vague also. People might be called *educated,* for example, if they have had a good deal of formal schooling or if they have acquired considerable knowledge through their own study. But in addition to having these two fairly distinct meanings, which make the word ambiguous, it is also vague because neither meaning has a definite boundary. How much schooling (or individual study) does it take before one can be properly called *educated*?

We can contrast this kind of unclarity of meaning and the kind of "shift" in meaning that can result, to the kind of unclarity and the kind of shift that can result from vagueness. A vague expression like *tall* is unclear because of the haziness of the boundary between things that are tall and those that are not. By "shifting in meaning," we meant that a vague term like *tall* can make a shift from premise to premise in the range of objects to which it refers. In the case of ambiguity, it might be unclear which of two distinct meanings a word like *dream* should be given in a particular premise, and a word might shift from one distinct meaning to another within an argument.

Ambiguity is less likely than vagueness to lead to difficulties in an argument. If an expression has wildly different meanings, then using it as though the meanings were the same would be too obvious to fool most listeners. Problems can arise, however, if the meanings are closely related. For example, there is a family of terms used in both legal contexts and moral contexts—*responsible, right, entitled,* and so on. It is easy to slip from one context to the other, giving these terms a slightly different meaning, as in the following argument:

Example 7.6 *If you bought the car from me, then I'm entitled to the money. And if I'm entitled to the money, then it isn't wrong for me to ask for it now.*

The speaker in this argument might be shifting from a legal to a moral context in using the word entitled. The first statement has to do with a legal right to payment. But the person being addressed might be complaining about the ethical propriety of being asked for the money in special circumstance—being in dire need, for example, or having just been insulted by the person who is owed the money. If the first premise depends on a legal sense of *entitled,* but the second premise requires that entitled be used in a moral sense, then it wouldn't follow that it's permissible for me to ask for the money now. This is an example of an ambiguous expression leading to equivocation in an argument.

INTERPRETING AND EVALUATING: A DIALOGUE PROCESS

It can be seen from the discussion of these examples that when an argument contains unclear terms, the tasks of evaluating it and determining what the unclear terms mean are not separate. This point can be brought more clearly into focus through a discussion of another argument that you already attempted to criticize in Exercise 4.4. It might have been reconstructed in the following way:

Example 7.7

(1) Getting married involves promising to live with a person for the rest of one's life.

(2) No one can safely predict compatibility with another person for life.

(3) If two people aren't compatible, then they can't live together.

(4) No one should make a promise unless she or he can safely predict that she or he can keep it.

∴ *No one should get married.*

As we will see, an adequate evaluation of this argument and an interpretation of its unclear terms are two parts of a dialogue process in which each part affects the other. We call this a dialogue process because it simulates a dialogue that might actually occur if the author of the argument were present. We imagine the critic asking the arguer what is meant by certain expressions, and the arguer responding in turn by clarifying his or her meaning. The critic then assesses the implications of this interpretation for the argument as a whole.

It is possible simply to dismiss some of the premises in the argument given in Example 7.7 (and in many others) by interpreting vague or ambiguous expressions in ways that make the premises false. But by seeking interpretations (within reason) that will make the premises true, we can try to discover whether the argument advanced is making a point worth our consideration. This approach, which might be seen as an extension of the Principle of Charitable Interpretation, supports our objective of using critical reasoning to determine what is reasonable to believe rather than to defeat opponents in argument.

Since a written text provides no opportunity for a real dialogue, the reader must play the arguer's role as well as his or her own in interpreting and evaluating this document. The first premise of our argument states that *Getting married involves promising to live with a person for the rest of one's life*. But the term *marriage* is broad (that is, vague) enough to cover common-law marriages and the recent phenomenon of self-styled marriage contracts that include no such promise. These cases suggest that the premise is false.

This criticism has a point; the first premise is at best misleading as stated. But it is both interesting and worthwhile to give the arguer the benefit of the doubt by interpreting getting married in a sense that restricts the term to cases involving the traditional vow "until death do us part" or some equivalent. This interpretation now makes the first premise true since traditional marriages do seem to involve a promise—that is, a marriage vow.

The second premise may also be subjected to the dialogue process. It states that *No one can safely predict compatibility with another person for life.*

The expression *safely predict* is vague here. Would a prediction with 90 percent certainty be a safe prediction? 80 percent? 51 percent? Again, we can pick a meaning that will make Premise 2 false since we can predict compatibility if we set the level of safe prediction low enough. But let us see where a more generous interpretation might lead us.

We can pick a level of certainty high enough to make the second premise true—one such that no one will be able to safely predict compatibility for life. But notice that the same expression—safely predict—is used again in Premise 4. We must interpret it in the same way there.

Now a problem emerges. The high standards of predictability that were necessary to make Premise 2 true make it less likely that *No one should make a promise unless she or he can safely predict that she or he can keep it.* We might be justified, for instance, in promising to return a book even though we know that a variety of factors, such as a house fire, might make the promise impossible to keep. To demand nearly absolute certainty of being able to keep a promise would rule out all but a few promises. Such a stipulation, if actually carried out in practice, would virtually eliminate the useful custom of making promises.

We are now left with the question of whether there is a range of "safe prediction" low enough to make this premise about promises true but high enough that it is also true that no one can safely predict compatibility with another person for life. It's doubtful that there is such a range.

There is a problem of interpretation regarding Premise 3 as well. It maintains: *If two people aren't compatible, then they can't live together.* We have the same dilemma with *compatible* that we had with *safely predict.* For Premise 3 to be true, we would have to call people "compatible" unless they had extremely serious conflicts. After all, many people continue to live together in spite of minor incompatibility. But by interpreting the notion of "compatible" in a broad way, we make Premise 2 less plausible—many people might be able to safely predict that they won't have serious conflicts (especially if they share a great many values and have known each other for some time). Therefore, an interpretation that makes Premise 3 more plausible makes Premise 2 less plausible.

What is the outcome of our dialogue process? Even being generous with the meanings of unclear terms, we judge the argument in question to be unsound—some premises are implausible. But reaching this conclusion through a dialogue process that makes every effort to find truth in the argument's premises is more important than jumping at easy ways to dismiss the argument. As an added benefit, the dialogue process has raised interesting questions about the nature of commitment in marriage. In actual practice, you need not act out a dialogue to interpret an argument. But you should try to provide a sympathetic, even generous, interpretation of crucial expressions.

The discussion of this example should have made clear how interpreting the words used in an argument, and evaluating the argument itself, are interrelated. We can often choose one of several meanings for an expression, and the choice we make can affect the truth or falsity of premises. But we must make our choices consistent to preserve the validity of an argument.

EXERCISE 7.1 **Criticizing Arguments That Contain Unclear Words or Expressions**

A. Discuss the ways vague or ambiguous expressions might be clarified in the following statements. Suggest how assigning different interpretations affects their truth or falsity.

1. Man is born free.
2. Exceptional children should be given special attention by the public education system.
3. Suicide, whether direct or indirect, should be strongly condemned.
4. The average American family has 3.2 members.
5. The war on poverty was no war.
6. The Obama administration yesterday, amidst all this record-setting cold weather, proposed a new agency to study and report on the changing climate, also known as global warming. . . . They're having to delay setting up the office [of Climate Service] because they're expecting another 16 to 20 inches [of snow] in Washington. I mean, this is absurd.[2]
7. Marriage is a bond of trust between equals, but the partners in a marriage are rarely equal.
8. The accused argued that he should not be required to pay the parking ticket because the sign said, "Fine for Parking" (from Mike Mailway, *Seattle Post-Intelligencer*).
9. The public school system can never treat students equally; they come to the schools unequal in talent, experience, and family background.
10. America did not become a democracy until the 1960s. Women could not vote until the Nineteenth Amendment was ratified in 1920, and it was only in 1965 that a Voting Rights Act was passed that did away with property qualifications and literacy tests, and paved the way for the genuine participation of all people, regardless of race, creed, or national origin.

B. Write a brief critical assessment of the following arguments, focusing particularly on possible shifts in meaning of vague or ambiguous terms. Try to create a dialogue—suggesting possible meanings of unclear terms, evaluating the argument in the light of these stipulations of meaning, and suggesting alternative interpretations that might get around any objections. Refer to the discussion of Example 7.7 for a model of this kind of dialogue.

1. The United States is a democracy. This follows from the fact that the United States is ruled by the people and *democracy* means "government ruled by the people."
2. If the average couple has more than two children, the population will rise drastically. But we should prevent the population from rising drastically. So we should prevent the average couple from having more than two children. *(Note that this argument has been altered from the version presented in Chapter 4 so that the shift in wording has been eliminated.)*

---

[2]Rush Limbaugh, February 9, 2010 broadcast of his radio program.

3. Space cannot be expanding unless it is finite. But space is not finite. Hence, space cannot be expanding.
4. Equal rights for women should not be constitutionally guaranteed. This follows from the fact that men and women are different physiologically and emotionally. But if this is so, then men and women are not equal. And if men and women are not equal, then they should not be called "equal" by the law.
5. Nobody should undertake college education without at least some idea of what she wants to do and where she wants to go in her life. But our world is full of change. We can't predict which fields will provide job openings in the future. If we can't confidently predict future employment, then we can't form a reasonable idea of what to do with our lives. So nobody should go to college.
6. A game is time-bound. . . . It has no contact with any reality outside itself, and its performance is its own end. Further it is sustained by the consciousness of being a pleasurable, even mirthful, relaxation from the strains of ordinary life. None of this is applicable to science. Science is not only perpetually seeking contact with reality by its usefulness, i.e., in the sense that it is applied, it is perpetually trying to establish a universally valid pattern of reality, i.e., as pure science.[3] **(Hint: Assume that the conclusion being argued is that science is not a game.)**
7. "Man is born free," said Rousseau, "and is everywhere in chains," but no one is less free than a newborn child, nor will he become free as he grows older. His only hope is that he will come under the control of a natural and social environment in which he will make the most of his genetic endowment and in doing so most successfully pursue happiness.[4] **(Hint: Assume that Skinner is arguing in this passage for the conclusion that happiness does not involve freedom from control.)**
8.

LETTERS TO THE EDITOR

Health Care Fiasco

Obama and the Democrats are proposing to have the government run more of the health care system in the U.S. This amounts to socialism. We all know about the failures of socialism in other countries, so we can clearly see that Obama and the Dems are headed on the wrong path. Not only that, but they are also proposing to cut a half-trillion dollars from Medicare to pay for this fiasco.

Tom T. Bagley
City

---

[3]John Huizinga, *Homo Ludens: A Study of the Play Element in Culture* (Boston: Beacon Press, 1955), 203.

[4]B. F. Skinner, *About Behaviorism* (New York: Knopf, 1974), 201.

ARGUMENT AND DEFINITION

At the beginning of this chapter we pointed out that when an argument has been presented and the meanings of terms are challenged, the discussion is likely to get frustrating and confused. Some people become impatient with further discussion because they believe there is an easy resolution: a trip to the dictionary. Other people see the debate over meaning as pointless ("mere semantics") because they believe that definitions are arbitrary; anyone can use a word to mean almost anything he or she wants. We believe both points of view are mistaken.

Consider first the view that substantial problems of meaning can all be solved by consulting a dictionary. This presumption is faulty in two ways. First, dictionary entries often do little more than provide synonyms whose meaning is closely allied to the term being defined. As such, they often fail to clarify meaning, as is illustrated in the following series of dictionary entries:

> **recondite**—incomprehensible to one of ordinary understanding or knowledge
>
> **incomprehensible**—impossible to comprehend; unintelligible
>
> **unintelligible**—not intelligible; obscure
>
> **obscure**—not readily understood or not clearly expressed; abstruse
>
> **abstruse**—difficult to comprehend; recondite

Second, dictionaries give precise definitions for only a limited range of scientific or technical terms. They can define precisely, for instance, specially coined terms from physics, such as:

> **pion**—a short-lived meson that is primarily responsible for the nuclear force that exists as a positive or negative particle with mass 139.6 MeV/c^2 (273.2 times the electron mass) or a neutral particle with mass 135.0 MeV/c^2 (264.2 times the electron mass)

But dictionaries give only incomplete analyses of more familiar terms:

> **marriage**—the institution whereby men and women are joined in a special kind of social and legal dependence for the purpose of founding and maintaining a family

Even if we overlook the vagueness of certain terms (*social and legal dependence, family*), this dictionary entry faces difficulty. It is inadequate because people can be married without intending to found or maintain a family (that is, without intending to have children). It is not even clear that marriage must customarily be associated with intending to have children. To fix the dictionary entry to avoid this problem, we would need to investigate more closely the connection between the concept of marriage and related concepts such as that of a family or social and legal dependence. The latter part of this chapter examines techniques that can be used to improve our understanding of crucial concepts used in arguments. The dictionary, however, as we have seen, provides little help in resolving uncertainty about concepts.

A second perspective is taken by those who believe that discussion about meaning and definition should be dismissed because they are merely a matter of semantics. Such skeptics assume that we are free to attach whatever meaning we like to the words and statements we use, and for that reason believe that inquiry into meaning (and definition) must be fruitless.

An unlikely but well-known supporter of this perspective is Humpty Dumpty, as recorded in his discussion of the matter with Alice in Lewis Carroll's classic *Through the Looking Glass.*[5] They have just finished a conversation about birthdays and un-birthdays (did you know we have 364 days for un-birthday presents?).

> *"And only one for birthday presents, you know. Here's glory for you!"*
>
> *"I don't know what you mean by glory," Alice said.*
>
> *Humpty Dumpty smiled contemptuously. "Of course you don't—till I tell you. I meant 'there's a nice knock-down argument, for you!'"*
>
> *"But 'glory' doesn't mean 'a nice knock-down argument,'" Alice objected.*
>
> *"When I use a word," Humpty Dumpty said, in rather a scornful tone, "it means just what I choose it to mean—neither more nor less."*
>
> *"The question is," said Alice, "whether you can make words mean so many different things."*
>
> *"The question is," said Humpty Dumpty, "which is to be master—that is all."*

This snippet illustrates an extreme version of the thesis that the meaning of words reflects the momentary intentions of speakers. Alice raises the telling question of whether we *can* mean what we choose at the moment. A certain stability is necessary for communication to be possible at all. Communication is possible only if people can share meanings for the words they use and hence share concepts. If people use words as they please, with no regard for the meaning recognized by others, then they limit the amount of communication possible. Some people might be momentarily amused by a strange, unorthodox use of expressions, but they would quickly tire of the game. If you give words meaning according to a personal code, you make it virtually impossible for others to understand you. But even more generally, if the "words" (that is, sounds) people use are completely arbitrary and unsystematic, they won't even be able to begin to communicate. They won't be speaking a language but merely babbling sounds.

Of course, sometimes it is useful to specify or choose a meaning. Such specifying is commonly done within a field through its technical vocabulary; we do it as well when we stipulate a meaning for a vague expression or select among the meanings of an ambiguous expression. Such choices need not be arbitrary. But extensive use of technical expressions, especially those that have nontechnical meanings as well, can make communication difficult. Learning to use words in a technical manner is like learning to use another language.

This emphasis on stability is not meant to suggest that meanings are unchanging over time, or from person to person, or group to group; people can miscommunicate. The process of examining the meaning of crucial concepts in

---

[5]Lewis Carroll, *The Annotated Alice* (New York: Clarkson N. Patter Inc., 1960), 268–269.

an argument is designed to limit faulty communication. The process presupposes a certain amount of agreement between the person producing an argument and those to whom the argument is directed. If there is no such agreement on the application of a concept to even a single case (either real or imagined), then we should conclude that the people involved have different concepts—even though they might employ the same words to express them. This is what most people are prepared to do with Humpty Dumpty. His concept of "glory" is certainly not theirs (however much they might relish a "nice knock-down argument").

One minimal requirement for fruitful communication is that the meaning of terms in an argument or argumentative passage is consistent. This *consistency criterion* is violated in the case of equivocation. As we saw in the previous section, if the meaning of a key term changes in various premises or the conclusion of an argument, the argument commits a fallacy. More broadly, if an argumentative passage contains several arguments that employ a certain key term, then the consistency criterion requires that these different applications use the term consistently as well.

Evaluating Definition-like Premises

At the beginning of this chapter we pointed to three kinds of situations in which considerations of meaning can affect our appraisal of an argument. The first two we discussed involved unclear expressions that are used more than once in an argument, raising the possibility of equivocation, or misleading definition. The comments just made concerning argument and definition are intended to clear the way for a discussion of the third kind of situation. That is, a premise of an argument might make or imply a claim about the meaning of an expression. When this occurs, a part of our appraisal of the argument is to consider whether this claim about meaning is acceptable. We have just made a case that this cannot be done by simply consulting a dictionary, but neither are meanings so arbitrary that words can mean whatever we want them to. So how do we decide whether to accept a claim concerning meaning?

Let's consider again the argument we posed at the beginning of the chapter, in which the acceptability of some premises depends on the meaning or definition of concepts.

Example 7.3 *(repeated)*

The YourFriends.com website contains images of people in sexually provocative poses. Since such images contribute to lewd desires, it follows that the YourFriends.com website is pornographic.

or in standard form:

(1) The YourFriends.com website contains images of people in sexually provocative poses.

(2) Images of people in sexually provocative poses arouse lewd desires.

(implicit) *(3) Any material that arouses lewd desires is pornographic.*

∴ The YourFriends.com website is pornographic.

Imagine how we might explore the truth of these premises. We could test Premise 1 by looking at the website to see whether they contain pictures of people in sexually provocative poses. Premise 2 is more difficult to assess. Presumably it depends at least on some sort of psychological investigation. Such a claim might well rest on the observations and theories of psychologists concerning the causes of "lewd desires." Thus Premises 1 and 2 can both be interpreted as needing justification that appeals to features of the world and, either directly or indirectly, to observation of it. The term *empirical* is often used to mark this dependence. Premise 3, on the other hand, is more a matter of definition. Appeal here is to the meaning of the concept of pornography. Further, part of the process of assessing the truth of not only Premise 3, but Premise 2 as well, depends on making clear the meaning of lewd desires.

In deciding whether to accept the premise *Any material that arouses lewd desires is pornographic,* we could simply test it like any other universal generalization—we could try to find a counterexample to it. We could point out that for some people who are readily inclined to lewd desires, almost anything remotely related to sex could arouse such desires—pictures of fully clothed but physically attractive people, for example. For someone not disposed to lewd desires, material that many would call "pornographic" might only arouse disgust.

In many situations in which a definition-like premise is to be evaluated, this sort of testing by counterexample will probably suffice. But our discussion of the inadequacy of dictionary definitions raises a deeper question than how to determine whether a particular claim about meaning is acceptable. We might wonder how a particular claim could be supported—what kind of theory would provide a basis for a claim about the meaning of *pornographic,* or of *lewd desires,* or of any other concept. To address this deeper question, we present the following analysis of conceptual theories and discuss techniques for reconstructing and evaluating them. Even when evaluation of argument does not initially seem to depend on the meaning of a key term, as we have seen assumptions about meaning might be lurking in the background. Our discussion of marriage and promising in Example 7.7 raises questions about what the concept of marriage includes.

RECONSTRUCTING CONCEPTUAL THEORIES

Conceptual theories are seldom stated fully and explicitly in ordinary argumentative passages or discourse, although they are common in such disciplines as philosophy, logic, and mathematics, where conceptual clarity is essential. In those disciplines, a conceptual theory will be offered where there is conceptual uncertainty. A philosopher wonders which laws are just and which objects should be considered works of art; a logician wonders which arguments should be considered acceptable; a mathematician wonders how to give an account of a concept such as "finite number."

We are also called on to make conceptual distinctions in ordinary, less formal contexts. The local community wants to encourage recycling, cut down on the amount of material sent to the local landfill, and generate usable compost. It announces that "lawn and garden wastes" can be brought to a specified site. What are lawn and garden wastes? If someone brings a broken water heater, the item is clearly outside the boundaries of the concept. Leaves, grass clippings, and old tomato plants are clearly within it. What about pesticide containers and old fertilizer bags? What about large tree limbs or stumps? Even though the pesticide containers and fertilizer bags are wastes attendant to the lawn and garden, they pose a danger to those who would use the compost and would for this reason be inappropriate. The limbs and stumps, though recyclable in the long run, take such a long time that, without special processing, they too would be inappropriate. The town could articulate more fully the requirements for using the recycling facility. They might add that the site is for "recyclable vegetable matter from lawns and gardens." This might help, at least if the citizens were clear about what counted as recyclable vegetable matter. They might even specify it in more detailed ways—for example, require that it be less than one inch in diameter and three feet in length.

This example suggests some important features of conceptual reasoning that apply not only in the more abstract speculation of philosophers, logicians, and mathematicians, but in more everyday contexts. First, we had some clear cases in mind: water heaters were out (though they might be recyclable in a different project); leaves and grass clippings were in. Furthermore, we might raise issues that would help decide less clear-cut cases—for instance, trees and stumps. In trying to clarify the concept, we face the danger that our attempt might not be illuminating, if for instance, the public doesn't already have an idea of what "recyclable vegetable matter" might be. Finally, we might want to make somewhat arbitrary decisions on borders for ease of use. If a one-inch-diameter branch is acceptable because it would decay in a reasonable amount of time, a one-and-one-eighth-inch branch would not take much longer. The exact point at which one draws the boundary might not be critical, though having a boundary might be necessary for actually using the concept as a tool for admitting waste into the public compost pile. If the context changed, for example, if the city bought a wood chipper—then the boundary for acceptable wastes might be altered significantly.

We borrow the model of conceptual theory[6] from the disciplines of philosophy, logic, and mathematics in order to set out a systematic way of reconstructing definition-like claims found in arguments, even everyday arguments, and as a way of seeing what these claims look like when fully articulated. This way of reconstructing these claims also helps promote critical assessment. In later sections, we suggest several techniques for criticizing conceptual theories and tie these criticisms into the larger task of reconstructing and criticizing whole arguments.

A Model for Conceptual Theories

Ideally, a conceptual theory designates precisely the conditions under which a certain concept applies to an object. Some conceptual theories (not necessarily adequate ones) might be:

Example 7.8 *A film is <u>pornographic</u> if and only if it provocatively depicts sex acts.*

---

[6]We use the uncommon expression *conceptual theory* (rather than the term *definition*) for the full account of the meaning of a concept, in order to distinguish it from a simple dictionary definition.

Example 7.9 *A law is just if and only if it is passed democratically.*

Example 7.10 *An object is a work if and only if*

(1) It is made by humans;

(2) It resembles an object in nature;

AND

(3) It is beautiful.

Example 7.11 *An argument is valid if and only if the conclusion follows from the premises.*

Often it is not an isolated concept that is unclear, but rather a group of related concepts. In such a case, a conceptual theory tries both to state the way the concepts are related and to designate which objects are to be included under each of the concepts. For example, an ethical theory might try to explain what acts are right, what things are good, and the relation between right and good, in the following way:

Example 7.12 *An act is right if and only if it produces more good than any alternative.*

Something is good if and only if

(1) It is happiness;

OR

(2) It produces happiness.

Each of these theories is stated in a standard form useful for clearly expressing conceptual theories. The part of the statement that comes before *if and only if* indicates what is being explained: the use of a certain concept in a certain context. The word or phrase designating the concept is underlined in these examples. This first part of the statement, before *if and only if*, also indicates the context. In Example 7.8, the conditions under which the concept of pornography applies to any film are being explained. In Example 7.9, the concept of justice is being explained in the context of law. The theory explains the conditions under which a law is just. In Example 7.10, the context is not limited. What is being explained (not necessarily adequately) are the conditions under which the concept of being an artwork can apply to any object whatsoever.

The middle phrase in each stated theory—*if and only if*—indicates that what follows is a set of *requirements, or conditions to be met;* these select precisely those objects to which the concept applies. The part of the statement following *if and only if* is the list of requirements or conditions. The theory in Example 7.10 claims that the conditions an object must meet to be a work of art are:

1. It is made by humans.
2. It resembles an object in nature.
3. It is beautiful.

It is claimed that, taken by itself, each condition is *necessary*, in the sense that an object *must* meet this condition to be a work of art. There may be other conditions as well, but nothing can be a work of art without satisfying this one. For instance, the theory in Example 7.10 claims that it is necessary for an object to be made by humans to be a work of art. But each condition by itself is not enough to make the object a work of art. All the conditions must be met in order for an object to qualify fully as art. In this sense, while each condition is *necessary*, the entire list of conditions is said to be *sufficient* to ensure that an object is a work of art.

The preceding discussion might be misleading in that it represents conceptual theories as being rather simple, brief formulations standing by themselves; nothing has been said about the context in which a conceptual theory is developed. Typically, a conceptual theory is not offered in isolation from a discussion of (1) why it was chosen, (2) what alternatives were considered and why they were rejected, (3) how the analysis in question is related to a broader area of inquiry, and (4) further conclusions or implications that can be drawn from it. Example 7.12, for instance, is a simplification of an ethical theory that has been the focus of attention in hundreds of books and essays. In these writings, a rationale for choosing this theory over others is carefully discussed. Possible objections to the account are raised, and the reasons for overriding the objections are presented. The analysis or theory of valid arguments, introduced in Chapters 2 through 5, has been developed through ongoing work in the field of symbolic logic.

Much of the development of a conceptual theory takes place in the context of the dialogue process discussed in this chapter. In such a dialogue an inadequate account is rejected and a stronger one is constructed to meet objections. You will understand this process better after we explain how a conceptual theory is criticized.

Reconstructing Fragmentary Theories

In an ideal case (in a careful philosophical essay, for example), a conceptual theory will be presented completely and precisely. If it is not presented in the form we have discussed, it is at least apparent how the theory will fit into this form. In less formal discourse, however, theories are sometimes presented in a fragmentary, loosely expressed manner. It is often helpful to reconstruct such a theory in order to organize the task of criticism. To do this, we determine how the writer's or speaker's statements can be fit into the form we have discussed, while both preserving the meaning and making the theory as defensible as possible.

Suppose someone has written

Example 7.13

When can we consider two people to be married? This is a particularly difficult question in this age which has seen the rise of self-styled marriage contracts and even homosexual marriage. I would venture to say that marriage requires cohabitation. But it also requires having the intention of sharing love—by which, to be explicit, I mean sexual love.

As with reconstructing an argument, a good portion of the task is eliminating remarks that are incidental. The first part of the passage conveys the difficulty of saying what marriage is, but it does not state a theory. From the second half of the passage we can elicit the following theory:

Reconstruction

Two people are <u>*married*</u> *if and only if*

(1) They live together;

AND

(2) They have the intention of sharing sexual love.

Consider a second example that is more fragmentary and therefore requires more extensive reconstruction.

Example 7.14

Some people claim that the institution of marriage has not declined. But this is due to a misunderstanding of the true nature of marriage: it is a lifelong commitment.

Again, we must eliminate remarks that are not a part of the theory. The first statement in this example is not part of the conceptual theory being reconstructed, although it presents the position the author is criticizing. On the basis of the second statement, however, we could take the writer to be asserting.

Reconstruction 1

Two people are <u>*married*</u> *if and only if they have made a lifelong commitment.*

But we should presume that the writer is more reasonable than this. First, the writer probably has in mind not just any commitment, but the specific commitment to live together. Second, the writer probably sees this as only one condition necessary for marriage—so that, for example, two brothers or sisters would not necessarily be married just because they had made a lifelong commitment to live together. Often, fragmentary theories present only the most important or controversial conditions. In this case, since the writer has not spelled out the remaining necessary conditions, we should reconstruct only the incomplete theory:

Reconstruction 2

Two people are <u>*married*</u> *if and only if*

(1) They have made a lifelong commitment to live with each other;

AND

(2) other (unspecified) conditions.

We can also use a somewhat similar pattern of reconstruction when we interpret a passage as setting out one of several possible conditions sufficient for us to apply a concept.

Example 7.15

All people born within the boundaries of the United States are U.S. citizens.

This can be reconstructed by adding "OR other (unspecified) conditions."

Reconstruction

A person is a U.S. citizen if and only if

(1) He or she is born within the boundaries of the United States;

OR

(2) other (unspecified) conditions (for example, he or she is born abroad of parents who are U.S. citizens).

You may find it easier to see the kinds of glaring weaknesses that should be avoided in reconstructing fragmentary theories after we examine the kinds of criticisms that can be made against conceptual theories. We turn to this topic in the next section.

EXERCISE 7.2

Reconstructing Conceptual Theories

Reconstruct the conceptual theory presented in each of the following passages and present it in the form illustrated in the text. In each case, begin by asking what concept is being discussed in the passage. The words designating this concept should be underlined. Second, look for the condition(s) that explains the concept. The condition(s) should be listed after the phrase *if and only if.* Try to make your statement of conditions as brief as possible. This may require substantial summarizing and rephrasing of some passages. Eliminate any irrelevant material and be as charitable as possible.

1. It is easy to see that squares are precisely those figures with four sides of equal length.
2. Much of the trash hung in art galleries these days is not really art, for to be art something must represent an object found in the real world.
3. It cannot be argued whether this law is just. It is obvious that it is just, since it was passed democratically.
4. Many questions of ethics could be resolved if people would be mindful that an act is right if it produces happiness and wrong if it produces unhappiness.
5. Traffic gridlock is a total standstill of traffic for at least fifteen minutes extending eight blocks or more in any direction.[7]
6. A family is a group of persons of common ancestry living under the same roof.
7. A work of art can be characterized by noting two features. First, works of art are the product of man's activity, i.e., they are artifacts. But unlike most tools, which are also artifacts, a work of art is an artifact upon which some society or sub-group of a society has conferred the status of candidate for appreciation.[8]

---

[7]Adapted from *Science* 84 (October 1984): 84.
[8]Adapted from George Dickie, "Defining Art," *American Philosophical Quarterly* 6 (1969): 253–255.

8. There are certain indicators of humanhood, included among them are an IQ of at least 20 and probably 40, self-awareness, self-control, a sense of time, and the capability of relating to others.[9]
9. The "positive" sense of the word "liberty" derives from the wish on the part of the individual to be his own master. I wish my life and decisions to depend on myself, not on external forces of whatever kind. I wish to be the instrument of my own, not of other men's acts of will. I wish to be a subject, not an object; to be moved by reasons, by conscious purposes which are my own, not by causes which affect me, as it were, from outside. I wish to be somebody, not nobody; a doer—deciding, not being decided for, self-directed and not acted upon by external nature or by other men as if I were a thing, or an animal, or a slave incapable of playing a human role, that is, of conceiving goals and policies of my own and realizing them.[10]
10.

Autism Spectrum Disorder[11]

Must meet criteria 1, 2, and 3:

1. Clinically significant, persistent deficits in social communication and interactions, as manifest by all of the following:
   a. Marked deficits in nonverbal and verbal communication used for social interaction;
   b. Lack of social reciprocity;
   c. Failure to develop and maintain peer relationships appropriate to developmental level.
2. Restricted, repetitive patterns of behavior, interests, and activities, as manifested by at least TWO of the following:
   a. Stereotyped motor or verbal behaviors, or unusual sensory behaviors.
   b. Excessive adherence to routines and ritualized patterns of behavior.
   c. Restricted, fixated interests.
3. Symptoms must be present in early childhood (but may not become fully manifest until social demands exceed limited capacities)

[9]Adapted from Joseph Fletcher, "Indicators of Humanhood: A Tentative Profile of Man," *Hasting Center Report* 2(5) (November 1972).
[10]Isaiah Berlin, "Two Concepts of Liberty," *Four Essays on Liberty* (Oxford: Oxford University Press, 1958), 16. Reprinted with permission.
[11]American Psychiatric Association Proposed Revision for DSM V (Diagnostic and Statistical Manual of Mental Disorders), 5th edition expected 2013. From the APA website http://www.dsm5.org/ProposedRevisions/Pages/proposedrevision.aspx?rid=94.

11.

What Is Death with Dignity?[12]

The dictionary shows that the word [dignity] is derived finally from Latin meaning worthy. The definition includes the following:

1. *The quality or state of being worthy of esteem or respect.*
2. *Inherent nobility and worth:* ***the dignity of honest labor.***
3.
   a. Poise and self-respect.
   b. Stateliness and formality in manner and appearance.
4. *The respect and honor associated with an important position.*
5. *A high office or rank.*

So one would wonder what is the expression used these days "death with dignity" could possibly mean. When we use dignity in that expression, surely we are not talking about a person's high office, rank or necessarily an important position nor would we be considering stateliness and formality in manner or appearance. We must be talking about being worthy of esteem or respect by others and also, perhaps, poise and self-respect.

Could these elements be what is missing when a death is not dignified? Can a person in great pain, suffering, perhaps mentally obtunded to varying degrees demonstrate personal poise and self-respect? Probably not. Beyond what the person is presenting as him/herself is what others consider is common consideration of all human beings: esteem, the holding a human as a high value for the potential of a human and respect, as a civilized notion, for the values, rights and beliefs of all persons. With regard to the dying person, this esteem and respect by others should be shown in care and concern about seeing that no further discomfort, anguish or alteration of the physical body, appearance or condition occurs. This esteem and respect should carry over to the person once deceased. If these elements of dignity expressed through the patient's self or by others are missing then the death is undignified, something we, who are not in the patient's condition at the moment, should not ignore. . . .

---

[12]From contributor Maurice, http://bioethicsdiscussion.blogspot.com/2005/10/what-is-death-with-dignity.html. Saturday, October 8, 2005. Reprinted by permission.

THE CRITICISM OF CONCEPTUAL THEORIES

Some of the most effective ways of criticizing a conceptual theory are:

1. Presenting a counterexample.
2. Pointing out that the theory uses concepts that are as difficult to understand as the concept being explained (that is, the theory *does not elucidate*—it does not make things clear).
3. Showing that the theory contains incompatible conditions.

The application of these techniques can be illustrated by considering some examples. Suppose someone offers the following theory to explain what things qualify as works of art.

Example 7.16 *An object is <u>a work of art</u> if and only if*

(1) It is made by an artist;

AND

(2) It expresses the emotions of the artist.

Criticism 1: Presenting a Counterexample The first kind of criticism—presenting a counterexample—was introduced in Chapter 4. It can be done in either of two ways. First, an object that clearly is a work of art but does not satisfy the two conditions stated can be described. Or second, an object can be described that clearly is not a work of art but does satisfy the two conditions. The theory asserts that these two groups of objects are equivalent; either kind of counterexample just described shows that they are not.

Something that is a work of art but does not satisfy both conditions is a painting with a purely geometrical design, expressing no emotion whatsoever. This would fail to satisfy the second condition. Something that would not count as a work of art but *would* satisfy the two conditions would be a note written by an artist demonstrating affection or hostility inartistically.

Although we have provided two counterexamples, even one clear case is enough to show that a conceptual theory is inadequate. No matter how many instances are covered by it, a full-fledged conceptual theory does not merely describe the characteristics of *some* of the objects that fall under a concept. Such a theory would not be particularly interesting. A conceptual theory ideally states that a concept applies to *all and only* those objects having certain specified characteristics.[13]

Criticism 2: Showing That a Theory Fails to Elucidate The second kind of criticism points out that the theory uses concepts as difficult to understand as the concept being explained (that is, the theory fails to elucidate). As in

[13]There is a related criticism that notes the "inapplicability" of a concept in a particular domain. We could, for instance, have an interest in studying political behavior of legislators who are resistant to change and offer the following "stipulative" definition: *A legislator is refractory if and only if he or she refuses to admit any grounds for changing policy.* The problem here is not so much that we have a counterexample, but that given this stipulation it is unlikely that any actual legislator is *refractory*. The concept is inapplicable to the "real" world of actual legislators.

the case of criticizing an argument for lack of clarity, this criticism should not be overused. It is always possible to quibble about terms and to claim that a certain term has not been defined. What is more interesting to point out is that a person who did not already understand the concept being explained would not understand the explanation being offered. For instance, in the theory presented as Example 7.16, the term *artist* is used in the explanation of what a work of art is. To apply the theory to determine what things to count as works of art, we need to know what an artist is. But if we really did not know what things to count as works of art, we most likely would not know which people to count as artists either, so the theory is not very helpful.[14] For this kind of criticism to be justified, it is not necessary for a theory to use a concept as closely related to the one being explained as "artist" is to "art." For example, if someone were to explain the concept of "morally right action" simply as "an action that has good consequences," it would be appropriate to point out that "good" is a concept that is not clearer than "right," so if the theory is going to explain "right" in terms of "good," the theory should also explain what things are good.

Criticism 3: Showing That Conditions Are Incompatible The third kind of criticism is typically useful when a conceptual theory specifies more than one condition or is part of an elaborate conceptual analysis that focuses on several concepts. In these cases there may be conflict. In the more extreme instance, we can derive an explicit *contradiction* from the theory with the addition of some noncontroversial definitions or conceptual statements.

Example 7.17 *Capital punishment is morally justified if and only if*

(1) It takes the life of a person who deserves to die;

AND

(2) It does no harm (to anybody).

Even if an adequate elucidation is provided for the concept of "deserving to die," this example faces a further liability: the condition leads to a contradiction.[15] Since taking the life of a person is quite plausibly held to do the person harm, the statement Capital punishment does harm follows from condition 1. This explicitly contradicts condition 2 in that both cannot be simultaneously true, and one or the other must be true.

It is unusual to find an explicit contradiction following so easily from the analysis of a single concept. More often it is present in ambitious attempts to

---

[14]A particularly vivid example of this failing arises if someone characterizes a work of art as the product of an artist and goes on to characterize an artist as a person who produces a work of art. Such a process is clearly circular and does not help to explain what a work of art is. For this reason, these so-called circular definitions should be avoided.

[15]As we indicated in Chapter 5, a contradiction is sometimes represented as any pair of statements of the form *A and not A*.

analyze several interrelated concepts. Imagine a complex passage that contains, among other things, conceptual theories that can be reconstructed as follows:

Example 7.18

An aggregation of people is a <u>society</u> if and only if most people are committed to common norms and cultural ideals.

America is an <u>anomic society</u> if and only if

(1) It is a society;

AND

(2) Most of its members are uncommitted to common norms and cultural ideals.

Once these conceptual theories are placed next to each other it is easier to see the incompatibility of the conditions for an anomic society. Condition 1, by virtue of the definition of a society, implies:

(1) Most Americans are committed to common norms and cultural ideals.

but condition 2 states:

(2) Most Americans are uncommitted to common norms and cultural ideals.

Again we have an explicit contradiction. Either most Americans are or are not committed, but not both. Such an incompatibility makes the proposed analysis of the two concepts unacceptable. Should we want to modify our analysis, we could alter either our theory of the concept of a society or, in this case, more plausibly alter our analysis of an anomic society to allow that a society can be anomic when a "substantial fraction" (though not necessarily most) of its members are uncommitted to common norms.

Attempts at conceptual theory can have incompatible conditions even when they do not entail explicit contradictions. The conditions might entail *inconsistent* statements. Two inconsistent statements cannot both be true, but unlike contradictions, neither statement in an inconsistent pair need be true. To say something is "all red" is inconsistent with saying that it is "all blue." However, neither might be true—for example, if it is "all green." Examine this conceptual theory.

Example 7.19

A character in a work of fiction is a <u>tragic hero</u> if and only if

(1) The character suffers or dies during the work;

(2) The character is typical of the ordinary person in the society;

AND

(3) The character exemplifies rarely realized ideals of the society.

The theory of the tragic hero is faulty (assuming that the crucial terms can be adequately elucidated) because conditions 2 and 3 are inconsistent. It is impossible for a character to be typical of the ordinary person in a society and at the same time be highly atypical (that is, exemplify rarely realized ideals). We have an inconsistency, rather than a full contradiction, because there is the possibility that a character is neither typical nor highly atypical. A character could be uncommon, but not extraordinary. Nevertheless, this analysis of the tragic hero is unacceptable because of the inconsistency it contains.

Finally, conditions can be incompatible in a subtler way. Suppose, for example, a conceptual theory asserted that:

Example 7.20 *A society is <u>just</u> if and only if*

(1) The liberty of citizens is maximized;

AND

(2) Wealth is divided equally.

As they stand, conditions 1 and 2 are not contradictory or inconsistent, but it could be argued that they are incompatible because an inconsistency arises when we add other statements that are true to these two conditions. We could add, for example, the statement that given human social psychology, a continuing state of equal distribution of wealth could be maintained only if some restriction is placed on citizens with regard to their liberty to buy and sell and to spend or save. If so, condition 2 is possible only if some liberties are restricted. This shows that against the background of certain plausible assumptions about human nature, condition 2 is incompatible with condition 1. Both could not be true simultaneously (unless human nature changed). Similarly, we could argue that if condition 1 were realized and the liberty of citizens was maximized, then (again given human nature as we know it) wealth could not long remain divided equally. The conceptual theory is shown to be inadequate because it characterized a just society in such a way that it is impossible for any such society to exist (at least for human beings).

Types of Criticism for Conceptual Theories

1. Presenting a counterexample
2. Showing that the theory fails to elucidate
3. Showing that conditions are incompatible

EXERCISE 7.3 Criticism of Conceptual Theories

A. Criticize each of the following conceptual theories by finding a counterexample (actual or imagined). Counterexamples may be generated in two ways:

- By describing an uncontroversial example to which the concept applies but that does not satisfy at least one condition.
- By describing an example that satisfies all the conditions, but to which the concept does *not* apply.

Sample: An action is morally right if and only if it is legal.

Counterexample:

(i)	Jaywalking in order to give first aid	is morally right	but is *not* legal
(ii)	Insulting a depressed friend to make the friend even sadder	is *not* morally right	but is legal

1. A figure is a square if and only if it has four equal sides.
2. A law is just if and only if it is passed by majority vote.
3. A group is a society if and only if it is composed of members who live close to each other.
4. A film is pornographic if and only if it provocatively depicts sex acts.
5. A person is a compulsive gamer if and only if nothing for that person is worthwhile except time spent playing computer games.
6. An argument is valid if and only if it has true premises.
7. A person is intelligent if and only if the person scores above 130 on the Stanford-Binet IQ test.
8. An object is a work of art if and only if
   (1) It is made by humans;
   (2) It resembles an object in nature;
   AND (3) It is beautiful.
9. A belief is true if and only if
   (1) It is accepted by most people;
   AND (2) It is supported by some evidence.
10. A society is democratic if and only if
    (1) It has a constitution;
    (2) It has a court system;
    AND (3) It has elected officials.
11. A person is courageous if and only if
    (1) The person has been in a position of danger;
    (2) The person acted with disregard for personal safety;
    AND (3) The person did so for some noble purpose.

B. For each of the following determine whether the conceptual theory should be criticized for failing to elucidate. If it should, indicate which term or terms lack clarity.

1. An argument is valid if and only if it follows from the premises.
2. An action is morally right if and only if it is the sort of action a morally upright person in possession of all the facts would choose.
3. Something is good if and only if
   (1) It is happiness itself;
   OR (2) It produces happiness.
4. Someone is lascivious if and only if the person is wanton.
5. A policy is just if and only if it provides for a fair distribution of benefits and liabilities.

6. An object is beautiful if and only if it is aesthetically successful. An object is aesthetically successful if and only if it springs from the creative imagination.
7. A line is an arc if and only if it is part of a circle. An object is a circle if and only if it is a locus of points in a plane equidistant from a given point.
8. A group of organisms is a society if and only if its members can communicate about their wants and expectations.
9. An organism communicates with another if and only if its behavior results in the transmission of information from this other organism.
10. An object is a work of art if and only if
    (1) It is an artifact;
    AND
    (2) Some society or subgroup of a society has conferred the status of candidate for appreciation on it.[16]
11. An object is appreciated if and only if, in experiencing it, someone finds it worthy or valuable.
12. A book is pornographic if and only if
    (1) It offends standards of decency;
    AND
    (2) It has no redeeming social value.

C. For each of the following indicate whether the conceptual theory contains incompatible conditions. If so, discuss the character of this incompatibility.

1. A society is free if and only if
    (1) Everyone is permitted by the society to do as he or she pleases;
    AND
    (2) Everyone is encouraged by the society to realize his or her potential.
2. A decision is democratic if and only if
    (1) It reflects the sentiments of the majority;
    AND
    (2) It protects the rights of the minority.
3. A work of art is aesthetically successful if and only if
    (1) It would be appreciated by most people;
    AND
    (2) It enlarges people's aesthetic sensibilities by teaching them something new.

CONCEPTUAL CLARIFICATION AND ARGUMENT

The soundness of an argument can depend on an assertion about meaning. Consider this argument about the showing of a film.

Example 7.21 *The film Last Tango in Paris shouldn't be shown at the university because it is pornographic. It is quite provocative in its portrayals of sexual acts.*

[16]Adapted from George Dickie, "Defining Art," *American Philosophical Quarterly* 6 (1969): 253–255.

This argument can be restated as follows:

Example 7.22

(1) Last Tango in Paris *contains provocative portrayals of sexual acts.*

(implicit) *(2) Any film that contains provocative portrayals of sexual acts is pornographic.*

(implicit) *(3) Pornographic films shouldn't be shown at the university.*

∴ Last Tango in Paris *shouldn't be shown at the university.*

Controversy over this argument is most likely to arise concerning Premise 2. Since the argument is valid, the argument's soundness hinges primarily on this premise. The conceptual theory implicit in the premise can be reconstructed in this way:

Example 7.23

A film is <u>pornographic</u> if and only if

(1) It contains provocative portrayals of sexual acts;

OR

(2) Other unspecified conditions.

First, we might criticize this theory by pointing out that it contains the expression *provocative portrayals of sexual acts*. Although this expression might not need further elucidation in many contexts, its application is questionable in the case of *Last Tango in Paris*. That film contains, for example, little nudity but highly suggestive bodily movement. The question of whether such portrayals of sexual acts are "provocative" might be as difficult to answer as the question of whether the film was pornographic. So this theory fails to elucidate.

Second, we could hold that condition 1 is not a sufficient condition for being a pornographic film. We could cite counterexamples, such as medical films or films having substantial redeeming social and cultural value.

To the extent that we could maintain these criticisms of the conceptual analysis, we have provided grounds for rejecting the premise contained in the passage cited. If this premise is questionable, the soundness of the argument that contains it is also questionable.

REVIEW

In this chapter, we have looked at three main ways in which the success of an argument depends on the meaning of a word or phrase. (1) When an unclear expression is used in more than one premise, we need to determine whether the expression must shift its meaning in order for each premise to be true. If there is such a shift, then the argument is an equivocation, and the conclusion doesn't follow. (2) When an unclear expression is used in a premise and the conclusion, the premise might only be true if the expression is given a special meaning—different from what the audience would ordinarily take it to mean—and the conclusion is only true if this special meaning is preserved. It is misleading, then, to assert the conclusion without stipulating this special meaning even if the argument appears valid, as for instance in the argument with the conclusion that Frank is not a war veteran. (3) The premise of an argument might make or imply an assertion about the meaning of an expression. To evaluate such a premise, it is necessary to judge whether this claim about meaning is acceptable. Sometimes a simple counterexample will show that the premise is false. In other cases, it is helpful to reconstruct the claim about meaning as a conceptual theory and then evaluate the theory.

EXERCISE 7.4

Reconstructing and Criticizing Conceptual Theories and Arguments Based on Them

A. This exercise will give you the opportunity to apply all the techniques of reconstruction and criticism you have learned in this chapter. For each of the following passages, write a paragraph or two in which you first present a reconstruction of the conceptual theory, then apply all criticisms that are appropriate. Several passages were presented earlier for reconstruction only.

1. Listen then, Thrasymachus began. What I say is that "just" or "right" means nothing but what is to the interest of the stronger party. Well, where is your applause? . . .[17]
2. Love is a deep and vital emotion resulting from significant need satisfaction, coupled with a caring for and acceptance of the beloved and resulting in an intimate relationship.[18]
3. Any adequate account of morality must concern itself with both what is right and what is good. They are related in this way; a morally right action produces more good than any available alternative. But this leaves open the question of just what counts as good. Ultimately the goodness of something must be measured in terms of the pleasure it produces in normal individuals.
4. A work of art can be characterized by noting two features. First, works of art are . . . artifacts [made by humans]. But unlike most tools, which are also artifacts, a work of art is an artifact upon which some society or sub-group of a society has conferred the status of candidate for appreciation.[19]
5. There are certain indicators of a humanhood, including among them an IQ of at least 20 and probably 40, self-awareness, self-control, a sense of time, and the capability of relating to others.[20]
6. Family: Any sexually expressive or parent–child relationship in which people live together with commitment, in an intimate interpersonal

[17]Plato, *The Republic,* I.338, trans. Francis Cornford (Oxford: Oxford University Press, 1945).
[18]Mary Ann Lamanna and Agnes Riedmann, *Marriages and Families,* 5th ed. (Belmont, CA: Wadsworth, 1994), 86.
[19]Adapted from George Dickie, "Defining Art," *American Philosophical Quarterly* 6 (1969): 253–255.
[20]Adapted from Joseph Fletcher, "Indicators of Humanhood: A Tentative Profile of Man," *Hasting Center Report* 2(5) (November 1972).

relationship. Family members see their identity as importantly attached to the group, which has an identity of its own.[21]

7. Cross Examination of David Blankenhorn by plaintiffs' attorney David Boies Day 12 of the Federal Trial in United States District Court, *Perry et al v. Schwarzenegger et al*, Jan 27, 2010. The plaintiffs challenged California Proposition 8, the 2008 ballot initiative that reinstated a California ban on same-sex marriage. Q = David Boies, A = David Cross examination of David Blankenhorn by plaintiffs' attorney David Boies, Day 12 of Blankenhorn[22]

page 2879

Q . . .
Now, what are the three main rules that you believe define marriage?

A. Well, the first is what you might call the rule of opposites. That was the man — what is the customary man/woman basis of marriage.

Q. And second?

A. Two, that is, marriage is two people.

Q. Okay. And the third?

A. It's a sexual relationship.

page 2880

Q. Okay. Now, let me ask you about those three rules that you used to define marriage.
First, with respect to the rule of opposite —

A. By the way, I want to just clarify. I'm not saying that those three rules constitute a definition of marriage. What I'm referring — that was the term you just used in your question or your statement.
What I'm saying is that those are the three essential foundations of the marital institution or the three essential structures of the marital institution, and that's where we get into this concept of rules. So that's what I'm trying to say.

Q. Okay. The three essential structures of the institution of marriage, is that an acceptable terminology?

A. Yes, sir.

---

[21]Mary Ann Lamanna and Agnes Riedmann, *Marriages and Families*, 5th ed. (Belmont, CA: Wadsworth, 1994), 645.

[22]From the transcript of *Perry et al v. Schwarzenegger, et al*, United States District Court. Northern District of California, Vol 12, January 27, 2010.

3.

What Is Marriage? Six Dimensions[23]

MARRIAGE HAS AT LEAST SIX IMPORTANT DIMENSIONS:

- *Marriage is a legal contract.* Marriage creates formal and legal obligations and rights between spouses. Public recognition of, and protection for, this marriage contract, whether in tax or divorce law, helps married couples succeed in creating a permanent bond.
- *Marriage is a financial partnership.* In marriage, "my money" typically becomes "our money," and this sharing of property creates its own kind of intimacy and mutuality that is difficult to achieve outside a legal marriage. Only lovers who make this legal vow typically acquire the confidence that allows them to share their bank accounts as well as their bed.
- *Marriage is a sacred promise.* Even people who are not part of any organized religion usually see marriage as a sacred union, with profound spiritual implications. "Whether it is the deep metaphors of covenant as in Judaism, Islam and Reformed Protestantism; sacrament as in Roman Catholicism or Eastern Orthodoxy; the yin and yang of Confucianism; the quasi-sacramentalism of Hinduism; or the mysticism often associated with allegedly modern romantic love," Don Browning writes, "humans tend to find values in marriage that call them beyond the mundane and everyday." Religious faith helps to deepen the meaning of marriage and provides a unique fountainhead of inspiration and support when troubles arise.
- *Marriage is a sexual union.* Marriage elevates sexual desire into a permanent sign of love, turning two lovers into "one flesh." Marriage indicates not only a private but a public understanding that two people have withdrawn themselves from the sexual marketplace. This public vow of fidelity also makes men and women more likely to be faithful. Research shows, for example, that cohabiting men are four times more likely to cheat than husbands, and cohabiting women are eight times more likely to cheat than spouses.
- *Marriage is a personal bond.* Marriage is the ultimate avowal of caring, committed, and collaborative love. Marriage incorporates our desire to know and be known by another human being; it represents our dearest hopes that love is not a temporary condition, that we are not condemned to drift in and out of shifting relationships forever.
- *Marriage is a family-making bond.* Marriage takes two biological strangers and turns them into each other's next-of-kin. As a procreative bond, marriage also includes a commitment to care for any children produced by the married couple. It reinforces fathers' (and fathers' kin's) obligations to acknowledge children as part of the family system.

In all these ways, marriage is a productive institution, not a consumer good. Marriage does not simply certify existing loving relationships, but rather transforms the ways in which couples act toward one another,

[23]From *Institute for American Values The Marriage Movement: A statement of Principles* pp. 8–9. http://www.americanvalues.org/pdfs/marriagemovement.pdf. This statement grew out of a conference held January 2000. Reprinted by permission.

toward their children, and toward the future. Marriage also changes the way in which other individuals, groups, and institutions think about and act toward the couple. The public, legal side of marriage increases couples' confidence that their partnerships will last. Conversely, the more marriage is redefined as simply a private relationship, the less effective marriage becomes in helping couples achieve their goal of a lasting bond.

8. The "positive" sense of the word "liberty" derives from the wish on the part of the individual to be his own master. I wish my life and decisions to depend on myself, not on external forces of whatever kind. I wish to be the instrument of my own, not of other men's acts of will. I wish to be a subject, not an object, to be moved by reasons, by conscious purposes which are my own, not by causes which affect me, as it were, from outside. I wish to be somebody, not nobody; a doer—deciding, not being decided for, self-directed and not acted upon by external nature or by other men as if I were a thing, or an animal, or a slave incapable of playing a human role, that is, of conceiving goals and policies of my own and realizing them.[24]
9. [The original position] is understood as a purely hypothetical situation characterized so as to lead to a certain conception of justice. Among the essentials of this situation is that no one knows his place in society, his class position or social status, nor does anyone know his fortune in the distribution of natural assets and abilities, his intelligence, strength, and the like. I shall even assume that the parties do not know their conception of the good or their special psychological propensities. The principles of justice are chosen behind a veil of ignorance. . . . I shall maintain . . . that the persons in the initial situation would choose two rather different principles; the first requires equality in the assignment of basic rights and duties, while the second holds that social and economic inequalities, for example inequalities of wealth and authority, are just only if they result in compensating benefits for everyone, and in particular for the least advantaged members of society. . . .

   The first statement of the two principles reads as follows.

   First: each person is to have an equal right to the most extensive basic liberty compatible with a similar liberty for others.

   Second: social and economic inequalities are to be arranged so that they are both (a) reasonably expected to be to everyone's advantage, and (b) attached to positions and offices open to all.[25]

[24]Isaiah Berlin, "Two Concepts of Liberty," *Four Essays on Liberty* (Oxford: Oxford University Press, 1958), 131. Reprinted with permission.
[25]John Rawls, *A Theory of Justice* (Cambridge, MA: Harvard University Press, 1971), 12, 14, 60.

10. Selection from *Memorandum for Alberto R. Gonzales, Counsel to the President*[26]

> You have asked for our Office's views regarding the standards of conduct under the Convention Against Torture and Other Cruel, Inhuman and Degrading Treatment or Punishment as implemented by Sections 2340-2340A of title 18 of the United States Code. . . . In Part I, we examine the criminal statue's text and history. We conclude that for an act to constitute torture as defined in Section 2340, it must inflict pain that is difficult to endure. Physical pain amounting to torture must be equivalent to intensity to the pain accompanying serious physical injury, such as organ failure, impairment of bodily function, or even death. For purely mental pain or suffering to amount to torture under Section 2340, it must result in significant psychological harm of significant duration, e.g., lasting for months or even years. We conclude that the mental harm also must result from one of the predicate acts listed in the statute, namely: threats of imminent death; threats of infliction of the kind of pain that would amount to physical torture; infliction of such physical pain as a means of psychological torture; use of drugs or other procedures designed to deeply disrupt the senses, or fundamentally alter an individual's personality; or threatening to do any of these things to a third party. The legislative history simply reveals that Congress intended for the statute's definition to track the Convention's definition of torture and the reservations, understandings, and declarations that the United States submitted with its ratification. We conclude that the statute, taken as a whole, makes plain that it prohibits only extreme acts.

B. The following passages contain arguments that depend on definitions or conceptual analyses. (1) State the underlying conceptual theory on which the argument depends. (2) Reconstruct the argument. (3) Criticize the argument by criticizing the underlying conceptual analysis.

1. The Museum of Modern Art in New York City shouldn't show any of the French Impressionists. Its mandate is to collect and exhibit the best of modern art, but the French Impressionists painted during the nineteenth century.

---

[26]Jay C. Bybee, Assistant Attorney General in the U.S. Department of Justice's Office of Legal Counsel, Memorandum submitted to Alberto Gonzales, Counsel to the President, George W. Bush, August 1, 2002. Leaked to the press June 2004; provided by findalaw.com. http://fl1.findlaw.com/news.findlaw.com/hdocs/docs/doj/bybee80102mem.pdf.

2. People shouldn't be given capital punishment for treason. The state is justified in taking a life only as a penalty for murder. Since treason involves no killing, a traitor doesn't deserve the death penalty.
3. Since a valid argument is a good argument, all valid arguments must have a true conclusion.
4. Public sale of pornography violates the civil rights of women. Pornography involves the sexually explicit exploitation of women whether graphically or in words. As such, it promotes the sexualized subordination of women.
5. The hope of computer scientists to create Artificial Intelligence is misguided. Computers must be programmed. If they're programmed, they can't be creative. If they're not creative, then they can't be intelligent. Perhaps *artificial* intelligence is the correct term. Computer intelligence must remain artificial, not genuine.
6. Gay marriage is unacceptable. Marriage is a union between a man and a woman, sanctioned by the state, in accordance with the laws of God.
7. Discussion between Jon Stewart (JS), host of *The Daily Show* and Newt Gingrich (NG), former Republican House Speaker on whether to have trials of accused terrorists in military or civilian courts.[27]

JS: I'm not suggesting that military tribunals don't have their place and might not be an option. But why do we suggest that using our justice system is radical? How do you make this [interruption]

NG: Because it defines the terrorist in a criminal context instead of in a war context.

JS: Doesn't defining in this way in a war context honor them and give them more credibility and credence? Aren't they thugs? Aren't they [interruption]

NG: These people are our mortal enemies. Putting the rights of terrorists legally ahead of figuring out how to save Americans is seen by most Americans to be a fairly radical re-definition.

JS: That's a very emotional way of putting it. But wouldn't it, wouldn't you consider it [interruption]

NG: That's part of our job to reset the emotions of the American people.

JS: I think that's wise. And don't let reality get in the way.

---

[27]The Daily Show Feb 9, 2010 transcribed from the television broadcast.

8.

WHY IS TORTURE WRONG?

by Jim Manzi[28]

Or more precisely, why is the belief that the torture of captured combatants is wrong compatible with anything other than some form of pacifism? I mean this an actual question, not as a passive-aggressive assertion.

It can't just be that it involves inflicting horrible pain and suffering. The moment before an enemy combatant surrenders, it is legal (under the current rules of war which govern U.S. military operations as I understand them), to shoot this person in head, launch burning petroleum jelly onto him that is carefully designed to stick to his skin and clothing, or deviously hide explosives that will maim him (but intentionally not kill him) when he steps on a landmine, in order to slow the advance of the group that must then carry him, and also to make it easier to subsequently kill both him and the person who assists him.

It can't just be that the prisoner is helpless, or that the imbalance of power between the inflictor and recipient of the suffering is so high. The whole point of maneuver in warfare is often to put yourself in a position where you can cause massive causalities from a protected position. It is normally a retreating army that suffers the worst causalities. After all, it is legal (as I understand it) to drop a bomb from a virtually invulnerable aircraft at 30,000 feet onto an enemy combatant who has dropped his rifle and is running away at high speed. Presumably, it is actually illegal *not* to do this if so ordered by a superior officer.

Why is it that if this person turns around looks up at the plane and says the words "I surrender" that it suddenly becomes wrong to punch him in the face hard enough to make him bleed? Not prudentially foolish, but morally wrong?

It can't just be that "hitting somebody hard in the face is really awful, seems mean, and is not something I would want done to me", because everybody but a pure pacifist agrees that we have the right after he surrenders to lock him in a prison camp and deprive him of liberty for an indefinite period (basically, as I understand it, until hostilities have ended). Going to prison is unpleasant, and is not something I would want done to me.

So apparently it's OK to inflict (the most extreme imaginable) violence when the guy is totally helpless in combat, but suddenly upon his saying the words "I surrender", any serious violence beyond confinement becomes wrong. Now, the natural justification for this is, I assume, that until he surrenders, if you let him run away, he might very well come back to try to kill you later. Therefore, once you have operationally captured him you are entitled to imprison him for the duration to prevent this future plausible attempt to kill you, but that is all. Why is that all? What changed when he said "I surrender". After all, he might escape from the prison camp. It might be your judgment that killing him, or intentionally injuring him short of death while he is imprisoned – as per landmines – might

---

[28]Jim Manzi. *The American Scene*, April 27, 2009. http://theamericanscene.com/2009/04/27/why-is-torture-wrong.

serve your purposes better. One could imagine all kinds of prudential reasons why one might make the judgment that war aims are better served by torturing such a captured combatant. What is the moral reason that you should not pursue such a course of action?

You may be bound by an agreement that you (collectively, as a national unit) have made to treat prisoners in this way. But, either that treaty had a prudential motivation, or it was made, in part, because (at least some of) the signatories viewed torture of captured combatants as morally wrong. So, we've just kicked the can back one step: why did the national unit consider torture of captured combatants to be morally wrong?

You may argue that torture, as a practical matter, is never confined to the intended cases, and leads to corruption. But this is a prudential argument—it doesn't say that some specific acts of torture are immoral. You might argue that torture is so dehumanizing that it inevitably morally corrupts those who do it. But, how does this distinguish it from lots of other things done in war to other human beings (see prior paragraphs)?

Maybe I'm morally obtuse about this (again, I mean that non-rhetorically), but I don't see how a non-pacifist makes the moral case against torturing captured combatants. Of course, there are at least two ways to interpret that. One is that torture of captured combatants is not morally wrong. The other is to see this as an example of why we should be skeptical about moral reasoning as a way to answer the question; that is, of why we must rely on moral intuition and the traditions of our society.

CHAPTER 8

Arguments That Are Not Deductive: Induction and Statistical Reasoning

In previous chapters, we have focused on how to evaluate arguments that traditionally have been called *deductive*. The primary aim of this chapter and the next is to explain how to evaluate several kinds of arguments that are not deductive. These include arguments that are commonly called *inductive* (including sampling arguments and arguments with statistical premises), as well as causal arguments, convergent arguments, and arguments from analogy. As we discuss how to evaluate nondeductive arguments, we will at the same time be continuing our survey of strategies for criticizing premises of deductive arguments. This is because the conclusions of inductive and other types of nondeductive arguments often serve as premises for deductive arguments.

For example, one kind of nondeductive argument, commonly called *inductive*, moves from a premise that cites particular observations to a conclusion that is more general.

Example 8.1 ***Inductive Sampling Argument (Particular to General)***

Premise *(1) In studies of 5,000 people, those who had more exposure to environmental smoke had a higher frequency of lung cancer.*

Conclusion *(likely) People who have more exposure to environmental smoke generally have a higher frequency of lung cancer.*

The conclusion of this inductive argument would serve as a premise in the following deductive argument:

Example 8.2 ***Deductive Argument (Modus Ponens)***

Premise *(1) People who have more exposure to environmental smoke generally have a higher frequency of lung cancer.*

Premise *(2) If (1), then we should restrict smoking in public places.*

Conclusion *∴ We should restrict smoking in public places.*

In evaluating this deductive argument, we need to decide whether to accept Premise 1. One way of doing this would be to evaluate the inductive argument on which this premise is based.

It is useful to place arguments like 8.1 in a separate category from deductive arguments like 8.2. We reconstruct them somewhat differently, apply specifically tailored criticisms, and also employ different criteria for their success. Notice that Argument 8.1 moves from a single premise that reports what has been observed in specific studies to a conclusion about a larger population that has not been directly observed. The term *likely* is used rather than the sign ∴ to indicate that inductive arguments do not guarantee the truth of the conclusion. We might accept Argument 8.1 as successful, even though we acknowledged that the premises could be true and the conclusion false.

In this chapter, we discuss two kinds of nondeductive arguments. The first kind moves from a premise or premises that describe *particular* observations to a more *general* conclusion (as in Example 8.1). A second kind of nondeductive argument moves from a *general* premise to a *particular* conclusion. An example is the argument *Most teachers enjoy talking, and Mario is a teacher. So Mario probably enjoys talking.* Both of these kinds of arguments are called **inductive** although the term is used most commonly for the first. In Chapter 9 we will examine some special cases of nondeductive arguments: causal arguments, arguments from analogy, and arguments of the type we called *convergent.*

TWO TYPES OF INDUCTIVE ARGUMENTS

We use inductive reasoning frequently in our everyday lives. Suppose Robin examines the top two layers in a container of strawberries at a local market and finds most of them delightfully ripe. Robin concludes that probably most of the berries in the whole container are ripe. Again, the premise of this argument states a particular observation, while the more general conclusion goes beyond what has been observed.

Example 8.3 *Inductive Argument (Particular to General)*

(1) Most of the strawberries in the first two layers are ripe.

(likely) Most of the strawberries in the whole container are ripe.[1]

A less obvious version of this argument pattern moves from evidence about the past to a conclusion that applies not only to the past, but also to the future:

Example 8.4 *Inductive Argument (Past to Anytime)*
Variation of Particular-to-General Argument

(1) In the 1960s, big tax cuts were followed by significant job growth.

(2) In the 1980s, big tax cuts were followed by significant job growth.*

(3) In the 1990s, big tax cuts were followed by significant job growth.

(4) In the first part of the "noughts" (2000s), big tax cuts were followed by significant job growth.

(likely) Big tax cuts will always be followed by significant job growth.

*Note that there were no big tax cuts in the 1970s.

As in the previous example, this form of sampling argument generalizes from information about a certain sample of cases to a conclusion that goes beyond the evidence.

The conclusion of such inductive arguments is called an *inductive* or *empirical generalization*.[2] It is important to notice that a *leap* is made from premises (evidence) about particular cases to a conclusion that applies *generally*—not just to these specific instances. Not all such leaps are equally justified, and we will discuss techniques later in this chapter for criticizing inductive arguments that make them.

Both of the examples of inductive reasoning we have just considered move from *particular to general*—that is, from statements about particular instances (particular layers of strawberries or particular decades) to a generalization based on those statements. But some inductive arguments move from *general*

---

[1]The conclusion is asserted to be likely relative to the evidence provided in the premises. Against a wider background of evidence, the conclusion may be unlikely.

[2]The process of moving from statements about particulars to a statement about a larger class that contains the particulars is called *generalizing*. To call a statement *general* means that it applies to a number of individuals rather than to a particular or specific case. Generalizations can apply to all cases, such as *all animals with hearts have kidneys*. (These are also called *universal empirical generalizations*.) But in some contexts, generalizations can also speak of *some*, *a few*, or *a certain percentage of cases*—for example, *30 percent of adult Americans are overweight; some stocks are too speculative;* a *few TV programs are worthwhile*.

to particular; they contain a *statistical* generalization as a premise.[3] The argument applies this generalization to a particular person or situation and reaches a conclusion about him or it.

Example 8.5 *Argument from Statistical Premises (General to Particular)*

(1) Most 103-year-old persons who have major surgery suffer serious complications.

(2) Didi is a 103-year-old person who has had major surgery.

(likely) Didi will suffer serious complications.

Assuming the truth of the premises, this argument provides good reasons for believing the conclusion, but like the examples discussed earlier, the truth of the premises doesn't guarantee that the conclusion will be true, but only makes it likely.

Deductive versus Nondeductive Arguments

In previous chapters we stated that a successful deductive argument has two principal properties.[4]

1. The conclusion follows from the premises. (*If all the premises are true, it is impossible for the conclusion to be false.*)
2. The premises are true.

As we have indicated, for nondeductive arguments the requirements for success are somewhat different. A fully successful inductive argument has true premises, but the connection between premises and conclusion is not as strong. If the premises are true, then it is improbable or unlikely that the conclusion is false. For a deductive argument the truth of the premises assures us of the truth of the conclusion; for a nondeductive argument the truth of the premises makes the conclusion likely or probable, although there is always the possibility that the premises are true and (unlikely as it seems) the conclusion is false.

This characterization is true of nondeductive arguments generally and of the subcategory called *inductive* arguments in particular. Compare these two candidates, one billing itself as a deductive argument, the other as an inductive argument:

---

[3]The term *statistical* is used broadly to include not only those cases in which some specific percentage is mentioned, but also premises that include some unspecific statistical terms such as *many, most, a few, seldom,* and so on, in contrast to the universal empirical generalizations that contain terms such as *all, every, always, no, none,* and *never*. The universal generalizations discussed in Chapter 7 are more definitional than empirical.

[4]In addition, it needs to be legitimately persuasive to be fully successful, as indicated in Chapter 6.

Example 8.6

Deductive Argument	*Inductive Argument with Statistical Premises*
(1) All human beings need potassium in their diets.	*(1) Most adults can tolerate moderate amounts of sugar in their diets.*
(2) Alvin is a human being.	*(2) Alvin is an adult.*
∴ Alvin needs potassium in his diet.	*(likely) Alvin can tolerate moderate amounts of sugar in his diet.*

The principal difference is that if the premises of the deductive argument are true, then the conclusion must be true. But the premises of the inductive argument may both be true and the conclusion false. For example, if Alvin is diabetic, then the conclusion of the inductive argument is false, even though both premises are true.[5]

EXERCISE 8.1

Generalizations, Descriptions of Particulars, and Inductive Arguments

A. The previous section distinguished several kinds of statements. To practice finding the differences among them, determine which of the following statements are generalizations and which are descriptions of particular states of affairs. Indicate which of the generalizations are *universal* (apply to all, every, or none) and which are *statistical* (apply to some—that is, not all or none). Remember that statistical generalizations can include terms such as *most, many, few,* and *some percentage.* It might be debated whether some statements are general or particular. Provide a brief justification of your choice in these cases.

1. Alvin bought the strawberries on June 15.
2. Most people don't trust government.
3. Seventy percent of the people who live in Texas like chili.
4. Dale always parties on Friday nights.
5. Smoking is hazardous to your health.
6. People don't get everything they like.
7. Bianca and James usually treat each other lovingly.
8. Few people enjoy having their gallbladder removed.
9. Alice will not go out to dinner tonight.
10. Every animal with a heart is an animal with kidneys.
11. Children always suffer in a divorce.

[5]A common misconception distinguishes *inductive* from deductive reasoning by holding that induction moves from particular to general and deduction from general to particular. As Examples 8.3 and 8.4 demonstrate, certain inductive arguments can move from general to particular. We can also construct deductive arguments that go from particular to general—for instance, *If Al can do it, then anybody can do it. Al can do it. So anybody can do it.*

12. Brenda voted Republican and Mike voted Democratic.
13. Human beings do not live by bread alone.

B. Label the arguments in the following passages as deductive or inductive. (One passage contains both kinds of argument.) Among the inductive, note which are sampling arguments (particular-to-general arguments), which are arguments with statistical premises (general-to-particular arguments), and which include both.

1. Most people under thirty-five can jog without special precautions. Debra is young, so she can begin running right away.
2. The outlook for education in America is bleak. Educational disaster will be avoided only if people give up their desire for more tax cuts. But Americans are not willing to do that.
3. A reporter is seldom able to get a politician to admit his or her real motives. The *Daily Herald* story about the mayor doesn't tell the whole story.
4. Alvin should pay at least half his income in taxes because everybody who has more than a $1 million income, whether from wages or some other source, should pay at least 50 percent in taxes no matter what his or her deductions.
5. You should buy a Chevy. Jerry and David each had one and they were great cars.
6. Any time population increases in a state, the housing demand increases as well. Population has been increasing in Wyoming, Utah, and Texas. So we can expect the demand for housing to increase in those states.
7. The mayor really doesn't care about the poor in spite of her pious pronouncements. If she were truly interested, she would be actively seeking to bring more jobs into the city.
8. Willie was late on Monday and late on Tuesday. We shouldn't expect him to be on time today.
9. It is decision time at Widget, Inc. The company president says: "Our market research department has just completed a test of the new and improved Widget in three test market areas: Dallas, Detroit, and Denver. In all three cities the consumers preferred the new Widget over the old two to one. I think we should go for it."
10. "The Survey of Consumer Finances shows that the top 1 percent of households controls roughly 42 percent of the country's nonhome wealth in 2004."[6] If so, a targeted marketing campaign designed to induce these individuals to buy Widgets should improve the bottom line for Widget, Inc.

---

[6]*Federal Reserve 2004 Survey of Consumer Finances.*

CRITICIZING ARGUMENTS THAT GENERALIZE: SAMPLING ARGUMENTS

Arguments that move from statements about particular samples to more general statements about populations can be criticized in four ways. As in the case of deductive arguments, such pieces of inductive reasoning may be shown unsuccessful (1) by indicating that some of the premises are false, that is, by *disputing the data,* and (2) by showing that the conclusion does not follow—typically because the sample is not likely to be representative of the larger population from which it is drawn. In addition, it is appropriate at times (3) to point out that there is a *shift* between what the premise is about and what the conclusion is about, or even (4) to attack the conclusion directly (independently of any argument that might be put forward to support it) by offering *counterevidence.*

Attacking the Premises (Disputing the Data)

One means of criticizing an argument that generalizes is by *disputing the data*—that is, showing that the "evidence" used as a basis for the generalization does not really exist or has been misinterpreted. Recall the example of Robin and the strawberries. Robin examined two layers of strawberries in a container and found most of them ripe, generalizing that most of the berries in the whole container were ripe. A person versed in new horticultural technologies could criticize this reasoning by pointing out that the berries might be the newly developed hybrid California red strawberries that have the red color of the ripe, traditional berry even when they are hard and undeveloped. This horticultural commentator is disputing Robin's interpretation of the evidence used in support of the generalization (the berries looked ripe but weren't). Of course Robin might be suspicious of such an improbable story. Observing the berries more carefully to see how hard they were might resolve the issue. The technique of criticism employed by the commentator is similar to questioning the soundness of a deductive argument by challenging the truth of a premise.[7] This first kind of criticism often requires specialized knowledge or research. The following kind of criticism can more often be made against a bad particular-to-general argument, on the basis of commonly held knowledge.

Questioning the Representativeness of the Sample

Even if we accept the data, we can challenge some generalizations by pointing out that illegitimate reasoning is involved. Typically, generalizations go beyond the data used to support them to make claims that apply to a wider class of cases. This type of reasoning is an instance of *sampling:* the evidence about an observed sample is a premise. This premise is generalized to a larger

---

[7]Perhaps a more plausible criticism of Robin's reasoning could be given by a cynical consumer advocate, who might point out that fruit vendors sometimes put the unripe, green fruit at the bottom of the container. Such a comment concerns whether the top layers are representative of the whole container. The next section will consider this kind of criticism.

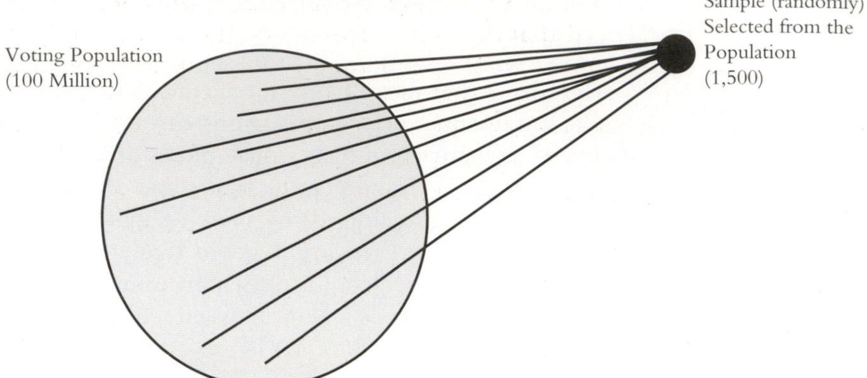

FIGURE **8.1** A sample is selected from a population

population in the conclusion. The conclusion is not supported if the sample is not representative of the larger population.

One of the most familiar instances of sampling is the political poll. Prominent pollsters, such as the Gallup, Harris, and Zogby organizations, try to make generalizations about the beliefs of large numbers of people. It would be time consuming and expensive (indeed virtually impossible) to question all the people who might vote in an election. Instead, the polling organization looks at a much smaller group (the *sample*) which it expects to represent the beliefs of a much larger group (the *population* of prospective voters). Just before the election, 1,500 people might be polled about their presidential preferences (Figure 8.1). Let's say that 45 percent of the people who indicate that they are planning to vote prefer candidate A, 47 percent prefer candidate B, and 8 percent are undecided. The polling organization would be prepared to generalize from its sample to the whole voting population (perhaps 100 million people).[8]

The move from sample to population is justified if we can be assured that the sample is *representative* of the population from which it is taken. Two factors are important in judging whether a particular sample is representative: its *size* and whether it was selected in an *unbiased* or *random* fashion.

Suppose that a young man has arrived at a Woody Allen view of life (that women will always reject him) on the basis of unsuccessful dates with only two women, and he uses this two-case sample to generalize to all women.

---

[8]Typically, polling organizations hedge their bets by announcing a margin of error (with the usual Gallup poll, 1,000–1,500 people constitute the sample, and the margin of error is considered to be 3 percent). If we use a 3 percent error in our example, then in 95 percent of the cases, the actual percentage of the population is likely to be within 3 percent of the number listed: between 42 and 48 percent favoring candidate A (that is, 45 ± 3), 44–50 percent favoring candidate B (that is, 47 ± 3). The larger the sample, in general, the lower the margin of error. Statistical theory can be used to determine the interval in which we can have this confidence.

The generalization that all women will reject him can be criticized by pointing out that the sample (two cases) is not sufficiently large to justify the inference to the whole population of all women he might date. This criticism should be used sparingly, however, because properly constituted samples need not be particularly large. A sample of 1,500 is often used by social scientists to support generalizations about the entire American population, and a sample of millions may be unrepresentative of the whole country if it is selected from a restricted geographical region or limited to a certain income group. For purposes of certain statistical tests, though, a sample of less than thirty is especially suspect because it may distort the findings.

Ordinarily, there is a trade-off among three factors: (1) the size of the sample required, (2) the *margin of error* that is acceptable, and (3) the *level of confidence*[9] that can be placed in the generalization. As the sample size goes up, the margin of error can narrow or the level of confidence can increase, or both. As the size goes down, the opposite occurs. A narrow margin of error and a high confidence level mean that the sample was large enough to produce a good fix on the population characteristic, but such samples can be difficult and costly to obtain, so researchers typically make compromises when selecting sample size.

There is no automatic rule for deciding among these trade-offs. How big a margin of error should we have? To know that 45 percent of the prospective voters prefer a candidate with a range of plus or minus 30 percent is not much help in predicting a close election. But we might be willing to live with a range of plus or minus 5 percent, or 4 percent in some circumstances. In others, we could demand even tighter boundaries, in which case we would need a larger sample. What level of confidence should we expect? Again, it depends on the reasoning involved. The level for a largely academic piece of research that is only looking for tendencies might be as low as 90 percent—that is, we might be willing to live with the likelihood of being wrong one time in ten. In medical research where a life might depend on our reasoning, we could demand a 99.9 percent confidence level (only one chance in 1,000 of an incorrect finding).

Similar considerations apply when we use sampling, not to estimate just a single property of the population (for instance, the percentage supporting a particular candidate), but also to estimate an association between two characteristics. What, for example, is the relationship between gender and support for a particular candidate? On the basis of a survey, a pollster might conclude that there is a difference in level of support for a candidate among women and men. This result of sampling can be reported by saying the level of support is associated or correlated with gender. If a sample is large enough and selected by appropriate (random) procedures, we can conclude that it is likely that

---

[9]In technical literature, the confidence level is given in terms of the probability of making an error in accepting the results of the sample. A 95% confidence has a 5% chance of error, that is, a probability of .05. This probability is called the "level of significance." The branch of statistics that studies this topic is called *inferential* statistics. It examines under what conditions we are justified in going from judgments about the sample to conclusions (inferences) about the population from which it is drawn and provides some estimate of the likelihood that we might be making an error.

there is a difference between women and men in the population from which the sample is drawn and that even a small difference is not due to just chance factors.

Example 8.7

(1) In the sample, gender is associated with preference for candidate A.

(likely) In the population, gender is associated with preference for candidate A.

When appropriate sampling is carried out, it might be said that there is a "statistically significant" difference in the level of support for candidate A. This point might be made by saying that women have a significantly higher level of support for candidate A than men do. It is important to realize, however, that when the term "statistical significance" or just "significance" is used in reporting the results of sampling, it does not mean the results are significant in a broader sense. There might be a statistically significant difference between those who take an experimental drug and those who don't. But if this difference is very small, the drug might not be a very good choice as a medication. Similarly, a new reading program might produce an increase in reading scores that is statistically significant compared with the standard method of teaching reading. But if this difference was between an average grade of 3.2 for the old method and 3.24 for the new one (on a 4-point scale), we would not say that this was an important enough difference to justify changing the policy on the reading curriculum, especially if this change would be costly. Such small differences could be statistically significant (meaning that they are likely to exist in the population from which our experiment sampled) without being scientifically significant or policy significant. In general, if the random sample size is very large, even small differences will be statistically significant. Whether they are significant in the sense of "important" is not answered by statistics alone.

Even if our sample is large enough, it still might not be representative. To be justified in going from data obtained about a sample to a conclusion about a larger population, the sample must resemble the population in terms of the characteristics measured. But a person doing sampling can't directly know whether the sample is representative.[10] One way to improve the likelihood that it is representative is to select the sample on a random basis. Random sampling helps eliminate sources of systematic bias that over- or underestimate certain parts of the population, and thereby helps ensure a sample with greater odds of being significantly like the population from which it was selected.

Drawing a random sample is not as easy as might initially be imagined. Picking numbers out of a telephone directory in what might seem to you to be a random pattern will not do (fatigue, for instance, might result in an under-selection of people with numbers near the end of the book). A more respectable technique uses a computer or a table of random numbers to pick

---

[10]Direct knowledge that a sample is representative would involve comparison of the sample with the population. But this would defeat the whole purpose of sampling. A sample is used because it is impossible or impractical to measure the whole population.

out the sample.[11] Other more elaborate methods of sampling have been developed to produce a sample that is as representative as possible in a number of different situations. One common variant is a stratified random sample, which tries to ensure that certain characteristics known to hold for the whole population, such as distribution of gender, age, or race, are replicated within the sample. If 20 percent of the population is between thirty and forty years old, then approximately 20 percent of the sample should also be between thirty and forty years old. Selection of individuals within each of the strata remains random. Of course, for such a procedure to work, we need to know the distribution of age or other stratifying characteristic in the population as a whole.

An argument based on a sample that is too small or that is selected in a biased way is open to criticism. But how do we know whether the size is adequate or the sample unbiased? The answer depends on background knowledge. A biologist might be prepared to generalize about some characteristics from a sample of one or two members of a newly discovered species to a conclusion about the whole species because she knows that some characteristics—number of chambers in the heart, for instance—vary little among members of the same species. Similarly, if a political scientist believes that attitudes about economic matters do not vary widely among Republicans, he may be able to determine Republican attitudes toward a new economic proposal from a smaller sample.

Conversely, a large sample may be needed if we seek information that is strongly influenced by narrow geographical or regional considerations. Whether there is much or little variation in a given characteristic is often a matter of expert knowledge.[12] Sometimes our common, everyday knowledge is sufficient to call a generalization into question because the generalization is based on too small a sample, as in the case of the young man who generalized from two dates to all women. Notice, however, that the size of the sample we demand depends on the nature of the case. Suppose that instead of basing a judgment about a person's prospects on dating two women, we were considering a judgment about his suitability for marriage on the basis of two unsuccessful marriages. Here, we might expect relatively little variation. Two failed marriages might indeed be good evidence that the person has difficulties in maintaining the sustained commitment required of a lasting marriage.

Background knowledge is also relevant to questions about the representativeness of a sample. If we have a complete listing of all the individuals in a population being examined, it is relatively easy to pick out a random or scientific sample using a table of random numbers, but such a complete list

---

[11]A table of random numbers can be used to generate telephone numbers. Such random digit dialing has an advantage over selection from a directory because unlisted numbers are polled. But such a method will still be somewhat biased—people without phones or people who spend large amounts of time away from home will not be adequately represented.

[12]Given assumptions about this variability, statistical theory can give a precise answer to the question of how large the sample must be to produce a result with a given error factor.

(sampling frame) is often unavailable.[13] In its absence, we are forced to rely on our judgment about factors that might distort the results. Suppose we were sampling by randomly selecting telephone numbers out of a directory and conducting a phone interview. As we stated earlier, we would miss people without phones and those with unlisted numbers. We need additional knowledge to estimate how many people were left out of our sampling frame. The results of other surveys and telephone company figures would be helpful in determining how significant this number is. The importance of such background knowledge or speculation is even more conspicuous for stratified random sampling. If we are unsure about the racial makeup of a community, then a stratified sample that attempts to reflect a certain racial distribution will also be suspect.

Criticizing an argument by questioning the representativeness of the sample on which it is based might sometimes demand expert knowledge, but in other situations the nonexpert has background enough. Conclusions about community attitudes drawn exclusively from interviews at noon in the financial district or, alternatively, at 5:30 in a tavern near the docks are suspect even if the number of people interviewed is quite large. It is common knowledge that the people present at those times and in those places are not likely to be representative of the community as a whole. An argument that assumes they are is unsuccessful.

Finally, a sample of citizens interviewed at a particular time in order to determine public opinion on a policy issue might not accurately represent an ***enduring and stable attitude*** even if the sample of people interviewed is randomly selected and accurately reflects a momentary attitude by a broader population. Suppose the issue of cutting taxes on businesses is being debated heatedly in the media, with strong arguments being aired by one side on one day and being staunchly refuted by opponents on the next. If opinion is generally split on the issue, the majority view could be swinging from one side to the other as the debate proceeds. It would be misleading to use a poll taken when opponents of the tax cuts have just scored significantly in a widely covered press conference to claim without qualification that a majority of the public favors or opposes cutting business taxes. This is a slightly different criticism than claiming that the sample of subjects interviewed is not representative of the population. Rather, the situation at the time when the sample is taken might not be representative of the situation at succeeding times. If an opinion is volatile, then a momentary snapshot should not be used in a broader argument that presupposes the opinion to be enduring and stable.

Pointing to a Shift in the Unit of Analysis

The results of well-constructed sampling can be misused in a sampling argument if the premises and the conclusion are statements about different kinds of things, technically called "units of analysis." For example, suppose a student

---

[13]A sampling frame is a listing of a population from which a sample is drawn (e.g., all the students currently registered at a university) or the potential population that could be sampled using a certain sampling method (e.g., those having a "land line" phone number).

newspaper carried out a survey about whether courses at the university included an exam. Most of the courses surveyed did. The newspaper concluded that most teachers give exams. We can reconstruct the argument in this way:

Example 8.8

(1) Most courses sampled at the university give exams.

(likely) Most teachers in the university give exams.

The premise is about courses; that is, **courses** are the unit of analysis. To be acceptable the conclusion needs to be about courses as well; it should be *Most* ***courses*** *in the university give an exam* rather than *Most teachers give exams.* That is, the same "unit of analysis" should occur in the statement about the sample (the premise) and in the statement about the larger population (the conclusion).[14] Indeed, it could be that most courses included exams, but that these courses were taught by a relatively small number of the junior faculty, whereas most faculty taught more advanced courses and offered research opportunities that used papers rather than exams.

Consider a second, somewhat different case:

Example 8.9

(1) 20 percent of schools sampled across the United States fail to meet the Average Yearly Progress requirement of the No Child Left Behind Act.

(likely) 20 percent of school districts across the United States fail to meet the Average Yearly Progress requirement of the No Child Left Behind Act.

Again the error is the shift in units of analysis from **schools** to **school districts.** This move is faulty even though school districts are composed of individual schools. The problem becomes more obvious when we realize that some districts have only a few schools and some have a very large number of schools. It could be the case that the 20 percent of schools are concentrated in a small percentage of the districts, in which case the percentage of districts having failing schools might be smaller than 20 percent. Alternatively, if a district failed if just one school in it failed, then the opposite could be true. In either case, the move from schools to school districts can be criticized.

Challenging the Truth of the Conclusion[15]

Even when we are not in a position to question the sample size or its representativeness, we may be able to undermine an argument that leads to a generalization by directly challenging the generalization itself, irrespective of the argument offered on its behalf. The most effective way of doing so is to show that the alleged regularity described by the generalization does not exist. What is needed is counterevidence from other samples that don't support

---

[14]This is akin to the fallacy of equivocation discussed in Chapters 6 and 7.

[15]Note that attacking the conclusion is appropriate only for inductive arguments. The ineffectiveness of doing so for deductive arguments was explained in Chapter 4.

the generalization. This could be in the form of samples drawn from the same population that do not support the generalization in question.

Often, many different researchers will investigate the degree to which a certain population has a particular feature. For example, many studies, based on independent samples, have been conducted to determine the rates of various crimes in the United States. If one particular study involving rates of sexual assaults is at odds with all other studies, this alone is grounds for doubting the conclusion of this study. As a second example, if someone claims that a survey sample indicates that most homeowners in the Far Horizons gated community prefer a dog-leash ordinance, others might have conducted their own surveys, using random sampling, that indicate weak support for such an ordinance. Ideally, a *census* (an examination of all or almost all of the population) could be carried out that would discredit a generalization based on sampling.[16] But it is precisely because a census is difficult to carry out that we so often rely on sampling.

Summary of Criticisms

In this section we have discussed the following types of criticism that are appropriate to sampling arguments . Successful criticism depends in part on our background knowledge, but often an amateur knows enough to advance a compelling objection.

Criticisms of Sampling Arguments

1. ***Attacking the premise.*** Is the evidence cited in the premise true or can the data be disputed?
2. ***Questioning the representativeness of the sample.***
   a. **Size of sample.** Is the sample large enough that it is likely to mirror the population (given the variability of the factors being generalized)?
   b. **Sample selection.** Was the sample selected in an appropriate way, using random sampling techniques, so as to accurately mirror the population? Or is it likely to be biased in such a way as to over- or underestimate some significant segment of the population? What was done to ensure representativeness? What are the potential biases that might affect the results? Are there alternative sampling frames that might have produced a more representative sample?

Note: Arguments that generalize on the basis of unrepresentative samples (particularly those that are too small or selected without

[16]If the census indicated that, for example, 53 percent favored the ordinance, then the counterevidence is less conclusive. Is 53 percent most of the homeowners?

appropriate randomization or appropriate sampling frames) are sometimes held guilty of the fallacy of *hasty generalization.*

3. ***Pointing to a shift in the unit of analysis.*** Are the objects referred to in the premise the same kind as the objects referred in the conclusion or is there a shift to a related, but different grouping?
4. ***Challenging the truth of the conclusion.*** Is the generalization presented in the conclusion made doubtful by counterinstances or counterevidence.

EXERCISE 8.2

Criticizing Sampling Arguments

A. The following passages describe situations in which a generalization is made on the basis of sample. For each case, reconstruct the argument. The premise(s) will report an observation of a sample. The conclusion will be a generalization about a larger population. If specific percentages are given, state the argument in the form:

(1) x percent of P_1s in the sample are P_2s

(likely) x percent of P_1s in the population are P_2s

Criticize any faulty reasoning exhibited in the following passages, and, where appropriate, describe how a more appropriate sample might be obtained.

1. A student studied with ten teachers at the university. Six of the ten were women. The student assumes that more than half of the teachers at her university are women.
2. A quality control engineer closely examines a random sample of automobiles produced on Tuesdays and Wednesdays at the Youngstown plant. He finds that only 3 percent of the cars in this sample are faulty and concludes that only 3 percent of all the cars produced at this plant are faulty.
3. In 1936 the *Literary Digest,* a popular magazine among the well-to-do and well educated, conducted a poll. The people surveyed were selected from among those included on their subscription records, in telephone books, and on automobile registration lists. They got responses from almost 2 million people and concluded that Franklin Roosevelt would not be elected.
4. The widely cited Harvard Medical Practice Study examined 31,429 records sampled from more than 2.5 million cases in New York hospitals. It found that about 1 percent of the cases involved adverse outcomes due to negligence. We should conclude that it is likely that about 1 percent of the doctors are guilty of malpractice.
5. Bruce examined records of several countries and determined that in Uganda, Rwanda, and Nigeria, being female was not associated with

greater life expectancy. Males and females had about the same life expectancy. He concluded that, in general, being female is not associated with greater life expectancy than being male.

6. A student newspaper conducted a survey by asking students a series of questions. The survey was conducted at noon in front of the student center and involved 250 students out of a student body of 8,000. The interviewers were careful to get a sample with a racial, gender, and religious breakdown similar to that of the university as a whole. In the survey, 53 percent of the students interviewed said they opposed abortion. The newspaper presented the results of its survey in an article that was headlined "Majority of Student Body Opposes Abortion."
7. A random sample of cities and towns in the United States indicated an increase in the number of bank robberies. This trend was noted in a lead story in local TV news broadcasts with the announcement, "The number of bank robbers in the United States has increased."
8. A San Francisco area survey of randomly selected individuals seeking treatment for gout indicated that contrary to tradition, most gout sufferers are not addicts of rich gourmet food and beverages.
9. Al had trouble in high school math and didn't do a very good job in college algebra. He'll never make it as a math major.
10. All bachelors are unhappy. They just interviewed the guys down at the Beta fraternity house and they turned out to be unhappy. They got the same results down at Bernie's Tavern.
11.

Age of Autism: A Pretty Big Secret posted by "Luddite"[17]

CHICAGO, Dec. 7 (UPI)—It's a far piece from the horse-and-buggies of Lancaster County, Pa., to the cars and freeways of Cook County, Ill. But thousands of children cared for by Homefirst Health Services in metropolitan Chicago have at least two things in common with thousands of Amish children in rural Lancaster: They have never been vaccinated. And they don't have autism.

"We have a fairly large practice. We have about 30,000 or 35,000 children that we've taken care of over the years, and I don't think we have a single case of autism in children delivered by us who never received vaccines," said Dr. Mayer Eisenstein, Homefirst's medical director who founded the practice in 1973. Homefirst doctors have delivered more than

[17]*Lancaster On-Line: TalkBack*. Lancaster County PA, online version of *Intelligencer Journal/Lancaster New Era/Sunday News*. Posted by Luddite, 13 December 2005, under label "Age of Autism: A Pretty Big Secret."

> 15,000 babies at home, and thousands of them have never been vaccinated.
>
> The few autistic children Homefirst sees were vaccinated before their families became patients, Eisenstein said. "I can think of two or three autistic children [for] who[m] we've delivered their mother's next baby, and we aren't really totally taking care of that child—they have special care needs. But they bring the younger children to us. I don't have a single case that I can think of that wasn't vaccinated."
>
> The autism rate in Illinois public schools is 38 per 10,000, according to state Education Department data; the Centers for Disease Control and Prevention puts the national rate of autism spectrum disorders at 1 in 166—60 per 10,000.

(Hint: There is both a sampling argument and an implicit causal argument in this passage. Reconstruct the sampling argument. In your reconstruction take as the sample the unvaccinated Amish and Cook County children that are mentioned in the passage; take as the population all unvaccinated children.)

B. Design a sampling procedure that can serve as a basis for successful arguments leading to generalizations on the following topics. Indicate what techniques you are going to use to ensure representativeness. List some of the factors that might contribute to a bias in sampling. If possible indicate how to set up a sampling frame (a comprehensive list) from which to draw the sample.

1. The number of minority-group members living in the United States.
2. The attitude at your school toward substantial tax cuts.
3. The attitude in your neighborhood toward abortion.
4. The number of people in a class using this book who have used illegal drugs.
5. The attitude toward global warming in your city.
6. The support in your community for eliminating smoking in all enclosed areas open to the public.

ARGUMENTS WITH STATISTICAL PREMISES

The second major type of inductive argument we introduced in this chapter moves from general to particular, and in some forms is called a "statistical syllogism." As we stated earlier, this type contains "statistical" premises (those with *most, many*, *few*, a certain percentage of cases, rather than *all* or *none*). Unfortunately, no one has produced a theory that does for them what the theory of validity does for deductive arguments. No limited set of rules or techniques allows us to demarcate, in a foolproof way, good and bad patterns of reasoning for these cases. The basis for this difficulty lies at the very foundation of empirical reasoning. Our judgments about them rely on our background knowledge in a crucial way.

Criticisms of Arguments with Statistical Premises

Three criticisms apply to arguments with statistical premises: calling premises into doubt, indicating that a sequence of premises dilutes the likelihood of the conclusion, and showing that the argument does not use all the available relevant evidence. The first two are only occasionally applicable, the third is more widely useful.

Doubtful Premises; Diluted Probability First, as in the case of deductive arguments and inductive arguments that move from the particular to the general, you can simply call one or more of the premises into doubt. Second, even when all the premises are true, arguments with statistical premises can be dismissed without recourse to background knowledge, when the premises do not make the conclusion more likely. The likelihood of the conclusion is diluted by having an excessive number of premises, each of which is only somewhat likely. Each step in the argument lessens the likelihood of the conclusion. It is only in these complex cases that the opportunity to criticize structurally faulty arguments is likely to arise.

Example 8.10

(1) Many air traffic controllers are under great stress.

(2) Many people under stress are heavy drinkers.

(3) Many heavy drinkers lose their driver's licenses.

(4) Many people who lose their license are bad insurance risks.

(5) Many people who are bad insurance risks live in New York City.

(6) Fran is an air traffic controller.

(likely) Fran lives in New York City.

This string of premises does not make the conclusion more likely, and the longer the series of such connections, the more questionable the inference.

Meeting the Requirement of Total Available Relevant Evidence A successful argument from statistical premises must meet the Requirement of Total Available Relevant Evidence. The principal method of criticizing arguments with statistical premises is showing that it does not do so. The requirement can best be put in focus by noting that two inductive arguments of this type can have all their premises true and yet yield incompatible conclusions.

Example 8.11

Argument A	**Argument B**
(1) Most people who have their gallbladder removed recover without serious complications.	*(1) Most 103-year-old persons who have major surgery suffer serious complications.*
(2) Didi is about to have her gallbladder removed.	*(2) Didi is a 103-year-old person about to have major surgery for gallbladder removal.*
(likely) Didi will recover without serious complications.	*(likely) Didi will suffer serious complications.*

Background knowledge is important in this case. If all we know about Didi is that she is about to have her gallbladder removed, then Argument A seems successful (given the truth of both premises); however, given the additional knowledge that she is 103 years old, we can produce Counterargument B that leads to the incompatible conclusion that Didi will suffer serious complications.[18] This counterargument provides more specific information that points out that the case is an exception to a statistical premise. Given our common knowledge about surgery for the elderly, Didi's age makes her a plausible exception to the premise that most people who have their gallbladder removed recover without serious complications.

Similar considerations apply to some arguments that present "shocking statistics." For example, somebody says to Mike, "Do you realize that a murder is committed every 32 minutes? So be careful, you are in danger of being murdered."[19] Given appropriate knowledge of Mike's circumstances, we can produce a counterargument.

Example 8.12

Argument Criticized	**Counterargument**
(1) A murder is committed in the United States every 37 minutes (that is, murder is frequent in the United States).	*(1) A murder has never been committed in Serenityville.*
(2) Mike lives in the United States.	*(2) Mike lives in Serenityville.*
(likely) Mike is in danger of being murdered.	*(likely) Mike is in little danger of being murdered.*

[18]This situation has no analogue in the case of deductive arguments. Two deductively sound arguments cannot come to incompatible conclusions. In this case, we have arguments with true premises in which the conclusion of each is likely relative to the premises, but that have incompatible conclusions.

[19]Rate based on the FBI's figure of 14,137 murders in 2008 from the *Uniform Crime Reports* 2008 (http://www.fbi.gov/ucr).

Here again the counterargument introduces more specific information that suggests that a premise in the argument being criticized does not directly apply.

Similar consideration apply to arguments cast in more statistical form.[20] For example,

Example 8.13

Argument Criticized	**Counterargument**
(1) 60 percent of college graduates get a high-paying job after graduation.	*(1) 75 percent of college binge drinkers do not get a high-paying job after graduation.*
(2) Sybil is graduating.	*(2) Sybil is a college binge drinker.*
(60 percent likely) Sybil will get a high-paying job after graduation.	*(75 percent likely) Sybil will not get a high-paying job after graduation.*

The counterargument here succeeds because it leads to a more likely conclusion.

Our commonsense background knowledge sometimes provides us with the appropriate materials needed to construct a counterargument, but in other cases arguments can be challenged (if at all) only on the basis of expert knowledge. Consider the following argument.

Example 8.14

(1) Most long-time, heavy smokers suffer from smoking-related health problems.

(2) Bruce is a long-time, heavy smoker.

(likely) Bruce will suffer from smoking-related health problems.

Given the results of numerous scientific studies that have been cited by the Surgeon General of the United States, such an argument might seem conclusive (assuming that the premise about Bruce is true). But perhaps Bruce has a rare genetic makeup that enables his body to resist the health-destroying effects

---

[20] The "statistical syllogism" comes in several forms. The most "general" is

(1) Most P_1's are P_2's.
(2) m is a P_1.

(likely) m is a P_2.

But we can be more specific about how likely the conclusion might be

(1) N% P_1's are P_2's.
(2) m is a P_1.

(N% likely) m is a P_2.

of heavy cigarette smoking. Should this be the case, a sophisticated scientist might launch a counterargument along the following lines:

Example 8.15

(1) Most people with the "lucky" gene configuration will resist the health-sapping consequences of smoking.

(2) Bruce has the "lucky" gene configuration.

(likely) Bruce will resist the health-sapping consequences of smoking.

The important point here is that the criticism of arguments with statistical premises may depend on expert knowledge. The mere possibility that an expert might ultimately discover some new, relevant information is not in itself a reason for rejecting an argument that is otherwise acceptable. In a sense, these arguments are always open to question because additional evidence can always be made available in principle. But we can strengthen an argument that has statistical premises by using all available, relevant evidence. If we don't have the time or energy to marshal all available evidence, we can still bring the conclusion within an acceptable margin of error. We can do this more readily if we believe that additional evidence is only minimally important and that additional factors are unlikely to appear. If an argument does not live up to the requirement of using all available, relevant evidence, it is open to criticism.

In this section we considered three criticisms appropriate to arguments with statistical premises:

Criticisms of Arguments with Statistical Premises (general-to-particular argument)

1. Attacking the premises.
2. Noting that the number of premises dilutes the strength of the conclusion.
3. Pointing out the total available evidence was not used (as shown by a counterargument).

EXERCISE 8.3

Criticizing Arguments with Statistical Premises

Which of the following arguments are acceptable? Sketch out your criticisms of those that you think are not. Use the information provided in the premises, or alternatively, make use of your own background knowledge to develop any appropriate counterarguments.

1. *(1) Most auto fatalities are the result of the driver drinking.*

   (2) Armand was in an auto fatality at 9:30 on Sunday morning.

   (likely) Armand's death was the result of the driver drinking.

2. *(1) Most sexually active women who take birth control pills according to directions do not conceive.*

   (2) Edna is a sexually active woman who takes birth control pills according to directions.

   (likely) Edna will not conceive.

3. *(1) Most areas with low unemployment rates have higher wages.*

   (2) American cities with a strong service economy have low unemployment.

   (likely) American cities with a strong service economy have higher wages.

4. *(1) Most incumbents are reelected in the United States if they decide to run.*

   (2) Mayor Armwrestler is an incumbent running for reelection who has long stood for increasing expenditures on social programs.

   (likely) Mayor Armwrestler will be reelected.

5. *(1) Most students will benefit materially from a college education.*

   (2) Sandy is a college student studying Greek and Latin.

   (likely) Sandy will benefit materially from a college education.

IDENTIFYING INDUCTIVE AND DEDUCTIVE ARGUMENTS IN NATURAL PROSE PASSAGES

Sometimes it is fairly easy to determine whether an argument is best construed as inductive rather than deductive. You can look for indicator words associated with the conclusion such as *probably* or *likely*. As we will see, the language of sampling or polling suggests induction. But in some natural prose passages it is difficult to determine whether the conclusion of an argument is presented by the arguer as only made probable by the premises, or whether the conclusion is presented as guaranteed by the truth of the premises. For example,

Example 8.16 *Fran must be pretty well off. Lexus owners have higher-than-average incomes and Fran owns a Lexus.*

Deductive Version	***Inductive Version***
(1) All Lexus owners have higher-than-average incomes.	*(1) Most Lexus owners have higher-than-average incomes.*
(2) Fran is a Lexus owner.	*(2) Fran is a Lexus owner.*
∴ Fran has a higher-than-average income.	*(likely) Fran has a higher-than-average income.*

There is no direct clue in the passage to suggest which version the arguer intends. If it were in an advertising brochure in a section titled "Lexus Owners Tend to Be Brighter and Wealthier," the inductive version would be more clearly indicated because of the word *tend*. Reference to tendencies in this and related contexts suggests that something often (but not always) takes place. In the absence of even this type of clue, we are left only with an application of the Principle of Charitable Interpretation, which asks us to interpret the argument so that the premises support the conclusion. In the deductive version, the first premise would be hard to accept. It is difficult to believe that every single Lexus owner is well-off. Some older models of Lexus are no doubt owned by students with relatively low incomes. To treat the passage as containing an obviously unsound deductive argument rather than a much more plausible inductive argument, however, would be uncharitable. The charitable course, other things being equal, is to interpret an argumentative passage as a plausible inductive argument (one with no obvious faults) rather than as an unsuccessful (unsound) deductive argument. The author, of course, is ultimately responsible for guiding the interpretation of an argument. In some contexts you might not be able to tell whether the author intended to present a weak deductive argument or a somewhat less weak inductive argument. In either instance, however, the argument might be open to criticism.

A More Complex Passage

Complex examples of empirical reasoning may include both types of inductive arguments—sampling (particular to general) and arguments with statistical premises (general to particular)—as illustrated in the following passage and reconstruction.

Example 8.17

A recent poll of a random sample of Americans of voting age indicated that 68 percent favored stricter gun control legislation. With such a large approval rating, it is only a matter of time before stricter gun control legislation ultimately passes into law. This is because most proposed legislation that has substantial public support ultimately gains ratification.

Reconstruction

Sampling Argument (Implicit)

(1) Sixty-eight percent of the eligible voters sampled in the poll favored stricter gun control legislation.

(likely) About 68 percent of the eligible voters in America favor stricter gun control legislation.

Argument with Statistical Premises (Implicit)

(1) About 68 percent of the eligible voters in America favor stricter gun control legislation.

(2) Most measures supported by a large portion of the American public become law.

(likely) Stricter gun control legislation will ultimately be ratified.

This passage makes a prediction—*stricter gun control legislation will ultimately be ratified*. The conclusion of the first reconstructed argument is the premise of the second.

Finally, the conclusion of a sampling argument or an argument with statistical premises can be used as part of an overall deductive argument. In an interview of President Obama by Matt Lauer shortly after the final vote on the health insurance reform bill, Lauer stated:[21]

Example 8.18

This version of health care reform did not receive one single Republican vote. You almost have to say that again to let it really sink in: Not one Republican vote and a lot of people wonder how a bill, now a law, can be good for the American public in general when it didn't receive a single Republic vote and when a recent poll said 50% of people are not in favor of the plan.

The argument implicit in this passage can be reconstructed as a deductive argument supported by a sampling argument.

Reconstruction of Example 8.18

Sampling Argument

(1) 50% of people recently polled were not in favor of the health care reform bill.[22]

(likely) 50% of all Americans are not in favor of the health care reform bill.

Deductive Argument

(1) The health care reform bill did not receive any Republican votes.

(2) 50% of all Americans are not in favor of the health care reform bill.

(3) If (1) and (2), then the bill (now a law) is not good for the American public.[23]

∴ The health care reform bill is not good for the American public.

The sampling argument supporting Premise 2 of the full deductive argument can be criticized by noting that public opinion can be quite volatile and quickly change. A poll taken at a time when those sampled have been exposed

---

[21]Taken from a March 30, 2010 broadcast of Matt Lauer's interview with President Obama on NBC's *Today* program.

[22]This claim references the results of a *USA Today*/Gallup Poll reported on the USA today website. "In the poll, 50% call passage of the bill 'a bad thing' and 47% say it was 'a good thing.'. . . The margin of error is +/− 4 percentage points." http://content.usatoday.com/communities/onpolitics/post/2010/03/poll-half-say-passage-of-health-care-law-a-bad-thing-/1 March 29, 2010

[23]This could be stated more generally as *Any bill that has no Republican support and is opposed by 50% of Americans is not good for the American public.*

to considerable negative publicity regarding the bill might not represent a stable and enduring opinion of 50% of the American public.[24]

The third premise of the deductive argument is also open to criticism. It is doubtful that even if about half of the American public opposed the bill at the time it was passed, then it follows that it is not good for the country. Legislators who have studied a particular area of public policy might be better able to make judgments than the public at large. President Obama himself, in the interview, focused on the connection between Republican opposition and whether the health care reform provisions were good for the public. He maintained that "the Republican party made a calculated decision, a political decision, that they would not support whatever we did. There was a quote by a well-known Republican senator that said that this was going to be Obama's Waterloo. We're going to bring him down the same way we brought down Bill Clinton, by making sure that health care fails. . . . I think that if you actually break down the specifics of the bill you will see that it has historically had a lot of Republican support."

Review: Types of Inductive Arguments

Sampling Argument
Particular-to-general argument

(1) In studies of 5,000 people, those who had more exposure to environmental smoke had a higher frequency of lung cancer.

(likely) People who have more exposure to environmental smoke generally have a higher frequency of lung cancer.

Argument with Statistical Premises
General-to-particular argument

(1) Most long-time, heavy smokers suffer from smoking-related health problems.
(2) Bruce is a long-time, heavy smoker.

(likely) Bruce will suffer from smoking-related health problems.

EXERCISE 8.4 Reconstructing and Evaluating Arguments Contained in Complex Prose Passages

Reconstruct and evaluate the main argument in each of the following passages. If a premise of the main argument is itself supported by a sampling argument or an argument with statistical premises, reconstruct and evaluate this subsidiary argument as well.

1. America is a democracy, and most democracies will not long permit substantial differences in wealth. Since roughly 59 percent of America's

[24]Furthermore, the difference between the 50% not in favor and the 47% in favor is within the margin of error. As a consequence, the poll does not rule out that more people in the American population actually favor than are against the health care reform bill. It certainly does not *strongly* support the view that a majority does not favor the law.

wealth is owned by the top 5 percent of households, it is likely that legislation to alter this distribution, at least somewhat, will be produced.[25]

2.

Study Links Alzheimer's To Childhood[26]

Hardship during childhood may contribute to Alzheimer's later, researchers say.

Early growth has far-reaching effects on many diseases, said study leader Victoria Moceri of the University of Washington in Seattle. Her team of researchers found that factors such as family size and location point to a role for childhood and teenage living conditions in the risk of getting Alzheimer's.

In the study, published Tuesday in the journal *Neurology,* researchers carefully matched 393 Alzheimer's patients with 377 healthy people the same age. All the participants were over 60; the average age was 79.

Compared with those who grew up in rural or urban areas, people from the suburbs had 45 percent of the chance of developing Alzheimer's.

"Living outside the city in the suburbs in the 1920s was associated with a better standard of living."

(Hint: Take as the sample the 770 individuals in the study—both the Alzheimer's patients and the healthy people.)

3.

"Sex Was Forced on Us" 19 Percent Say in College Poll[27]

Boston (AP)—A fifth of some 1,500 undergraduate women surveyed at Harvard said they had been forced into sexual activity they didn't want, according to a report published yesterday. Fifty-seven percent of the women polled also said they consider themselves sexually active, the *Boston Globe* reported. Nearly 1,500 women undergraduates, or 54 percent of the female undergraduate population, answered the questionnaire passed out in September 1983, the *Globe* reported. University Health Services and Radcliffe College sponsored the Women's Health and Sexuality Survey.

Nineteen percent of respondents answered yes to the question, "Have you ever been forced into any sexual activity you didn't want?"

That percentage was "frighteningly high," said the survey's author, Michelle J. Orza.

"These are young women. How many will answer yes when they are 30?"

---

[25]As indicated in Edward Wolff's June 2004 Working Paper 205, *Recent Trends in Household Wealth in the United States: Rising Debt and the Middle-Class Squeeze* using data from the *Federal Reserve 2004 Survey of Consumer Finances.*

[26]Gannett News Service, "Study Links Alzheimer's to Childhood," *The Olympian (Wash.),* January 26, 2000, A8.

[27]Associated Press, *Seattle Post-Intelligencer,* 18 November 1984. Reprinted by permission.

Seven percent of the respondents answered yes to the question, "Since you have been at Harvard, have you ever been the recipient of undue and/or unwanted personal attention from a faculty member, teaching fellow or administrative officer of the university?" the *Globe* said. Forty percent of women undergraduates answered yes to a similar question in a study last year, the Globe reported.

4. The following passage contains several examples of nondeductive arguments.
   (a) Reconstruct the sampling argument used in the U.S. Supreme Court majority opinion in *Gregg v. Georgia*.
   (b) Justice Thurgood Marshall presents a deductive argument in the second paragraph. Reconstruct and evaluate this argument.
   (c) The authors of the passage present research results that can be used to support Justice Marshall's conclusion. Reconstruct the sampling argument and indicate how it can be used as a premise in support of Marshall's conclusion.

Attitudes Toward Capital Punishment[28]

In *Gregg v. Georgia,* the seven justices in the majority noted that both the public and state legislatures had endorsed the death penalty for murder. The Court stated that "it is now evident that a large proportion of American society continues to regard it as an appropriate and necessary criminal sanction." Public opinion data indicates that the Court was correct in its assessment of the level of support for the death penalty. In 1976, the year that *Gregg* was decided, 66 percent of the respondents to a nationwide poll said that they favored the death penalty for persons convicted of murder. By 1997, three-quarters of those polled voiced *support* for the death penalty. Although the exoneration of death row inmates and subsequent decisions to impose a moratorium on executions (discussed later) led to a decline in support, in October of 2003, 64 percent of Americans still reported that they favored the death penalty for persons convicted of murder.

The reliability of these figures has not gone unchallenged. In fact, Supreme Court Justices themselves have raised questions about the reliability and meaning of public opinion data derived from standard "do you favor or oppose?" polling questions. Justice Marshall observed in his concurring opinion in *Furman* that Americans were not fully informed about the ways in which the death penalty was used or about its potential for abuse. According to Marshall, the public did not realize that the death penalty was imposed in an arbitrary manner or that "the burden of capital punishment falls upon

---

[28]Samuel Walker, Cassia Spohn, and Miriam DeLone, *The Color of Justice: Race, Ethnicity and Crime in America*, 4th (Cengage Learning, 2007), Ch. 8. Published with Permission.

the poor, the ignorant, and the underprivileged members of society." Marshall suggested that public opinion data demonstrating widespread support for the death penalty should therefore be given little weight in determining whether capital punishment is consistent with "evolving standards of decency." In what has become known as the "Marshall Hypothesis," he stated that "the average citizen" who knew "all the facts presently available regarding capital punishment would . . . find it shocking to his conscience and sense of justice."

Researchers also have raised questions about the poll results, suggesting that support for the death penalty is not absolute, but depends upon such things as the circumstances of the case, the character of the defendant, or the alternative punishments that are available. Bowers, for example, challenged the conclusion that "Americans solidly support the death penalty" and suggested that the poll results have been misinterpreted. He argued that instead of reflecting a "deep-seated or strongly held commitment to capital punishment," expressed public support for the death penalty "is actually a reflection of the public's desire for a genuinely harsh but meaningful punishment for convicted murderers." In support of this proposition, Bowers presented evidence from surveys of citizens in a number of states and from interviews with capital jurors in three states. He found that support for the death penalty plummeted when respondents were given an alternative of life in prison without parole plus restitution to the victim's family; moreover, a majority of the respondents in every state preferred this alternative to the death penalty. Bowers also found that about three-quarters of the respondents, and 80 percent of jurors in capital cases, agreed that "the death penalty is too arbitrary because some people are executed and others are sent to prison for the very same crimes." Bowers concluded that the results of his study "could have the critical effect of changing the perspectives of legislators, judges, the media, and the public on how people think about capital punishment." Consistent with Bowers' results, recent public opinion polls reveal that most Americans believe that innocent people are sometimes convicted of murder. These polls also suggest that respondents' beliefs about the likelihood of wrongful convictions affect their views of the death penalty. A Harris poll conducted in July of 2001 found that 94 percent of those polled believed that innocent people are "sometimes" convicted of murder; only 3 percent stated that this "never happens." When respondents were asked, "If you believed that quite a substantial number of innocent people are convicted of murder, would you then believe in or oppose the death penalty for murder," 53 percent said that they would oppose the death penalty, compared to 36 percent who stated that they would continue to support it.

CHAPTER 9

Causal, Analogical, and Convergent Arguments: Three More Kinds of Nondeductive Reasoning

Chapter 8 focused on inductive arguments, both particular-to-general and general-to-particular. This chapter looks at three additional kinds of nondeductive arguments: causal, analogical, and convergent arguments. They all are nondeductive in that the conclusion does not follow necessarily from the premises. For each kind of argument there are considerations that make the conclusion more or less likely; we attend to these considerations in evaluating the argument.

Causal arguments move from a premise that two things are associated or correlated (for example, exposure to high levels of secondhand smoke and lung cancer) to a conclusion that the first is not merely correlated with, but causes, the second.

Example 9.1 ***A Causal Argument***

(1) Exposure to high levels of secondhand smoke is correlated with lung cancer.

(likely) Exposure to high levels of secondhand smoke causes lung cancer.

It is tempting to move from correlation to cause. How else, we might think, can we account for the regular association between exposure to secondhand smoke and cancer? Although regular association might create a presumption of causation in many cases, judgments of causation do not follow necessarily from correct judgments of correlation. The crowing of a rooster on a farm might be regularly associated with sunrise, but we shouldn't conclude that the crowing caused the sunrise. As we shall see, steps can be taken to determine that the conclusion is more likely, and in their absence causal arguments are open to criticism.

Arguments from analogy rest on a comparison of two things. They typically begin with a premise asserting that two objects are similar in certain important respects and conclude that some additional properties of one are similar to properties of the other. For example, as we suggested in Chapter 2, the universe can be compared to a clock. Both have order and precision. According to a version of this argument from analogy, since clocks have makers, we can conclude that it is likely the universe had a maker. (Traditionally, this maker of the universe is said to be God.)

Example 9.2 ***An Argument from Analogy***

(1) The universe is like a clock in order and precision.

(2) Clocks have makers.

(likely) The universe has a maker.

This kind of argument is not deductive because being similar in some respects does not *guarantee* that things will be similar in other respects. At most, the premises make the conclusion likely. Although seeing comparisons can be very useful in extending our thinking, the conclusion of an argument from analogy does not follow necessarily from the premises. The success of such arguments depends on whether there are dissimilarities between the objects that make it unlikely that the additional feature cited (having a maker, for example) can be appropriately extended from one to the other.

Finally, this chapter will examine convergent arguments, which offer multiple independent premises in support of a conclusion. An argument from circumstantial evidence in criminal cases is such an argument.

The prosecution argues that the defendant has motive, means, and opportunity and concludes, even though there might be counter-evidence, that he is guilty.

Example 9.3 ***A Convergent Argument***

(1) The defendant was deeply in debt.

(2) The defendant knew the location of the household safe.

(3) The defendant was not at work.

(likely) The defendant committed the burglary.

In this type of nondeductive argument the conclusion does not necessarily follow from the premises, although each of the independent premises makes the conclusion more likely.

All three kinds of arguments advance conclusions that go beyond the premises. In doing so, they face special, additional requirements and can be criticized when these requirements are not met. This chapter will discuss the arguments in greater detail and consider the criticisms that can be raised against them.

CAUSAL ARGUMENTS

Causal arguments are of special interest because they often play a central role in a debate about what should be done. We want to know whether smoking, exposure to asbestos, or exposure to electromagnetic radiation *causes* cancer, not merely for the sake of the knowledge itself but also because knowledge of cause provides a basis for *control*. If we know that exposure to asbestos is the major cause of mesothelial cancer, then we can prevent or limit this cancer by intervening to control exposure to asbestos.[1]

As we indicated in Chapter 8, the premise that a correlation exists is typically justified in part by using sampling procedures. For example, a sample of individuals suffering from mesothelial cancer might be examined to determine whether they had been exposed to asbestos. If our sample is large enough and is representative of those having this form of cancer, then we might be justified

[1]Mesothelial cancer is a particularly rare form of cancer that attacks the lining of the lungs, heart sac, and some tissues on the inside of the abdomen. A number of studies have indicated that a majority, and perhaps as many as 72 percent, of the victims have had substantial exposure to asbestos particles. Of even greater significance is the fact that about 10 percent of the workers in the asbestos insulating industry contracted the disease. See International Labour Office, *Asbestos: Health Risks and Their Prevention* (Geneva: International Labour Office, 1974), 6, 37.

in asserting that the rate of mesothelial cancer is associated with exposure to asbestos, and in such a case statisticians say that there is a statistically significant difference between the mesothelial cancer rates of those exposed to asbestos and those who do not have such exposure. When we make such a judgment, we hold that a property observed in the sample (for example, difference in cancer rate among those exposed to asbestos) was found because the population actually has this property rather than as a result of some random factors (random error or "luck of the draw"). Samples are virtually never exact duplicates of the population—they don't represent it perfectly. But if the sample is properly selected we are justified in holding that it is a fairly good representation of the population.

We have been describing how the premise of a causal argument (the claim that A is correlated with B) can be based on sampling procedures. But no matter how well-established this premise is, the conclusion that A causes B might not follow. In the case of asbestos and cancer, there is not only a strong basis for the premise that they are correlated but also (as we shall see) a strong basis for the conclusion that the first causes the second.

The problems that can occur in moving from the premise of correlation to the conclusion of cause are better illustrated by a second example. In a radio interview, a critic of sex education in the public schools argued that sex education programs had caused an increase in sexually transmitted diseases (STDs). She based this claim on the correlation between increases in the amount of sex education offered in high school curricula and increases in the rate of STDs such as gonorrhea.

The expert was correct in asserting that rates of STDs (at least of gonorrhea) increased dramatically in the 1960s and 70s. There was also, no doubt, an increase in the number of sex education classes during this period, but accurate information about the nature and extent of sex education programs in U.S. high schools was difficult to obtain and, unfortunately, she did not provide any sources. For purposes of illustration, we can use a graph to display the actual increase in gonorrhea as estimated in the U.S. Statistical Abstract, along with some largely fictional data that would support the critic's claim about a strong correlation.[2] The data that underlie this example do support the generalization that increases in the number of gonorrhea cases are correlated with increases in the number of students in high schools with sex education programs. This is shown visually by the roughly parallel lines in Figure 9.1. Obviously, however, the critic was concerned to assert more than the mere correlation of sex education and gonorrhea. She is interested in showing that sex education courses are a major causal factor in the spread of STDs and that we can control the incidence of the disease by eliminating sex education from the schools. But such a jump from correlation to cause is, at best, suspect.

---

[2]An unpublished National Institute of Education study suggests that perhaps 36 percent of the schools offered sex education programs in the mid-1970s, according to Douglas Kirby and others, *An Analysis of U.S. Sex Education Programs and Evaluation Methods* (Bethesda, MD: Mathtech, Inc., 1979).

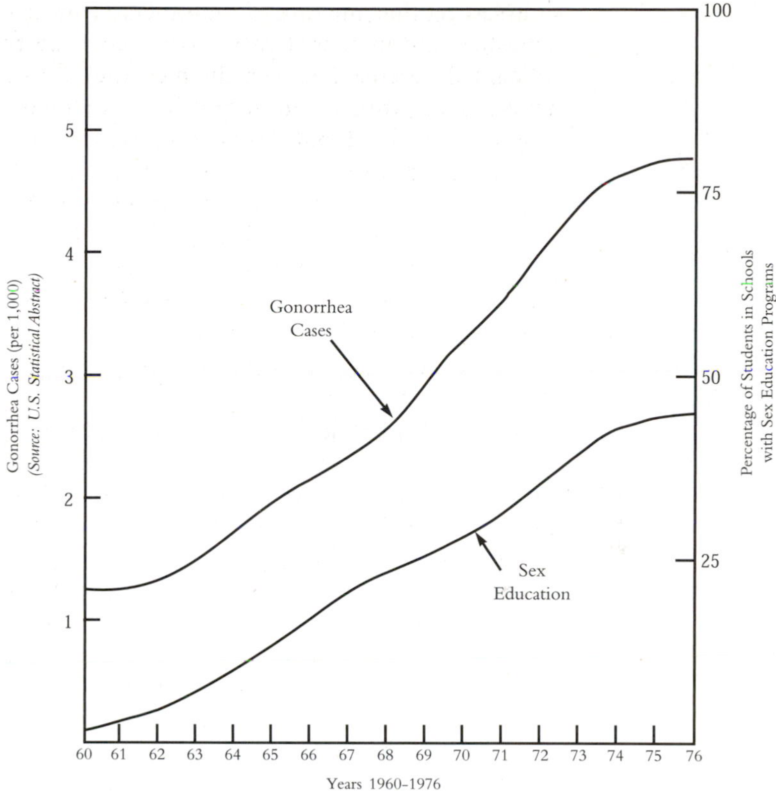

FIGURE **9.1** Rate of gonorrhea cases per 1,000 population (actual estimates) and percentage of students (largely fictional estimates) in high schools with sex education programs

FIVE WAYS IN WHICH CAUSAL REASONING MIGHT FAIL

The argument about the relationship of gonorrhea and sex education has the form

Example 9.4

(1) Increases in sex education are ***correlated*** *with increases in gonorrhea (in the United States, 1960–76).*

(likely) Increases in sex education courses ***caused*** *increases in gonorrhea (in the United States, 1960–76).*

One reason the argument could fail is because the premise is unjustified. The premise could be based on faulty sampling procedures of the type we discussed in Chapter 8. However, even if the sampling procedure is correct, and if we are justified in believing that there is indeed a correlation between increases in sex education and gonorrhea rates, the conclusion might be false—there might be a correlation but not a causal relation. This could come about in five different ways.

1. The correlation might be *coincidental*. The two characteristics might be accidentally correlated rather than genuinely connected. An increase in the national debt is also correlated with increases in gonorrhea, but few are tempted to say that increases in the debt caused the increase in gonorrhea. The correlation between sex education and gonorrhea might be similarly coincidental.
2. The items might be correlated because they are *both effects of the same underlying cause*. For example, both the increase in gonorrhea and the increase in sex education courses might have been caused by changes in the sexual attitudes of the young. Increased sexual activity might have spread the disease and simultaneously moved school officials to develop sex education programs. In technical terms a correlation between items related in this way is called *spurious*.
3. The causal relation might be genuine but *insignificant*. Sex education courses might have induced only a few people to engage in the sexual activity that led to the transmission of gonorrhea. In this case, sex education would be a causal factor, but it would not be a major causal factor in the sense that eliminating it would not significantly affect the spread of gonorrhea.
4. The causal relation might be in the *wrong direction*. Perhaps the increase in gonorrhea, and other factors, caused the increase in sex education courses by alarming parents and school officials, rather than the other way around. (Remember, to say that A is correlated with B implies that B is also correlated with A. So correlation alone does not tell us the direction of causation.)
5. The causal relation might be *complex*. An increase in sex education might have caused changes in sexual attitudes that led to increased sexual activity and, ultimately, to the spread of gonorrhea. But increases in gonorrhea might have simultaneously caused the development of expanded programs of sex education.

An argument that simply moves from correlation to cause is never adequate unless the preceding considerations can be ruled out. (Later we will discuss a main strategy for ruling them out: a controlled experiment.) When they are not taken into account, the author of the argument is sometimes said to be guilty of the fallacy: *post hoc, ergo propter hoc,* meaning "after this, therefore because of this."

Criticism of causal arguments presented by researchers often demands special background, but even the general consumer of such arguments should be aware of possible faults and on occasion can rely on more general background knowledge to raise telling criticism. The most readily employed criticism is that there is a plausible X-factor—an underlying cause—that might account for the correlation even though the elements are not causally related. Secondly, the nonexpert might point out that the direction of causation might plausibly be the opposite of what is presented. The remaining faults may be more difficult to establish.

Our suspicion that the correlation is coincidental is most prominent when the connection is very unclear; for example, a correlation between which baseball league won the World Series and which party won the presidential election is unlikely to be a causal relationship, because it is difficult to see what kind of causal steps might link them.[3] In order to establish that the correlation is coincidental, you might point out that the correlation existed only in some studies or is likely to exist only for a certain period of time. Ideally, you would point out what the underlying factor or genuine cause actually is. This certainly would take additional research. Such additional research is generally needed as well to justify the criticism that the correlation betokens a genuine but insignificant cause or reflects causal complexity.

EXERCISE 9.1

The Faulty Move from Correlation to Cause

Indicate whether these passages contain a faulty move from correlation to cause. If so, state your criticism. If you are claiming that a correlation might be due to an X-factor, say what this X-factor might be, and explain how it could account for the correlation.

1. Texting while driving has been correlated with traffic accidents. So texting while driving causes traffic accidents.
2. There is a correlation between heavy consumption of coffee and heart attacks. So coffee drinking causes heart attacks.
3. People who get a flu shot every year live longer than those who do not, so it is likely that it is the flu shots that cause them to live longer.
4. There is a significant correlation between going to the hospital and dying, so hospitals are important causal factors in the occurrence of deaths.
5. There is a significant correlation between the increase in the number of hours children watch TV and a decrease in the college admission test scores, so TV watching caused the lower scores.
6. An article in the *Seattle Times* (April 24, 2003) cites a study by the American Cancer Society of more than 900,000 people nationwide for 16 years. The article says that the study provided "the first definitive understanding of the role of obesity in causing cancer." It indicated that men in the highest weight category (a Body Mass Index—BMI—score above 30) were 52 percent more likely to die from cancer than those of normal weight (BMI 18.5–24.9), and women in the highest groups were 62 percent more likely to die from cancer.

---

[3]The fact that we can't imagine what the connection might be, however, is not a completely compelling reason for rejecting the conclusion. More scientific research might establish such a connection. Thirty years ago, the association between red wine consumption and lower incidence of heart disease might have seemed accidental, but recent evidence about the role of antioxidants (which occur in red wine as well as other foods) suggest that they can lower the risk of heart disease.

7. Staying happy and positive can help ward off heart disease, a new study has suggested. . . The new research showed that people who are usually happy, **enthusiastic** and content are less likely to develop heart disease than those who tend not to be happy.[4]
8. A survey by the Sleep Disorder Clinic of the VA Hospital in La Jolla, California (involving more than 1 million people), revealed that people who sleep more than ten hours a night have a death rate 80 percent higher than those who sleep only seven or eight hours. Men who sleep less than four hours a night have a death rate 180 percent higher, and women with less sleep have a rate 40 percent higher. This might be taken as indicating that too much and too little sleep cause death.

9.

Study Links Homicide with TV Use[5]

Seattle (AP)—Television viewing "is a factor" in about half of the 20,000 homicides and many other violent crimes that occur each year in the United States, according to a psychiatrist who studied statistical links between homicides and the rise in television ownership.

The study, published Tuesday in the April issue of the *American Journal of Epidemiology,* is billed by the University of Washington as the first study ever to look at the statistical relationships between exposure to television and acts of violence for the entire country.

The study by Dr. Brandon Centerwall, a member of the psychiatry faculty at the University of Washington School of Medicine, also indicates that as many as half of other violent crimes—including rapes and assaults—are related to exposure to television.

"Television is a factor in approximately 10,000 homicides each year in the United States," Centerwall told a news conference Tuesday.

"While television clearly is not the sole cause of violence in our society, and there are many other contributing factors, hypothetically if television did not exist there would be 10,000 fewer homicides a year."

To arrive at this conclusion, Centerwall studied the white population of South Africa, where television was not introduced until 1975. Using statistics from 1945 to 1974, he compared homicide rates among South African whites to the rates among U.S. whites and the entire Canadian population.

He found that homicides remained roughly flat in South Africa before television was introduced. In the United States and Canada, however, homicide rates doubled within 20 years after the widespread introduction of television, Centerwall said.

It took Centerwall seven years to complete his study.

Centerwall said he hypothesized that if television ownership is followed by an increase in violence, then those populations

[4]Neka Sehgal, "Happiness key to a heathy heart." February 18, 2010, http://buzz7.com/health-science/happiness-key-to-a-healthy-heart.html
[5]Associated Press, *Daily Olympian (Wash.),* 5 April 1989. Reprinted with permission.

that had television earlier should have had an earlier increase in violence.

He tested his theory by comparing the change in homicide rates among white and minority populations in the United States. According to Centerwall, televisions were widespread in American white households about five years before they appeared in minority homes. Accordingly, homicide rates among minorities rose four years after the rates went up among whites, he said.

Centerwall said regions of the United States that had widespread television before the rest of the country also saw earlier increases in homicide rates.

"There is a strong relationship between when a region acquired television and when its homicide rates went up," he said.

According to Centerwall, the homicide rates among South African whites in 1983—the last year for which statistics were available—were 56 percent higher than in 1974—the year before the introduction of television, indicating a trend similar to what occurred in the United States after the introduction of television.

In addition to the fact that South Africa did not introduce television until as late as the mid-1970s, it was an appropriate country to choose for the study because it is a prosperous, industrialized Western country similar in many respects to the United States, Centerwall said. He limited his study to South African whites because South African blacks and other minorities live under very different conditions.

Centerwall said he found there was a lag of 10 to 15 years between the time television was introduced in the United States and the rapid increase in homicide rates. He explained that other studies have determined that children are most likely to be strongly influenced by television. Homicide, however, is generally an adult crime, so the initial "television generation" would have had to age 10 to 15 years before it would have been old enough to affect the homicide rate, he said.

10.

Ear Hair Linked to Heart Attacks[6]

Boston (UPI)—Dark hair in and around the hole leading into a person's inner ear indicates they may be at greater risk of having a heart attack, a Boston University doctor said yesterday.

A study of 43 men and 20 women found that those people with ear hair often had heart attacks. The findings were published as a letter to the editor in the *New England Journal of Medicine.*

People with a crease running across their ear lobe, it had been shown in earlier studies, also may be more likely to have heart attacks. The latest study found 90 percent of all people studied with both traits have had a heart attack.

(Hint: What might the "X-factor" be?)

[6]United Press International, *Seattle Post-Intelligencer,* November 14, 1984. Reprinted with permission.

11.

Type A's Must Change to Avoid Heart Attacks[7]

Miami Beach, Fla.—Teaching heart attack victims to conquer their hostility and impatience, hallmarks of Type A personality behavior, cuts their risk of suffering another seizure by half, a researcher has reported.

"I think that when this is confirmed, it will almost be considered malpractice not to try to alter Type A behavior in the patient who has already had a coronary," said Dr. Meyer Friedman, of Mount Zion Hospital and Medical Center in San Francisco. He released his findings at a meeting of the American Heart Association.

People with Type A behavior tend to approach life with a sense of urgency. They are impatient, aggressive and often hostile.

About three-quarters of all Americans are said to show some degree of Type A behavior. However, the link between this kind of personality and heart disease is still controversial.

In the latest study, doctors randomly assigned 891 heart attack survivors to two groups. Some received ordinary cardiac care, while the rest also were counseled by psychiatrists in an effort to change their behavior.

After three years, 9 percent of those who stuck with the counseling program had suffered new heart attacks, compared with 20 percent of the people who had received medical care alone. And of those who dropped out of the behavior training, 26 percent had heart attacks.

"What a person feels and thinks may be as important as what he eats or inhales in respect to heart disease," Friedman said.

SUPPORTING CAUSAL ARGUMENTS

What then are the requirements necessary to establish causation? It is difficult to list the requirements in an enlightening definition of *cause*. Philosophers have long debated about what, if anything, is meant by saying that one thing causes another, other than that they are correlated in certain ways. To determine whether something is a cause in the sense of a controlling factor, we characterize it as a *condition without which the effect would not have occurred*. Treated in this way, the connection between judgments of causation and questions of control is made more manifest. If an effect would not have occurred without the cause, then, in principle, one way of controlling the effect is (or would have been) to eliminate the cause.[8]

---

[7]Associated Press, *Seattle Post-Intelligencer*, November 18, 1984. Reprinted with permission.

[8]Although this characterization will serve the purpose of dealing with arguments from correlation to cause, it is inadequate as a general characterization of cause. It could be objected, for example, that smoke inhalation might cause a person's death even though the person would have died from the burns received anyway. So our rough characterization needs refinement. We might say that the death would not have occurred at the time it did without smoke inhalation.

In practice, of course, it might be impossible to control an effect even if we know the cause. We know that nuclear fusion causes radiation from the sun and other stars, but it is unlikely that we will be able to control, or prevent, solar radiation. Consequently, it is a mistake to think that merely establishing a cause permits us to control the effect in all or even most cases.

Our purpose is to examine how causal generalizations may be justified and how arguments that support them may be criticized. By concentrating on causal arguments themselves rather than on any attempt to formally define causality, we can avoid many of the issues that have complicated the philosophical debate on this subject.

THE CONTROLLED EXPERIMENT: HANDLING THE X-FACTOR

It is helpful to see the task of defending and criticizing causal arguments as an instance of the dialogue process we discussed in Chapter 7. The initial argument that is open to criticism moves from a statement of correlation or association to a statement of cause.

Example 9.5 *(1) A is correlated with B.*

(likely) A causes B.

The burden of responsibility to respond shifts to one or another party in the dialogue—the proponent or critic of the causal generalization—depending on the background or context in which the generalization is advanced. The bare argument of the form displayed in Example 9.5 is open to the general criticism that the correlation is spurious. It might be that both A and B are the effects of some underlying cause, X. Alternatively, X might be the cause of B and also have a strong association with A. Either possibility would explain how A and B could be correlated without A causing B. The defender of the causal argument must handle this X-factor criticism.

The classical way of eliminating X-factors is by the *controlled experiment.*[9] If properly carried out, such an experiment forms a background context that shifts the burden of responsibility from the proponent to the opponent or critic. Such experiments use random assignment procedures and close monitoring of possible interfering factors to blunt possible criticism. The virtue of the controlled experiment is that it transfers the onus of responsibility to the critic, who must now provide some reason why it is plausible that an X-factor is at work. Causal arguments that move from correlation to cause without any further support are weak, and the critic has the upper hand. But if the correlation is established by a controlled experiment, the critic must do more. It is not enough to suggest that there might be an X-factor; some attempt must be made to establish its existence.

To illustrate the controlled experiment, suppose we wish to establish that a new acne medicine (AcneX) taken in a certain dosage over a certain period of time

---

[9]Laboratory experiments in the physical sciences typically provide a model for such experiments.

causes a reduction in acne-related skin problems.[10] To do so, we randomly assign test subjects from some sampling list (say, adolescents) to one of two groups: the experimental group or the control group against which it is compared. The initial skin conditions of all the participants in both groups are determined. The experimental group is then treated with the new medicine in the required dosage, and the control group is not. If after the designated period of time the experimental group has fewer skin problems than the control group, we would be tempted to generalize the results by saying that the new acne medicine caused the reduction in acne-related skin problems. Our confidence in this causal generalization will be increased even more if the results can be duplicated in other studies.

The argument moves from a statement about association or correlation to a causal generalization as a conclusion.

Example 9.6

(1) Treatment with ***AcneX is correlated with*** *reduced acne-related skin problems.*

(likely) Treatment with ***AcneX causes*** *reduction in acne-related skin problems.*

The basic model for the controlled experiment that could support the causal claim in the conclusion can be depicted as follows:

Example 9.7 ***Controlled "True" Experiment (before–after design)***[11]

	Initial examination (pretest)	*Experimental intervention*	*Outcome examination (posttest)*
Experimental Group (randomly assigned)	*Condition of skin determined*	*Treatment with AcneX*	*Reduced acne-related skin conditions*
Control or Comparison Group (randomly assigned)	*Condition of skin determined*	*No treatment*	*No change in acne-related skin conditions*

Random assignment strengthens the case for the causal generalization because it rules out a number of possible criticisms against it. These *threats to the causal claim* include the following:[12]

maturation
historical circumstance
moderation of extreme conditions

---

[10]Such a controlled experiment assumes that we can accurately measure the degree or amount of acne-related skin conditions, for example, the number of eruptions or percent of the body covered by irritations. A precise statement of what would count as such a condition is sometimes called an *operational definition* in which we specify operations for applying the term such as counting the number of eruptions or measuring the irritated area.

[11]This is called a *before–after* design because it measures the experimental and control groups both before and after the intervention (in contrast to an *after–only* design that examines the groups only after the intervention).

[12]Researchers call them *threats to internal validity.* The concept of validity is used differently here than in discussing deductive arguments. A longer list can be developed, but these three are important and illustrative.

We know that acne tends to lessen as part of the normal human developmental process as people get older. *Maturation* could account for the experimental differences if the experimental group were significantly older than the comparison group. We know that people who volunteer to take an experimental drug are apt to be different from those who do not. The volunteers might be especially concerned with treating acne, and as a consequence, they might be influenced by *historical circumstance* (advertisements or education programs) to take better care of their skin or might be willing to change their diet more readily than people in a comparison group who were not as eager to participate. In such a case, it is incidental advertisements and education, not the new drug, which account for the improvement in the skin of the experimental group. Finally, we know that if people are suffering from a particularly severe episode of acne it is likely that their condition will moderate even without special medication, given the ebb and flow of the disorder. If people were selected for the program (or self-selected) because of an especially severe episode, then we would expect a *moderation of extreme conditions* even if the test medication had no effect.[13]

Random assignment of individuals to the experimental and control groups makes it very unlikely that these threats to the causal claim apply. Of course, it is still possible that in spite of random assignment, those who are older, more eager, or suffering from an especially acute episode will be selected, by chance, for the experimental group and those without these conditions will fall into the comparison group. But this is also very unlikely. Unless the opponent has *specific reasons* for believing that this is the case, the person's criticism amounts to little more than the weak assertion that it is *possible* that some X-factor exists. The burden of responsibility shifts to the critic to show some specific and significant differences between the experimental and control groups.

Even though random assignment handles certain threats, it does not handle all of them. It remains possible that expectations *bias* observation of results. Determining whether a particular patch of irritated skin is an acne-related skin disorder might not always be easy. Judgment calls need to be made, and even a conscientious investigator might be subtly biased if she expected reduction of acne in the experimental group and no reduction in the control group. To handle this possibility, *double-blind* experiments are conducted in which neither the person treated nor the judge of pre- and posttest results is aware of whether medicine has actually been given. To attain this state, a placebo (often a sugar pill) that looks like the real medication is given to those in the control group.[14] The use of a placebo is not possible in many experiments involving human subjects—students in a new type of educational program typically know they are being experimented upon, though testers could be kept ignorant of whether they were.

---

[13]Researchers call this *regression toward the mean.*

[14]An even more elaborate extension of this design is the *double-blind with crossover.* In this version, sometime during the experiment, treatment is withheld from the experimental group and initiated for the control group. If the medicine works, the experimental group should improve and then return to the initial state; the control group should remain the same and then improve.

There are additional problems that arise in experiments with human subjects. The pretest might affect them in a way that influences the outcome. Measuring the acne in the control group might cause its members to take better care of their acne and thus lead to an underestimation of the effect of the new medicine. In some cases, it is possible to rule out this threat by having two more groups—another experimental and another control group that get only a posttest.[15] If these precautions are taken, the move from association or correlation to cause is even more strongly supported, and the task for the critic even more demanding.

WHAT HAPPENS IF CONTROL IS LIMITED?

A fully controlled experiment is difficult to carry out in many circumstances. Since acne is not life-threatening and the medicine in question is not (we can assume) likely to have serious side effects, we can administer or withhold the medicine with few qualms. But consider the case of mesothelial cancer and asbestos exposure cited earlier. Even if practical problems concerning the length of time between exposure and onset of the cancer could be handled by having a long-term experiment, further obstacles would remain. We could not morally or practically subject a sufficiently large random sample of people to asbestos exposure to determine whether they develop significantly more mesothelial cancer than a control group that is not so exposed. Rather, we have to rely on a so-called natural experiment. Nobody exposed people to asbestos to determine whether it had adverse health effects. But given that this exposure (the "intervention") actually occurred, we can investigate the health consequences. To do so it is necessary to compare the rate of mesothelial cancer among those exposed to those who have not been exposed.

Example 9.8 ***Design of a "Natural" Experiment***

	"Natural" intervention	*Outcome examination*
Experimental Group: Asbestos insulation workers	*Prolonged heavy exposure to asbestos*	*10% incidence of mesothelial cancer*[16]
Control or Comparison Group: People not exposed to asbestos	*No exposure to asbestos*	*1% incidence of mesothelial cancer*[17]

[15]This is sometimes called a *Solomon Four-Group Design.*

[16]International Labour Office, *Asbestos.*

[17]The figure is virtually zero because mesothelial cancer is extremely rare. This is an unusual situation. A more common situation is the one faced by researchers looking into smoking and lung cancer. Nonsmokers do get lung cancer, but at a much lower rate. The importance of cigarettes as a causal factor is indicated by this substantially higher incidence of lung cancer among heavy smokers. Further evidence is provided if we consider a second experimental group of moderate smokers. Their lung cancer rate is intermediate between those of the nonsmokers and the heavy smokers.

Research into mesothelial cancer also differs from the acne case in that members of the experimental group are not randomly selected (though members of the control group might be). As a consequence, it is somewhat more likely that an X-factor exists that is systematically responsible for the outcome—perhaps some other material commonly found in the workplace.

Even so, unless there is some other identifiable factor plausibly attributed to the experimental but not the comparison group, the response of the critic will be relatively weak.

The critic is in an even stronger position when assignment to the experimental and control groups is based on self selection, that is, non-random.[18] Suppose there is a new method of producing reading improvement. Instead of the traditional classroom divided into poor, average, and good readers, a system is introduced for using interactive computer terminals for self-paced, individualized instruction. An appropriate evaluation of the success of this experimental alternative to the traditional method would employ an argument along these lines:

Example 9.9

(1) Exposure to computer-assisted reading instruction is correlated with improvement in reading.

(likely) Computer-assisted reading instruction causes improvement in reading.

Imagine that this inference is backed up by the following research design:

Example 9.10 ***Controlled Experiment Without Random Assignment***

	Initial examination (pretest)	*Intervention*	*Outcome examination (posttest)*
Experimental Group: Self-selected from available subjects	*Reading score on a standardized test—measurement of other factors*	*Computer-assisted instruction in reading*	*Reading score on another version of the standardized test—possible re-measurement of other factors*
Control or Comparison Group: Self-selected from available subjects	*Reading score on a standardized test—measurement of other factors*	*No special instruction—traditional methods*	*Reading score on another version of the standardized test—possible re-measurement of other factors*

[18]This design is sometimes called *quasi-experimental*. It provides more support than a *non*experimental design that merely compares outcome scores and in which the experimental group might have begun with higher scores. It is not as resistant to criticism as the "true" experiment with random assignment.

Given that the experimental group was self-selected and given our knowledge about possible factors associated with willingness to participate, the burden of responsibility shifts to the proponent of the causal generalization who has to rule out the possibility that change is really the result of some other factor, such as intelligence or parental involvement. If further information is available to rule out these factors, the burden shifts back to the critic to produce some additional reasons for rejecting the inference. The more knowledge we have about the case, the better position we are in to confidently accept or reject the inference. The advantage of a fully controlled ("true") experiment is that it allows us to get by without much specific, additional knowledge about the experimental and control groups.

Problems with Generalizing Causal Claims

Even if we can be confident, however, that the intervention is causally related to the outcome in a particular case, we may not be able to generalize as broadly as we would like. A particular drug rehabilitation program that worked for clients in Des Moines, Iowa, might not work for clients in New York City. To generalize to broader contexts, it is necessary not only to have random assignment to experimental and control groups but also random selection from the population to which we want to generalize.[19]

For instance, the program might work not because of its nontraditional structure, but because of the special characteristics of the administering staff. Thus, although a controlled experiment might show that the program had a causal impact in curbing continued drug abuse among those randomly assigned to it, we aren't justified in concluding that programs with that nontraditional structure cause rehabilitation by virtue of their structure. Similarly, in Example 9.9, any claims that the intervention of computer-assisted instruction is the sole cause of the change depends on background assumptions. It is presupposed, for example, that any improvement results solely from computer-assisted instruction without regard to unknown factors. If it produces results only when some other unexpected factor is operating, then clearly we would be mistaken in predicting that it will work in the future, for this unknown factor might no longer be present. For instance, computer-assisted instruction using a TV screen as a terminal might work only in a culture in which there is a great deal of recreational TV watching as well. As long as both the control and experimental groups are drawn from a population that has had massive exposure to TV, we are apt to miss this connection. Of course, the greater our understanding of the factors affecting learning—that is, the better our theories—the better we will be able to determine whether the control and experimental groups are alike in relevant respects. Only by having an adequate theory can we minimize the possibility that there is some X-factor affecting our results.

There is a second way that a theory is assumed when causal inferences are made. The outcome or effect must be measured, and this measurement

[19]If you select from an appropriate population, then your results are said to have "external" validity.

often relies on a theory that justifies the measuring instrument. It is assumed in the computer-assisted instruction example, for instance, that the standardized reading test is a good measure of reading ability.[20] Such background assumptions about instruments or techniques of measurement are commonplace in the natural sciences, as for example when a spectrophotometer—an instrument for measuring the wavelength of emitted light—is routinely used in the course of some laboratory experiment. Unless there is a reason for believing the apparatus is broken, the scientist assumes that the spectrophotometer is accurately measuring wavelength.

These assumptions about the measuring instrument depend on appeal to a theory concerning its operation that is well known and well accepted. And generalizations that rely on experiments employing such instruments presuppose the adequacy of these underlying theories. When doubt can be raised about measuring instruments such as a survey research questionnaire or an IQ test, it may be difficult to justify a generalization based on their use.[21] For example, a Gallup poll conducted during the 2010 congressional debate over finance reform[22] asked: "Do you favor or oppose Congress passing a law that would give the federal government new powers to [A] Regulate large banks and major financial institutions [OR B] Regulate Wall Street banks?" Where half the split sample was given the A option and the other half the B option, the response to the A Form was 46% Favor, 43% Oppose, and 12% No Opinion; and the response to the B Form was 50% Favor, 30% Oppose, and 15% No Opinion. This clearly shows how sensitive questionnaire items are to actual wording. If we wish to use a poll to make generalizations about attitudes concerning government regulation, we need to be clear about the extent to which the poll question provides an adequate measure of the attitude or belief we are trying to measure.

Chapter 10 contains a detailed discussion of empirical theories of the type that are often assumed by causal inferences. Unless a causal generalization is backed up by appropriate controlled experiments and acceptable theories about relevant factors and instruments, it remains open to question. An argument that blithely moves from correlation to cause may always be criticized. The most impressive criticism will at least sketch out how the correlation could be obtained even though there is no causal relationship. It is not enough to merely point out that it is *possible* that the argument fails in the ways mentioned above, especially if the argument in question seems to be based on a controlled experiment.

---

[20]The question whether the instruments used to measure a certain property adequately do so is said to concern *construct validity:* Does an IQ test adequately measure intelligence or a poll question adequately determine whether a person has a certain belief or attitude? A specific procedure or protocol for measurement is often called an *operational definition.*

[21]Further, even if we establish that some intervention actually causes some change in a population, as noted on page 222, we have not yet established whether the amount of change is significant. Suppose, for instance, that the acne medicine we described in example 9.7 reduced skin problems, on average, one-quarter of a skin eruption per person per month. Is that significant enough to take the medicine? Probably not.

[22]http://www.gallup.com/poll/127448/Banking-Reform-Sells-Better-Wall-Street-Mentioned.aspx. April 22, 2010.

Review of Criticisms of Arguments from Correlation to Cause

Most common criticisms for the nonexpert:

- *Joint effect of an underlying cause.* Some underlying factor is shown to be directly or indirectly responsible for the items correlated. That is, the apparent relation is spurious.
- *Wrong direction.* The correlation is shown to support a causal inference in which cause and effect are the opposite of what has been claimed.

Additional criticisms, often requiring actual research:

- *Coincidental correlation.* When it is implausible that there could be a connection between the items correlated, so that the correlation is likely to exist only for a limited period of time, or the correlation is not found in additional studies, the correlation is probably accidental.
- *Genuine but insignificant cause.* Other factors are shown to be of greater importance in producing the effect in question.
- *Causal complexity.* It is shown that factors correlated are not related to each other in a straightforward way. Other factors might be involved, and several criticisms might apply at once.

EXERCISE 9.2 **Supporting Causal Arguments**

1. Select two of the causal claims in Exercise set 9.1, and devise a controlled experiment to test the causal claim.

ARGUMENTS FROM ANALOGY

Arguments from analogy like the one presented at the beginning of this chapter (Example 9.2) typically claim that two kinds of things are alike in many respects and that the first has some further characteristic. It then moves to the claim that the second thing shares this characteristic.

How can an argument from analogy be criticized? Let's begin with a simple example. A U.S. vice president once claimed that he never expressed disagreement with the president's policies because "You don't tackle your own quarterback." His argument rested on an analogy between presidential administrations and football teams, in which the role of the president is parallel to that of quarterback. As with many arguments from analogy, it is left to the audience to think of other ways these two kinds of organizations are similar. We might note, for example, that both "teams" include members who perform specialized tasks and whose actions must be coordinated and that both teams are often required to respond to situations quickly and decisively. We might incorporate such considerations into an argument along the following lines:

Example 9.11

(1) Organizations like presidential administrations and football teams have common characteristics A, B, C. . . .

(2) A football team has the additional characteristic that it functions best if the leader is obeyed uncritically.

(likely) A presidential administration functions best if the leader is obeyed uncritically.

This and other arguments from analogy share the following form:

General Form of an Argument from Analogy

(1) Both Thing 1 and Thing 2 have characteristics A, B, C. . . .

(2) Thing 1 has the additional characteristic Z.

(likely) Thing 2 has characteristic Z.

Note, however, that it is not the number of characteristics the two things have in common that will strengthen an argument from analogy. A stuffed animal and a real animal can have countless trivial similarities—color, shape, size, number and proportion of limbs, and so on. But these similarities don't make it more likely that since the real animal has a brain, the stuffed animal has a brain also. There must be a genuine connection between the shared characteristics and the additional characteristic in question.[23]

We must keep a similar point in mind when we criticize an argument from analogy. It might seem that we can criticize this kind of argument by simply pointing out a large number of ways in which the two objects in question are *not similar*. The problem, however, is that some dissimilarities are relevant but others are not. In attacking the analogy between the presidential administration and a football team, it is surely irrelevant to point out that there are more people in a presidential administration than there are members of a football team. But it *is* relevant to point out that there is no close similarity

---

[23]The nature of this connection is a complicated matter to explore thoroughly. In biology, for example, where analogies are drawn between one biological system and another, certain important characteristics are seen as serving a necessary function in the preservation of the whole. These characteristics can be seen as genuinely connected in our special sense in that they cannot be eliminated without substantially affecting each other. For instance, food intake and locomotion are connected in this way. Roughly speaking, if two systems are of the same type, then any characteristics that serve a necessary function in one will have an equivalent in the other. The football analogy treats both the football team and the presidential administration as instances of a certain kind of system and holds that uncritical obedience to the person serving the leadership function is essential to maintaining the strength and effectiveness of the group.

between winning a football game and some function or purpose of a presidential administration. What makes the latter a relevant criticism but not the former?

Basically, a dissimilarity is relevant if it makes *less likely* the particular similarity asserted in the conclusion of the argument. The fact that a football team has fewer members than the administration doesn't make it less likely that the quarterback and the president should both be uncritically obeyed. But the fact that the administration aims (or *should* aim) at making wise policy decisions rather than winning contests is relevant. Whereas tackling the quarterback is obviously detrimental (normally) to winning football games, criticizing the president (in private) might actually play a helpful role in arriving at wise policy decisions.

Such considerations lead to a counterargument to the argument from analogy in Example 9.11:

Example 9.12

(1) Most activities that aim at making wise policy decisions demand critical consultation.

(2) A presidential administration aims at making wise policy decisions.

(likely) A presidential administration demands critical consultation.

Another approach to criticizing an argument from analogy is to *challenge the premises*. As we have construed such arguments, the premises are of two kinds: one cites similarities between objects and the other attributes a certain additional characteristic to one of the objects. To challenge the first kind of premise, you can simply raise the question of whether the supposed similarities really hold.[24] Concerning the "universe-as-clock" analogy, you might ask whether the universe really has the kind of precise order and uniform motion that a clock has, or whether it is not in fact much more chaotic.

The second kind of premise, which attributes an additional characteristic to one of the objects (as in "You don't tackle your own quarterback"), might also be subject to doubt. Tackling your own quarterback is just the thing to do if the quarterback is running in the wrong direction. In such a criticism, we *accept the basic analogy but maintain that it needs to be extended in another way.* We point out that if the analogy is developed properly, we can justify criticizing the president in certain extreme circumstances. Such criticism not only takes support away from the conclusion of the argument, it can actually make the conclusion unlikely. For if the analogy between the two objects holds, and if it is sometimes justified to tackle your own quarterback, then it is probably justified also for a vice president to criticize the president. This would be the case if the president were working against the proper goals of the administration.

Criticizing a sophisticated analogy may take some ingenuity, particularly when you attempt to point out a relevant dissimilarity between the objects that have been compared. We have not attempted to point out, in the "universe-as-clock" analogy, any relevant dissimilarities that would make

---

[24]Arguments that depend on appropriate similarities that don't hold are sometimes treated as falling prey to the *fallacy of faulty analogy.*

it less likely that the universe had a maker. We leave this as a problem in Exercise 9.2 to test your ingenuity.

Finally, analogies can be usefully employed in the reasoning process even when analogical arguments based on them are open to criticism. Through most of the book, we have concentrated on reconstruction and criticism. We have said little about creating arguments or, more generally, coming up with new and interesting ideas. It is in the discovery or creating phase of reasoning that analogies might be most important. Often we can get insight into new domains by seeing them as analogous to more familiar territory. We might, for instance, get insight into special features of human memory by seeing it as analogous to computer memory, which at least the computer scientist understands well. But this insight might only be a starting point. Even if the analogical argument in itself is unconvincing, the analogy might suggest a new hypothesis or theory about human memory. This hypothesis might not be defensible by appeal to the analogy alone but could be *independently tested* by carefully studying human memory. Because analogies can play this role in creative thinking, the best analogies are often held to be those that are *most fruitful* in generating new, interesting, and unexpected connections.

General Form of an Argument from Analogy

(1) Both Thing 1 and Thing 2 have characteristics A, B, C. . . .

(2) Thing 1 has the additional characteristic Z.

(likely) Thing 2 has characteristic Z.

Ways of Criticizing Analogies

1. Point out dissimilarities that make it unlikely that Thing 2 has the characteristic Z.
2. Challenge the premises:
   a. Question whether the similarities hold.
   b. Cast doubt on whether Thing 1 has characteristic Z.

EXERCISE 9.3

Criticizing Arguments from Analogy

Criticize the following arguments from analogy:

1. A country is like a ship with the president as captain. Just as a captain should be obeyed without question during a storm, the president should be given special powers in periods of crisis.
2. In the politics of confrontation the rules of poker apply. Once you begin to run a bluff, never show the slightest hesitation.
3. The finances of a government are like the finances of a family. A family can't go on spending more than it takes in.

4. In life as in basketball you cheat if you can get away with it—that way you have a better chance of winning.
5. An analogy is like a rented tuxedo. It never quite fits.
6. Spending a great deal of money to provide medical care for the aged is like wasting money on a car. When a car is all worn out, needs a new engine, transmission, and body work, it's just better to junk it. The same goes for people.
7. The vice president is the spare tire on the automobile of government.[25]
8. Just as it is rational for a single individual to maximize his happiness, so it is rational for the entire body of society to maximize the happiness of the whole.
9. The human mind is like a computer. It slows down when it has to confront too many alternatives.
10. The universe is like a clock. Both are systems of moving parts, set in a precise order, balanced, and having repeated, uniform motion. Since clocks have makers, it is likely that the universe had a maker.
11. If a "war on rats" that relies solely on a killing strategy will fail, so will a "war on terrorism" that aims at killing terrorists without removing the "garbage" on which they feed.[26]
12. So, you say, government should be run like a business. Does this mean that many of the programs should fail the way small businesses do?
13. No one knows where the borderline between non-intelligent behavior and intelligent behavior lies; in fact, to suggest that a sharp borderline exists is probably silly. But essential abilities for intelligence are certainly:

    to respond to situations very flexibly;
    to take advantage of fortuitous circumstances;
    to make sense out of ambiguous or contradictory messages;
    to recognize the relative importance of different elements of a situation;
    to find similarities between situations despite differences which may separate them;
    to draw distinctions between situations despite similarities which may link them;
    to synthesize new concepts by taking old concepts and putting them together in new ways;
    to come up with ideas that are novel.

    Here one runs up against a seeming paradox. Computers by their very nature are the most inflexible, desireless, rule-following of beasts. Fast though they may be, they are nonetheless the epitome of unconsciousness. How, then, can intelligent behavior be programmed? Isn't this the most blatant of contradictions in terms? One of the major theses of this book is that it is not a contradiction at all. One of the major purposes of this book is to urge each reader to confront the apparent contradiction head on, to savor it, to turn it

---

[25]Douglas R. Hofstadter, *Gödel, Escher, Bach: An Eternal Golden Braid* (New York: Basic Books, Inc., 1979), 670.

[26]Kenneth Janda, excerpt from a commentary in *Chicago Tribune*, Chicago, Ill; July 4, 2004, p. 9. (The full essay appears in Chapter 11, Exercise 11.1 of this book.)

over, to take it apart, to wallow in it, so that in the end the reader might emerge with new insights into the seemingly unbreachable gulf between the formal and the informal, the animate and the inanimate, the flexible and the inflexible.

This is what Artificial Intelligence (AI) research is all about. And the strange flavor of AI work is that people try to put together long sets of rules in strict formalisms which tell inflexible machines how to be flexible.

What sorts of "rules" could possibly capture all of what we think of as intelligent behavior, however? Certainly there must be rules on all sorts of different levels. There must be many "just plain" rules. There must be "metarules" to modify the "just plain" rules, then "meta-metarules" to modify the metarules, and so on. The flexibility of intelligence comes from the enormous number of different rules and levels of rules. The reason that so many rules on so many different levels must exist is that in life, a creature is faced with millions of situations of completely different types. In some situations, there are stereotyped responses which require "just plain" rules. Some situations are mixtures of stereotyped situations—thus they require rules for deciding which of the "just plain" rules to apply. Some situations cannot be classified—thus there must exist rules for inventing new rules . . . and on and on. Without doubt, Strange Loops involving rules that change themselves, directly or indirectly, are at the core of intelligence. Sometimes the complexity of our minds seems so overwhelming that one feels that there can be no solution to the problem of understanding intelligence—that it is wrong to think that rules of any sort govern a creature's behavior even if one takes "rule" in the multilevel sense described above.[27]

CONVERGENT ARGUMENTS

Simple *convergent* arguments are ones in which independent reasons are given for a conclusion, each providing some support. In Chapter 1 we contrasted convergent arguments to *linked* arguments, in which the premises, combined together, support the conclusion, rather than each supporting it independently. The deductive arguments we have studied are linked arguments. The difference between linked and convergent arguments can be seen more clearly by considering the following examples:

Example 9.13

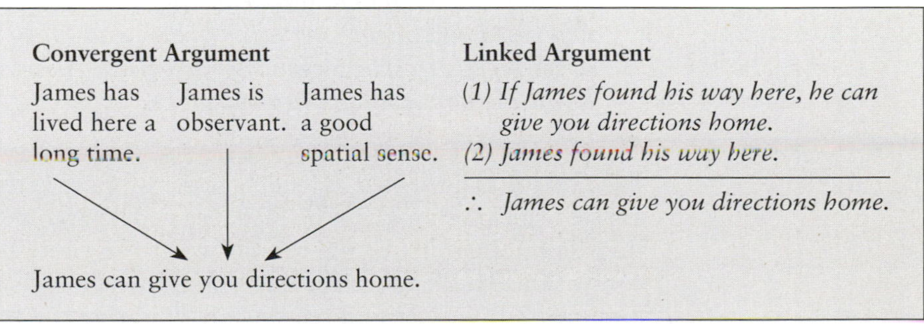

Convergent Argument
James has lived here a long time.
James is observant.
James has a good spatial sense.
James can give you directions home.
Linked Argument
(1) If James found his way here, he can give you directions home.
(2) James found his way here.
∴ James can give you directions home.

[27]From Douglas R Hofstadter, *Gödel, Escher, Bach: An Eternal Golden Braid*. Copyright ©1979 by Basic Books, Inc., Publishers. Reprinted by permission of the publisher.

In the linked argument, the premise *If James found his way here, he can give you directions home* doesn't support the conclusion by itself, but when combined with *James found his way here*, it does. By contrast, each of the premises in the convergent argument supports the conclusion.

Are convergent arguments deductive or not? Initially, there seems to be a key difference between deductive and convergent arguments: In a deductively valid argument, the premises support the conclusion in a way that makes it impossible for the premises to be true and the conclusion false. If a deductive argument such as the linked one above adequately supports its conclusion (that James can give you directions home), then no counter-considerations, such as James now being in a disoriented state, can outweigh the truth of this conclusion without making one of the supporting premises false. Convergent arguments appear to be different, in that the pro-considerations can all be granted as true but outweighed by counter-considerations. For example, the fact that James is now disoriented (maybe he has been misled about which direction he is facing) could make the conclusion false in Example 9.14 even though all the premises are true.

In reply to the claim that convergent arguments are nondeductive, someone could suggest that there is an implicit premise linking the stated premises to the conclusion, such as "If James has lived here a long time, is observant, and has a good spatial sense, then he can give you directions home." Once this premise is added, then if a counter-consideration makes the conclusion false, it also makes this linking premise false. This sort of move can always be used to make an argument deductive. After discussing a few more examples we will ask what is gained or lost by adding a linking premise to make convergent arguments deductive, as opposed to simply leaving them as they stand.

A common kind of convergent argument gives several independent reasons why we should or shouldn't do something. For example, Chapter 2 presented an argument in which three separate reasons were given against legalizing physician-assisted suicide:

Example 9.14 *Legalizing physician-assisted suicide would lead to (1) helping disabled people die who are not terminally ill, (2) helping people die who are depressed and might later want to live, and (3) helping people die in order merely to save on medical expenses. These are all reasons against legalizing physician-assisted suicide.*

Each reason is presented as lending some support to the conclusion: physician-assisted suicide should not be made legal. The argument leaves open the question of whether any of the reasons is strong enough by itself to support its conclusion. This leads to the question: How should we evaluate a convergent argument? If we can find reasons for doubting the premises, are we justified in rejecting the conclusion? If we can give reasons against the conclusion, how damaging is this to the argument?

Representation of Example 9.14

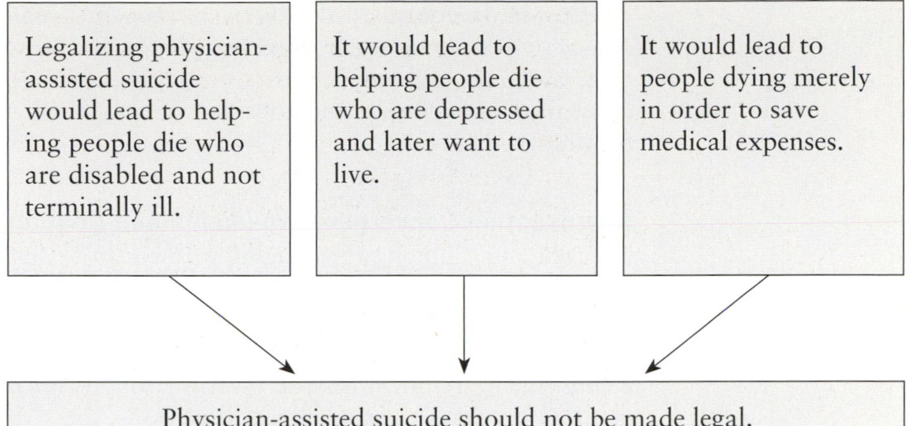

Evaluation of Convergent versus Deductive Arguments Evaluating convergent arguments is different from evaluating typical deductive arguments in two important ways. First, to criticize a convergent argument we may *either* cast doubt on the premises *or* raise counter-considerations against the conclusion. When we criticize Example 9.14, one strategy would be to challenge the first and second premises by suggesting that restrictions against helping people die who are merely disabled or depressed could be built into the legislation that would permit physician-assisted suicide. Raising this point is no different from attacking the premises of a deductive argument. However, finding grounds for rejecting *some* premise(s) in a convergent argument isn't necessarily grounds for rejecting the entire argument. The remaining premise(s) might be judged strong enough to support the conclusion.

In addition to attacking the premises, it would also be appropriate to attack the conclusion—to give reasons in favor of legalizing physician-assisted suicide. We could point out that as long as physician-assisted suicide is kept illegal, many patients will go through a long period of suffering who would really rather die and that for many of them this preference for dying is reasonable, not the result of temporary depression. We could claim that even if all three reasons in Example 9.14 are acknowledged, the benefit of preventing suffering is more important.

Attacking the conclusion, then, is acceptable when criticizing convergent arguments but not when criticizing deductive arguments. This reflects a key difference between these two kinds of arguments. If we can't find grounds for rejecting at least one premise of a deductive argument, we are compelled to accept the conclusion. By contrast, we could reject the conclusion of a convergent argument (because of counter-considerations), even if we accepted all the premises.

Another way in which convergent arguments are evaluated differently is in judging how strong the connection is between the premises and the conclusion. In contrast to deductive arguments, judging the strength of this connection is not a matter of seeing whether the argument fits a correct pattern. Rather, it is simply a matter of judging the weight of considerations in favor of the conclusion and considerations against. There is no general rule for doing this.

Representing Convergent Arguments and Counter-Considerations This metaphor of "judging the weight" of pros and cons suggests a way of diagramming convergent arguments and criticisms. We might think of setting out the pros on one side of a scale (or teeter-totter) and setting the cons on the other side. The existence of considerations that count against a conclusion of a convergent argument isn't necessarily grounds for rejecting the entire argument. Oftentimes in an argumentative essay, the writer will actually lay out an argument and its opposition and claim that the considerations on one side outweigh those on the other. This same diagramming device can be used to illustrate a convergent argument and counter-consideration.

Example 9.15

Dropouts Ought to Repay Part of Grant[28]

Requiring college dropouts to repay a portion of a federal grant that allowed them to go to college makes sense.

Pell grants for low-income students have, until now, been handed out with no strings attached. The Department of Education has proposed requiring that students who don't finish their education give back a modest amount of their awards. Currently, the maximum grants are $3,125 an academic year.

The amount dropouts would have to repay is relatively small. Only students who didn't complete at least 60 percent of the academic term would be expected to return any money. The student wouldn't have to pay back tuition, nor even the full amount awarded beyond the tuition cost.

For instance, take a student given a grant of $1,500 for a college term. If tuition were $1,000 for that term, that amount would be subtracted from the total, leaving $500. If the student completed half the college term before dropping out, the amount is pro-rated to $250. Then, students are asked to pay back half that amount, or $125. That is hardly an onerous sum, even for a low-income student, considering how much the government has invested in the dropout's education.

But the symbolism is appropriate. Pell grants shouldn't be considered a free lunch,

[28]Editorial, *Omaha World-Herald*, November 6, 1999. Reprinted by permission.

to be accepted or discarded frivolously. They should be used by low-income students to better themselves, to gain the education they need to make a better life and contribute to society.

Critics of the new federal rule have suggested that the threat of repayment could keep some deprived teenagers from using the Pell grants to go to college. If the payback provision is explained properly and if the students want an education, that shouldn't be a problem.

The rule should encourage the wise use of the Pell funds and underline the importance of working hard to stay in college.

Pell grants have enabled many people to go to college and graduate to become productive members of the workforce. It doesn't seem likely that the minimal repayment requirement being instituted by the Department of Education would have discouraged many of them. Neither should it hurt grant recipients in the future.

It is a good way to emphasize that students who take the grants have responsibilities as well as privileges.

Diagram of Convergent Argument with a Counter-Consideration (from Example 9.15)

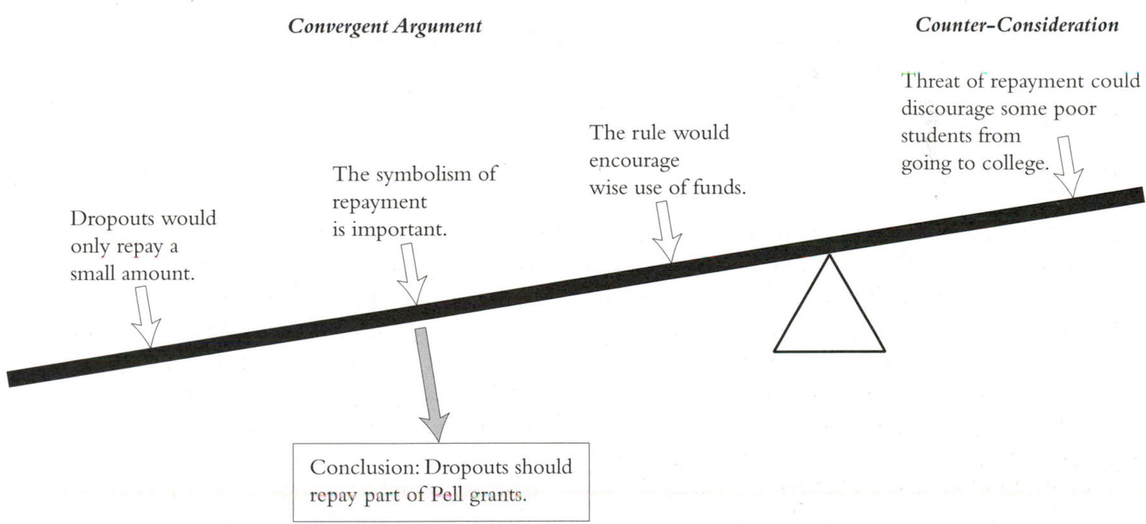

We can return now to the question of what is gained by interpreting an argument as convergent as opposed to adding a linking if–then premise to make it deductive. Does a deductive interpretation invite counter-considerations? A deductivist could argue that any counter-considerations that are brought against the conclusion of a convergent argument can also be brought against the if–then premise of the deductive version. In Example 9.14, the claim that prevention of suffering outweighs the drawbacks of assisted suicide could be given as a reason against an implicit premise: *If assisted suicide has the three disadvantages that are listed, then it should not be made legal.* And the counter-consideration in Example 9.15—the claim that the threat of repayment could discourage some poor students from going to college—could be given as a reason against an implicit premise in the deductive version of the argument: *If a requirement to repay Pell grants has these three advantages, then repayment should be required.*

The deductive reconstruction leaves room for these kinds of counter-considerations as criticisms, but it doesn't clearly invite them. The convergent approach sets out an issue as being a matter of pros versus cons: Here are some reasons in favor, now what are some reasons against? Which are stronger? The convergent approach more clearly invites counter-considerations, and this is an advantage. Furthermore, the convergent approach provides a way of picturing the two sides of an argument that are presented in an essay such as 9.15, and this two-sided approach is common in argumentative writing.

This advantage held by the convergent approach of inviting counter-considerations is even more apparent if we remember how difficult it was for the deductive approach to handle arguments such as: *We should lower the speed limit, because if we don't, there will be more highway deaths.* As was pointed out in the discussion in Chapter 4, pp. 102–3, a deductive reconstruction would add the premise: *There shouldn't be more highway deaths.* But this can't be taken to mean simply that *more highway deaths would be undesirable.* We have to construe this premise as asserting *that the disadvantage of highway deaths outweighs any good that would result from keeping the speed limit at its present level.* This interpretation is clearly not a natural one, so it is a disadvantage of the deductive approach that it does not naturally prompt us to make a kind of criticism that is clearly relevant, that is pointing to advantages of keeping the speed limit where it is.

On the other hand, the deductive approach has the advantage of clearly raising the question of whether the considerations advanced in the premises of an argument are supposed to be compelling. We suggest that the convergent approach is often better for *interpreting* what is being offered by the arguer(s) in the early stages of a discussion; while the deductive approach is better in the later stages, after the pros and cons are all on the table, and the critic is trying to decide finally what to believe. We are presenting the convergent approach in addition to the deductive approach that was laid out in detail in Chapters 2 through 6, so that you will have both of these critical tools available to you.

Applying Criticism to Convergent Arguments with Counter-Considerations: A Four-Step Process The convergent approach is especially useful when you deal with complex exchanges or debates in which a variety of considerations, both pro and con, support or undermine a certain conclusion. Suppose you are listening to a forum on the topic of capital punishment. You might arrange the considerations you have heard as a convergent argument with counter-considerations along these lines:

Step 1: Presenting the Convergent Argument with Counter-Considerations

Convergent Argument

Counter-Considerations

Capital punishment is a deterrent to murder.

Capital punishment guarantees that murderers are permanently off the streets.

Capital punishment leads to innocent persons being killed—as recent evidence from Illinois shows.

Capital punishment desensitizes society to killing.

Conclusion: Capital punishment should be maintained.

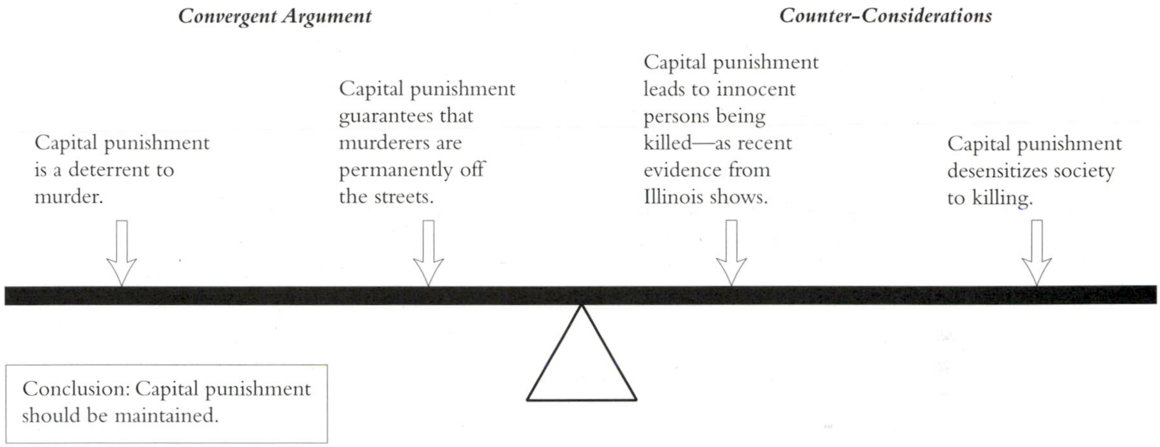

We can assess such a convergent argument through a four-step process: First, consider whether to add further considerations. When you are criticizing an argument presented by someone else, these additional considerations are typically counter-considerations, but if you are deciding what to ultimately believe about an issue you might add pro-considerations as well. For example, the initial representation of the capital punishment argument can be transformed into the Step 1 representation by adding some ethical considerations on both sides: just retribution and cruelty.

Step 2: Adding Further Considerations

Convergent Argument

Counter-Considerations

Capital punishment is a deterrent to murder.

Capital punishment guarantees that murderers are permanently off the streets.

Capital punishment provides just retribution for murder—an "eye for an eye."

Capital punishment leads to innocent persons being killed—as recent evidence from Illinois shows.

Capital punishment desensitizes society to killing.

Capital punishment is cruel.

Conclusion: Capital punishment should be maintained.

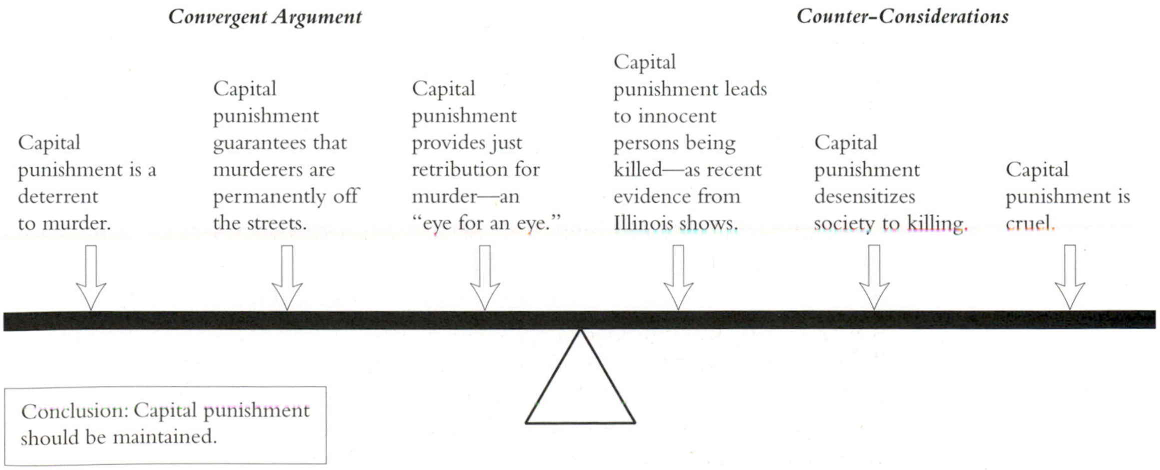

Once we have a more complete list of considerations, we should determine if the premises in support of the conclusion (or the counter-considerations) are true or at least acceptable. You might point out, for example, that it is not at all clear that capital punishment is a better deterrent than life imprisonment. States with comparable demographics, some of which have capital punishment and some of which do not, don't vary significantly in their murder rates.

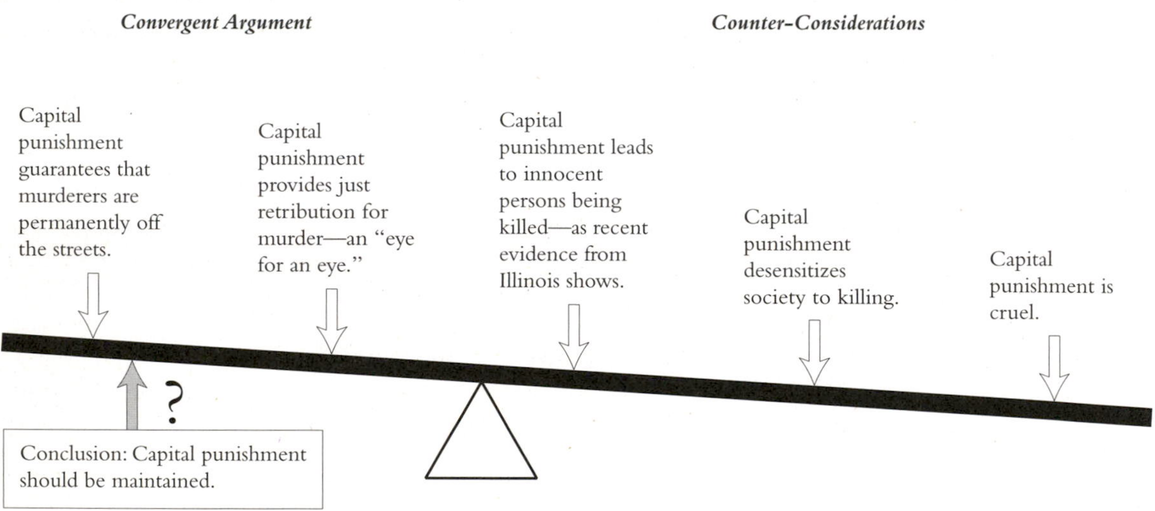
Step 3: Eliminating Doubtful Considerations
Convergent Argument
Counter-Considerations
Capital punishment guarantees that murderers are permanently off the streets.
Capital punishment provides just retribution for murder—an "eye for an eye."
Capital punishment leads to innocent persons being killed—as recent evidence from Illinois shows.
Capital punishment desensitizes society to killing.
Capital punishment is cruel.
?
Conclusion: Capital punishment should be maintained.

Just eliminating that pro-consideration doesn't alone tip the scales away from capital punishment. We can't just count up the considerations on either side and say that we have two pro-considerations and three counter-considerations. What is important is how weighty the considerations are. We could blunt the pro-considerations by maintaining that although *capital punishment guarantees that murderers are permanently off the street*, this consideration is relatively insignificant because life without the possibility of parole does likewise or, on the other side, even though *capital punishment has*, *in the past, led to innocent persons being killed,* new forensic tests such as DNA matching at trial has significantly reduced the likelihood of such errors in the future. Similarly, even if we admit that *capital punishment desensitizes society to killing,* slightly, this factor is insignificant compared to the effect of violence on TV and in films.

Step 4: Blunting or Promoting Considerations

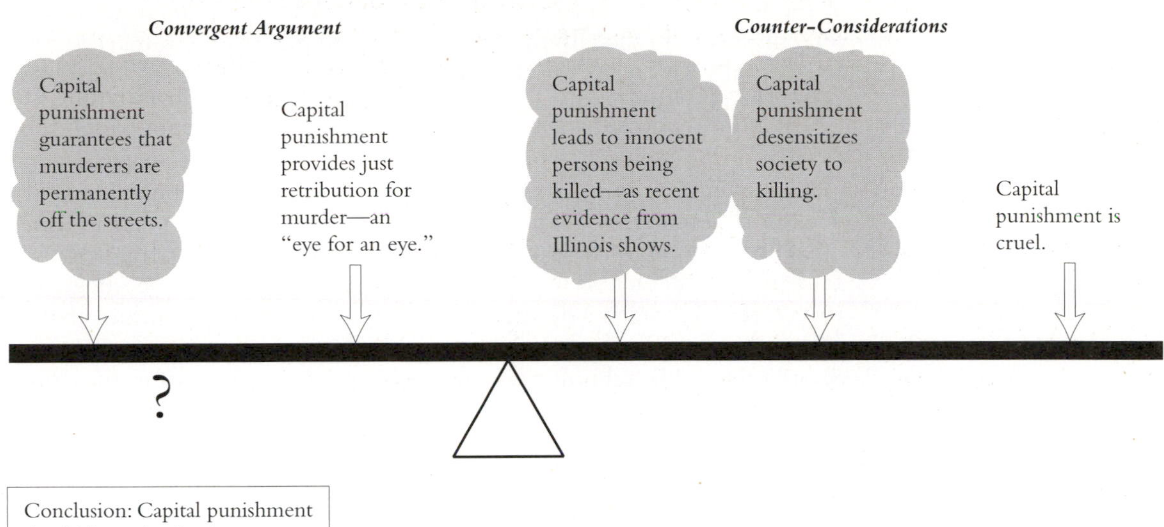
Convergent Argument
Counter-Considerations
Capital punishment guarantees that murderers are permanently off the streets.
Capital punishment provides just retribution for murder—an "eye for an eye."
Capital punishment leads to innocent persons being killed—as recent evidence from Illinois shows.
Capital punishment desensitizes society to killing.
Capital punishment is cruel.
?
Conclusion: Capital punishment should be maintained.

Such a pattern of criticisms leaves us with two major considerations to weigh against each other: the claim of just retribution versus the claim of cruelty of punishment. Now we must consider whether either or both of these claims is acceptable, and if both are, we have to decide which is more important or weighty. There is no set of general rules that will tell you how to weigh the remaining considerations. Indeed, the weighing might be different in different contexts. But the three-step process of criticism we have advanced in this section has focused attention on the most important elements to be ultimately weighed.[29] The following exercises will provide some practice in using this convergent approach.

Criticizing Convergent Arguments

1. Present the initial convergent argument and counter-considerations.
2. Add further considerations.
3. Eliminate doubtful considerations.
4. Blunt or promote considerations.

---

[29]The problem of how to weigh them is no different than the problem the deductivist faces in deciding whether to accept an *if–then* premise that connects the pro-consideration to the conclusion. A simple deductive reconstruction of the argument would be

(1) If capital punishment provides just retribution, then capital punishment should be maintained.
(2) Capital punishment provides just retribution.

∴ *Capital punishment should be maintained.*

EXERCISE 9.4

Reconstructing and Criticizing Convergent Arguments

All of the following passages contain arguments that could be interpreted as convergent. Diagram them in the manner of Example 9.15. Arrange the premises horizontally, and write the conclusion beneath the premises. If the passage contains counter-considerations, include them in the diagram on the right side of a scale, as in Example 9.17. Then write an evaluation of each argument, assessing individual premises as well as the relative weight of the pros and cons using the four-step process discussed at the end of the section.

1. Teaching courses on the web is a bad idea. Students don't experience face-to-face interaction with professors, there aren't adequate safeguards to ensure that students do their own work, and many institutions that offer online courses have instructors of poor quality.
2. Should the public schools maintain zero-tolerance policies for infractions such as fighting and bringing a weapon to school? There are two good reasons against such policies. First, a mild, borderline infraction such as bringing a table knife in a lunchsack or punching a classmate on the shoulder could result in suspension—a much more severe penalty than is deserved. Second, zero tolerance is unrealistic given the lack of maturity of school-age children. It must be granted that a zero-tolerance policy would be a better deterrent, but that's not enough to outweigh these two potential injustices.
3. Many people who were adopted as children would like to know the identity of their birth parents. But this benefit must be weighed against other considerations before we decide to give adoptees the legal right to this information. Would fewer women be willing to go through with a pregnancy and put their babies up for adoption if they don't have the option of remaining anonymous? Probably so. Furthermore, parents who adopt might prefer that their adopted children focus on them as their full-fledged parents, rather than dividing their concern between their adopted parents and their birth parents.
4. The plea bargaining passage in Chapter 1, page 9, of this book.
5. A convergent argument from an editorial or column from a newspaper or website.

Review: Types of Nondeductive Arguments

Inductive

Sampling Argument *Particular-to-general argument*	(1) In studies of 5,000 people, those who had more exposure to environmental smoke had a higher frequency of lung cancer. ——— (likely) People who have more exposure to environmental smoke generally have a higher frequency of lung cancer.
Argument with Statistical Premises *General-to-particular argument*	(1) Most long-time, heavy smokers suffer from smoking-related health problems. (2) Bruce is a long-time, heavy smoker. ——— (likely) Bruce will suffer from smoking-related health problems.
Causal Argument	(1) Exposure to computer-assisted reading instruction is correlated with improvement in reading. ——— (likely) Computer-assisted reading instruction causes improvement in reading.
Argument from Analogy	The presidential team is like a football team.You don't tackle your own quarterback. If you are in the administration, you don't challenge the president.
Convergent Argument *multiple independent premises supporting a conclusion*	Legalizing physician-assisted suicide would lead to helping people die who are disabled and not terminally ill. It would lead to helping people die who are depressed and later want to live. It would lead to people dying merely in order to save medical expenses. ↓ Physician-assisted suicide should not be made legal.

CHAPTER 10

Explanation and the Criticism of Theories

In this chapter, we focus on how to evaluate theories.[1] Since the premise of an argument is sometimes a theoretical statement, we are continuing our account of how to evaluate different kinds of premises by discussing how to evaluate theories. But the techniques for evaluating theories can be applied not only when a theory is used as premise in an argument to persuade you, but also when a theory is used to explain to you why something happens. In fact, even to evaluate a theory used in an argument to persuade, it is necessary to examine how well the theory can perform this role of explanation.

To better understand the distinction between these two ways a theory might be used—to persuade or to explain—consider the following examples. First, suppose you and a friend are discussing the relationship of a couple, Sarah and Tom. The point at issue is who has more decision-making power. Your friend might draw on a sociological theory to *persuade* you that Sarah has more power, by making the following argument:[2]

---

[1]Specifically, we address empirical theories, which are used to explain or predict regularities (patterns of events) in the observable world. Chapter 7 discussed conceptual theories, which explain the meaning of concepts.

[2]Adapted from *Marriage and Families: Making Choices and Facing Change* by Mary Ann Lamanna and Agnes Riedmann.

Example 10.1 ***Theory Used as a Premise in an Argument***

Theory Statement

(1) The partner who needs the other partner least has more decision-making power in a marriage.

(2) Sarah needs Tom less than he needs her.

∴ Sarah has more decision-making power than Tom in their marriage.

In Example 10.1, the first premise expresses a theory, or at least a portion of a theory. To decide whether to accept the argument's conclusion, you would want to evaluate this theory.

Consider now a second kind of situation—one in which this same theory about power in marriage is used not to persuade but rather to explain. Suppose you and your friend are both well aware that Sarah has more decision-making power than Tom. What is at issue is not *whether* Sarah has more power, but *why*. Your friend notes that Sarah and Tom need all the money they earn to support their lifestyle, and that Sarah earns more and is more secure in her job than Tom. That is why Sarah has more decision-making power than Tom and why higher-earning partners like her generally have more power than their spouses. The partner who needs the other least is the one who has the most power. You wonder whether this really is the reason.

We could view the structure of this explanation in the following way:

Example 10.2 ***Theory Used to Explain a Pattern of Behavior***

Theory Statement — *The marriage partner who needs the other least has more decision-making power.*

Regularity Being Explained — *Generally, when a couple depends more on one partner's earnings, that partner makes more decisions.*

Particular Events Being Explained — *Sarah, who makes more money than Tom, also makes more decisions in the marriage than Tom.*

In Chapter 8, we discussed the relationship between empirical generalizations (that is, statements of regularity) and observation of particular events such as those in the lower two levels of Example 10.2. The observation of a representative sample of particular couples, their income pattern, and their decision-making behavior, could inductively support the generalization that when a couple depends more on one partner's earnings, that partner makes more decisions. In this chapter, we turn to the relationship between regularities and theories, or between statements such as the middle one in Example 10.2 and the top one.

Essentially, an empirical theory is judged by how well it explains or predicts regularities—patterns of behavior such as the one claimed to occur in Example 10.2. Even when a theoretical statement occurs as a premise of an argument rather than in an explanatory passage, it must be evaluated in terms of how well it would succeed in predicting and explaining regularities. In order to evaluate the theory that is used as a premise in Example 10.1—that the partner with less need has more power—it would be necessary to judge how well this theory can perform in explaining patterns of behavior such as the one stated in Example 10.2 (if it is a pattern that does in fact occur). It is for this reason that this chapter focuses on the explanatory role of theories. We will return in Chapter 11 to the role of theories as premises of arguments.

"THAT'S *JUST* A THEORY"

Before we discuss how to identify and evaluate theories, we should address a common misconception about theories. It is sometimes believed that simply to identify a statement as a theory is grounds for rejecting it. This view is expressed when someone dismisses a claim by saying, "That's just a theory." In fact, some theories are well supported by evidence and are deserving of belief, while other theories are not. It must be admitted that the evidence for theories is less direct and less conclusive than is the evidence for particular, concrete assertions about the world. But it does not follow that no theory deserves belief; and it certainly does not follow that all theories are equally doubtful.

Consider for example some theories that have been used to explain the spread of disease. At one time in history, people explained the onset of disease by appeal to an act of God or correlatively to the moral fault of those who became sick.[3] We might call these the Divine Intervention or Moral Fault Theories of disease. Most of us today embrace another theory—the Germ Theory—of disease (at least for a wide variety of diseases). According to this theory, infectious disease symptoms are typically caused by the presence of large numbers of germs (now including those called viruses, bacteria, fungi,

---

[3]This contrast assumes a simple connection between divine judgment of moral fault and divine punishment: disease. A more elaborate version of the Divine Retribution Theory might be compatible with the Germ Theory of disease. God, it could be said, uses natural means, germs, for His purposes.

and prions). Such a theory allows us to explain why lack of hygiene leads to the spread of disease: lack of hygiene promotes the transmission of germs from one person to another.

If all theories were to be dismissed simply because they were theories, we would have to be equally doubtful of the Germ Theory and the Moral Fault Theory of disease. Clearly, this is not justified. Some theories are more deserving of belief; some are less so. Our aim is to improve your ability to identify and evaluate theories. Criticism of technical theories that are well developed by scientific research usually requires special expertise or at least sustained efforts that few of us have the ability to marshal. Nevertheless, we are regaled on a regular basis by less-well-developed theories about which we possess sufficient expertise or knowledge. Even though this chapter will use theories of this sort as examples, the approach we present could be used to understand and evaluate more sophisticated theories as well.

PICKING OUT THEORIES

Actual passages containing theories are not always easy to interpret. When presented with passages such as Example 10.3, in which a theory is used to provide explanation, the general tactic for identifying theory statements is to determine *what is explained* and *what does the explaining*. When this is difficult, it is helpful to look for *indicator words*. Some common words to look for are *because, accounts for*, or simply *explains*. Here is an example.

Example 10.3 *The political boss and his political machine flourished in cities like Chicago even after the age of reform in the early part of this [20th] century, because political patronage served to integrate new immigrants into American life. After the New Deal programs of the 1930s, this function was less important, and the political boss and his machine gradually died out though vestiges remained until the end of the century.*[4]

Here the word *because* indicates that what precedes it is explained by what follows it. The success of the institution of political bossism in American cities is explained by the theory that political bosses served an essential function in maintaining the social life of the country, namely, introducing and socializing new members.

As we noted in Chapter 2, expressions such as *because* and *for the reason that* can sometimes indicate the premise of an argument. We are now pointing out that these same expressions—*because* and *for the reason that*—can also indicate an explanation. The difference is that the premise of an argument is presented to *convince* someone of a conclusion. By contrast, an explanation is presented not to convince the audience of something, but rather to say *why* it happened. For example, consider the statement *Alice quit going out with Miguel, because he is always late*. This would not be offered to convince the listener that Alice quit going out with Miguel, but rather to say *why* this occurred.

---

[4]Adapted from Robert Merton, *Social Theory and Social Structure* (Free Press: New York, 1968), 130–131.

Another common device for calling attention to theories is the explicit use of the *why?* question. The answer to the question presents a theory.

Example 10.4 *Why did the political bosses continue to have power in U.S. cities long after the Progressive Era that brought reform to many other aspects of U.S. government? Quite simply, they served an essential function in bringing new immigrants into the social life of the country in a period that had no other social welfare programs.*

In addition to this main strategy of seeing what statement does the explaining, three further aids can be used for identifying theories:

Theories Have Broader Scope We can sometimes identify a theory by noting that it is capable of providing an explanation for more than one pattern or regularity. The Germ Theory accounts for the transmission of such diverse diseases as syphilis, stomach flu, leprosy, athlete's foot, and mad-cow disease. Newton's laws (theory) of motion helped explain phenomena as disparate as the movement of the planets, the falling of objects like apples, the trajectory of cannonballs, and the swing of clock pendulums. Such theories have especially wide scope; they explain a wide range of phenomena. This feature helps us identify the theory in the following passage.

Example 10.5 *People living alone are more likely to commit suicide than those living with others. The norms and rules imposed on us by others give us a sense of purpose and belonging. If norms and rules are absent, our appetites are unrestricted and our goals are unattainable, leading to disillusionment and self-destructive urges. This also explains why people who practice religions like Catholicism or Orthodox Judaism, which have a more extensive and well-defined system of rules have a lower suicide rate than those of Protestant faiths such as Lutheranism, whose rules and norms are less-clearly defined.*[5]

Here the theory that a system rules and norms protects a person from self-destructive urges can be identified by virtue of its scope. It applies to both the suicide rate of people living alone and to the suicide rate of members of certain religions. Further, such a theory of social support would apply, presumably, not merely to suicide but to a variety of other psychological conditions.

Theories Are More Remote from Evidence Germs (bacteria, viruses, fungi, and prions) are unobservable to the unaided senses, while the symptoms—high fever, headache, vomiting, and so on—that are explained by the Germ Theory can be observed directly. This is a natural consequence of the fact that theories are constructed to explain events or processes whose occurrence is puzzling to us; we theorize in the first place by trying to get at what is "behind" the apparent symptoms or effects, since their explanation is not evident on the surface. One

---

[5]Loosely based on ideas articulated in Emile Durkheim's classic, *Le Suicide* first published in 1897. See the English translation Suicide: A study in Sociology, edited by George Simpson, translated by John Spaulding and George Simpson, (New York, New York: Free Press, 1951).

reason theories can have broader scope than what they explain is that they use concepts less closely tied to observation or other concrete,[6] direct evidence and involve making inferences. In Example 10.5, a system of rules and norms is more remote from direct evidence than instances of committing suicide, living alone, or practicing Protestantism (although in any given case it might be difficult to determine whether a death was a suicide or if the person was a Protestant). Even the concept of self-destructive urges might be somewhat more remote from direct evidence if we allow for the possibility of urges that are not consciously felt.

It is often difficult to determine whether one concept is more remote from direct evidence than another, but the flavor of this distinction can be illustrated by some cases. Imagine a person interested in voting behavior who is somehow able to watch Calvin's activities on election day. This observer might describe Calvin's behavior in a number of ways.

Example 10.6

(1) The movement of Calvin's hand brought it about that the ballot was marked.

(2) Calvin cast a ballot.

(3) Calvin voted for his candidate.

(4) Calvin expressed his faith in the political process.

(5) Calvin exercised his political rights.

(6) Calvin overcame his political alienation.

Such a list is arranged according to proximity to direct evidence. The most observable (directly evidential) statement is the first. The last statement is the most remote from direct evidence. One way of characterizing this range is to say that, as the statements become increasingly remote from direct evidence, they become more prone to error. Movement of the hand is readily detectable (at least to our well-placed observer). Casting a ballot might not be so readily apparent. After all, Calvin could be testing the marking equipment. Even if he is casting his ballot, he might not be voting, if by vote we mean "cast a ballot that is officially counted, for the person he intended." After all, if Calvin marked his ballot incorrectly or some corrupt official discarded it, he didn't really vote for his candidate.

As we move even further down the list, the possibility of error or disagreement among similarly placed observers increases. More remote—or, as they are sometimes called, more "theoretical"—concepts are more subject to dispute. We could probably get agreement about whether Calvin was expressing faith in the political process (although this might be complicated) more readily than whether he overcame alienation. A person's testimony about his faith in the process would count as evidence of the former, but a person might not be cognizant of his alienation.

---

[6]Some might prefer to mark this distinction by contrasting more abstract or theoretical concepts with more concrete or more observational ones.

Notice as well that as we move down the list, the concepts cover an increasing variety of cases. There are ways of casting a ballot other than marking it (we could use a voting machine or punch card). And there are ways of voting other than using a ballot (voice voting or raising hands), other ways of expressing faith in the political process (working on a transition team), other ways of exercising political rights (picketing), and other ways of overcoming political alienation (working with a group to change a party platform). The use of concepts more remote from direct evidence enables statements of a theory to have a broader scope.

Theories Use Specialized or Technical Language Another clue we can use in identifying theory-statements is the use of specialized, technical or "theoretical" language. In creating or broadening a theory we often need to coin new terms to describe the range of objects, processes, or events we are grouping under the theory. This is most conspicuous in the natural sciences, where new terms are often created or old ones more precisely specified. Such terms are needed because no expression in the existing language has the scope required or because the language community has not developed a term for something so remote from direct evidence. It is sometimes possible to identify elements in the theory by finding such language.

Example 10.7 *Automobile engine blocks are apt to crack in very cold weather unless antifreeze is added to the radiator fluid. A block cracks when the pressure exerted by expanded ice exceeds the ultimate tensile strength of the metal out of which it is constructed. Antifreeze (usually ethylene glycol) freezes at much lower temperatures than water.*

In Example 10.7, the cracking of engine blocks is explained by a theory of sorts. The theory uses technical or "theoretical" expressions, such as tensile strength and ethylene glycol, whereas what it explains is characterized by more everyday terms, such as engine block, cold weather, and antifreeze, which are less remote from observational evidence. Even here, however, the term engine block is more specialized and technical than the expression cold weather.

Identifying Theories

Main Strategy: Look for statements that explain why regularities occur. (Indicator words such as "why," "because," "explains," "accounts for" can help.)

Additional Features That Help Identify Theories

1. Theories typically have a *broader scope* than that which they explain; many regularities can be explained by the same theory.
2. Theories are more *remote from direct evidence* than the events or processes they can be used to explain.
3. Theories commonly use *specialized or technical language.*

Levels of Explanation Thus far we have looked at the way theories can explain patterns or regularities. But we are often interested in explaining particular conditions. For example, why has John, in particular, remained a bachelor? Sometimes we answer a question like this by offering an *explanatory argument*[7] of general-to-particular inductive form. The purpose of such an argument is to show that the particular event follows from a more general pattern of events. Suppose you have a friend John who has remained a bachelor. We might attempt to explain John's condition by considering events in his childhood and how they fit into a more general pattern of regularities concerning families:

Example 10.8

Regularity (1) *Most men who have dominating mothers and weak fathers remain bachelors.*

Observed Data (2) *John had a dominating mother and a weak father.*

(likely) John is a bachelor.

Such an explanatory argument helps us understand John's condition by treating it as an instance of a general pattern. But we can also ask why this general pattern exists.

We might explain why the regularity in question occurs by appeal to some psychological theory. Sigmund Freud, for instance, might be taken as suggesting that strong mothers and weak fathers produce a situation in which the male child's attraction to his mother is not fully resolved, resulting in a condition in which the child grows up having difficulties relating to women.[8] This theory purports to explain why a certain family situation is likely to produce an adult who does not marry. This regularity in turn would help us understand and explain particular features of the world, such as why John is a bachelor.

This rough version of Freudian theory can be formulated more fully:

Example 10.9

(T_1) *All male children have a strong, positive emotional attachment to their mothers and a hostile reaction to their fathers.* (This is called the Oedipus complex.)

(T_2) *The Oedipus complex produces anxiety in male children.*

---

[7]As indicated earlier, an explanatory argument differs from a deductive argument aimed at persuasion in that the conclusion is not taken to be in doubt. The person offering the argument assumes that the audience does not need to be persuaded that the conclusion is true. Rather, the argument is offered to explain why the state of affairs expressed in the conclusion exists.

[8]Sigmund Freud (1856–1939), Austrian neurologist and founder of psychoanalysis, has suggested such an explanation with his theory of the Oedipus complex.

(T_3) *In normal personality development, the male child identifies with his father.* (This identification reduces the anxiety caused by the Oedipus complex and allows the child to develop satisfactory relations with women later in life.)

(T_4) *If the mother is especially dominating and the father is weak, the child does not identify with the father, and the anxiety caused by the Oedipus complex is not reduced.* (As a result the child does not develop satisfactory relations with women later in life.)

(T_5) *Bachelorhood (in our society) is often a sign of the inability to establish satisfactory relationships with women.*

We have at least two levels of explanation in Examples 10.8 and 10.9. In the former, a particular event is explained by appeal to a regularity captured by an empirical generalization. We might call this a theory of very narrow range—a theory about bachelors and their parents. This regularity or pattern is in turn explained by the latter, broader Freudian theory. We are not endorsing this Freudian theory as adequate (or indeed, even as an accurate representation of Freud's view), but it does illustrate how a narrower explanation of particular events fits into a larger scheme of explanation by theory.

The Freudian theory in Example 10.9 has only two levels of explanation. In more complex cases there may be many levels of explanation and hence many levels of theory. These correspond to increasingly broad answers to the question *why*? as in the series in Example 10.10.

Example 10.10

Why did Bruce's engine block crack?

The water in it expanded when it froze.

Why does water expand when it freezes?

It forms a crystalline structure that occupies greater volume than water in the liquid phase.

Why does water form such a crystalline structure?

It consists of a number of molecules of H_2O *that have an angle of 105° between the two hydrogen atoms.*

Why does the H_2O *molecule have this form?*

Quantum mechanics tells us . . .

This series of questions and responses provides explanation at increasingly higher levels of abstraction. We move from concrete notions, such as an engine block cracking, through a theory of water freezing, to a chemical theory of the hydrogen and oxygen atoms in a crystal, and ultimately to quantum mechanics and atomic physics. At each level a theory of broader scope with more abstract concepts helps explain a theory that is narrower, less abstract, and less remote from evidence.

EXERCISE 10.1 Identifying Theories and Regularities

A. For each of the following pairs of statements, identify the theory statement (the one that does the explaining) and the regularity statement (the pattern that is being explained).

1. i. Engine blocks containing water with no antifreeze tend to crack in very cold weather.
   ii. Water expands when it freezes.
2. i. Rules and norms imposed by others give people a sense of belonging and protect them from self-destructive urges.
   ii. People living alone are more likely to commit suicide.
3. i. Among college students in the 1970s and 1980s, women were less likely to smoke marijuana than men.
   ii. American society is less tolerant of women engaging in deviant behavior than it is of men, which tends to constrain deviant behavior in women.
4. i. Individuals who are better adapted to their environment tend to survive and pass their genes on to succeeding generations.
   ii. During the Industrial Revolution, as buildings in cities became covered with soot, populations of city-dwelling moths changed in color from white to gray.
5. i. The judge, prosecutor, and defense attorney form a workgroup that carries out shared goals such as disposing of its caseload.
   ii. In the United States, a high percentage of criminal defendants plead guilty in plea bargains.
6. i. Educators tend to vote for Democrats.
   ii. Americans identify with a group and vote for the party that represents that group's interests.

B. For each of the following passages, identify what is being explained as well as the theory or theories that are put forward to do the explaining. The theory in a given passage may consist of several statements and may be used to explain several regularities or particular events. As we have indicated, the mark of empirical theories is that they can be used to provide explanations. The statements that make up the theory can often be recognized in prose passages by certain clues: (1) the presence of indicator words, (2) a broader scope, (3) remoteness from direct evidence, and (4) specialized or technical language.

1. During the 1980s, numerous banks and savings and loans in the United States failed. Between 1981 and 1984, over 150 failed. Before that time, since the Great Depression, the number of bank failures for a typical three-year period had been much lower than 150. Why this increase in failures? One reason that has been suggested is that banks

had been largely deregulated, resulting in less-conservative practices by bankers willing to take risks.

2. It is well known that black Americans and members of labor unions tend to vote for Democratic candidates, and that businesspeople and religious fundamentalists tend to vote for Republican candidates. The reason is not difficult to find. In America people see themselves as primarily members of one group or another. When they go to vote they tend to choose parties that historically represent the interests of the groups of which they are members and that have an ideology similar to theirs.
3. On January 20, 1942, leaders of the Nazi Third Reich gathered at a villa on the Wannsee in Berlin. . . . the German leadership had been trying out various approaches, in an effort to solve what they termed the "Jewish problem." . . . The meeting at Wannsee was designed to share this decision with those officials whose fateful job it would be to translate into action a plan for the execution of millions of people. Yet the records of the meetings never actually mention the genocide. . . . Ever since the truth of the death camps became known more or less in its entirety, humans of reason have asked how and why these events came to pass . . . intentionalist historians trace the genocide to explicit, long-term plans on the part of Hitler and his closest Nazi henchmen. The functionalist historians (sometimes called the structuralists) are less impressed by long-term consistency and the operation of direct "top-down" chains of command. They call attention instead to the struggle among rival camps within the Nazi hierarchy to gain the approval of Hitler and his inner circle; to a series of ad hoc actions that were deemed unsuccessful or insufficient; and the final desperate lunge toward a decision that would render all other options unnecessary.[9]
4. **Explanation X** Many explanations have been advanced for the political apathy of Generation X [the American generation born from 1965 to 1978], but none seems to tell the entire story. One theory holds that television, which the average child now watches for forty hours a week, is to blame for the cynicism and lack of civic education among the young. Another is that growing up during the Reagan and Bush presidencies, when government-bashing was the norm, led many Xers to internalize a negative attitude toward politics and the public sector. A third theory blames the breakdown of the traditional family, in which much of the child's civic sensitivity and partisan orientation is said to develop. And, of course, the incessant scandals in contemporary politics deserve some blame for driving young people into political hiding. Each of these theories undoubtedly holds some truth, but a simpler and more straightforward explanation is possible—namely, that young Americans are reacting in a perfectly rational manner to their circumstances, at least as they perceive them.

[9]Howard Gardner, *The Disciplined Mind* (New York: Simon & Schuster, 1999), 141, 180.

As they enter adulthood, this explanation goes, Xers are facing a particularly acute economic insecurity, which leads them to turn inward and pursue material well-being above all else. They see the outlines of very real problems ahead—fiscal, social, and environmental. But in the nation's political system they perceive no leadership on the issues that concern them; rather, they see self-serving politicians who continually indenture themselves to the highest bidders. So Xers have decided, for now, to tune out. After all, they ask, what's the point?[10]

5. The [U.S.] Constitution survived only because it was frequently adapted to fit the changing social balance of power. Measured by the society that followed, the [U.S.] Constitution envisaged by the men at the [Constitutional] Convention distributed its benefits and handicaps to the wrong groups. Fortunately, when the social balance of power they anticipated proved to be illusory, the constitutional system was altered to confer benefits and handicaps more in harmony with social balance of power.[11]
6. Natural selection is an immensely powerful yet beautifully simple theory that has held up remarkably well, under intense and unrelenting scrutiny and testing, for 135 years. In essence, natural selection locates the mechanism of evolutionary change in a "struggle" among organisms for reproductive success, leading to improved fit of population to changing environments. (Struggle is often a metaphorical description and need not be viewed as overt combat, guns blazing. Tactics for reproductive success include a variety of non-martial activities such as earlier and more frequent mating or better cooperation with partners in raising offspring.) Natural selection is therefore a principle of local adaptation, not of general advance or progress.[12] **(Hint: Look for a theory that explains why the members of a species often have different characteristics at one time than their ancestors at a previous time.)**
7. The Greenhouse theory holds that an increase in the concentration of any of the greenhouse gases will lead to increased warming. No one disputes this, but the question is how much will it warm and are there any naturally occurring corrective phenomena? Nature is always unexpectedly complex, and we all too frequently underestimate its powers. Given the increases in carbon dioxide since the beginning of the Industrial Age, temperatures, according to the Greenhouse theory, should have gone up from 2 degrees to 4 degrees Centigrade over the past 100 years. They have not. The measurable overall increase is a trivial 0.5 degrees Centigrade or less. . . . Examination of temperature records, whether current or in the distant past, reveals a history of continual temperature oscillations. The facts do not support a claim of significant global warming. The . . . temperature

[10]Ted Halstead, "A Politics for Generation X," *The Atlantic Monthly*, 284 #2 (August 1999), 34.
[11]Robert Dahl, *A Preface to Democratic Theory* (Chicago: University of Chicago Press, 1956), 143.
[12]Stephen Jay Gould, "The Evolution of Life on Earth," *Scientific American* (October 1994), 85.

rise . . . is probably part of the slow recovery from the Little Ice Age of 1450–1850.[13] **(Hint: What alternative theory to global warming does this passage offer?)**

8. The struggle for civil rights temporarily submerged the potential conflict between the two principles. All that black Americans needed, some thought, was an equal chance. When experience revealed that decades of deprivation had taken their toll, so that those disadvantaged before needed more than an equal chance now, the demands shifted to equal results for black people as a group. It was no longer enough to be allowed to run in the race; it became necessary for a proportionate number of blacks to win. Racial quotas, which had been anathema, became acceptable. From this shift in the paradigm of equality flowed a sequence of important consequences. First, white, liberal support split into factions, one favoring "opportunity" and one favoring "results." Second, civil rights groups such as the Congress of Racial Equality (CORE) and the Student Nonviolent Coordinating Committee (SNCC) rejected white leadership. Thus a cadre of white activists, accustomed to leadership and trained to represent deprived groups, was left out of work and free to lead the fight against risks perpetrated by giant corporations and big government on the public at large. The major manifestation of their leadership became the public interest group.[14]
9. Our curiosity is naturally prompted to inquire by what means the Christian faith obtained so remarkable a victory over the established religions of the earth. To this inquiry an obvious but satisfactory answer may be returned, that it was owing to the convincing evidence of the doctrine itself and to the ruling providence of its great Author. But as truth and reason seldom find so favorable a reception in the world, and as the wisdom of Providence frequently condescends to use the passions of mankind as instruments to execute its purpose, we may still be permitted (though with becoming submission) to ask, not indeed what were the first, but what were the secondary causes of the rapid growth of the Christian Church? It will, perhaps, appear that it was most effectually favored and assisted by five following causes: (i) The inflexible and, if we may use the expression, the intolerant zeal of the Christian—derived, it is true, from the Jewish religion but purified from the narrow and unsocial spirit which, instead of inviting, had deterred the Gentiles from embracing the law of Moses. (ii) The doctrine of a future life, improved by every additional circumstance which could give weight and efficacy to that important truth. (iii) The miraculous powers ascribed to the primitive church. (iv) The pure and austere morals of the Christians. (v) The union and

[13]Dixey Lee Ray with Lou Guzzo, *Environmental Overkill: Whatever Happened to Common Sense?* (New York: HarperCollins, 1993), 17–21.
[14]Mary Douglas and Aaron Wildavsky, *Risk and Culture* (Berkeley: University of California Press, 1983), 164. Reprinted with permission.

discipline of the Christian republic, which gradually formed an independent and increasing state in the heart of the Roman Empire.[15]

C. Select an explanatory passage from a textbook, website, or other source. Clearly state the theory by listing in your own words the more theoretical statements that do the explaining. Provide as well the statements describing the regularities or observations that are explained.

CRITICISM OF THEORIES

Finding theories is only a first step toward our main task of evaluating them. Should we believe Freud's theory of the Oedipus complex? Or the theory that the marriage partner who needs the other least has the most power? We discuss four common kinds of criticisms that can be raised against theories. In narrowing our focus to these four, we are assuming that the regularities that a theory is initially designed to explain do in fact occur. Of course, if they do not, then this also would be a reason for rejecting the theory.

If, for example, it turned out that men with strong, dominating mothers and weak fathers didn't tend to remain bachelors, then this would count against Freud's theory. It could well be that Freud mistakenly generalized this claim about bachelors and their parents from a small, unrepresentative sample of his patients. But we have already discussed (in Chapter 8) how to evaluate empirical generalizations based on observation of a sample. Our focus in this chapter is on the evaluation of theories designed to explain the patterns expressed by these generalizations.

We divide criticisms of theories into two kinds: first-stage and second-stage criticisms. When a theory has been presented as a way of explaining some regularity, critics can initially challenge it by pointing out that there is an alternative way of explaining this same regularity. For example, it could be pointed out that if men who had strong dominating mothers and weak fathers tend to remain bachelors, we don't need the elaborate Freudian theory of the Oedipus complex to explain this regularity. Another plausible explanation is that men from this kind of family background received an unhappy impression of family life, so they tend to remain bachelors simply because they see single life as more enjoyable. Furthermore, critics can suggest that if a proposed theory were true, we would expect certain other regularities to occur—regularities that seem unlikely. Critics of the theory that power in marriage arises from relative need could suggest that if this theory were true, then when one member of a two-career couple suffers a loss of employment, the other would enjoy a substantial gain in power. The critic could question whether this pattern occurs.[16]

---

[15]Edward Gibbon, "The Decline and Fall of the Roman Empire," *The Portable Gibbon*, ed. Deros Saunders (New York: Viking, 1952), 261–2. First published between 1776 and 1788. Reprinted with permission of the publisher.

[16]Of course, the criticism is not substantiated unless evidence can be gathered showing that these regularities probably do not occur.

Second-stage criticisms typically occur later, as part of a dialogue between the theory's supporters and its critics. When critics claim that a theory is committed to predicting patterns of behavior that are unlikely, supporters of the theory often try to get around this apparently damaging evidence. They might alter their theory so that it no longer predicts the regularities that are unlikely. If this move is made by supporters, critics might claim that the defense is *ad hoc*. That is, the defensive move is made just to avoid this criticism. Alternatively, supporters might claim that their theory can't be tested in the particular ways that turn out to be damaging. In reply to this move, critics might raise the question of whether the concepts employed by the theory are applicable or testable at all. Occasionally this question of testability is raised by critics at the outset, when a theory has first been presented. However, we suggest first interpreting a theory charitably, lending some plausible, testable meaning to its terms and judging whether, as interpreted, the theory makes doubtful predictions. If a defender of the theory rejects this interpretation of the theory's terms, the charge of untestability can then be considered.

Four Criticisms of Empirical Theories

1. There is a plausible alternative theory. 2. The theory makes doubtful predictions.	*First-Stage Criticisms*
3. Defense against doubtful predictions is *ad hoc*. 4. The theory is untestable.	*Second-Stage Criticisms*

FIRST-STAGE CRITICISMS—PLAUSIBLE ALTERNATIVE; DOUBTFUL PREDICTIONS

1. There is a plausible alternative theory. Just because the Greenhouse theory could explain why the global temperature has tended to rise in recent years, it doesn't follow that this is the only theory that could explain this pattern. As is noted in passage 7 of Exercise 10.1, this rise could also be explained by the theory that there are continual oscillations in global temperature. When the Greenhouse theory is presented to us and we see that it could explain this rise, the theory seems convincing. But as soon as we see that there is an alternative explanation, the original theory loses some of its grip. At this point, if all we know is that the temperature has risen and that this could be explained either by the greenhouse effect or as a part of a larger pattern of rises and falls, then it is no more reasonable for us to choose one theory than the other. This is a first-stage criticism in that more information and reasoning is needed in order to decide which theory (if either) to accept.

The theory that political patronage served to integrate new immigrants into American life (Example 10.3) is intended to explain why political bosses and political machines flourished in cities like Chicago in the early part of the 20th century. An alternative theory would be that opportunities for political corruption were presented first as the rule of law in cities had difficulty keeping up with rapid social and economic changes, and that the underground economy of the Prohibition Era then allowed political machines to tighten their grip. Simply stating this theory does not make it true, but it does reveal how the same pattern—political machines in cities like Chicago—could initially be explained in more than one way. After the alternative theories are presented, choosing among them depends to a large degree on which one makes other predictions that turn out to be substantiated.[17]

2. The theory makes doubtful predictions. Because of the generality of theories, any empirical theory can be used to make many predictions. We must look beyond the regularities that the theory is designed to explain and ask what else we would expect to occur if the theory were true. To the extent that these predictions turn out to be false, the theory is discredited. The theory of the Oedipus complex would seem to predict that if a strong father figure is absent from the home, a male child will have difficulty relating to women. Suppose we conducted research on this issue and found that men from homes with the father absent marry at the same rate as men from homes with a strong father figure. This finding would discredit the theory.

The prediction that men from homes with the father absent would have difficulty relating to women is not one we can claim to be doubtful without conducting the appropriate research. We can say only that this is a criticism we *could* raise depending on our findings. In other cases, however, we might see that a theory is committed to predictions that, given our background knowledge, are simply implausible. The theory of voting behavior in Exercise 10.1 B2 claims that people identify with a group, and that they tend to vote for a candidate whose party historically represents the interests of that group. This theory would seem to predict that unless large numbers of voters shift their group identification, the same party should continue to win election after election. But the winning party in U.S. presidential elections, for example, has shifted frequently. It is implausible that this was never due to a skillful campaign by a candidate who, as an individual, was appealing to voters; but always by a shift in the group identification of voters that would align them with a different political party.

Making either of the criticisms we have just discussed requires inventiveness. There is no rote procedure for creating an alternative theory that would explain a pattern or regularity. Why did political machines flourish in cities like Chicago? We need to marshal our understanding of how politics works

[17]There are other criteria as well for choosing among theories, such as breadth of scope, systematic unity and fruitfulness in stimulating additional research.

and discover a mechanism that could explain this. Some knowledge of the subject matter in question is necessary. And similarly, there is no automatic way of generating predictions from a theory. Some degree of inventiveness is needed to see that the theory of the Oedipus complex would imply that men from homes with the father absent would have difficulty relating to women. Simply thinking about the voting-behavior theory doesn't automatically generate the prediction that the same party would keep winning elections unless there were significant shifts in the ways voters identified with groups. Even in this case, there is a little leap from the theory to the prediction.

EXERCISE 10.2

Applying First-Stage Criticisms to Theories

The following selections each contain at least one empirical theory and (at least implicitly) some statements describing regularities or patterns that the theory is supposed to explain. For each selection, create a two-column chart like the one displayed below that lists theory statements from the passage in the upper-left section and regularity statements—a list of the patterns being explained—in the lower left. Then fill in the sections on the right with appropriate criticisms—a plausible alternative theory in the upper right, and predicted regularities that might not occur in the lower right.

Sample Passage[18]

> The ideas of bargaining, market, and resources used to describe relationships such as marriage come to us from exchange theory. . . the basic idea of exchange theory is that whether or not relationships form or continue depends on the rewards and costs they provide to the partners. Exchange theory must fight the human tendency to see family relationships in far more romantic and emotional terms. Yet, dating relationships, marriage and other committed partnerships, divorce, and even parent-child relationships show signs of being influenced by the relative assets of the parties. Money is power, and the children of wealthier parents are more likely to share their parents' values. Marriages tend to take place between equal status. Decision making within a marriage, as well as decisions to divorce, are affected by the relative resources of the spouses. People without resources or alternatives to the relationship defer to the preferences of others, and are less likely to leave it.

[18]Mary Ann Lamanna and Agnes Riedmann, *Marriage and Families*, 5th ed. (Belmont, CA: Wadsworth, Inc., 1994), 31, 193.

Sample Criticisms

Initial Theory Being Evaluated

Relationships tend to form or continue when exchanges are equitable.

Plausible Alternative Theory

Regularity 1. This could be explained by pointing out that people of similar social status are in closer contact with each other than people of different social status, so they are more likely to date and eventually marry.

Regularity 2. Presumably, exchange theory would predict that the partner with fewer resources will defer decision-making to the other partner as a way of compensating for the imbalance. But it is also likely that the partner with more resources is better educated and is in a more powerful position at work. The other partner might defer decision-making because the partner with more resources is a better decision-maker.

Regularities Being Explained by Both Initial Theory and Alternative Theory

1. *Marriages tend to take place between people of relatively equal status.*
2. *The partner with more resources tends to make more decisions.*

Regularities Predicted by Original Theory That Might Not Occur

If the theory were true, then relationships would be strained or severed any time one partner received a promotion and raise or any time one partner became debilitated by accident or illness. Both these regularities seem unlikely.

Passage 1

Explanation X

In Exercise 10.1 you identified the theory and the regularities in this passage. Now go a step further and apply the first-stage criticisms.

Many explanations have been advanced for the political apathy of Generation X [the American generation born from 1965 to 1978], but none seems to tell the entire story. One theory holds that television, which the average child now watches for forty hours a week, is to blame for the cynicism and lack of civic education among the young. Another is that growing up during the Reagan and Bush presidencies, when government-bashing was the norm, led many Xers to internalize a negative attitude toward politics and the public sector. A third theory blames the breakdown of the traditional family, in which much of the child's civic sensitivity and partisan orientation is said to develop. And, of course, the incessant scandals in contemporary politics deserve some blame for driving young people into political hiding. Each of these theories undoubtedly holds some truth, but a simpler and more straightforward explanation is possible—namely, that young Americans are reacting in a perfectly rational manner to their circumstances, at least as they perceive them.

As they enter adulthood, this explanation goes, Xers are facing a particularly acute economic insecurity, which leads them to turn inward and pursue material well-being above all else. They see the outlines of very real problems ahead—fiscal, social, and environmental. But in the nation's political system they perceive no leadership on the issues that concern them; rather, they see self-serving politicians who continually indenture themselves to the highest bidders. So Xers have decided, for now, to tune out. After all, they ask, what's the point?[19]

Passage 2

If we look at the history of colonialism in Africa and Asia we find that the earliest revolts against colonialism took place in the countries with the best, not the worst, social and economic conditions. Similarly, if we look at the history of riots in the United States—those springing from both racial conflict and labor disputes—we find that disorder occurred much more often in places where the social and economic conditions were better, rather than where they were worse. These counterintuitive results can be explained when we realize that the violence results not from oppression alone, but from the perception that better conditions are possible. Frustration comes when people first have their expectations increased, and then realize that these new, higher aims cannot be immediately satisfied.

Passage 3

French sociologist Emile Durkheim undertook a study of suicide. Included among his data was evidence from various European countries about the relationship of suicide to marital status and religion. For example, the recorded suicides for Catholics in Austria for 1852–1859 were 51.3 per million persons and 79.5 per million for Protestants. Similarly, in Prussia for the years 1849–1855 the recorded suicides were 49.6 per million for Catholics and 159.9 per million for Protestants. He also found that during this period the recorded suicides for unmarried men were 975 per million, while there were only 336 per million for men with children. He used this and other evidence to support the view that in general Catholics have a lower recorded suicide rate than Protestants, and that married persons living with spouses have a lower recorded suicide rate than single persons living alone. Why? He believed that suicide rates are a function of detachment; a sense of not belonging, which he called "anomie." When we are members of a closely-knit group with well-defined norms, we have a sense of belonging; of knowing the expectations of the group. When norms are not present, our appetites become unrestricted and we have no means of satisfying them. This leads to disillusionment and self-destruction.

---

[19]Ted Halstead, "A Politics for Generation X," *The Atlantic Monthly,* 284 #2 (August 1999), 34.

Passage 4

What Is Gender?

While sex refers to the biological dimension of being male or female, **gender** *refers to the social dimension of being male or female.* Two aspects of gender bear special mention—gender identity and gender role. **Gender identity** *is the sense of being male or female, which most children acquire by the time they are 3 years old.* A **gender role** *is a set of expectations that prescribe how females and males should think, act, and feel. . . .*

Parents are only one of the many sources through which the individual learns gender roles (Beal, 1994). Culture, schools, peers, the media, and other family members are others. Yet it is important to guard against swinging too far in this direction because—especially in the early years of development—parents are important influences on gender development.

Identification and Social Learning Theories Two prominent theories address the way children acquire masculine and feminine attitudes and behaviors from their parents. **Identification theory** *is the Freudian theory that the preschool child develops a sexual attraction to the opposite-sex parent. By approximately 5 or 6 years of age the child renounces this attraction because of anxious feelings. Subsequently, the child identifies with the same-sex parent, unconsciously adopting the same-sex parent's characteristics. . . .*

The **social learning theory of gender** *emphasizes that children's gender development occurs through observation and imitation of gender behavior, and through the rewards and punishments children experience for gender appropriate and inappropriate behavior.* Unlike identification theory, social learning theory argues that sexual attraction to parents is not involved in gender development.[20]

Passage 5

For this passage, state Gottman's criticism of the theory that active listening and validation enhance a relationship, and state Markham's defense of this theory. Discuss which position you favor. Finally, suggest a new theory to explain why couples tend to be happy when the male partner gives in.[21]

The Secret to a Happy Marriage? Men Giving In

Los Angeles Times

Husbands, forget all that psychobabble about active listening and validation.

If you want your marriage to last for a long time, the newest advice from psychologists is quite simple: Just do what your wife says. Go ahead, give in to her.

Active listening, in which one partner paraphrases the other partner's concerns — "So what

---

[20]John W. Santrock, *Life-Span Development,* 7th ed. (McGraw-Hill Companies, 1999), 248.

[21]*Omaha World-Herald*, 21 February 1998. Copyright © 1998 Los Angeles Times. Reprinted by permission of Tribune Media Services.

I hear you say is . . ." —is unnatural and requires too much of people in the midst of emotional conflict," says psychologist John Gottman of the University of Washington. "Asking that of couples is like requiring emotional gymnastics," he said.

Gottman and his colleagues studied 130 newlywed couples for six years in an effort to find ways to predict both marital success and failure.

Couples who used such techniques were no more likely to stay together than couples who did not, they report in the *Journal of Marriage and Family*, which is published by the National Council on Family Relations.

"We need to convey how shocked and surprised we were by these results for the active listening model," the team said in the article. In fact, Gottman and his colleagues have long recommended active listening to couples seeking counseling and had expected that its use would be a predictor of success in marriages.

That it was not a predictor, he said suggests that its widespread use in marital counseling should be abandoned.

"We found that only those newlywed men who are accepting of influence from their wives are ending up in happy, stable, marriages," Gottman said. The autocrats who failed to listen to their wives' complaints, greeting them with stonewalling, contempt and belligerence, were doomed from the beginning, they found.

But the study did not let wives completely off the hook. Women who couched their complaints in a gentle, soothing, perhaps even humorous approach to the husband were more likely to have happy marriages than those who were more belligerent. "That type of (belligerent) response is even more exaggerated in violent marriages," he said.

The fact that happily married couples do not normally use active listening is not a surprise, according psychologist Howard Markman of the University of Denver, author of the 1994 book "Fighting For Your Marriage." "We've found that in our own studies," he said.

In fact, he says the Gottman is setting up a "straw man" in the study of active listening and validation, which is another form of recognizing the legitimacy of a spouse's opinions. "When the listening is taught, it is not because happy couples use it," Markman said, "we use it to help couples disrupt the negative patterns that predict divorce."

Gottman said he is "very sympathetic" to that idea. "If you can genuinely listen and be empathetic when your are the target of the complaint that can be very powerful," he said. But for the average person, he said, "it is just too hard. The average person meets anger with anger."

The differences between Gottman and Markman are typical of the turmoil in the field of marital counseling. A 1993 report said that marital therapy has a relapse rate so high "that the entire enterprise may be in a state of crisis." A recent Consumer Reports study indicated that people who underwent such therapy were the least satisfied among people who have undergone any form of psychotherapy.

Gottman's study was designed to identify the factors that naturally contribute to a successful marriage, so those might be brought into play in therapy, thereby making it more successful.

"If you want to change marriages, "he said, "you have to talk about the 'emotionally intelligent' husband. Some men are really good at accepting a wife's influence, at finding something reasonable in a partner's complaint to agree with." That group represents perhaps a third of all men, he said.

SECOND-STAGE CRITICISMS—*AD HOC* DEFENSE; UNTESTABILITY

3. Defense against doubtful predictions is *ad hoc*. Suppose I hold the Moral Fault Theory of disease and you present damaging evidence against the theory. If I defend the theory solely by changing it to accommodate this damaging evidence, my defense is *ad hoc*. You might point to a number of cases in which infants, too young to be guilty of serious wrongdoing, contracted horrible diseases. If I replied that in these cases the infants are being punished for past sins of the parents, then you could justifiably claim that my defense was *ad hoc*—that I was adding something to the theory just in order to get around the evidence against it. This is a second-stage criticism in that it would be presented after a defender of the theory has replied to the criticism that the theory produces doubtful predictions.

Another example of this *ad hoc* move is the defense of the Divine Creation Theory of the origin of animal and plant species that was offered to escape the apparently conflicting evidence presented by Charles Darwin and other evolutionists that fossils of more complex creatures were located only in rock strata closer to the surface. Some creationists replied that fossils had apparently been planted by the devil to tempt people away from their faith. If it were not for the way the existence of fossils threatened their theory, the creationists would have no reason to claim this particular origin for fossils.

In cases of *ad hoc* defense such as these, there is no independent reason given for the proposed addition to or alteration of the theory, aside from the fact that it would save the theory from damaging evidence. By contrast, scientists are sometimes justified in modifying their theories in the face of counterevidence. Paleontologist Stephen J. Gould has argued, contrary to some versions of Darwin's theory of evolution, that evolutionary change is not gradual, but occurs in fits and starts. There may be periods of relatively rapid evolutionary change as the result of environmental catastrophe, such as a large meteor hitting the earth, followed by periods of only gradual or limited change. We have found evidence that such an event occurred 65 million years ago (at the end of the "Age of Dinosaurs"). This alteration of classical Darwinian theory, however, is backed by additional evidence—for example, mammals evolved relatively rapidly after the extinction of dinosaurs, which might well have been the indirect result of a large meteor striking the earth.

4. The theory is untestable. If a theory can't be tested by observation, even indirectly, then it can't be used to make predictions. There would be no way of knowing whether the predictions were correct. Suppose I hold the Moral Fault theory of disease, and you point out that, contrary to what the theory would predict, disease sometimes strikes people who are leading virtuous lives. I might stubbornly reply that each of these individuals must be guilty of some serious wrong that we can't detect, such as secretly wishing that someone be harmed. If we can't identify some procedure for determining whether these wishes occurred and whether they really distinguish these individuals from others who haven't wished for harm to others, then there is no way of knowing that disease occurs as punishment for moral fault.

The charge of untestability is a second-stage criticism in that it typically occurs after an attempt to test the theory has produced apparently damaging evidence.[22] Defenders of the theory might counter that the theory can't be tested in that way, which raises the question: Can the theory be tested at all? It was suggested earlier that the theory of the Oedipus complex would seem to predict that men who had no father in the home would have difficulty relating to women. Suppose research indicated that this was not the case. A proponent of the theory might reply that presence or absence of a father in the home is not a good test of whether a child had identified with the father. Or the proponent could speculate that male children from homes with an absent father must consistently identify with some older male as a father figure, whether or not this identification is observable. By making these defensive moves, the Freudian theorist exposes the theory to the charge of untestability. Unless there is a way of translating the theory's predictions into a description of what we can expect to observe, then the theory can't be accepted as truly predicting and explaining anything.

EXERCISE 10.3

Applying Second-Stage Criticisms to Theories

A. The following passages contain responses to criticism of theories. In each case indicate (i) the theory being defended, (ii) the criticism (evidence) against which it is being defended, (iii) how the original theory is defended, and (iv) briefly discuss whether the defense appears to be *ad hoc.*

1. **Psi:** A neutral term for parapsychological phenomena. Psi, psychic, and psychical are synonyms. Psi is not an acronym! *Why aren't psychics breaking the bank in Las Vegas casinos?* The theoretical house advantage for some casino games is fairly small, e.g., about 1% for optimally-played craps. This means that over the long term, a good craps player might get back 99 cents for each dollar they play. If they hit a "hot streak," they might even win some money. In practice, the actual house take for most games is fairly large (about 25% for table games) because people rarely play consistently, they reinvest their winnings, and the casino environment is intentionally designed to be noisy and visually distracting. Thus, for a given psychic to make any notable differences in long-term casino profits, they would have to (a) understand the strategies of each game they play, (b) consistently play according to those strategies, (c) stop when they are ahead, and (d) consistently apply strong, reliable psi.

   Over the long term casino profits are predictably stable, but given that some psi effects are known to be genuine, in *principle* a good,

[22]Even though the problem of testability is typically raised by opponents as a second-stage criticism (after apparently damaging evidence has been rejected by proponents of a theory), the problem is faced also at the time the theory is being developed. Unless proponents of a theory are willing to accept some way of making testable predictions from it, the theory faces the charge of not really being an *empirical* theory.

consistent psychic (who knows how to play the casino games) might make some money by gambling. In addition, many people applying weak psi may cause small fluctuations in casino profits, but testing this would require analyzing an enormous amount of casino data, and such data is difficult to obtain.[23]

2. *Because We See Galaxies Billions of Light-Years Away, Isn't the Universe Billions of Years Old?* The logic behind this common question has several hidden assumptions. . . . Has starlight always traveled at the present speed?. . .

   Historical Measurements. During the last 300 years, at least 164 separate measurements of the speed of light have been published. Sixteen different measurement techniques were used. Astronomer Barry Setterfield of Australia has studied these measurements, especially their precision and experimental errors. His results show that **the speed of light has apparently decreased so rapidly that experimental error cannot explain it!**[24]

3. The extreme rarity of transitional forms in the fossil record persists as the trade secret of paleontology. The evolutionary trees that adorn our textbooks have data only at the tips and nodes of their branches; the rest is inference . . . Yet Darwin was so wedded to gradualism that he wagered his entire theory on a denial of this literal record. . . . Paleontologists have paid an exorbitant price for Darwin's argument. We fancy ourselves as the only true students of life's history, yet to preserve our favored account of evolution by natural selection we view our data as so bad that we almost never see the very process we profess to study. . . . The modern theory of evolution does not require gradual change. In fact, the operation of Darwinian processes should yield exactly what we see in the fossil record. It is gradualism that we must reject, not Darwinism.

   The history of most fossil species includes two features particularly inconsistent with gradualism:

   1. *Stasis.* Most species exhibit no directional change during their tenure on earth. They appear in the fossil record looking much the same as when they disappear; morphological change is usually limited and directionless.
   2. *Sudden appearance.* In any local area, a species does not arise gradually by the steady transformation of its ancestors; it appears all at once and "fully formed."[25]

---

[23]Adapted from Psi Explorer website (http://www.psiexplorer.com/faq.htm) April 28, 2010.
[24]Adapted from Walt Brown, *In the Beginning: Compelling Evidence for Creation and the Flood*, 8th ed., 2008 Center for Scientific Creation website (http://www.creationscience.com onlinebook/FAQ16.htm), April 28, 2010.
[25]Stephen Jay Gould, *The Panda's Thumb* (New York: W. W. Norton, 1980), 181–2.

4. The Bible is clear. The ancestors of every animal that ever lived were created during Creation week. Each basic animal type was created "after his kind" and all subsequent individual animals, including dinosaurs, descended from these created categories. . . .The land and flying dinosaurs could only have survived on . . . [Noah's] Ark, only to disembark at the end of the flood into a strange and hostile world. We can surmise that the environmental conditions, with the sparse vegetation, the destruction of the pre-flood water canopy, and the temperature extremes during the ensuing Ice Age would have caused many animal types to become extinct, a process that continues today. Evidently the dinosaurs just didn't make it![26] **(Hint: This passage takes the biblical theory of the creation and flood as asserting that all animals [including dinosaurs] were created in the same week and were preserved on Noah's Ark during the flood. A critic might claim that the theory would then be committed to dinosaurs existing now. How does the passage defend the theory against this apparently damaging evidence? Is this defense ad hoc?)**
5. *Can Radioisotope Dating Be Trusted?* For decades creation scientists have shown that the answer to this question is a clear NO! Its results have been shown to be inconsistent, discordant, unreliable, and frequently bizarre in any model. Creationists have, in particular, pointed out the weak assumptions on which the method is based, and the contradictory nature of its results.

   Assumption One: The radioisotope decay rates have been constant throughout the past. . . .

   Assumption Two: No parent or daughter material has been added to or taken from the specimen. . . .

   Assumption Three: No daughter material was present at the start. . . .This assumption actually denies the possibility of creation when, in fact, God may have created an array of radioisotopes, which, if analyzed with false assumptions, could be misinterpreted as age.[27]

B. The following passages raise questions about testability. Briefly describe whether, and if so, how, the following theories might be tested.

1. Suppose we theorize that individual organisms have a personal space, a kind of "shell" surrounding them that is especially "intimate" and provokes "strong," generally negative reaction when another organism enters it. For example, human beings often react negatively when another (particularly a stranger) is "too" close. On this view, the boundary of their personal space is the distance at which they

---

[26]Adapted from John D. Morris, "Did Dinosaurs Survive The Flood?," May 1, 1993. Institute for Creation Research website (http://www.icr.org/article/did-dinosaurs-survive-flood/) April 28, 2010.

[27]Adapted from John D. Morris, "Can Radioisotope Dating Be Trusted?," August 1, 1997. Institute for Creation Research website (http://www.icr.org/article/can-radioisotope-dating-be-trusted/) April 28, 2010.

become uncomfortable and will typically move back a little or otherwise react to express their discomfort, so as to remove the errant individual from their personal space. The size of the personal space might vary by individual, gender, cultural background, context, and other characteristics.

2. It has become increasingly difficult to find politicians who are morally virtuous. The culture of the last half of the twentieth century has served to undermine moral education. Of course, politicians want to appear morally upright and may even believe that they are, but ordinary citizens, even friends, of the politician can never be sure. A person may appear to be morally incorruptible, but fail to live up to moral standards when great temptation is placed before them.
3. How are fossils to be explained? One early defender of the biblical account, a nineteenth-century naturalist named Philip Henry Gosse, suggested that God created the earth with the fossils already in it.[28]
4. It is sometimes argued that "misery loves company"; unhappy people tend to congregate with each other.
5. Parapsychologists D. Scott Rogo and Raymond Bayless have recently discovered a startling fact: that dozens of people have had telephone calls from the dead. . . . Their new book, *Phone Calls From the Dead,* describes fifty such cases. Unfortunately, if the person receiving the call realizes that he is speaking to a spirit from the Beyond, the call is usually over within seconds, they say. Some postmortem calls arrive, appropriately enough, over dead telephone lines. Rogo believes that these calls occur when a spirit manipulates electrical impulses in the phone to reproduce the sound of its own voice. "We've stumbled on a whole new method of psychic communication!" says Rogo.[29]

C. Use your favorite web browser to find examples of a theory on one of the following topics: creationism, parapsychology, Taos hum, telekinesis, UFOs. Develop appropriate criticism of the passage you select.

REVIEW OF TECHNIQUES FOR CRITICIZING THEORIES

We have described two initial ways of criticizing a theory: (1) by offering an alternative theory to explain the same patterns that the theory in question has been designed to explain, and (2) by suggesting some doubtful predictions that the theory in question would make. We have also discussed two further criticisms that are sometimes appropriate to raise after a theory has been defended against apparently damaging evidence: (1) that the defense is *ad hoc,* and (2) that the theory is untestable. Even though successful criticism of a well-developed scientific theory often requires sophisticated techniques and sustained research, attempting to apply the criticisms we have described can be helpful in understanding a theory and its implications.

[28]Cited in Daisie Radner and Michael Radner, *Science and Unreason* (Belmont, CA: Wadsworth, 1982), 6.
[29]*The Skeptical Inquirer* (Summer 1979): 15. As quoted in Radner and Radner, ibid.

Four Criticisms of Empirical Theories

1. There is a plausible alternative theory.
2. The theory makes doubtful predictions.

} *First-Stage Criticisms*

3. Defense against doubtful predictions is *ad hoc*.
4. The theory is untestable.

} *Second-Stage Criticisms*

Central Concepts for Chapter 10

Empirical Theory—a set of statements of broad scope that explains why patterns or regularities occur (Example: *Relationships tend to form and continue when exchanges are equitable.*)
Regularity—a pattern of behavior that is explained by a theory (Example: *Women who work tend to make more decisions in their families than women who do not.*)
Observed Data—the specific instances that form the basis for determining that a regularity occurs (Example: *Fran works and makes more decisions in her family than Alice who does not.*)
Explanation—an attempt to indicate why or how something occurred, rather than to justify our belief that it did
***Ad Hoc* Defense**—an attempt to save a theory being criticized by modifying it just in order to avoid damaging counter-evidence
Testability Criticism—pointing out that there is no procedure for determining whether predictions made by the theory do in fact occur

EXERCISE 10.4 **Criticizing Empirical Theories in Longer Passages**

The following four selections each contain at least one theory that is intended to explain certain regularities or patterns. In each case you should undertake these tasks:

1. List the most important aspects of the theory (that which is put forward in the passage to provide explanation) as well as any significant regularities or patterns explained or predicted by the theory.
2. Sketch criticisms of the theory using the techniques discussed in this chapter.
3. (Optional) If appropriate, assess some of the arguments in the passage.

Passage 1

Benefit of Handguns[30]

What evidence is there that handguns in private hands protect the lives and property of innocent persons? First of all, there is the burglary data. The chart below sets forth crime and suicide rates for several nations, per 100,000 population.

Crime and Death Rates in Various Countries

Country	*Homicide*	*Suicide*	*Total Death*	*Rape*	*Robbery*	*Burglary*
Japan	0.8	21.1	21.9	1.6	1.8	231.2
England & Wales	1.1	8.6	9.7	2.7	44.6	1639.7
Scotland	1.7	10.2	11.9	4.4	86.9	2178.6
Canada	2.7	12.8	14.5	10.3	92.8	1420.6
Australia	2.5	11.8	14.3	13.8	83.6	1754.3
New Zealand	1.7	10.8	12.5	14.4	14.9	2243.1
Switzerland	1.1	21.4	20.5	5.8	224.2	976.8
United States	7.9	12.2	20.1	35.7	205.4	1263.7

FIGURE **10.1** Crime and suicide rates for several nations, per 100,000 population

While the United States has much more violent crime than the other nations (including crimes such as rape, which rarely involve guns), the United States anomalously has less burglary. In terms of burglaries perpetrated against occupied residences, the American advantage is even greater. In Canada, for example, a Toronto study found that 48 percent of burglaries were against occupied homes, and 21 percent involved a confrontation with the victim; only 13 percent of U.S. residential burglaries are attempted against occupied homes. Similarly, most Canadian residential burglaries occur in the nighttime, while American burglars are known to prefer daytime entry to reduce the risk of an armed confrontation. After Canada's stricter 1977 controls (which generally prohibited handgun possession for protection) took effect, the Canadian overall breaking and entering rate rose 25 percent, and surpassed the American rate, which had been declining. A 1982 British survey found 59 percent of attempted burglaries involved an occupied home (again compared to just 13 percent in the United States).

Why should American criminals, who have proven that they engage in murder, rape, and robbery at such a higher rate than their counterparts in other nations, display such a curious reluctance to perpetrate burglaries, particularly

[30]David B. Kopel, "Peril or Protection? The Risks and Benefits of Handgun Prohibition," *Saint Louis University Public Law Review*, vol. 12, pp 344–7. Reprinted with permission of the Saint Louis University Public Law Review © 1993 St. Louis University School of Law, St. Louis Missouri.

against occupied residences? Could the answer be that they are afraid of getting shot? When an American burglar strikes at an occupied residence, his chance of being shot is equal to his chance of being sent to jail. Accordingly, a significant reduction in the number of Americans keeping loaded handguns in the home could lead to a sharp increase in the burglary rate, and to many more burglaries perpetrated while victim families are present in the home.

(Hint: Apply first-stage criticisms [alternative theory and doubtful predictions]. For this and the remaining passages, you will find it helpful to construct a chart such as the following, with the theory you are evaluating in the upper-left section, the regularities being explained in the lower-left section. Write your criticisms in the right-hand part of the chart: alternative theory or theories in the upper-right section and doubtful predictions in the lower-right section.)

Initial Theory Being Evaluated	**Plausible Alternative Theory**
Handguns in private hands (in the United States) protect property and property owners' lives from burglars.	
Regularities Being Explained	**Regularities Predicted by Original Theory That Might Not Occur**
1. *The United States has a higher rate of murder, rape, and robbery but a lower burglary rate than other countries listed.* 2. *Burglaries in the United States tend to be committed during daylight hours.*	

Passage 2

Effect of Cohabitation Before Marriage[31]

. . . evidence accumulated in recent years suggests that, contrary to Margaret Mead's hopes, "trial marriage" may have a negative effect on marital success. A panel study (Booth and Johnson, 1988) based on a national sample of married people interviewed in 1980 and again in 1983 found that cohabitation was negatively related to supportive marital interaction and was associated with marital disagreement and increased probability of divorce. No sex difference or effect of length of marriage was found in this study.

The researchers thought that what some cohabitants bring to marriage might explain the negative relationship between cohabitation and successful marriage. Drug, money, legal, and unemployment problems; risk-taking; parental disapproval; and lesser commitment to marriage were more characteristic of cohabitants than noncohabitants. Still, much remained unexplained by the data, suggesting that further research might find the cohabitation process itself to be contributing to marital weakness.

In a subsequent study, Thomson and Colella (1992) used 1988 National Survey of Families and Households (NSFH) data to analyze the relationship between prior cohabiting and the likelihood of divorce among 714 couples in first marriages. Researchers classified these couples according to whether and for how long they had lived together before marrying. Respondents were also asked the following question: "It is always difficult to predict what will happen in a marriage, but realistically, what do you think the chances are that you and your husband/wife will eventually separate or divorce?" Response

Perceived Likelihood of Divorce by Cohabitation Experience

		Months Cohabited			
	Did Not Cohabit	*1–5*	*6–11*	*12–23*	*24+*
Likelihood of divorce					
Very Low	61.2%	50.9%	49.6%	36.0%	38.8%
Low	27.0	28.2	29.6	48.2	39.2
Even or higher	11.8	20.9	20.8	15.8	22.0
Valid cases	714.0	90.0	57.0	68.0	75.0
Percent of couples	71.8	9.0	5.7	6.4	7.0

NOTE: Respondents were couples in their first union and marriage, married less than ten years.

FIGURE **10.2** Perceived likelihood of divorce by couples in their first union of marriage

[31]Mary Ann Lamanna and Agnes Riedmann, *Marriage and Families*, 5th ed. (Belmont, CA: Wadsworth, Inc., 1994), 216–219. Reprinted with permission.

options included: "very low," "low," "about even," "high," or "very high." The table above shows the results. Whereas 61.2 percent of those who had not cohabited said the likelihood of divorce was "very low," only 38.6 percent of those who had cohabited for two years or more said so. Generally, those who had cohabited were less satisfied with their marriages and less committed to the institution of marriage; their dissatisfaction increased with the length of time they had lived together before marrying. Wives who had cohabited had more individualistic views (as opposed to family-oriented views) than those who had not.

Thomson and Colella (1992) did not disagree with explanations offered by Booth and Johnson (1988) but rather added to them. It is possible, they suggested, that the experience of cohabiting adversely affects subsequent marital quality and stability inasmuch as the experience actually weakens commitment because "successful" cohabitation (ending in marriage) demonstrates that reasonable alternatives to marriage exist" (Thomson and Colella (1992), 266). Put another way, experiencing cohabitation may lead to more individualistic attitudes and values. . . .

Passage 3

What if Women Ran the World?[32]

Both men and women participate in perpetuating the stereotypical gender identities that associate men with war and competition and women with peace and cooperation. As sophisticated feminists like Jean Bethke Elshtain have pointed out, the traditional dichotomy between the male "just warrior" marching to war and the female "beautiful soul" marching for peace is frequently transcended in practice by women intoxicated by war and by men repulsed by its cruelties. But like many stereotypes, it rests on a truth, amply confirmed by much of the new research in evolutionary biology. Wives and mothers can enthusiastically send their husbands and sons off to war; like Sioux women, they can question their manliness for failing to go into battle or themselves torture prisoners. But statistically speaking it is primarily men who enjoy the experience of aggression and the camaraderie it brings and who revel in the ritualization of war that is, as anthropologist Robin Fox puts it, another way of understanding diplomacy.

A truly matriarchal world, then, would be less prone to conflict and more conciliatory and cooperative than the one we inhabit now. Where the new biology parts company with feminism is in the causal explanation it gives for this difference in sex roles. The ongoing revolution in the life sciences has almost totally escaped the notice of much of the social sciences and humanities, particularly the parts of the academy concerned with feminism, postmodernism, cultural studies, and the like. While there are some feminists who believe that sex differences have a natural basis, by far the majority are committed to the idea

[32]From Francis Fukuyama, "What if Women Ran the World?". *Foreign Affairs* (September/October 1998), 33–39. Reprinted by permission of the publisher.

that men and women are psychologically identical, and that any differences in behavior, with regard to violence or any other characteristic, are the result of some prior social construction passed on by the prevailing culture. . . .

Once one views international relations through the lens of sex and biology, it never again looks the same. . . . The basic social problem that any society faces is to control the aggressive tendencies of its young men. In hunter-gatherer societies, the vast preponderance of violence is over sex, a situation that continues to characterize domestic violent crime in contemporary postindustrial societies. Older men in the community have generally been responsible for socializing younger ones by ritualizing their aggression, often by directing it toward enemies outside the community. . . . Channeling aggression outside the community may not lower societies' overall rate of violence, but it at least offers them the possibility of domestic peace between wars.

The core of the feminist agenda for international politics seems fundamentally correct: the violent and aggressive tendencies of men have to be controlled, not simply by redirecting them to external aggression but by constraining those impulses through a web of norms, laws, agreements, contracts, and the like. In addition, more women need to be brought into the domain of international politics as leaders, officials, soldiers, and voters. Only by participating fully in global politics can women both defend their own interests and shift the underlying male agenda.

The feminization of world politics has, of course, been taking place gradually over the past hundred years, with very positive effects. Women have won the right to vote and participate in politics in all developed countries, as well as in many developing countries, and have exercised that right with increasing energy. In the United States and other rich countries, a pronounced gender gap with regard to foreign policy and national security issues endures. . . . It is difficult to know how to account for this gender gap; certainly, one cannot move from biology to voting behavior in a single step. Observers have suggested various reasons why women are less willing to use military force than men, including their role as mothers, the fact that many women are feminists (that is, they're committed to a left-of-center agenda that is generally hostile to U.S. intervention), and partisan affiliation (more women vote Democratic than men). It is unnecessary to know the reason for the correlation between gender and antimilitarism, however, to predict that increasing female political participation will probably make the United States and other democracies less inclined to use power around the world as freely as they have in the past.

Will this shift toward a less status- and military-power-oriented world be a good thing? For relations between states in the so-called democratic zone of peace, the answer is yes. Consideration of gender adds a great deal to the vigorous and interesting debate over the correlation between democracy and peace that has taken place in the past decade. The "democratic peace" argument, which underlies the foreign policy of the Clinton administration as well as its predecessors, is that democracies tend not to fight one another. While the empirical claim has been contested, the correlation between the degree of consolidation of liberal democratic institutions and interdemocratic peace would seem to be one of the few nontrivial generalizations one can make about world politics. Democratic peace theorists have been less persuasive about the reasons democracies are pacific toward one another. The reasons usually cited—the rule of law, respect for individual rights, the commercial nature of most democracies, and the like—are undoubtedly correct. But there is another factor that has generally not been taken into account: developed democracies also tend to be more feminized than authoritarian states, in terms of expansion of female franchise and participation in political decision-making. It should therefore surprise no one that the historically unprecedented shift in the sexual basis of politics should lead to a change in international relations. . . .

The feminization of democratic politics will interact with other demographic trends in the next 50 years to produce important changes. . . . While the median age for America's population was in the mid-20s during the first few decades of the twentieth century, it will climb toward 40 by 2050. The change will be even more dramatic in Europe and Japan, where rates of immigration and fertility are lower. Under the U.N. Population Division's low-growth projections, the median age in Germany will be 55, in Japan 53, and in Italy 58.

The graying of the population has heretofore been discussed primarily in terms of the social security liability it will engender. But it carries a host of other social consequences as well, among them the emergence of elderly women as one of the most important voting blocs courted by mid-twenty-first-century politicians. . . .

By the middle of the next century, then, Europe will likely consist of rich, powerful, and democratic nations with rapidly shrinking populations of mostly elderly people where women will play important leadership roles. The United States, with its higher rates of immigration and fertility, will also have more women leaders but a substantially younger population. A much larger and poorer part of the world will consist of states in Africa, the Middle East, and South Asia with younger, growing populations, led mostly by younger men.

Passage 4

Science, Proof, and the Ancient Astronaut Hypothesis: The Case for von Däniken[33]

It is common knowledge that it is both possible and probable that intelligent beings exist elsewhere in the universe. Even Carl Sagan admits that. To assume otherwise is to regress to the Middle Ages, when it was believed that the earth was the center of the universe and man the supreme creation.

Historian Will Durant, in his *Story of Civilization*, suggests that we are not necessarily the descendants of the primitive cultures to which archaeologists

[33]Adapted from Pasqual S. Schievella, "Science, Proof and the Ancient Astronaut Hypothesis," *Philosophy of Science and the Occult*, ed. Patrick Grim (Albany: State University of New York Press, 1982), 268–270. Reprinted with permission of the author.

and anthropologists like to attribute our ancestry. His thesis, and the mysteries that science has not explained, suggest the possibility that ancient space travelers visited earth. No argument based on such data as problems of intergalactic travel and the vastness of space has yet proved that superior intelligence could not accomplish what we, with our few centuries of limited scientific technology and theory, believe to be impossible.

It is both possible and probable that ancient astronauts did visit earth. This cannot be denied unless one holds that evolution is impossible, or that there is no evolution and God created only us (a point that raises questions on which no evidence could be brought to bear), or that such evolution as there has been took place only on earth, or that except for us, there are no astronauts or other intelligences in the universe, or that the evidence is all in as to our origin, or that we have absolute knowledge about these things, and the like. Surely no enlightened person could hold such medieval ideas.

Unless we deny the possibility of evolution elsewhere in the universe or pretend to have an absolute knowledge regarding our past, we must recognize at least the possibility that technologically advanced civilizations may have arisen elsewhere and that they may have visited us in the remote past.

The ancient astronaut hypothesis, then, is at least possible. As to proof of von Däniken's theories, it must be noted that the ancient astronaut hypothesis cannot be expected to follow the rigid rules and standards of proof set for natural science. Its modes of proof are primarily like those in the social sciences, such as psychology, sociology, and anthropology. To expect formal rigidity in such informal disciplines is to demand what cannot be. Nevertheless, one would expect scientists to permit von Däniken to extrapolate from his data, since they themselves accept extrapolation as a kind of evidence permitting further advances in science.

What could constitute proof for the ancient astronaut hypothesis? We are not likely to find an ancient astronaut. As von Däniken points out, "crashed" spaceships from the distant past would probably long ago have disintegrated or possibly have been carried away piecemeal. What then?

Von Däniken's thesis explains hitherto inexplicable mysteries, none of which has received any elucidation from academic minds fettered by prejudices and preconceptions. It is not fatal to the hypothesis that critics find errors. Taken as a whole, von Däniken's findings point convincingly to the likelihood of extraterrestrial interference in man's distant past. That is not to deny that von Däniken manipulates many of his facts to adapt them to the ancient astronaut hypothesis. But what scientist does not do this when he formulates a theory?

The ancient astronaut hypothesis is little different from most of recorded history. The hypothesis requires only "validation" of the reported data through correlation of those data with the unexplained and wondrous technical artifacts of the distant past. The proofs of the ancient astronaut hypothesis can be found in the logic of both possible and probable events, in the historical, even though predominantly religious, documents that are held in such high historical esteem throughout the world, and in the ancient artifacts that cannot be explained in terms of the supposed knowledge and capabilities of antiquity.

Any mythologist will readily insist that much of mythology is but disguised history. There remains only to break the code of the expressions of antiquity and to translate them into the speech patterns of a space-age language. As George Sassoon explained, even the word *Glory* in the scriptures turns out to be a highly probable reference to a spacecraft. All these, studied as a body of coherently describable data, point to extraterrestrial intervention. Furthermore, the descriptions in ancient documents, when coupled with empirical data, considerably weaken the argument that terrestrials are responsible for those artifacts which obviously were beyond their linguistic, conceptual, and technical abilities. Let us consider some of those wonders. A few should suffice.

At the Bay of Pisco, south of Lima, Peru, there is an enormous trident engraved on the side of a hill pointing (we can now say with accuracy, thanks to the intensive research of Josef Blumrich) directly at a small island by the name of Isla Blanca. In addition, not far from the small city of Nazca, Peru, one can find what are now called the Nazca ground drawings. Inscribed on approximately thirty square miles of arid Nazca pampas are huge drawings of a spider, a monkey, a hummingbird, and the like. They are so large that they can be recognized only from the air. Other drawings could easily be mistaken for aircraft landing strips. Some are merely straight (often parallel) lines running across rough terrain and up mountainsides, appearing to deviate not an inch—sometimes almost ten kilometers (6.21 miles) long, as if cut by a laser beam from on high. As to their source and meanings, there are no accepted explanations. A NASA engineer, Robert Earle, claims to have determined that most of the lines point to important geographic locations on the earth.

Another unexplained mystery is that of the Terraces of Baalbek in Lebanon where huge stone blocks sixty feet long and said to weigh 2,000 tons have been moved into place. They are so massive that even our modern technology could not handle them.

Then there are the so-called "fortress" walls at Sacsayhuaman, outside the city of Cusco in Peru. There are thousands of enormous irregularly shaped stones, many tons in weight, fitting together as closely and as neatly as the pieces of a jigsaw puzzle, without any kind of connecting adhesive. The thin edge of a sheet of paper could not be inserted between them.

Another marvel is the recessed quadrangular wall at Tiahuanacu, outside of La Paz, Bolivia. The inside surface is studded with sculptured faces apparently representing every racial type on earth. There are many hundreds of other unexplained mysteries which most scientists show no inclination to investigate. I shall mention only one more: the mystery of the existence of models of sophisticated aircraft. Some of these models show a separation space indicating the possible existence of nuclear engines. Such models, which are in museums throughout the world, have been tested and found to be aerodynamically accurate in design. They are amazingly interesting artifacts because they correlate so well with the many scriptural descriptions of flying machines emitting smoke, fire, and thunderous noise. Even if we accept the claim that all these things originated with terrestrial beings, we would be hard-pressed to explain the disappearance of such superior civilizations. We have found no documentary evidence or, indeed, evidence of any kind to support a terrestrial origin for such technological achievements.

It seems, then, as von Däniken reiterates, that it is time to bring to bear upon these fascinating mysteries, and the descriptions of them in the languages of antiquity, new perspectives and viable hypotheses made possible by the more sophisticated language and knowledge of our day.

If scientific and religious institutions would allow it, and if governments or foundations would advance funds to support it, researchers could feed data from all over the world into computers to determine the comparative similarities among empirical descriptions of "gods from space" and to determine whether these descriptions are, as the critics prefer to believe, nothing more than the creations of insane minds or over-fertile imaginations. Supplemented by computers, experts in comparative linguistics, translation, ancient cultures, and ancient languages should be able to determine whether the technical data, concepts, and achievements found in museums, existing at archaeological sites, and described in historical and religious documents could have originated with a prescientific people who spoke only non-technical and unsophisticated language. Surely such an effort would bring more probable results than will the expenditure of hundreds of millions of dollars from an impulse technology attempting to discover evidence of the existence of extraterrestrial intelligences—an effort with which I nevertheless heartily agree. However, there is even less of a "smidgen," to use a favorite word of Carl Sagan's, of evidence in space. In fact, there is *no* evidence except for the "evidence" of extraterrestrial interference (in the development of man) right here on Earth as it had been offered throughout our history by ancient astronaut theorists.

As it stands now, the ancient astronaut hypothesis is primarily a historical hypothesis and peripherally a scientific one. It is founded on documentary and circumstantial evidence and, in some cases, on hard evidence that may not be denied except by stretching the facts beyond reason and probability.

CHAPTER 11

Putting It All Together: Six Steps to Understanding and Evaluating Arguments

The previous ten chapters have presented various techniques for understanding and evaluating arguments. Chapters 2 and 3 concentrated on extracting arguments from a text. Chapter 4 outlined the task of evaluating arguments, broadly describing the criteria for soundness—validity and truth of premises—and Chapter 5 focused more specifically on the concept of validity. Chapter 6 considered how we might be taken in by fallacious reasoning. Chapters 7 through 10 discussed the evaluation of specific kinds of premises: definitional premises, empirical generalizations, and theory-based statements, as well as conclusions based on analogical or convergent arguments. Now we can bring these parts together in a sequence of steps illustrated by the flowchart in Figure 11.1.

Much of the earlier discussion of particular steps in reconstructing or evaluating arguments concentrated on relatively short, stylized passages in which each sentence played a role as a premise or conclusion. We will now survey the whole six-step procedure represented on the flowchart and adapt it to understanding and evaluating arguments found in longer passages, such as essays and editorials.

Preliminary step. This step directs you to read the passage in question carefully. The importance of this step should not be overlooked. One of the first things you need to determine is whether a passage does in fact

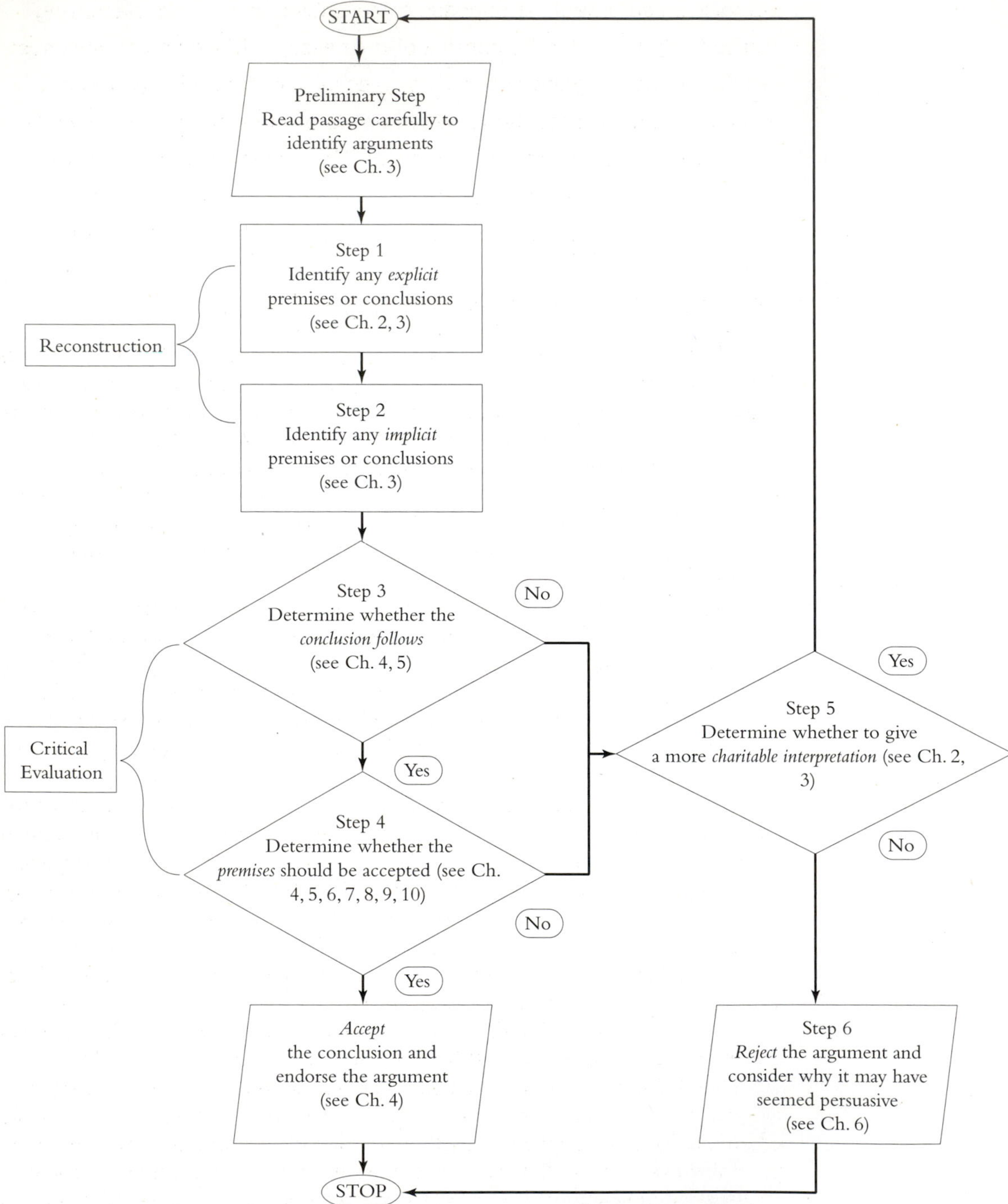

FIGURE **11.1** Six steps to understanding and evaluating deductive arguments put forth an argument, as opposed to describing, explaining, classifying, and so forth. Consider the context of the passage. Make use of hints such as titles or recurring themes. You can also initially determine (without fully reconstructing any arguments) whether there is one argument or several and how different arguments are related. You might need to read a passage carefully *several times* before you understand it well enough to identify any arguments it contains and to begin reconstructing them.

THE SIX-STEP PROCEDURE FOR EVALUATING ARGUMENTS

Step 1. You should identify any *explicit* premises or conclusions, but this doesn't mean copying sentences out of a passage exactly as they are written. More likely, you will paraphrase or restate assertions made by the passage. In actual practice, the distinction between identifying explicit and implicit premises is not as sharp as in the stylized passages we dealt with, where whole sentences *could* be copied as premises. But even if no premises can be copied word for word from the passage, some premises might be strongly suggested and easily paraphrased from what is actually written. This will allow you to begin your reconstruction.

Step 2. We pointed out in Chapter 3 that the step of identifying *implicit* premises typically amounts to adding any premises that are needed to make the conclusion follow (insofar as this *can* be done without radically distorting the meaning of the passage being interpreted). Adding an implicit conclusion consists of adding a conclusion that *would* follow from the interpreted premises, if the conclusion is not already stated in the passage. This will lead to a full reconstruction.

Step 3. Given what we just said about Step 2, determining whether the conclusion follows will often be carried out in the process of adding implicit premises or an implicit conclusion. The premises and conclusion of the argument might have been stated so explicitly, however, that Step 2 is unnecessary, and a negative answer to the question in Step 3 (Does the conclusion follow?) might be unavoidable. Or (as happens more frequently), the argument might contain an unclear expression that occurs more than once. If so, you will probably make several quick loops through Steps 3, 4, and 5, and back through 1 and 2, to determine whether a single meaning that makes all the premises acceptable can be assigned to this expression (see Chapter 7).

Step 4. Determining whether the premises should be accepted or rejected was discussed in general in Chapter 4. More detailed techniques for evaluating additional kinds of premises—particularly definitional premises and empirical generalizations—as well as convergent arguments and scientific theories were investigated in Chapters 7, 8, 9, and 10. If you decide that the premises should be accepted, then you are done with your evaluation. If you decide to reject the argument, you move to a reassessment stage at Step 5. What do you do if you can neither clearly accept nor reject the argument? You have two options again. You might move to Step 5 and try another interpretation, or, especially if you have tried various interpretations, you might quit and decide to remain uncommitted to the conclusion until a better argument is given.

Step 5. If you find that the conclusion of an argument does not follow or the premises are unacceptable, the flowchart directs you to consider giving a more charitable interpretation of the argument. This procedure is in keeping with the rationale for critical reasoning that has been promoted throughout this book: being presented with an argument should be taken as an opportunity to determine what is reasonable to believe, not as a contest in which the object is to defeat the person who has presented the argument.

If an argument can be interpreted in such a way that the conclusion follows and the premises are acceptable, then the flowchart calls for the conclusion to be accepted. If, on the other hand, there is no reasonable way of interpreting the argument so that it passes these tests, the argument should be rejected.

Step 6. However, if an argument is rejected, the flowchart calls for the additional step of considering why the argument may have seemed persuasive. This is a particularly helpful step in a direct exchange with someone who has offered an argument or with an audience that might have been persuaded by it. It is much more likely that you will be able to sell your negative appraisal of the argument if you can explain why the arguer or audience was tempted to accept it in the first place. For this purpose, the discussion of fallacies in Chapter 6 should be helpful, since that analysis was aimed at explaining why people tend to be persuaded by certain kinds of bad arguments. Step 6 can also serve as an occasion to suggest what direction might be taken to improve the argument being examined. Often some core of reasonableness that the presenter of the argument was not able to adequately express lies behind the argument being offered. Perhaps even the Principle of Charitable Interpretation won't permit the argument to be revised radically enough to capture this reasonableness. But in applying the six-step procedure you might have developed some ideas about how a different but related argument could be constructed that *would* be acceptable.

A SAMPLE APPLICATION OF THE SIX-STEP PROCEDURE

It might be helpful to see how the entire six-step procedure can be applied to a sample argument found in a newspaper editorial.

Suppose you came across the editorial included as Passage 11.1 and decided to consider carefully what it is claiming and to evaluate its main arguments. How could the six-step procedure be used to carry out this task?

The way you would proceed depends in part on the particular purpose you had in analyzing the editorial. You might intend to write a reply, discuss the editorial with someone interested in the topic of prayer in the public schools, or simply figure out whether to accept the point of view being advanced by the writer. For many purposes, the following analysis is probably more detailed than you would need to go through, but the steps you would take would be essentially the same.

Preliminary Step: Read Passage Carefully to Identify Arguments Even though the main points of this editorial are reasonably clear, a careful reading will lead you to see beyond some surface features that might mislead the casual reader.

The first two paragraphs set out the case at issue. A Georgia schoolteacher intentionally disobeyed a new law requiring a "moment of silence" at the beginning of the school day, was suspended from teaching, and planned to appeal his suspension on constitutional grounds. The third paragraph indicates that this case involves freedom of religion, in particular "the propriety of requiring prayer, moments of silence and similar observances in public schools." It is useful but not essential to understanding the passage to realize that the teacher's action has taken place against a background of Supreme Court decisions apparently prohibiting prayer in the public schools. The Georgia law could be seen as an attempt to get around these decisions.

Passage 11.1

A Selfish Way of Looking at the Law[1]

1 In Georgia, a teacher of American government chose a poor way to deal with a law with which he disagreed. He broke it. He went right on teaching while other members of the faculty were observing a moment of silence, as required by the new law.

2 The teacher was suspended with pay. He said he planned to sue the school system, saying the suspension violated his First Amendment rights.

3 Yes, the teacher has every right to disagree with the law. Reasonable people differ over the propriety of requiring prayer, moments of silence, and similar observances in public schools. But what a wonderful opportunity he had to teach his students about the responsibilities of a citizen to obey a disagreeable law while working within the system to change it. And how thoroughly he blew that opportunity.

4 Certainly breaking a law is one way to protest its existence. Civil disobedience has a long history in the movements to abolish slavery, win civil rights, and end unpopular wars. Civil disobedience is one way to get the question before the court. It's also a way to stir up public support for one's position.

5 But if the teaching of American government is worthwhile, it shouldn't convey the impression that civil disobedience is the first line of attack. There should be lessons on majority rule and how it affects the making and changing of laws. The students should look at the role of political parties and special interest groups in building a consensus for change. There should be attention to the option of running for office or supporting candidates who are committed to changing the law. And finally, young people need to know that they can't always have their way. Some laws must

be tolerated even though a few people might disagree with them.

6 Those approaches may lack the drama of "taking a stand." But when a dramatic, attention getting gesture is depicted as superior to working within the system and building a consensus a harmful message is delivered. This teacher's example said it's permissible to pick and choose among the laws obeying or disobeying as one sees fit. If everyone followed that selfish notion, the result would be chaos.

Paragraph 3 sets up an opposition between the teacher's action, which is later characterized as "civil disobedience," and the alternative of working within the system. The final sentence—which says he "blew" the opportunity to work within the system—indicates the conclusion of the argument in the editorial: *the teacher should have worked within the system to change the law.*

Paragraph 4 summarizes some of the reasons why a person might want to carry out civil disobedience, and Paragraph 5 sets out the alternative open to a teacher in criticizing the law without breaking it.

Finally, Paragraph 6 argues that the teacher shouldn't have committed civil disobedience in this case. It suggests that picking and choosing which laws to obey would result in chaos.

A careful reading leads us to an initial interpretation of the main argument along the following lines. The central conclusion is that the teacher should have worked within the legal system to change the laws. Paragraphs 3 to 5 set out the alternatives and suggest that civil disobedience should not have been carried out in this case. The final paragraph provides a reason for holding that an act of civil disobedience should not have occurred; namely, that such civil disobedience would result in chaos.

Step 1: Begin Reconstruction by Identifying Any Explicit Premises or Conclusions in Overall Argument As we discussed in chapter 3, the distinction between explicit and implicit premises and conclusions is not sharp when you are reconstructing an argument from a complex prose passage. Nowhere in the essay is it explicitly stated that "the teacher should have worked within the legal system to change the law." Rather, evaluative comments such as "he blew that opportunity" or the title "A Selfish Way of Looking at the Law" suggest that the editorial is arguing in favor of working within the system. Even though no *either–or* sentence is given, the two alternatives being considered—civil disobedience and working within the system—are fairly explicit in the text. This suggests the premise

(1) *Either the teacher should have committed civil disobedience or he should have worked within the legal system to change the law.*

Selections from Paragraphs Containing Main Argument 1

3 Yes, the teacher has every right to disagree with the law. Reasonable people differ over the propriety of requiring prayer, moments of silence and similar observances in public schools. But what a wonderful opportunity he had to teach his students about the responsibilities of a citizen to obey a disagreeable law while working within the system to change it. And how thoroughly he blew that opportunity.

4 Certainly breaking a law is one way to protest its existence. . . .

5 But if the teaching of American government is worthwhile, it shouldn't convey the impression that civil disobedience is the first line of attack.

Step 2: Complete Reconstruction by Adding an Implicit Premise to the Main Argument On reviewing the premise as stated above and the conclusion we identified in the preliminary step, we can recognize that we have two of the three statements needed for a disjunctive argument fitting the pattern:

(1) A or B.

(missing) *(2) Not A.*

∴ B.

To interpret the argument in this form, we would need to add as an implicit premise: *The teacher should not have committed civil disobedience.*

First Interpretation of Passage 11.1

(suggested by Paragraphs 3–5) *(1) Either the teacher should have committed civil disobedience or he should have worked within the legal system to change the law.*

(implicit) *(2) The teacher should not have committed civil disobedience.*

∴ The teacher should have worked within the legal system to change the law.

Premise 2 in this reconstruction is itself the conclusion of a supporting argument.

Paragraph Containing Supporting Argument

6 But when a dramatic, attention getting gesture is depicted as superior to working within the system and building a consensus a harmful message is delivered. This teacher's example said it's permissible to pick and choose among the laws, obeying or disobeying as one sees fit. If everyone followed that selfish notion, the result would be chaos.

Applying Steps 1 and 2 to the Supporting Argument The argument in Paragraph 6 supports the conclusion that *The teacher should not have committed civil disobedience* (which was the implicit premise of the main argument). And we have already identified the explicit premise that *if it is permissible for everyone to pick and choose among laws, then chaos would result*. Implicit in the argument is the assumption that *chaos shouldn't occur* and a link between the teacher's civil disobedience and the notion that it is permissible for everyone to pick and choose among laws.[2]

Supporting Argument

(implicit) *(1) If the teacher should have committed civil disobedience, then it is permissible for him to pick and choose among laws.*

(implicit) *(2) If it is permissible for him to pick and choose among laws, then it is permissible for everyone to do so.*

(paragraph 6) *(3) If it is permissible for everyone to do so, then chaos would occur.*

(implicit) *(4) Chaos shouldn't occur.*

∴ *The teacher should not have committed civil disobedience.*

Applying Steps 3, 4, and 5 to the Arguments As will often be the case, we have interpreted these arguments in such a way that the implicit premises we add permit the conclusions to follow from the premises. Indeed, we could have combined the main and supporting arguments into one integrated argument, as we discussed in Chapter 3.

Integrated Argument

(suggested by Paragraphs 3–5) *(1) Either the teacher should have committed civil disobedience or he should have worked within the legal system to change the law.*

(implicit) *(2) If the teacher should have committed civil disobedience, then it is permissible for him to pick and choose among laws.*

(implicit) *(3) If it is permissible for him to pick and choose among laws, then it is permissible for everyone to do so.*

(paragraph 6) *(4) If it is permissible for everyone to do so, then chaos would occur.*

(implicit) *(5) Chaos shouldn't occur.*

∴ *The teacher should have worked within the legal system to change the law.*

---

[2]The argument can be interpreted as an extended version of *modus tollens* that combines it with a chain argument, having the form:

(1) If A, then B.
(2) If B, then C.
(3) If C, then D.
(4) Not D.

∴ *Not A.*

The two fairly explicit premises—1 and 4 in the continuous version of the argument—appear quite acceptable. As Premise 4 suggests, if everyone were to pick and choose which laws to follow (for example, which traffic laws), then chaos would likely follow. And given that the teacher was going to respond to the law, civil disobedience or working within the system appear to be the two alternatives, as suggested in Premise 1. We should note, however, that a supporter of the Georgia law would maintain that the teacher had a third course of action open, namely, following the law. Hence, the argument might contain a false dilemma fallacy.

What about the implicit premises? Are they acceptable? Premise 5 is straightforward. It is easy to agree that social chaos shouldn't occur. Premise 3 is less easy to assess. But it is plausible to maintain that if the teacher can be permitted to pick and choose which laws to obey solely on the basis of his judgment, then it must be permissible for anyone to do so.[3] There is nothing special about this particular teacher.

We are left to assess Premise 2: *If the teacher should have committed civil disobedience, then it is permissible for him to pick and choose among laws.* This premise can be criticized by noting that the civil disobedience in this case is limited to a controversial law that is of dubious constitutionality. Furthermore, breaking of the law does not do direct, serious harm. We can hold that civil disobedience in such cases (those involving controversial laws of dubious constitutionality in which breaking of the law does no serious harm) is justified (and permitted) without holding that the teacher (or anyone else) is permitted to break all laws. Laws against murder, driving on the wrong side of the road, and even tax evasion do not involve controversial laws of dubious constitutionality, and in the case of murder and reckless driving breaking them would likely cause serious harm.

These considerations give us grounds for rejecting Premise 2 of the continuous version of the argument at Step 4 in the flowchart. This leads us to consider according to Step 5 whether a more charitable interpretation is possible. The title and choice of words in Paragraph 6 suggest another version of the argument:

A Second Version of the Argument in Passage 11.1

(suggested by Paragraphs 3–5) *(1) Either the teacher should have committed civil disobedience or he should have worked within the legal system to change the law.*

(implicit) *(2) If the teacher should have committed civil disobedience, then it is permissible to act selfishly.*

(implicit) *(3) It isn't permissible to act selfishly.*

∴ *The teacher should have worked within the legal system to change the law.*

---

[3]This premise embodies what is sometimes called the *Generalization Principle* in ethics: roughly, if it is right for someone to do something in a situation, it is also right for similar people to do similar things in similar situations.

Even if we accept Premises 1 and 3, there are problems with Premise 2. Exactly why is the teacher's act selfish? Many would hold that he is acting altruistically for what he perceives as a larger constitutional principle. Indeed, his suspension presumably caused him some amount of harm. It is true that he did what he wanted to do and believed was right to do. But this is not enough to make the act selfish. If anything, this version of the argument is less charitable than the first. This interpretation fails as well.

A third interpretation, which focuses on the issue of whether civil disobedience should be the first line of attack, is also suggested, particularly in Paragraph 5. This interpretation of the argument acknowledges that civil disobedience might ultimately be used, but not until a person has exhausted other avenues. It notes that teachers are especially well positioned to work within the system to change a bad law.

A Third Version of the Argument in Passage 11.1

(suggested by Paragraph 5) *(1) If a person can work within the system to change a bad law, then that person should not commit civil disobedience (as the first line of attack).*

(suggested by Paragraph 3 *(2) The teacher can work within the system to change a bad law.*

∴ The teacher should not commit civil disobedience (as the first line of attack).

As in the case of the first two interpretations, this version of the main argument has been constructed so that it is valid. It is an instance of modus ponens. What about the premises?

Premise 2 is certainly plausible. As Paragraph 5 indicates, the teacher can work toward changing the law by teaching students lessons about democracy and about their options in working toward a change of state law within it. We can criticize Premise 1 by pointing out first that even if a person can work toward something in a certain way, that doesn't mean that there is much chance of success using this route. If there is another more effective alternative, perhaps this should be carried out instead. For example, it might be the case that *if you win the lottery, you need not look for a job*. It does not follow that *if you try to win—that is, play the lottery—you need not look for a job*. So it can be true that *you play the lottery*, but false that *you need not look for a job*. Perhaps you should do both. Similarly, teaching a few students, even galvanizing them to act, might possibly be instrumental in changing state law, but like the lottery the prospects are not very good. Just as looking for a job is a viable alternative to trying to win the lottery, civil disobedience might be a viable alternative to working within the system as a teacher.

Second, even if the teacher could be successful in overturning Georgia state law by working within the system, there is the larger question about similar laws that might be passed in other states. The teacher is described as interested in the First Amendment. He is challenging the constitutionality of the law. If the Georgia law is overturned by the federal district court or the

U.S. Supreme Court, then his action would have an effect not just in Georgia but in other states as well. To raise such a constitutional issue it is necessary to have standing. By breaking the law, the Georgia teacher is in a position to appeal its constitutionality. Seen in this light, his action is actually necessary to achieving his larger aim. So the first premise is false on these grounds as well. Even though he could (successfully) work within the system to change the Georgia law, given his larger constitutional aim he should also commit civil disobedience (as the first line of attack).

Applying Step 6 to the Arguments To conclude the application of the flowchart to the three interpretations of the editorial, we should ask why they might have seemed persuasive. In addition to the false dilemma in premise 1 that we mentioned earlier, two premises from interpretation 1 can be seen as committing the slippery slope fallacy:

(3) If it is permissible for him to pick and choose among laws, then it is permissible for everyone.

(4) If it is permissible for everyone to do so, then chaos would occur.

These statements suggest that his act of disobedience with respect to a newly passed law of questionable constitutionality might somehow encourage widespread law-breaking, which would then lead to chaos. A single act of civil disobedience is unlikely to produce this effect.

The second argument depends on the premises

(2) If the teacher should have committed civil disobedience, then it is permissible to act selfishly.

(3) It isn't permissible to act selfishly.

They contain an equivocation involving the concept of a selfish act. Premise 3 depends on the common interpretation of a selfish act as one that is done to benefit oneself at the expense of others. Premise 2 seems to assume that any act that occurs for one's own reasons is selfish.

Similarly, Argument 3 might seem plausible because of an equivocation as well. The term *system* is used differently in the two premises.

(1) If a person can work within the system to change a bad law, then that person should not commit civil disobedience (as the first line of attack).

(2) The teacher can work within the system to change a bad law.

In Premise 2 the "system" is the system of state laws and the political action that might change them. But as we pointed out in our analysis, the truth of Premise 1 is plausible only if the "system" includes the larger system of laws and their constitutional interpretation.

If you are discussing this editorial with someone who accepted the arguments it contained, you might be more effective in promoting your negative appraisal if you helped the person understand how these arguments could have misled him or her. The discussion above suggests some possibilities.

A SECOND APPLICATION: A CONVERGENT ARGUMENT CONTAINED IN A LINKED ARGUMENT

As we indicated in Chapters 8 and 9, a nondeductive argument can be used to support a premise of a deductive argument. In this section, we apply the six-step procedure to a passage in which the conclusion of a convergent argument serves as a premise in a larger, embracing deductive argument. In a case such as this, the techniques for criticizing a nondeductive argument are useful in evaluating a premise of a deductive argument. Passage 11.2 provides an example.

Passage 11.2

Today's Debate: Higher Education on the Web

Teachers assault online college, put self-interest over education[4]

Our View: Why fight learning at home—particularly when it is accredited?

The courses are taught on the Web. Students and faculty meet via e-mail. The library is digital, and the five students who earned degrees last spring got them at a cybergraduation. Now, Jones International University, the first college to function entirely in cyberspace, has acquired one crucial trapping of tradition—a seal of approval from a respected accrediting group.

That prize, awarded this spring after a four-year effort, marks a coming of age not only for Jones but also for students seeking a college education on this new frontier. It opens the way for Jones students to apply for federal aid not available at unaccredited colleges. And provides at least some assurance that a Jones degree will be worth something.

With all of that progress, professors should be cheering. Instead, Jones' accreditation is under fire by members of several national teachers associations who see it an affront to quality.

They focus on what's missing at an e-university: a traditional full-time faculty, a bricks-and-mortar library, personal interaction between professors and students. With students able to get federal loans, critics say, the unwary could end up with nothing more than a questionable degree and huge debts.

Certainly the pioneering cyber-universities are different, but that's just their point. They offer education to students who need to sign on from kitchens or home offices, during predawn hours or breaks at work. Most of the 600 students at Jones, for instance, are over age 28, with full-time jobs.

Working at an individual pace, students talk with faculty and each other in chat rooms or by e-mail. During one recent online forum, experts signed on from various locations and chatted with students in several

[4]*USA TODAY*. February 5, 1999. Reprinted by Permission.

Cybercollege

Jones International University, the first all-cyber college, offers a degree at about half the cost of a traditional college, when living and transportation are factored in.

Yearly costs	*Jones International*	*Four-year public college*
Tuition and fees	$3,908	$3,356
Books and supplies	$625	$681
Estimated Internet service	$300	0
Room, board, transportation	0	$4,730
Total	$4,833	$8,767

Source: Jones International University: The College Board. Graphic by Grant Jerding USA Today

countries, a more personal education encounter than a lecture to 500.

Jones' courses are developed by professors at well-known schools and taught by separate Jones faculty members, prompting a gripe that such duties shouldn't be divided. But Jones' professors often work in the fields they're teaching, adding real-world zest to the curriculum.

As to the fear that these may be little more than expensive diploma mills, that's a risk at any new college and a concern that accreditation is designed to ally.

Many top universities have joined the online rush, offering single courses or specialty degrees. What makes Jones different is its all-cyber existence, save for some business offices in Colorado. What makes it threatening to traditional colleges is its ability to offer courses for an accredited bachelor's degree at around $4,800 a year, about half the tuition, room and board costs at public colleges.

For now, Jones is a fledgling experiment. Most students drop in for a course or two, with only about 100 seeking degrees. Accreditation may help it thrive.

More important is what accreditation means to prospective students. Experts say cyber-diploma scams are growing fast, with a few e-schools moving offshore and paying foreign governments in an attempt to buy legitimacy.

Accreditation proves a needed yardstick to measure quality. In the new world of virtual colleges, it's good to know that real, live educators are checking them out.

Applying Steps 1, 2, and 3 After carefully reading this editorial on cyber education, we can identify a fairly explicit conclusion: Educators should be supporting, not criticizing, online college education. This is reflected in the headline ("Teachers Assault Online College, Put Self-Interest over Education"), the question posed in Paragraph 1 ("Why fight learning at home—particularly when it is accredited?"), and most explicitly in Paragraph 4 ("With all of that progress, professors should be cheering."). A supporting reason that looms large in the editorial is that Jones International University, an all-cyber college, has received accreditation. But a survey of the entire editorial reveals that this is only one of several convergent considerations in favor of viewing Jones International (and, potentially, other cyber colleges as well) as offering a quality education. This strongly suggested premise can be combined with an implicit *if–then* premise to form the following deductive argument:

(1) Jones International offers a quality education.

(2) If Jones International offers a quality education, then educators should be supporting, not criticizing, online education.

∴ *Educators should be supporting, not criticizing, online education.*

As is typically the case with deductive reconstruction, we are stating the argument in a way that makes the conclusion follow, so that Step 3 in the flowchart on page 314 is answered affirmatively.

To complete the reconstruction of the entire argument contained in the editorial, we add the following convergent argument, which is offered in support of Premise 1 above.

Diagram of Convergent Argument and Counter-Considerations in Passage 11.2

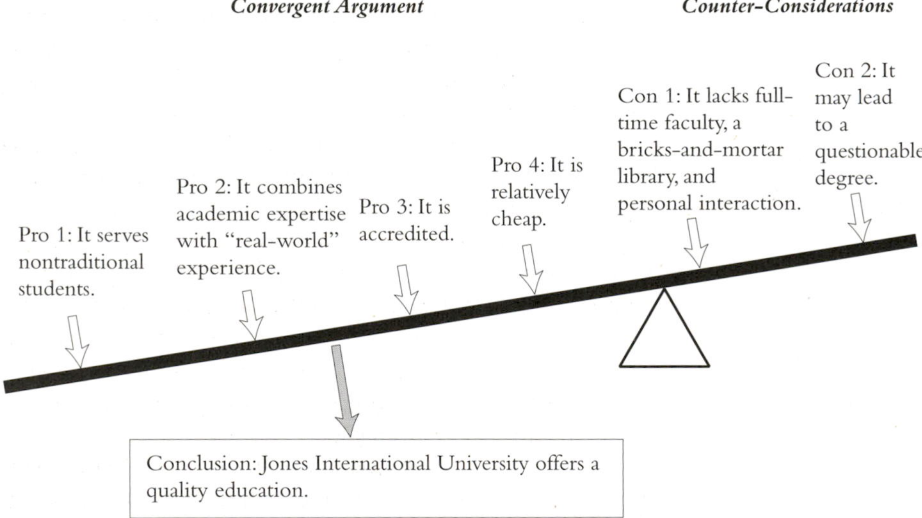

Convergent Argument
Counter-Considerations
Pro 1: It serves nontraditional students.
Pro 2: It combines academic expertise with "real-world" experience.
Pro 3: It is accredited.
Pro 4: It is relatively cheap.
Con 1: It lacks full-time faculty, a bricks-and-mortar library, and personal interaction.
Con 2: It may lead to a questionable degree.
Conclusion: Jones International University offers a quality education.

Applying Steps 4, 5, and 6 As the summary box indicates, we can criticize a convergent argument by showing that some considerations are doubtful. For example, we could challenge the claim that *Jones International University is relatively cheap* by pointing out that the chart contained in the passage itself shows that most of the difference in costs arise because the four-year college total contains cost of room and board and Jones International does not. But of course students using the cyber college will still be paying for food and shelter—perhaps even more than college students living on campus.

Criticizing Convergent Arguments (from Chapter 9)

1. Present the initial convergent argument and counter-considerations.
2. Add further considerations.
3. Eliminate doubtful considerations.
4. Blunt or promote considerations.

Even if we eliminate this pro-consideration, the article cites three other pro elements. The question is whether the remaining pros outweigh the cons. We can criticize the weighting in the article in two ways: *blunting* the pro-considerations or promoting the counter-considerations. For example, the article stresses that Jones International University is accredited, but a critic could point out that mere accreditation need not assure quality in education. The accrediting organizations determine only that an institution has met a minimum standard. This in itself does not give much support to the conclusion that it offers a "quality" education, only that it is not unacceptably bad education. Alternatively, a critic might try to *promote* the counter-consideration that the cyber college, at least at this point in time, offers a degree of questionable value for the students, both in terms of employment or graduate education, and that is of central importance. Sustained criticism of either of these types could shift the balance against the conclusion.

Additional criticism can be raised against the *if–then* premise of the deductive argument: *If Jones International offers a quality education, then educators should be supporting, not criticizing, online education.* Even if one grants the high quality of education at Jones International, it does not follow that educators should be supporting, not criticizing, online education. To suggest that one should either support or criticize is a false dilemma. One could support and promote the enterprise of developing online education because of its potential benefits for a particular student population—especially working students—but at the same time criticize particular aspects of online education. The consideration that such education lacks personal, face-to-face interaction is especially worrisome given the large body of evidence that links success in undergraduate education with a student's sense of connection to other students and to faculty. The editorial's premises could be seen as successfully supporting the modest conclusion that educators should support the development of online education for those to whom a traditional education is unavailable, but this conclusion is much less interesting just because it is uncontroversial.

EXERCISE 11.1

Applying the Six-Step Procedure

A. In Chapter 3, you applied the first two steps of the procedure to the passages in Exercise 3.3. Apply the remainder of the procedure to the arguments from these passages.

B. Apply the six-step procedure to the main *arguments* (not just the theories used to support the arguments) in Exercise 10.4, Passage 3 ("What If

Women Ran the World?") and Passage 4 ("Science, Proof, and the Ancient Astronaut Hypothesis . . .").

C. Apply the six-step procedure to one or more of the following longer passages. Supply appropriate reconstructions and sketch criticisms. Keep in mind the techniques explained in Chapters 4 through 10 for criticizing a wide array of premises: *if–then* premises, universal generalizations, *either–or* premises that are false dilemmas, as well as premises based on conceptual theories, empirical theories, and the various kinds of nondeductive arguments.

(Optional) Form your comments into a critical essay. Begin with an introduction of the topic being discussed. Next, identify the editorial or essay you are criticizing and restate briefly the argument(s) advanced. Present your critical comments, clearly identifying the specific premises you are attacking, and then conclude your essay.

1.

Gender Tests May Not Be Worth Risk of Misuse[5]

by Ellen Goodman

The woman beside me pats her rounded stomach and rolls her eyes to the ceiling, exclaiming, "Is she ever active today!" The "she" in this action won't be born until March. But my pregnant companion already knows the gender of this gestation.

I have grown accustomed to the attachment of a pronoun to a fetus by now. Most women I know of her age and anxiety level have had "the test" and gotten the results.

Over the past two decades, through amniocentesis and then CVS and sonograms, a generation of parents has received a prenatal exam, a genetic checkup on their offspring. They have all been given new information and sometimes new, unhappy choices.

But the "she" playing soccer in the neighboring uterus is a healthy baby. And the woman is more than pleased with both of those pieces of knowledge.

What if she were not? What if she and her husband had regarded the sex of this child as a devastating disappointment?

I wonder about this because, in the news, doctors report success on the road to developing a simple blood test on pregnant women to determine the sex of the fetus. The geneticists are excited because such a test could allow safer, widespread testing. It could help those worried about gender-linked inherited diseases.

But this test may increase the possibility of abortion for sex selection by those who regard gender—the wrong gender—as a genetic flaw.

The repugnance to abortion-by-gender runs deep in our culture. Both pro-choice supporters who believe that abortion is a serious decision and pro-life supporters who believe it is an immoral decision unite in opposing sex selection as the most frivolous or sexist of motives.

It is the rare person who defends it on the grounds of population control or pure parental choice. It is a rarer American who chooses it. Indeed, the only countries in which sex selection occurs in discernible numbers

[5]Ellen Goodman, "Gender Tests May Not Be Worth Risk of Misuse," *The New York Times*. © 1992 by The Boston Globe Newspaper Company/Washington.

have been those such as India or Korea where daughters have long been unwanted. It is almost always female fetuses that are aborted. But gender testing and the capacity for gender choosing—before and after conception—is an ethical issue in this country, too. This is the first, but hardly the last time, that the new technology will be available to produce designer babies. Today, genetic testing is valued in America because it leads to the diagnosis of diseases that cause pain and death and disability. Eventually it may lead to their cure. But in the future, we also are likely to have access to much more information about genes than we need medically. We may be able to identify the gene for height, hair color, eye color, perhaps even athletic ability or intelligence.

There will always be parents who, out of ego, or some perverse view of children as a perfect product, want to pick and choose genes according to a master plan. Should society encourage or allow that? Must doctors perform tests and turn over information to patients to do with as they will?

John Fletcher, an ethicist at the University of Virginia, suggests a line to be drawn around our right to know. "Any kind of genetic knowledge that isn't related to a genuine disease," he says, "is on the other side of the line."

Because gender, like hair color, is not a disease, he believes that the medical profession can refuse testing and disclosing for two reasons. To prevent abortion-by-gender and, in a wider moral context, to keep genetic research on the right track.

Americans haven't yet learned how to say "no" to knowledge. Doctors may feel uncomfortable, even paternalistic, withholding information from people about their own bodies, genes, fetuses. Pennsylvania has banned abortion for sex selection in a bill that goes into effect this month. Such a ban is not only impossible to enforce but says nothing about the future dilemmas of reproductive knowledge.

At the moment, the moral consensus against sex selection is holding. The medical profession should at least state, in public and in unity, a strong position against gender selection and a moral prohibition against genetic eugenics. But in the longer run, the rest of us may be called upon to ask whether our curiosity about gender is worth the risk that others will misuse that information. It may be wiser to learn if the baby is a "he" or a "she" the old-fashioned way.

2.

Selection from President Obama's 2010 State of the Union Address, January 27, 2010[6]

Next, we need to encourage American innovation. Last year, we made the largest investment in basic research funding in history—(applause)—an investment that could lead to the world's cheapest solar cells or treatment that kills cancer cells but leaves healthy ones untouched. And no area is more ripe for such innovation than energy. You can see the results of last year's investments in clean energy—in the North Carolina company

[6]http://www.whitehouse.gov/the-press-office/remarks-president-state-union-address. April 28, 2010.

that will create 1,200 jobs nationwide helping to make advanced batteries; or in the California business that will put a thousand people to work making solar panels.

But to create more of these clean energy jobs, we need more production, more efficiency, more incentives. And that means building a new generation of safe, clean nuclear power plants in this country. (Applause.) It means making tough decisions about opening new offshore areas for oil and gas development. (Applause.) It means continued investment in advanced biofuels and clean coal technologies. (Applause.) And, yes, it means passing a comprehensive energy and climate bill with incentives that will finally make clean energy the profitable kind of energy in America. (Applause.)

I am grateful to the House for passing such a bill last year. (Applause.) And this year I'm eager to help advance the bipartisan effort in the Senate. (Applause.)

I know there have been questions about whether we can afford such changes in a tough economy. I know that there are those who disagree with the overwhelming scientific evidence on climate change. But here's the thing—even if you doubt the evidence, providing incentives for energy-efficiency and clean energy are the right thing to do for our future—because the nation that leads the clean energy economy will be the nation that leads the global economy. And America must be that nation. (Applause.)

Third, we need to export more of our goods. (Applause.) Because the more products we make and sell to other countries, the more jobs we support right here in America. (Applause.) So tonight, we set a new goal: We will double our exports over the next five years, an increase that will support two million jobs in America. (Applause.) To help meet this goal, we're launching a National Export Initiative that will help farmers and small businesses increase their exports, and reform export controls consistent with national security. (Applause.)

We have to seek new markets aggressively, just as our competitors are. If America sits on the sidelines while other nations sign trade deals, we will lose the chance to create jobs on our shores. (Applause.) But realizing those benefits also means enforcing those agreements so our trading partners play by the rules. (Applause.) And that's why we'll continue to shape a Doha trade agreement that opens global markets, and why we will strengthen our trade relations in Asia and with key partners like South Korea and Panama and Colombia. (Applause.)

3.

The Price of This Beauty Is Too High[7]

A Web site auctioning the eggs of fashion models promotes an unhealthy idea. It encourages parents to fixate on their child's physical appearance.

Ron Harris, a fashion photographer, organized the auction. Bids start at $15,000 and can go as high as $150,000. Harris characterizes the sale of models' eggs as "Darwin at his very best." American society is obsessed with celebrity beauty, Harris says in trying to justify the sale. At the Web site, he writes: "If you could increase the chance of reproducing

[7]Editorial, *Omaha World-Herald*, October 27, 1999. Reprinted with permission.

beautiful children, and thus giving them an advantage in society, would you?"

He also states: "It is not my intention to suggest we make a super society of only beautiful people. This site simply mirrors our current society in that beauty always goes to the highest bidder."

The commercial aspect of Harris' enterprise isn't so unusual. Sperm has been available essentially as a commodity for years now. The most notorious example is the genius sperm bank which included donations form William Shockley, a Nobel Prize-winning scientist. Harris says, in fact, that he plans an online auction of sperm in the future.

It's also true that women who donate their eggs deserve monetary compensation for inconvenience and discomfort they experience as a result of hormone treatments and physical removal of the eggs. A payment in range of $2,500 to $5,000 is most common.

The last thing American society needs, however, is the shallow beauty worship Harris promotes. Harris is encouraging parents to engineer a desired appearance for their child—hardly a healthy philosophy around which to build a family. There's no guarantee, after all, that the children produced through Harris' project will meet the parent's expected standards of beauty. If the parents wind up with a boy or girl they considered an ugly duckling, the child could be weighed down by horrible burden.

Harris' beauty-obsessed rhetoric would have the world imagine that people with less-than-perfect features are somehow inferior. But modest physical attributes needn't stop individuals from achieving greatness. Consider the great good accomplished by Abraham Lincoln, whose physical appearance was such that his political foes derided him as an "ape." Albert Einstein had puffy hair, yet he turned modern science inside-out with his revolutionary thinking. Golda Meir may not have been a beauty queen, but she proved to be a strong leader of Israel.

Parents often discover that their child falls short in one regard or another, or that their child has developed interests far different from what the parents had expected—and yet the parents' love remains undiminished.

Harris urges parents to look on their children as physical objects. Well-adjusted parents, however, regard their offspring as individuals—precious yet imperfect individuals. And they love them for what they are.

4.

Stop Subsidizing the Future Rich[8]

by John R. Lott, Jr.

College Station, Texas—The basic problem with government subsidized student loans is that they are a subsidy to future high income people. The loans students receive carry interest rates far below what even the most stable corporations pay.

While students, especially those from relatively poor families, do not have a high standard of living during college, they enjoy above-average earnings soon after receiving their degrees. Since the loans are slowly paid off after graduation, during a

[8]Copyright 1985 *USA TODAY*. Reprinted with permission. John R. Lott, Jr. was a visiting assistant professor of economics at Texas A&M University when he wrote this passage.

period of high earnings, subsidized interest rates seem unjustified. Why should factory-workers and secretaries be taxed so would be managers, lawyers, and doctors can be subsidized?

And subsidized federal loans are only a small part of our educational subsidies. Here at Texas A&M, each student pays only a small percentage of the $10,000-plus it annually costs the state of Texas. The great majority of these students come from relatively well-to-do families. In the cases of those few who do not, the argument about transfers to future high-income earners applies. It is important to distinguish loans *per se* from the currently heavily subsidized loans.

While *subsidized* loans are unjustified, a weak case can be made for government loan guarantees or possibly loans at unsubsidized rates. This is because of the problems created by current bankruptcy laws, which in some cases have allowed students to rid themselves of educational debt by simply declaring bankruptcy after graduation. Banks may therefore consider student loans too risky.

Unfortunately, these bankruptcy laws probably hurt children from poor families the most. For a student from a poor family, the parents' co-signature does not appreciably reduce the riskiness of the loan, since they do not own enough assets.

The simplest and best solution is to alter the bankruptcy laws to get rid of this problem. Private banks could then handle student loans entirely, with no role played by the federal government.

Evidence provided by Sam Peltzman of the University of Chicago suggests that abolishing subsidized loans will have little effect on the number of people attending higher education. The primary effect will be to end the unjustified taxing of people to subsidize the future wealthy of this country.

5.

Legal Drugs Unlikely to Foster Nation of Zombies[9]

by Stephen Chapman

There is good news and bad news about cocaine. The bad news is that captive monkeys given unlimited access to the stuff will spurn everything else to get high, until they die of starvation.

The good news is you're not a monkey. In a society of lower primates, which are incapable of prudent restraint in the use of mind-altering substances, legalizing cocaine and other illicit drugs would probably be a bad idea. When it comes to humans, the issue looks a bit different.

We know that a 20-year government effort to stamp out illicit drug use has been a colossal failure. We know it has swallowed vast amounts of money, prison space and

[9]Copyright 1990 by Stephen Chapman. Reprinted by permission.

police time. We know it has spawned epidemics of violent crime in the inner city, much as Prohibition sparked gangland wars.

What we don't know is what would happen if drugs were legal. Would we become a nation of zombies—a "citizenry that is perpetually in a drug-induced haze," as drug czar William Bennett predicts?

Bennett says we don't have to try legalization to know how horrible it would be: "We have just undergone a kind of cruel national experiment in which drugs became cheap and widely available: That experiment is called the crack epidemic."

But what keeps clean-living citizens like Bennett from becoming crackheads? Is it the fear of jail? If crack were sold at a legal outlet around the corner, would he pick up a case? Would Miss America?

Would you? Not likely. A poll sponsored by the Drug Policy Foundation asked Americans if they would try illicit drugs if they were legal. Of those who had never tried marijuana before, only 4.2 percent of those questioned said they would try it. Fewer than 1 percent of those who had never used cocaine said they'd take it out for a test drive.

That 1 percent can be mightily grateful to Bill Bennett for deterring them. The other 99 percent gain essentially nothing from the drug war. In fact, if they live in the inner city, the drug war puts them in danger every day by reserving the business for violent people with lots of guns and ammo.

The poll confirms the few experiments with drug tolerance. After the Netherlands practically legalized marijuana in 1976, its use declined. In the various U.S. states that decriminalized marijuana in the 1970s, pot grew less popular.

Even if everyone were tempted to sample the newly legal drugs, very few would imitate monkeys. The government's National Institute on Drug Abuse says 22 million Americans have used cocaine at least once. Of these, 8.2 million have used it in the last year. Just 862,000 use it every week. That doesn't sound like a ferociously addictive drug.

When it comes to crack, a smokable form of cocaine which is allegedly more tenacious in its hold, no one knows exactly how many addicts there are. But NIDA says fewer than one in every five of the 2.5 million people who have tried it are regular users, blasting off at least once a month. Bennett's "epidemic" has afflicted no more than one American in every 500.

Crack is supposed to be uniquely destructive because of the severe damage it does to fetuses. Propagandists for the drug war claim that 375,000 "crack babies" are born every year, requiring billions of dollars in extra medical care. But the government says there are fewer than half a million people who smoke crack regularly. Apparently we're supposed to believe that four out of every five of them give birth each year.

In fact, despite being cheap and widely available, crack hasn't produced mass addiction. Why not?

The best explanation comes from Dartmouth neuroscientist Michael Gazzaniga in a recent interview in National Review magazine. Only a small portion of the population is inclined to abuse drugs (including alcohol), and these people will systematically wreck themselves with whatever is at hand, he says. But those who aren't prone to abuse won't become addicts regardless of what drugs are legally available.

"In our culture alone," said Gazzaniga, "70 percent to 80 percent of us use alcohol, and the abuse rate is now estimated at 5 percent to 6 percent. We see at work here a major feature of the human response to drug availability, namely, the inclination to moderation." People allowed to make free choices generally make sound ones.

But a recognition that humans can use freedom wisely is not one of the distinguishing traits of those behind the drug war who can imagine all sorts of costs from legalization but can't see the real ones from prohibition. If the citizenry ever emerges from the haze produced by the drug war, it may realize that the greatest harms are the ones we've already got.

6.

Choose Least Harmful Biotech Options

The splitting of the atom and the unraveling of the DNA double helix represent the two premier scientific accomplishments of the twentieth century, the first a tour de force of physics, the second of biology. . . . If the century just passing was the age of physics and nuclear technology its crown jewel, then the century just coming into view will belong to biology and its premier technology will be genetic engineering. . . . While the twenty-first century will be the Age of Biology, the technological application of the knowledge we gain can take a variety of forms. To believe that genetic engineering is the only way to apply our newfound knowledge of biology and the life sciences is limiting and keeps us from entertaining other options which might prove even more effective in addressing the needs and fulfilling the dreams of current and future generations. . . . the question is what kind of biotechnologies will we choose in the coming Biotech Century? Will we use our new insights into the working of plants and animal genomes to create genetically engineered "super crops" and transgenic animals, or new techniques for advancing ecological agriculture and more humane animal husbandry practices? Will we use the information we're collecting on the human genome to alter our genetic makeup or to pursue new sophisticated health prevention practices? . . . Since it is impossible to be clairvoyant and know all of the potential ramifications and consequences that might accompany the many new technologies we might want to introduce, we should attempt to minimize regrets and keep open as many options as possible for those who come after us—including our fellow creatures. This means that when choosing among alternative technological applications, we are best served by taking the less radical, more conservative approach—the one least likely to create disruptions and externalities. "First, do no harm" is a well established and long revered principle in medicine. . . . Which of the two competing visions of biotechnology—genetic engineering or ecological practices and preventive health—is more radical and adventurous and most likely to cause disequilibrium and which is the more conservative approach and least likely to cause unanticipated harm down the line? The answer, I believe is obvious.[10]

[10] Jeremy Rifkin, *The Biotech Century: Harnessing the Gene and Remaking the World* (New York: Tarcher/Putnam, 1998), 231–234.

7.

A Case History on the Killing of Rats and Terrorists: If a "war on rats" that relies solely on killing fails, so will a "war on terrorism" that aims at killing terrorists without removing the "garbage" they feed upon.[11]

Rats and terrorists are similar in key respects: Both are widely despised and feared; both move underground surreptitiously; and both types of vermin can't be exterminated by killing them.

In the case of rats, history proves the futility of killing as a means of eradication. Robert Sullivan's recent book, *Rats*, contends that the only way to eliminate rats is to remove their source of food—that is, remove the garbage.

The Bush administration justifiably regards terrorists as rats, and few U.S. citizens object to killing terrorists when they surface. That policy seems fitting, but it is also insufficient.

If a "war on rats" that relies solely on a killing strategy will fail, so will a "war on terrorism" that aims at killing terrorists without removing the "garbage" on which they feed.

What nourishes terrorism? Why do terrorists kill innocent civilians in the U.S., Iraq, Pakistan, Russia, Ireland, Saudi Arabia, Israel, Turkey, France, Indonesia, Spain and elsewhere? Looking at the list of disparate countries suggests different answers to the question. Factors that motivated Protestant and Catholic terrorists during the "troubles" in Ireland clearly differ from the sources of terrorism in Israel.

President Bush did not help us to understand terrorism by describing Iraqi terrorists simply as "cold-blooded killers." After a bombing in Baghdad on Oct. 27, 2003, Bush said, "That's all they are. They hate freedom. They love terror."

That view does not explain terrorist acts in Saudi Arabia, which offers few freedoms to hate. And suicide bombers elsewhere probably don't kill themselves for the love of terror. The reasons why terrorists sacrifice themselves differ from Iraq to Israel to Spain. Bush's dismissal of terrorists as freedom-hating terror-lovers may have been a quick response to a gruesome bombing. But in his address to Congress on Sept. 20, 2001, he explained the Sept. 11, 2001, terror attack with similar words: "They hate our freedoms."

Bush's simplistic explanation is misleading but not entirely untrue. Freedom of expression in our mass media allows for excesses of material consumption, violence and nudity. Many Muslims, among others, view our free lifestyle as impious, if not profane.

But a more thorough explanation of the terrorists' motive lies in the United States' international reach and role: its foreign policies and its global economic and military power. We need to look there for the terrorists' nourishment—for the garbage that sustains them.

What aspects of our policies and power cause Muslim terrorists to hate us enough to take their own lives? Reporters have cited several reasons:

- Despite upholding democracy as an ideal, Washington supports authoritarian governments (e.g., Saudi Arabia) when it serves its interests.

[11]Kenneth Janda, professor emeritus of political science at Northwestern University. *Chicago Tribune*. Chicago, Ill.: Jul 4, 2004. pg. 9. Reprinted with permission.

- On almost every important conflict between the Palestinians and the Israelis, the United States sides with Israel.
- American culture, spread worldwide through mass media, tends to infect and smother other cultures. Even advocating that women everywhere enjoy civil and political rights—such as going to school, driving cars, voting and holding office—infuriates some in traditional societies.

Should we change all our actions to appease terrorists? Of course not. But we should review our policies while seeking to understand the differing bases for terrorism—different even in the Middle East.

Yet our nation is ill-equipped to understand our enemies there. For example, only 22 of 1.8 million graduates of American colleges in 2003 took degrees in Arabic.The *New York Times* quoted Richard Brecht, a former Air Force cryptographer and director of a language project funded by the Defense Department as saying,"Five billion dollars for an F-22 will not help us in the battle against terrorism. Language that helps us understand why they're trying to harm us will."

How we deal with terrorism should be based on an understanding of the issues that feed terrorists in different circumstances.

We can't solve a rat problem by trying to kill all the rats.

EXERCISE 11.2 Putting It All Together in the Classroom: "Fishbowl" Discussions and Critical Exchanges

This is a group exercise for the classroom. Its objective is to provide practice for using critical reasoning techniques in everyday discussions.

First, generate a short list of topics that students have actually been discussing recently with their peers, outside of class. From this list, pick a topic of interest to the class. Next, a few students who have discussed this issue should describe how the discussions have gone, recounting as much detail as possible.

At this point, arrange the chairs in the classroom so that all chairs face the middle of the room, with two chairs in the center, facing each other. This is where the students in the "fishbowl" will sit. Two students should be selected to act out one of the discussions that have been described.

The next step is for those who have observed the discussion to comment on to what extent the dialogue represented good critical reasoning. Students who have ideas about how the dialogue might have been improved can now take the places of those in the fishbowl, with each participant initially taking the position of the person he or she has replaced. This process of replacing participants can be repeated.

The exercise can be concluded with comments from the observers concerning which strategies appeared to be most helpful in facilitating the discussion.

Participating in a Critical Exchange

A good exercise for displaying your reasoning skills orally, rather than in writing, is a structured, critical exchange on an important issue such as whether a woman should have the right to have an abortion, whether capital punishment is ever justified, whether casual sexual relationships are worth pursuing, whether a woman should take her husband's name when she marries, or whether drugs should be legalized.

A structured, critical exchange is similar to a formal debate, except for a few crucial features. Most important, the object is not to win but to join with those participating in the exchange to determine what position is most reasonable to hold regarding the issue in question. To build this goal into the structure of the exchange, a period of time should be allowed, after the participants take an advocacy role on one side of the issue or the other, for each person to explain where she or he really stands on the issue, having considered all the arguments and criticisms raised.

In addition, the arguments presented should be developed cooperatively in advance of the presentation of the exchange, so that the participants representing each side can help make all the arguments (including those they will be criticizing) as strong and worthy of consideration as possible.

Here is a format for a critical exchange involving four people that can be used in an hour-long class period, and that allows time for questions and comments from the audience. The format incorporates the features mentioned above, which are aimed at minimizing competition and maximizing insight.

Preparation for the Exchange

1. Meet as a four-person team to decide on a topic. (You can use any of those listed above or another of interest to the team.)
2. Decide which two members will take the affirmative side and which two the negative side in presenting arguments on the issue. It is not necessary to take the side you feel initially inclined to support. Sometimes it is a better learning experience to argue for the other side.
3. After some brainstorming and background reading, the team should develop two arguments on the affirmative side and two arguments on the negative side. The arguments should be briefly stated and tightly structured, so that they can be written on the chalkboard or on a handout sheet for the audience.
4. As a team, discuss possible criticisms of the arguments. Obvious flaws in the arguments can be spotted at this time, and the arguments can be rewritten.

Presentation of the Exchange

1. *Affirmative team.* Each member takes about three minutes to present one argument in favor of the proposition being discussed. (An example of an argument might be: "The tradition of a woman taking her husband's last name upon marriage promotes sexism. Traditions that promote sexism should be abandoned. Therefore, the tradition of a woman taking her husband's last name upon marriage ought to be abandoned.")

Explain what is meant by each premise and why it is reasonable to believe that premise.

2. *Negative team.* Each member takes about three minutes to criticize the arguments that have been presented, applying the techniques of criticism learned in class.
3. *Negative team.* Each member presents an argument opposing the proposition in question (three minutes each).
4. *Affirmative team.* Each member criticizes the negative team's arguments (three minutes each).
5. *Concluding presentations.* Having considered all arguments and criticisms, each member states where she or he really stands on the issue. Replies to criticisms and additional reasons can be brought up at this time.
6. *Class comments.* Class members who have been listening to the exchange are allowed to make comments or address questions to the participants.

CHAPTER **12**

Making Reasonable Decisions as An Amateur in a World of Specialists

We will finish our investigation of critical reasoning by examining your role in society as an active reasoner and decision maker. To what extent should you develop this role, as opposed to relying on those who claim to be experts as the sources of your opinions and decisions?

Our discussion of a variety of critical techniques in previous chapters might seem to promote the passive role of sitting back and critically judging rather than actively creating new arguments and theories. You have been told that a *sound deductive argument* demands true premises and that the knowledge necessary to establish these premises often requires specialized inquiry, particularly when it depends on empirical theories. Given these suggestions, you might have lost confidence in your ability to make judgments yourself. You might be tempted to say: "In any area I pick to create arguments and theories, there are people who have much more knowledge and expertise than I. Why not just find out what opinions they hold and adopt them for my own? If I try to figure things out for myself, it is very likely that I will be wrong."

The idea of "leaving things to the experts" is tempting enough that we will spend some time exploring it. After all, given nearly any question you might have about any area of knowledge, there are probably people who have made this their area of specialization and who are better able to answer this question than you could ever hope to be. Unfortunately, we are faced with a serious dilemma. We have a need to understand the world, but we can't understand what the experts say about it. If we try to figure things out for ourselves, we are likely to be wrong. But if we simply leave things to the experts without understanding their theories, we have difficulty in deciding who the experts are, in determining what to believe if the experts disagree, and in limiting the influence of experts to its proper domain.

This dilemma is extremely difficult to resolve; neither alternative is completely satisfactory. But we maintain that in the face of this difficulty it is important not to hide from the problem—not to take the view that it doesn't matter what you believe since all opinions are uncertain, or the view that to escape the uncertainty of rational processes it is necessary to rely on faith in some set of dogmatically held beliefs or ideology. It is crucial to continue to pursue reasonable belief, even if such belief is never certain, because belief is connected to *action*. Responsibility for our beliefs stems from responsibility for our actions.

When we say certain people are "experts," we are not assuming that society is divided into two groups—those few who understand the world and the masses who do not. Even if you are an expert in one area, there are many other areas in which you are uninformed. We are not all equal in our general knowledge or in the breadth of our expertise, but for the purposes of this chapter we can consider each one of us to be in the position of an amateur in a world of specialization.

LEAVING IT TO THE EXPERTS

What do you really know about nuclear energy, the effect of tax policy on economic growth, or the most effective ways of combating crime? Chances are you have expressed opinions on some of these issues in casual conversation, and you probably think that some views on these issues are not correct (for example, that there are no dangers involved in nuclear energy; that tax policy has no effect on economic growth; that crime will stop by itself). You are probably quick to acknowledge, however, that there are people who know more about each of these issues than you do. Why not, then, simply leave these matters to people who do know more—who have made it their business to learn all they can about areas such as these? You could say that for each issue on which you might need to express an opinion, you will just wait until the occasion arises and then try to find out what the experts think about it and adopt their advice. Surely you would then have a greater chance of being right about each issue than if you spread out your time trying to learn a little about everything; and by leaving things to the experts you will have more time to do the things you really enjoy. What could be more sensible?

Let us imagine that we have adopted this policy of leaving things to the experts. What problems might we encounter?

Who Are the Experts?

Our first problem would be to determine who the experts are, so we could know whom to ask about the views we should adopt. Suppose the issue is how dangerous nuclear power plants are. As a starting point we might go to various professors of physics and of engineering and ask them who the best experts are on this issue. If there were some consensus as to who the experts are, and these experts all had about the same story concerning the major risks in nuclear power plants and the extent to which these risks could be minimized, we would probably feel confident that our strategy of leaving it to the experts had been successful. But what might go wrong in this process?

We might pick the wrong fields of study in our search for experts. Perhaps the biggest risks involving nuclear power don't have to do with science and engineering, but with security. Perhaps the technical problems of protecting against radiation leaks can be easily solved, but a terrorist group who wanted to gain power could get access to and control of nuclear power plants. How would we know this in advance when we began looking for experts? Perhaps the physicists and engineers we consulted would see the problem of political security and send us to the right experts on this part of the issue, but there is nothing to guarantee it. It is important to see that it would be helpful to know *something* about the dangers of nuclear power before we began looking for experts.

We might try to find someone who is an expert on who the experts are in a given field. In science journals, editors have played this role by picking "peer reviewers" for scientific papers. More recently, journalists with a background in a particular field have acted to endorse the expertise of those whom they cite. But with the proliferation of sources of information it has become increasingly difficult to determine who can be relied upon to point us to the experts.[1]

What If the Experts Disagree?

Second, we have a problem if the experts themselves disagree. Suppose the issue is whether tax policy can be revised so that long-term economic growth is enhanced while at the same time the deficit is reduced. Since this is an economic issue, we would try to find out who the leading economists in the country are and consult them. As a matter of fact, the answers we would get on this issue would be particularly varied, but this issue is hardly unique.

---

[1]For instance, when a supposed expert is chosen to be interviewed by the media, it is questionable to what extent the choice is based on genuine expertise as opposed to the ability to present commentary in a way that is entertaining to an audience.

Suppose we get three different answers from three widely renowned economists. How do we decide what to believe? We can ask for reasons to support the varying points of view, but these reasons will probably be embedded in different economic theories or ideological perspectives. We might even need to understand the theories or ideologies to evaluate the particular views on tax policy.

How Can We Control the Influence of Experts? Both of these problems—determining in which field an issue lies, and deciding among conflicting expert opinions—are related to a third, more difficult problem. If a supposed expert states a number of views on an issue, how can we tell which are based on expertise and which are based on personal political or moral preferences? That is, how do we prevent technical expertise from spreading into political power? And how do we prevent ideology from undermining legitimate technical expertise?

Consider the issue of the most effective means of controlling crime. We might go to a famous criminologist who has carefully studied the variation in crime rates with different kinds of punishments, rehabilitation programs, police procedures, social conditions, and so on. But this criminologist also happens to believe that no one should ever be punished because all actions are socially caused, and no one should be blamed for an act that is socially caused. Now this view about punishment is not based on criminological investigation; it just reflects our expert's view about the way things should be. But on the basis of this political opinion, the criminologist might alter the answer given about the most efficient way to control crime, in trying to influence political opinion in a particular direction. We might have the same problem with a physicist or an engineer *wanting* nuclear power production, or an economist *wanting* to minimize taxes. And in each case, by relying on expert opinion, we as a society might be setting experts up so that they have things the way they want them—no longer will they just be giving us factual advice and letting us decide how *we* want things to be.

THE DILEMMA

The dilemma, then, is this: If we try to create our own arguments and theories without relying on experts, we will very likely be wrong. If we just leave things to the experts to figure out, thinking that we will adopt their opinions as our own, we have difficulty in knowing who the experts are, in deciding who is right when the experts disagree, and in controlling the influence of the experts on whom we rely.

If, by adopting the opinions of experts, we came to understand all that the experts understand, our dilemma would be resolved. However, when we spoke of "leaving things to the experts" we assumed that no one has the time, energy, and intellectual ability to actually acquire more than a tiny fraction of the knowledge needed to have expert opinions in all areas. In this age of specialization, it is a rare scholar who can keep up with the major developments in just one discipline, such as psychology or physics. It is because of the rapid proliferation of knowledge that we run into the problems of determining who the experts are, resolving their disagreements, and so forth. We are forced to make these decisions in the absence of direct knowledge of the area in which we are seeking expert help.

How then are we to resolve this dilemma? Is some sort of compromise possible—a compromise between learning all that we can on our own, and combining this with selective reliance on expert opinion? Are there particular strategies that might be used to control the influence of experts while still making use of their expertise? And how does all this relate to creating our own arguments and theories? Before addressing these questions, we should say a few words about certain attitudes that are easy to embrace in the face of the difficulties we have been discussing, but that we think are important to avoid.

Two Ways of Not Facing the Dilemma

Some seek to avoid the dilemma by going to one of two extremes: the relativist view that one opinion is as good as another, or the absolutist view that a single doctrine contains the answer to everything.

Relativism A kind of disillusionment strikes many people as they come to realize how easily most opinions can be doubted. The fact that there is widespread disagreement, even among experts, on almost any issue of importance, is unsettling. Perhaps this situation is grounds for a kind of skepticism—that is, we should be guarded in our claims to knowledge, and realize how many of our beliefs are uncertain. But it is tempting to go from skepticism to a more extreme point of view: that one opinion is as good as another and it doesn't really matter what you believe. It simply doesn't follow from the fact that people disagree that no one's opinion is more reasonable than anyone else's. And even if we granted that all our beliefs are uncertain, it doesn't follow that all our beliefs are *equally* uncertain.

Often, the kind of absolute relativism to which we are objecting comes out when someone is challenged about the truth of an opinion. A common reply is that some things are "true for me," and other things are "true for you," but no one can say what is *really* true. This may be an appealing point of view as long as the discussion remains abstract. But most, if not all, of the particular opinions we hold have implications for how we should *act*. If you are riding in a car and you are of the opinion that it is heading for a cliff, but the driver doesn't share this opinion, it is doubtful that you will be satisfied to say that it is *true for you* that the car is headed for a cliff, but it isn't *true for the driver*, and that no one can tell what is really true in this case. Leaving aside questions of absolute certainty, one opinion is probably much more reasonable to hold than the other in this case, and it obviously makes a big difference which opinion you hold. The consequences of many opinions are less direct and less drastic. But the fact that your beliefs determine your actions should be reason enough to reject the view that it doesn't really matter what you believe.

The Dogmatism of the "True Believer" A second response to the problem of uncertainty and the difficulty of understanding the theories of experts is to adopt the attitude of the "true believer." The person who takes this path wants a firm doctrine to hang onto, does not find it through ordinary rational processes, and turns instead to an embracing doctrine that explains anything and everything.[2] And once he has accepted it, the "true believer" is blind to any weaknesses in it. Whether the doctrine is Marxism, religious fundamentalism, laissez-faire capitalism, or astrology, he holds it so ardently that no conceivable argument will diminish his belief. We are not claiming that a person who holds any of the beliefs we have just listed is irrational. We are concerned about the *way* this person maintains his or her doctrine. Perhaps she will undergo some personal change that will make her suddenly withdraw belief in one doctrine and put it equally wholeheartedly into another, but this will not be the result of hearing a good argument.

Two tendencies, both partly the result of the difficult situation of the amateur in a world of specialization, contribute to this faithful embrace of ideology. One is an insecurity resulting from the tentative nature of belief based on science. With experts disagreeing, one theory succeeding another, and most theories only partly understandable by the average person, many people feel they lack a satisfying system of beliefs. It is comforting to believe a single, simple, understandable doctrine that will explain a great many things and will tell you precisely where you stand in the scheme of things. But the fact that such a doctrine is comforting is not evidence that it is true.

The second tendency is the tendency to see faith as parallel to and in competition with reason. This idea is especially attractive to the dogmatist who sees the uncertainty of belief, which we have been discussing, as a weakness of reason, a weakness that can be remedied by choosing faith instead. We do not maintain that faith has no justifiable role in our lives, but it is a mistake to see faith and reason as competing paths to knowledge. The true believer who sees dogmatic faith as the path to knowledge is at a loss to answer one crucial question: Why have faith in one doctrine rather than another? The answer cannot be produced from within faith itself, it *must* be produced from within reason. Or if it isn't, it must be granted that the decision is arbitrary. It is not as though reason might choose one set of beliefs and faith another; faith does not choose.

Furthermore, the same point can be made against the dogmatic true believer as was made against the relativist: Your beliefs form the basis for your actions, and as such you have a responsibility to choose beliefs reasonably. Both relativism and dogmatic belief may be *understandable* reactions to the dilemma of the amateur in a world of specialization, but this does not make them justifiable reactions.

---

[2]The term "true believer" in the sense used here springs from Eric Hoffer's 1951 book *The True Believer*. Hoffer was a largely self-educated longshoreman who became a widely admired social critic.

COPING WITH THE DILEMMA

The first part of the dilemma we have presented is that if you try to figure things out for yourself you will probably be mistaken. Let's explore this half of the dilemma first, to see whether some of the problems associated with such a course can be remedied.

When we spoke loosely about "figuring things out for yourself," we had in mind developing your own arguments and theories. We did not suppose you would do this in a vacuum, with no help from other people and their writings. But even with this help, the arguments and theories you would develop are likely to be inadequate compared with those of experts in the different fields.

Even if your arguments and theories are inferior to those of experts, however, what is wrong with developing these inadequate opinions? The main drawback is that your opinions form the basis for actions, so you want to acquire opinions with the greatest chance of being correct. But is it necessary for us to use the opinions we develop on our own as a basis for action? Can't we develop our own arguments and theories, and maintain them tentatively, allowing them to be overridden by expert opinion when we decide that this is wise?

Developing Opinions Without Acting on Them

Consider a few examples. Suppose you were to read and think about physical health and how it should be maintained. You might adopt some theories of nutrition that you read about and came to understand; you might develop some opinions about exercise, based both on the theories of others and on your own experience and experimentation. You might form some ideas concerning your own ailments—what causes them and how they should be treated. You could do all this and yet, when it came to diagnosing a certain ailment and providing treatment for it, you could decide to let one of your own beliefs be overridden by that of a doctor.

Suppose you read and thought about certain questions in the field of economics. You might read magazine articles on the nation's economy, discuss economic questions with other people, take a course or two in economics at a university, read some books in the area. You could come to understand and adopt certain theories you read or heard about, and you could develop certain variations of these theories yourself. You might acquire your own unique overview of economics, while hardly considering yourself an expert. And throughout this development of your own ideas, you would probably remain ready to defer to someone you thought knew more about a certain issue than you did. If it came to giving investment advice, or even to voting for a political candidate who held an economic ideology different from yours, you might put your own opinions aside in favor of an expert's.

It seems clear, then, that it is possible to develop your own opinions in any area and still refrain from acting on them. But what would be gained from doing so? Is there a way we can fit this possibility into a strategy for coping with the dilemma that confronts us?

A Proposed Strategy

There are two things to be gained from developing your own opinions, even though you probably won't act on them. First, self-realization is important to anyone. Developing your own ideas, your own understanding of the world, is an important part of self-realization. There is a satisfaction—a feeling of autonomy—in taking the task of understanding the world into your own hands. This does not mean shutting out the opinions of others, but it does mean actively engaging in understanding rather than being a passive receptacle for opinion. In the process, you will develop your mental abilities more fully.

Second, you reduce the problems involved in relying on experts. This point brings us, now, to what we see as the best strategy for coping with the dilemma of either leaving things to the experts or figuring them out for ourselves. The strategy is to combine both practices. This is not a complete resolution of the dilemma because it leaves problems unsolved. But it does allow for self-realization while reducing the problems that arise from leaving things to the experts.

The more understanding you have, the better chance you have of minimizing the problems involved in relying on experts. The three major problems we anticipated were determining who the experts are, deciding what to do when the experts disagree, and controlling the influence of experts. Of these, the problem of disagreement among experts is probably the most difficult to overcome by gaining a limited understanding of the area in question.

Still a Problem: The Disagreement of Experts

When experts disagree, considerations beyond the credibility of the competing opinions may give us grounds for making a choice. If one physician advises that you have an operation but a second physician advises against it, there is an obvious reason for accepting the second opinion. It may also be possible to test competing opinions by putting each into practice for a trial period. A president, for example, might try one economic policy for a certain period and then shift to another. But the results of such trials are often difficult for the amateur to assess, and there is not always time to experiment. Furthermore, a disagreement among experts may be such that you would need to understand both competing theories as well as the experts themselves do in order to make a reasoned choice between them. The other two problems, however, do not seem so intractable.

Creating Arguments and Theories: Identifying the Experts

One fringe benefit of creating your own arguments and theories is that in the process of gaining the background knowledge on which to base them, you can become acquainted with a large number of areas. You can begin to understand how various academic disciplines, professions, and specialized occupations deal with the different sciences and their branches. This is precisely the kind of knowledge that is crucial in the age of specialization. Furthermore, by actually developing arguments and theories, you have a better chance of seeing the many different areas of expertise that apply to a particular issue.

There is a broad tendency to see generals as the experts on national defense issues, doctors as the experts on medical care issues, police chiefs as the experts on crime issues, and so on. In fact, all these issues have political, economic, and technological aspects that could be addressed by experts from dozens of fields. By attempting to develop your own ideas on these issues, you have a greater chance of seeing how diverse they are.

Creating Arguments and Theories: Controlling the Experts

The point that many different areas of expertise usually apply to a single issue is important when it comes to determining how to control the influence of experts. This is one of the few considerations that should give amateurs confidence when comparing themselves to experts. Very often, no one is an expert when it comes to seeing how the expert opinions from various fields should all be brought together to form a policy. And this is precisely the point at which the influence of experts can and should be controlled. At this point, the amateur who has tried to create arguments and theories concerning a broad issue need not defer to someone who is an expert on only one facet of the issue.

Furthermore, the relation between certain areas of expertise and their application to real-world issues might be indirect. Many academic disciplines develop abstract, technical theories and models whose relation to the real world may be poorly understood even by experts within the discipline. It is too often assumed that any behavioral psychologist can give you advice on child rearing, that any economist can help you with your investments, or even that any mathematical logician can help you evaluate an argument from a piece of informal prose. It is important that you see as best you can the limitations of each area of specialization. Experts themselves will not be anxious to limit their own influence—they might attempt to run a bluff, hoping that amateurs will be too meek to challenge them. The more you have adopted the habit of leaving things to the experts rather than developing your own arguments and theories, the greater the chance that such a bluff will succeed.

How Does One Create Arguments and Theories?

One central topic we have not addressed is how to go about creating arguments and theories. We won't discuss the *mechanics* of creativity—this topic is more suitable to a psychological study, or perhaps a biographical study of creative individuals. Nevertheless, the critical procedures described in the foregoing chapters can be used as a starting point in creating arguments and theories.

Criticizing and Creating Criticizing and creating are not completely independent processes. One way of criticizing a theory is to see that an alternative theory is more plausible; this involves conjuring up, or creating, the alternative. When you reconstruct a fragmentary argument as a step toward criticizing it, devising missing premises requires creativity. When you ask whether a premise is doubtful or whether it is reasonable to believe, you create tentative arguments in an attempt to support it, and then critically assess these arguments.

Also, criticism is a part of a dialogue process that is, on the whole, creative. You consider arguments or theories presented to you, reject them in part or entirely, and reconsider new or altered versions. This process is like an artist experimenting with a design. The artist might change it around haphazardly, and by using a critical eye to reject all bad configurations, arrive at (create) an artistically good one. This model of creativity is not completely accurate, however. An artist need not try different designs entirely at random. He has a sort of guiding intuition, making it possible to picture in advance the way the design should look. Similarly, in creating an argument or explanation you do not sort through random lists of statements to be used as premises or as parts of a theory. A kind of intuition guides you in seeing what would be plausible candidates for premises or for theoretical statements. Criticism plays a role, although a limited one, by rejecting poor candidates.

Criticism, then, if it is carried out well, involves you to some extent in creative activity. It is possible, furthermore, to pursue this aspect of criticism consciously. As a way of getting started at devising a theory to explain something, or an argument to support a belief, study theories that have been offered to explain the same phenomenon, or arguments that attempt to support the same opinion. Critically assess these arguments and theories and cultivate the creative aspects of this critical process—seeking more plausible alternative explanations; refining and altering the premises that support the conclusions; or, if they cannot be made adequate, either choosing other premises or considering arguments for rejecting the conclusion. Even going this far will do a great deal to bring about the benefits of "figuring things out for yourself," rather than "leaving it to the experts."

THE STRATEGY AND ITS PROSPECTS

The strategy we have recommended for the amateur in a world of specialization is one that combines creating your own arguments and theories with selectively and cautiously relying on experts. As we have stated, we are not entirely optimistic about the outcome of this strategy. The number of problems and issues to study and the number of areas of expertise to monitor are overwhelming. Perhaps it is possible to gain back a significant degree of control over experts who affect you most directly and personally—your doctor, your mechanic. But the social effects that a single individual can have by carrying out this strategy are practically negligible. What must be hoped for, as specialization increases, is an increased intellectual activism on the part of a significant portion of the population.

But this point—that one person can't do much to guard against the dangers of relying on experts—brings into focus an aspect of our dilemma about which we have said very little so far. That is, the dilemma we have presented is not simply that of a single individual who wonders how to best attain knowledge. Neither, however, is it a matter of bringing together the knowledge of all the individuals in a society. There is no repository for such an aggregation—society as a whole has no mind. If there were such a collective repository, it would be easy to combine the opinions of many experts to form a more complete and adequate body of knowledge than that which any single individual possesses. But in reality, each person must try to combine the opinions of experts from a position of relative ignorance. We each must to some extent guess which experts to trust. The problem becomes in part political—that is, power and influence become issues. How can each of us assemble a picture of the world that has the best chance of accuracy, but that is also not biased in favor of the personal preferences of experts?

Can Information Technology Dissolve the Dilemma?

A critic might respond that, contrary to what we have claimed, there *is* now, in the twenty-first century, a collective repository for the aggregate knowledge of a society. Or, at least, we are well on our way to constructing such a repository via information technology: the World Wide Web. Our critic would claim that the problems we have posed against relying on experts—determining who they are, deciding what to do when they disagree, and controlling their influence—can be solved by a series of web searches.

Suppose we are addressing a medical problem, such as how best to treat a certain disease. We can now access several website discussions or journal articles on nearly any such problem. Furthermore, at the rate that information technology is progressing, we should soon be able to check the qualifications of the authors, their educational backgrounds, and descriptions of research they have engaged in. We could even access references from other researchers in the field. We could use this information to judge the relative credibility of experts who offer conflicting opinions on the condition we are addressing. Arguably, we could address the problem of controlling the influence of experts by gaining information regarding their motives. As background information about experts becomes more and more accessible, we could determine, for example, whether one of the experts is engaged in research that is funded by a company that manufactures a drug used to treat the problem in question, so that the opinion put forth by this expert might be biased.

We would reply that information technology can indeed be useful in dissolving the dilemma, but only because it is helpful in carrying out the strategy we have proposed—creating your own arguments and theories while selectively and cautiously relying on experts. If one attempts to leave things to the experts, then using information technology will simply speed up the process of encountering the three problems we have raised.

To continue with the example from the field of medicine, if we encounter conflicting opinions from two supposed experts, it is likely that each of them will appear to the outsider to be qualified (to have academic degrees and publications) and that other apparent experts would vouch for their expertise. They might be advocates from different schools of thought within traditional medicine, or a recent, nontraditional alternative medicine. To make a judgment concerning whether any or all of them should be treated as experts about a particular medical disorder and its treatment, we would need to learn something about these rival approaches. If we were to actually read several articles from medical journals on the problem we are approaching, we would need to draw from our understanding of deductive and nondeductive arguments, and probably our understanding of theories as well, to understand the conclusions reached and their basis. To judge whether to discount the opinions of the expert whose research was funded by a pharmaceutical company, we should determine whether those opinions were reached on the basis of well-constructed, controlled experiments that can be replicated by other researchers. If so, then the charge of bias might be a fallacious ad hominem attack on the researcher.

Our point is that using information technology wisely is not a way of simply leaving things to the experts, but rather a convenient way of accessing material that can form the basis for one's own judgments concerning whom to treat as experts and whether to trust their opinions.

THE CONTEMPORARY PROBLEM OF KNOWLEDGE

Through much of history, the problem of knowledge and the problem of the good society have been dealt with separately. A division of philosophy called *epistemology* attempts to answer the question of what knowledge is and how it can be attained. Political philosophy and social philosophy, on the other hand, deal with such problems as *How can a group of individuals combine to form a good or just society?* In the modern world of specialization, the problem of how to attain knowledge becomes, in part, a social one.

One ancient philosopher who did stress the connection between knowledge and the good society was Plato. In his book *The Republic,* true belief and knowledge could be ranked in terms of how well they captured how things really are. Overly simple beliefs are not so much false as limited. For Plato, genuine knowledge about a "good computer" or a "good nuclear power plant" or a "good energy technology" would encompass not only the technical requirements, but would also examine how, if at all, they might exist in a good society. We are not accustomed to asking this general question about most of the objects, institutions, and policies that confront us. We don't typically move from a discussion about what is a good car (for us or for car manufacturers) to questions about whether a transportation system relying on the private auto is really in the public interest. The problem, of course, with such a move is that it raises the difficult question of how to gain knowledge about the "good society."

Plato solved this dilemma by envisioning a class of super-experts who sought knowledge about the good society. In the society Plato describes, this knowledge was concentrated in a few individuals who were especially suited to rule in the republic he described. In contemporary society, understanding of complex issues and the will to confront them with an eye to broad public interest is at best spread among many individuals. To put it pessimistically: For Plato, a few had the requisite knowledge to rule in the public interest, and they would rule society; for us in a democracy, no one has very much knowledge, but everyone must try to rule.

It is doubtful that many of us would want to transform our society into the one Plato envisioned. It is difficult for us to part with the ideal of democracy, and we are justifiably suspicious of the "knowledge" of those who would rule. But to give our society the best chance of persisting, we must cope with its problems. Not the least of these is the problem of avoiding overly simplistic solutions by reasoning both critically and creatively in spite of our limited perspectives as amateurs in a world of experts.

EXERCISE 12.1

Case Study for Individual Writing Exercise or Group Discussion

How would you resolve the dilemma of whether to rely on experts or to figure out for yourself what to do if you faced the following situation? You are raising a child who begins to have severe behavioral problems, such as frequent temper tantrums, refusal to follow instructions at school or at home, and fighting with other children. Would you seek expert advice? From whom? What if you get conflicting advice from two sources? How would you be able to tell whether the person advising you is manipulating you for his or her own ends, rather than helping you decide what is best for the child and you?

GLOSSARY

Ad Baculum ("To the stick")
See **Appeal to Force.**

Ad Hominem ("To the person")
See **Attacking the Person.**

Ad Misericordiam ("To misery")
See **Appeal to Pity.**

Affirming the Consequent Any argument that exhibits the following *invalid* pattern: (*See* Chapters 2 and 6.)

(1) If A, then B.
(2) B.

∴ *A.*

Ambiguity A term in a context is ambiguous if it has more than one relatively distinct meaning in that context. (*See* Chapter 7.)

Analogical Reasoning Reasoning that justifies the claim that an item has a certain characteristic by appeal to a sufficiently similar (analogous) item, which is known to have the characteristic in question. (*See* Chapter 9.)

Appeal to Authority Appealing to someone whose expertise is not relevant to the issue at hand, or appealing to someone who is famous or admired but not an expert on the issue at hand. (*Note:* We have just described *fallacious* appeals to authority. There are also *legitimate* appeals to authority—appeals to people who really are experts in the appropriate areas.) (*See* Chapter 6.)

Appeal to Force The arguer tries to get you to agree by indicating that *you* will be harmed if you don't agree ("*ad baculum*"). (*See* Chapter 6.)

Appeal to Pity The arguer tries to get you to agree by indicating that *he or she* will be harmed if you don't agree ("*ad misericordiam*"). (*See* Chapter 6.)

Argument A structured piece of discourse in which a certain statement can be identified as a conclusion and others can be identified as premises that provide reasons for believing the conclusion.

Attacking the Person Arguing that a person's point of view should be doubted because the person has bad traits of character or because the person has something to gain by being believed. (*Note:* There are *legitimate* as well as *fallacious* cases of attacking the person.) (*See* Chapter 6.)

Begging the Question An argument that rests on a premise that is either a restatement of the conclusion or that would be doubted for the same reasons that the conclusion would be doubted ("*petitio principii*"). (*See* Chapter 6.)

Causal Reasoning Reasoning that typically moves from the observation that one thing is correlated with another to the claim that the first causes the second. Such reasoning is not always justified and is best supported by controlled experiments. (*See* Chapter 9.)

Charitable Interpretation Principle Maxim for interpreting argumentative passages that enjoins you to give the arguer the "benefit of the doubt" if at all plausible. If you have a choice, you should interpret a passage so that the premises provide the best support possible for the conclusion. Sometimes an argument as presented is faulty—for example, invalid or unsound—in which case a charitable reconstruction would leave it faulty in this way. (*See* Chapter 2.)

Conceptual Theory A statement of the conditions under which a certain concept applies to an object. These theories are most plausible in domains in which clear boundaries can be drawn at least for some purposes. These theories are typically criticized by finding counterexamples and pointing to the need for a more extensive and illuminating statement of conditions. (*See* Chapter 7.)

Conditional A statement of the *if–then* form, represented by "A → B" in formal language. The "if" part is called the *antecedent* or condition; the "then" part is called the *consequent*. (*See* Chapters 4 and 5.)

Confound When a causal argument is advanced (A is correlated with B, so it is likely that A causes B), a confound is a third factor, X, that is the true cause of B, but which is also correlated with A, creating the appearance that A causes B. Controlled experiments help rule out confounds. (*See* Chapter 9.)

Conjunction A statement of the form "A and B" that links two other statements. "and" is represented by "&" in formal language. (*See* Chapter 5.)

Consistency A group of statements is consistent if it is possible for all of them to be true at the same time. If it is impossible for all of them to be true simultaneously, then the statements are inconsistent.

Contradiction A statement that cannot (logically) be true. It is inconsistent in all contexts. Often used of statements having the form "A and not A," where "A" stands for a sentence, or the form "*m* is P_1, and *m* is not P_1," where P_1 is a predicate.

Controlled Experiment An experiment designed to determine whether one thing causes another that helps rule out the X-factor as an alternative explanation. It involves comparing an experimental group to which the suspected causal agent is applied, to a control group to which it is not, all other conditions being the same. If assignment to the groups is unbiased (random), then any significant difference in the experimental groups can be attributed to the suspected causal agent. (*See* Chapter 9.)

Convergent Argument An argument in which independent (non-linked) premises are offered in support of the conclusion and give weight to it. (*See* Chapter 9.)

Correlation The association of two or more characteristics or events. That two events are correlated—that is, they typically occur together—does not in itself justify the conclusion that the first causes the second. (*See* Chapter 9.)

Counter-Consideration In a convergent argument, considerations weighing against the conclusion. (*See* Chapter 9.)

Counterexample As a criticism of a premise that expresses a universal generalization (for example, of the form "All P_1s are P_2s"), a clear example of a P_1 that is not a P_2. In a deductive argument, a counterexample is a clear case in which the premises are all true and the conclusion is false. It can be an argument that shares the same pattern as the one in question, or, for an argument pattern itself, it can be a truth table assignment or a Venn diagram configuration. (*See* Chapters 4 and 5.) For a conceptual theory, a counterexample either clearly fits the concept but not the conditions of the theory, or it fits the conditions of the theory but not the concept. (*See* Chapter 7.)

Counterinstance In common usage, this term is interchangeable with **counterexample.**

Deductive Argument An argument in which the premises are put forward to guarantee the truth of the conclusion in the strong sense that it is *logically impossible* for the premises all to be true and the conclusion to be false.

Denying the Antecedent Any argument that exhibits the following *invalid* pattern: (*See* Chapters 2 and 6.)

(1) If A, then B.

(2) Not A.

$\therefore$ *Not B.*

Disjunction A statement of the form "A or B". "or" is represented by "v" in a formal language. (*See* Chapter 5.)

Distraction Fallacy The general category of fallacies that tend to persuade by taking the audience's attention away from weak points of an argument. (*See* Chapter 6.)

Elucidation A criterion for evaluating conceptual theories. A conceptual theory can be criticized by showing that it uses terms that are no easier to understand than the concept supposedly being clarified (that is, the theory fails to elucidate). (*See* Chapter 7.)

Emotion Fallacies The general category of fallacies that tend to persuade by making it desirable to believe an argument's conclusion rather than giving evidence to support it. (*See* Chapter 6.)

Empirical Generalization A generalization based on particular observations.

Empirical Theory A set of statements of fairly broad scope that explains patterns or regularities established by observation. Empirical theories can be criticized by pointing out that expected regularities, predictions, or patterns do not occur or are questionable; by offering a plausible alternative theory; by pointing out that a defense against damaging evidence is *ad hoc*; or by showing that crucial concepts in the theory can't be tested. (*See* Chapter 10.)

Epistemology The philosophical study of the nature and conditions of knowledge.

Equivocation An argument in which an expression shifts its meaning from one premise to another, making the pattern invalid. Equivocation can exploit either ambiguity (more than one relatively distinct meaning) or vagueness (unclear boundary between objects to which the term applies and objects to which it does not). (*See* Chapters 6 and 7.)

Expertise Specialized knowledge in a restricted domain. Expertise is difficult to locate and dangerous to blindly pursue. The amateur—the nonexpert—needs to be able to reason critically to be able to use expertise when and where it is appropriate. (*See* Chapter 12.)

Explanation An attempt to indicate why or how something occurred, rather than to justify a belief that it did.

Fallacy An argument that tends to persuade us even though it is faulty and should not do so. Some fallacies tend to persuade by distraction, some by resemblance to a good argument, others by providing a motive for belief in place of evidential support. (*See* Chapter 6.)

False Dilemma The arguer claims that there are only two alternatives and one is unacceptable, so we should choose the other. But in fact, there are more alternatives than two. (*See* Chapter 6.)

Generalization A statement that applies to some number of individuals rather than to a particular case. *See* **Empirical Generalization, Statistical Generalization, Universal Generalization.** (*See* Chapter 8.)

General-to-Particular Reasoning. *See* **Statistical Premise Argument.**

Hasty Generalization A generalization that is asserted on the basis of an unrepresentative sample, either too small or selected in a biased way.

Implicit Premise An unstated premise. We determine that such a premise should be added to the reconstruction of an argument in accordance with the Principle of Charitable Interpretation. Typically, such a premise is needed to render the argument deductively valid.

Inconsistency A set of statements is inconsistent if it is impossible for all of them to be true simultaneously.

Inductive Argument An argument in which the premises are put forward to make the conclusion likely or probable but not logically guaranteed. The term is most commonly applied the sampling arguments, though arguments with statistical premises can also be considered inductive.

Linked Argument A deductive argument in contrast to convergent argument. The name suggests the logical links that connect all the premises with the conclusion.

Mere Disagreement Mere disagreement takes place when people assert opposing points of view without being open to having their minds changed by reasons. Each seeks to maintain a prior set of beliefs. This contrasts with a dispute subject to critical reasoning. (*See* Chapter 1.)

Misleading Definition A case in which an unclear expression is given an "unusual" or technical meaning in the premises of an argument but where that peculiarity is not marked by qualifications or hedges in the conclusion. (*See* Chapter 7.)

Modus Ponens ("Mode of affirming") A common, valid argument form in which we "affirm the antecedent" of a conditional (that is, *if–then*) statement. It should be clearly distinguished from the similar but invalid argument form called the "fallacy of denying the antecedent." (*See* Chapters 2–4.) *Modus ponens* is exhibited by this pattern:

(1) If A, then B.

(2) A.

∴ *B.*

Modus Tollens ("Mode of denying") A common, valid argument form in which we "deny the consequent" of a conditional (that is, *if–then*) statement. It should be clearly distinguished from the similar but invalid argument form called "affirming the consequent." (*See* Chapters 2–4.) *Modus tollens* is exhibited by this pattern:

(1) If A, then B.

(2) Not B.

∴ *Not A.*

Necessity What must occur; the opposite of which is *impossible* or *can't be*. The conclusion of a valid deductive argument follows with necessity. It is impossible for all the premises to be true and the conclusion to be false. A statement is *logically necessary* if its denial leads to a contradiction (a contradiction describes an impossible situation). Something is *physically necessary* in a situation if it is physically impossible for it not to happen.

Negation A sentence of the "not" form, which is represented by "¬" in formal language.

Nondeductive Argument An argument in which the premises are not put forward to logically guarantee the truth of the conclusion, but to make the conclusion more likely. Inductive arguments are one form of nondeductive arguments. (*See* Chapters 8 and 9.)

Non Sequitur ("It does not follow") The conclusion does not follow from premises though it purports to.

Operational Definition A definition of an expression which is stated in terms of a detailed procedure or protocol for measuring it, for example using a particular IQ test to measure "intelligence," or a series of questions to measure "degree of intolerance."

Particular-to-General Reasoning *See* **Sampling Argument.**

Petitio Principii ("Petitioning the premises") *See* **Begging the Question.**

Post Hoc, Ergo Propter Hoc ("After this, therefore because of this") The fallacious or unjustified move from correlation to cause. (*See* Chapter 9.)

Prejudicial Language The arguer uses language that biases you in favor of his or her position or against an opponent's position without giving evidence for his or her position or against the opponent's position. (*See* Chapter 6.)

Principle of Charitable Interpretation *See* **Charitable Interpretation Principle.**

Quantifier A symbol in a formal language used to represent the "quantity" to which a sentence applies. The universal quantifier (x) is used to formalize statements containing *all, every,* and related terms. It can be roughly translated "for all." The existential quantifier, (∃x), means roughly "There exists at least one thing such that" and is used to translate statements containing the term *some.* (*See* Chapter 5.)

Reconstruction Reformulation of arguments, conceptual theories, or empirical theories that makes their structure clearer. This can include making explicit elements that are only implicit in the original presentation. Such a reconstruction puts an argument or theory in *standard form.* (*See* Chapters 3, 7, 8, 9, and 10.)

Reductio ad Absurdum ("Reducing to the absurd") A technique of indirect proof that justifies a statement by showing that its negation leads to a contradiction (more broadly, to an absurdity). (*See* Chapter 5.)

Regularity A pattern to be explained by a broader empirical theory that is described by a less theoretical, more observational statement. (*See* Chapter 10.)

Relativism The belief that one opinion is always as good as another, and that when two people disagree, it can never be determined whose position is more reasonable to hold. (*See* Chapter 12.)

Representativeness of a Sample A sample is likely to be representative of (similar to) a population from which it is drawn if it is sufficiently large and drawn in an unbiased manner. (*See* Chapter 8.)

Requirement of Total Evidence In an inductive argument with statistical premises, the expectation that all available, relevant evidence will be included in picking relevant premises. (*See* Chapter 8.)

Resemblance Fallacy The general category of fallacies that tend to persuade by resembling good arguments. (*See* Chapter 6.)

Sample A selection of cases from a population. In particular-to-general inductive reasoning, statements about a sample are used as reasons to justify similar statements about the whole population from which the sample is drawn. If the sample is likely to be unrepresentative, too small, or biased, then the reasoning can be criticized.

A random sample of sufficient size improves such inductive reasoning. (*See* Chapter 8.)

Sampling Argument A particular-to-general inductive argument.

Sampling Frame A listing of a population from which a sample is drawn (e.g., all the students currently registered at a university) or the potential population that could be sampled using a certain sampling method (e.g., those having a "land line" phone number).

Slippery Slope The arguer says we shouldn't do something, because it probably leads to something else, which leads to a third thing, and so forth down the "slippery slope" to a final consequence that is clearly undesirable. But in fact, some of these steps are implausible. (*See* Chapter 6.)

Sound Argument A valid deductive argument with only true premises. In such an argument the conclusion follows, all premises are true, and hence the conclusion is true as well. (*See* Chapter 8.)

Standard Form For a deductive argument, standard form consists of a numbered listing of premises, separated by a line from a statement of the conclusion prefaced by the symbol meaning "therefore" (∴). For inductive arguments, the symbol for "therefore" is replaced by the term *likely.* For conceptual theories, standard form has an underlined designation of the concept to be defined followed by "if and only if," followed by the condition(s) of the conceptual theory. For an empirical theory, standard form consists of a list of separate theoretical statements, regularities, or patterns, and any observational support.

Statistical Generalization A generalization that applies to some, a few, or a certain percentage of cases.

Statistical Premise Argument A general-to-particular inductive argument that includes statistical premises in which some unspecific statistical terms such as *many, most, a few, seldom,* and so on are used, or some specific percentage is mentioned. *See* **Statistical Syllogism.**

Statistical Significance If we can infer from a sample, that a property of the sample is likely to be true of the population from which it is drawn, then the result obtained by sampling is statistically significant. We need to note that a difference detected in a sample, between say an experimental group and a control group, can be *statistically significant* without being scientifically or policy significant. If a sample is large enough, even very small differences could be statistically significant.

Statistical Syllogism A version of the argument from statistical premises having the following form. (*See* Chapter 8.)

(1) Most P_1's are P_2's.
(2) m is a P_1.

(likely) m is a P_2.

or

(1) N% of P_1's are P_2's.
(2) m is a P_1.

(N% likely) m is a P_2.

Straw Man The arguer makes a position appear strong by making the opposing position appear weaker than it really is. The arguer puts a weak argument in an opponent's mouth when stronger arguments are available.

Subordinate Conclusion In the reconstruction of a complex deductive argument, the conclusion of one argument that serves as a premise in another.

Successfulness A deductive argument is successful if it is valid (that is, the conclusion follows), has true premises, and is legitimately persuasive. An inductive argument is successful if its premises make the conclusion likely, its premises are true, and it is legitimately persuasive.

Theory *See* **Conceptual Theory** or **Empirical Theory.**

Truth Table A way to systematically indicate possible assignments of truth values to initial statements and to display the truth value of more complex statements constructed out of them using logical connections. It provides a way to systematically search for counterexamples that might show an argument to be invalid. An argument that can be represented on a truth table is valid just in case there is no line in which the truth value, for all the premises, is true (T) and that for the conclusion is false (F). (*See* Chapter 5.)

Universal Generalization A generalization that applies to all cases. A universal positive generalization contains words such as *all* or *every,* as for example in "All animals with hearts have kidneys" and "Everybody will be famous for at least fifteen minutes." A universal negative generalization uses terms such as *no* or *none* to indicate that all cases do not have a characteristic. An example is "No one lives forever," which means "Everyone does not live forever."

Vagueness A term is vague in a context if it is unclear where to draw the boundary between things to which the term does apply and those to which it does not. (*See* Chapter 7.)

Validity A deductive argument is valid if and only if it is impossible for all the premises to be true and the conclusion to be false. (*See* Chapters 4 and 5.) There is no counterexample showing that the premises are true and the conclusion is false. Truth tables or Venn diagrams can be used to determine validity for some arguments. (*See* Chapter 5.) In causal reasoning, "internal validity" exists when a conclusion is made more likely by employing a research design that eliminates threats to it, by using random assignment to experimental and control groups or other means of ruling out confounds such as maturation, specific historical circumstance or regression towards a mean; in arguments involving sampling, "external validity" exists when the results obtained can be applied outside the specific situation investigated, for example, when properties of a sample can be generalized to the larger population of interest to the research. "External validity" is also applied more generally to situations in which controlled experiments can be justifiably applied to the "real world." (*See* Chapter 9.); "construct validity" exists to the extent that the method of measuring or operational definition adequately captures that concept. (*See* Chapter 9.)

Venn Diagram A way of representing simple predicate arguments using overlapping circles to designate the sets of objects to which the predicates apply. The technique is useful in assessing validity and finding counterexamples to certain simple arguments that contain quantifiers. (*See* Chapter 5.)

X-Factor See Confound.

ANSWERS TO SELECTED EXERCISES

Chapter 1

Exercise 1.2 (pp. 12–18)
(Wording of answers will vary.)

A1. MAIN POINT: America cannot allow widespread outsourcing of jobs to other countries.

SUPPORTING CLAIM: America can narrow the gap between the wealthiest and the rest only if it does not allow widespread outsourcing.

SUPPORTING CLAIM: America needs to narrow the gap between the very wealthy and the rest of us.

A3. MAIN POINT: We should not judge political candidates by their position on the single issue of abortion.

SUPPORTING CLAIM: Other issues on which candidates differ are more important to the fate of the country.

Chapter 2

Exercise 2.1 (pp. 26–28)

1. *(1) Any friend of mine deserves my respect.*

   (2) Ed is a friend of mine.

   ∴ *Ed deserves my respect.*

(We have put items 3–15 into standard form, rather than circling and labeling.)

3. *(1) If your mind were organized, your desk would be organized.*

   (2) Your desk isn't organized.

   ∴ *Your mind isn't organized.*

5. *(1) An activity pays if the people who engage in it come out ahead economically more often than not.*

   (2) The people who engage in many crimes come out ahead economically more often than not.

   ∴ *Many crimes pay.*

7. *(1) If a murderer is wrong in killing his victim, then society is also wrong in killing the murderer.*

   (2) A murderer is wrong in killing his victim.

   ∴ *It is wrong for society to kill a murderer.*

9. *(1) If belief based on faith is belief without evidence, then belief based on faith is never justified.*

   (2) Belief based on faith is belief without evidence.

   ∴ *Belief based on faith is never justified.*

11. *(1) If privatizing schools would leave poorer, more-difficult-to-educate students at a disadvantage, then privatizing schools will only worsen the problems of the inner cities.*

    (2) Privatizing would leave poorer, more-difficult-to-educate students at a disadvantage.

    ∴ *Privatizing schools will [only] worsen the problems of inner cities.*

13. *(1) A nonwhite murderer whose victim is white is much more likely to be executed than a white murderer whose victim is either white or nonwhite.*

    (2) If that is the case, then either this kind of discrimination should be eliminated, or the death penalty should be abolished.

    (3) This kind of discrimination cannot be eliminated.

    ∴ *Capital punishment should be abolished.*

15. (1) *Judges shouldn't be influenced by campaign contributors.*

    (2) *If judges are chosen by election, then they will be influenced by campaign contributions.*

    ∴ *Judges shouldn't be chosen by election.*

Exercise 2.2 (pp. 30–31)

1. (1) *If you buy a fur coat, then you are supporting the fur industry.*

   (2) *If you are supporting the fur industry, then you are encouraging cruel treatment of animals.*

   ∴ *If you buy a fur coat, then you are encouraging cruel treatment of animals.*

3. (1) *Every person has the capacity to kill.*

   (2) *All those who have the capacity to kill should avoid keeping loaded guns around the house.*

   ∴ *Every person should avoid keeping loaded guns around the house.*

5. (1) *Anyone who is overly ambitious will alienate her friends.*

   (2) *Sheila is overly ambitious.*

   ∴ *Sheila will alienate her friends.*

7. (1) *Either the United States will effectively curtail illegal border crossings or it should effectively discourage employers from hiring illegal immigrants.*

   (2) *The United States will not effectively curtail illegal border crossings.*

   ∴ *The United States should effectively discourage employers from hiring illegal immigrants.*

9. (1) *Any anti-gun law gives advantage to lawbreakers.*

   (2) *Anything that gives an advantage to lawbreakers makes law-abiders less safe.*

   ∴ *Any anti-gun law makes law-abiders less safe.*

11. (1) *If capital punishment deterred murder better than life imprisonment, then states with capital punishment would have lower murder rates than states with life imprisonment only.*

(2) *States with capital punishment do not have lower murder rates than states with life imprisonment only.*

∴ *Capital punishment does not deter murder better than life imprisonment.*

Exercise 2.3 (pp. 36–38)

A. Argument patterns in Exercise 2.2

(2.2) 1. (1) *If A, then B.*

(2) *If B, then C.*

∴ *If A, then C.*

(2.2) 3. (1) *All* P_1*s are* P_2*s.*

(2) *All* P_2*s are* P_3*s.*

∴ *All* P_1*'s are* P_3*s.*

(2.2) 5. (1) *All* P_1*s are* P_2*s.*

(2) *m is a* P_1.

∴ *m is a* P_2.

(2.2) 7. (1) *Either A or B.*

(2) *Not A.*

∴ *B.*

(2.2) 9. (1) *All* P_1*s are* P_2*s.*

(2) *All* P_2*s are* P_3*s.*

∴ *All* P_1*s are* P_3*s.*

(2.2) 11. (1) *If A, then B.*

(2) *Not B.*

∴ *Not A.*

B1.	(1) *All P_1s are P_2s.*	(1) *Anyone who studies critical reasoning is bound to sharpen his argumentative skills.*
	(2) *m is a P_1.*	(2) *John is studying critical reasoning.*
	∴ *m is a P_2.*	∴ *John is bound to sharpen his argumentative skills.*
B3.	(1) *If A, then B.*	(1) *If Paul can find the strength to resist Sheila's advances, then he will be able to salvage some measure of self-respect.*
	(2) *A.*	(2) *Paul will find this strength.*
	∴ *B.*	∴ *He will salvage some self-respect.*
B5.	(1) *If A, then B.*	(1) *If your car had fuel, it would have kept running.*
	(2) *Not B.*	(2) *It didn't keep running.*
	∴ *Not A.*	∴ *Your car doesn't have fuel.*
B7.	(1) *All P_1s areP_2s.*	(1) *Any armed intervention has many innocent victims.*
	(2) *All P_2s are P_3's.*	(2) *Any activity that has many innocent victims should be entered only as a last resort.*
	∴ *All P_1's are P_3s.*	∴ *Any armed intervention should be entered only as a last resort.*
B9.	(1) *If A, then B.*	(1) *If a human being is created at the moment of conception, then abortion always kills a human being.*
	(2) *If B, then C.*	(2) *If abortion always kills a human being, then it is never justified.*
	∴ *If A, then C.*	∴ *If a human being is created at the moment of conception, then abortion is never justified.*
B11.	(1) *All P_1's are P_2s.*	(1) *Everyone who watches a lot of violent films eventually becomes desensitized to violence.*

Form	Instance
(2) m is a P_1.	*(2) Roberta watches a lot of violent films.*
∴ *m is a* P_2.	∴ *Roberta will eventually become desensitized to violence.*
C1. *(1) All* P_1*s are* P_2*s.*	*(1) [All] true conservatives resist spending for social programs.*
(2) m is not a P_2.	*(2) Our senator does not resist such spending.*
∴ *m is not a* P_1.	∴ *Our senator is not a true conservative.*
C3. *(1) All* P_1*s are* P_2*s.*	*(1) Anyone who has practiced law has been subjected to corrupting influences.*
(2) Some P_3*s are* P_1*s.*	*(2) Some judges have practiced law.*
∴ *Some* P_3*'s are* P_2*'s.*	∴ *Some judges have been subjected to corrupting influences.*
C5. *(1) Either A or B.*	*(1) Either you should take control of your own life or trust the advice of a mentor.*
(2) If B, then C.	*(2) If you trust the advice of a mentor, then you stand the risk of being used to fulfill the mentor's own dreams.*
(3) Not C.	*(3) You should not take that risk.*
∴ *A.*	∴ *You should take control of your own life.*

Exercise 2.4 (pp. 42–43)

(*Note*: There may be more than one acceptable reconstruction.)

1. *(1) If gun control is constitutional, then it is constitutional to restrict artistic expression.*

   (2) It is not constitutional to restrict artistic expression.

   ∴ *Gun control is not constitutional.*

3. *(1) If gender testing becomes widely accessible, then people must be able to resist using it for sex selection.*

   (2) People will not be able to resist using gender testing for sex selection.

   ∴ *Gender testing should not become widely accessible.*

Chapter 3

Exercise 3.1 (pp. 55–63)

A1. *(1) If A, then B.*

(2) [A]. — *[The Netwizard desktop computer runs VideoMaker software.]*

∴ *B.*

A3. *(1) If A, then B.*

(2) If [B], then [C]. — *If [I can't create DVDs and video for the Web],then [it doesn't meet my needs].*

∴ *If A, then C.*

[ALTERNATIVELY]

(1) If not A, then not B.

(2) If [not B], then [not C].

∴ *If not A, then not C.*

(The same words would fill the brackets, but the internal structure, "not A," "not B," "not C," is represented in the pattern shown at the left.)

A5. *(1) Either [A] or [B].* — *Either [I should buy an Econoplasma high-definition TV] or [I should buy a Primeoview high-definition TV].*

(2) Not B.

∴ *A.*

A7. *(1) All P_1s are P_2s .*

(2) All [P_2s] are [P_3s]. — *All [products guaranteed three years] are [products that give you a lot of protection against faulty engineering and workmanship].*

∴ *All P_1s are P_3s.*

A9. *(1) If A and B, then C.*

(2) [A]. — *[The Netwizard desktop computer can run VideoMaster software.]*

(3) [B]. — *[The Netwizard desktop computer is cheaper than the Hacker laptop.]*

∴ *C.*

A11. *(1) Either A or B.*

(2) If C, then not B.

(3) [C]. — *[This money was given to me for my education.]*

∴ *A.*

B1.	*(1) A.*	*(1) You promised to be here at 8:00.*
	(2) If A, then B.	*(2) If you promised to be here at 8:00, then you should have arrived at 8:00.*
	∴ *B.* (IMPLICIT)	∴ *You should have arrived at 8:00.* (IMPLICIT)
B3.	*(1) If A, then B.*	*(1) If you tell lies frequently, then you must remember not only what you have done but also what you said you have done.*
	(2) If B, then C. (IMPLICIT)	*(2) If you must remember not only what you have done but also what you said you have done, then your memory becomes burdened.* (IMPLICIT)
	∴ *If A, then C.*	∴ *If you tell lies frequently, your memory becomes burdened.*
B5.	*(1) All P_1s are P_2s.*	*(1) Any social institution that spends beyond the willingness of the public to pay is eroding its public support.*
	*(2) m is a P_1.** (IMPLICIT)	*(2) American universities are a social institution that spends beyond the willingness of the public to pay.* (IMPLICIT)
	∴ *m is a P_2.*	∴ *American universities are eroding their public support.*
	**[NOTE the use of predicate instantiation here. We are treating American universities as a kind of individual as opposed to, say, Canadian universities.]*	
B7.	*(1) A.*	*(1) There are not enough alternative fuel facilities under construction.*
	(2) If A, then B. (IMPLICIT)	*(2) If there are not enough alternative fuel facilities under construction, then we will face substantial energy shortages by the year 2020.* (IMPLICIT)
	∴ *B.*	∴ *We will face substantial energy shortages by the year 2020.*

B9.

(1) All P_1s are P_2s.	*(1) Every successful politician has to compromise his principles occasionally.*
(2) All P_2s are P_3s.	*(2) Everyone who has to compromise his principles occasionally loses integrity.*
∴ All P_1s are P_3s. (IMPLICIT)	*∴ Every successful politician loses integrity.* (IMPLICIT)

B11.

(1) If A, then B.	*(1) If the older generation accepts their responsibility for the future, it will limit the deficit.*
(2) If B, then C.	*(2) If the older generation limits the deficit, then the current generation in their 20s has a chance at avoiding impoverishment.*
(3) A. (IMPLICIT)	*(3) The older generation accepts their responsibility for the future.* (IMPLICIT)
∴ C.	*∴ The current generation in their 20s has a chance at avoiding impoverishment.*
	(NOTE: The order of premises is changed to match the pattern.)

B13. *(1) Everyone who takes mood altering prescription drugs is happy.*

(2) You are not happy. (IMPLICIT)

∴ You don't take mood altering prescription drugs.

B15. *(1) Alice has a new job in Minneapolis.*

(2) If so, then she'll be moving.

(3) If she'll be moving, then Bruce or Frank will get a promotion.

(4) Frank will not get a promotion. (IMPLICIT)

∴ Bruce will get a promotion.

B17. *(1) Public awareness about global warming, greenhouse gases, and oil spills is growing rapidly.*

(2) If public awareness about global warming, greenhouse gases, and oil spills is growing rapidly, then political incentives are sufficiently high.

(3) If political incentives are sufficiently high, then mobilization of technological resources will occur.

(4) *If mobilization of technological resources will occur, then the industrial nations will resolve the environmental crises that are looming for the near future.*

∴ *The industrialized nations will resolve the environmental crises that are looming for the near future.* (IMPLICIT)

B19. (1) *If a bad social environment causes people to become criminals, then everyone from a bad social environment would be a criminal.*

(2) *Not everyone from a bad social environment is a criminal.*

∴ *It isn't a bad social environment that causes people to become criminals.* (IMPLICIT)

C1. Reconstruction b is adequate. It uses all the premises in the argument. Reconstruction a does not use all the premises and includes a Premise 2 that is not mentioned in the passage. Further, the conclusion is at odds with the passage as a whole. Reconstruction c includes a conclusion that is compatible with the passage, but also contains Premise 2, which is not in the passage.

C3. Reconstruction c is adequate, although quite bold. Both a and b take the easy way out by using the *if–then* construction and therefore are restricted to Mervin only, rather than to characteristics of all people who are devoted to becoming famous journalists.

Exercise 3.2 (pp. 70–75)
(These arguments can be reconstructed in more than one way.)

A1. (1) *If something never existed, then it can't be restored.* (IMPLICIT)

(2) *Democracy in Haiti never existed.*

∴ *Democracy in Haiti can't be restored.*

A3. (1) *Sex is private and intimate.*

(2) *Whatever is private and intimate should not be publicized.* (IMPLICIT)

∴ *Sex should not be publicized.* (SUBORDINATE CONCLUSION)

(3) *If sex education is permitted, then sex will be publicized.* (IMPLICIT)

∴ *Sex education should not be permitted.*

A5. (1) *Making collective (i.e., racist) judgments harms innocent human beings and their quest for equality.*

(2) *Whatever harms innocent human beings and their quest for equality is wrong.* (IMPLICIT)

∴ *Making collective (i.e., racist) judgments is wrong.*

A7. (1) *If reporters aren't as skeptical of anti-smoking groups as of the tobacco industry, then they won't get at the truth.*

(2) *Reporters should get at the truth.* (IMPLICIT)

∴ *Reporters should be as skeptical of anti-smoking groups as of the tobacco industry.*

A9. (1) *Feminist literature can either prepare women for life in the counterculture, or for meeting primary economic needs.* (IMPLICIT)

(2) *If feminist literature prepares women for life in the counterculture, then when that life is over they are left in limbo.*

(3) *Women should not be left in limbo when life in the counterculture is over.* (IMPLICIT)

∴ *Feminist literature should prepare women for meeting primary economic needs.*

B1. Lecture Fragment—Plea Bargaining
Argument I (for eliminating plea bargaining):

(1) *Plea bargaining causes some innocent defendants to plead guilty.*

(2) *Plea bargaining makes no presumption of innocence.*

(3) *Plea bargaining substitutes negotiation of guilt for an adversarial process.*

(4) *Plea bargaining sacrifices the interests of society.*

(5) *Any practice that has the defects described in Premises 1–4 should be eliminated.* (IMPLICIT)

∴ *Plea bargaining should be eliminated.*

Chapter 4

Exercise 4.1 (pp. 89–90)

1.

	Invalid Pattern
(1) *Anyone who lives with a smoker has an above-average risk of heart disease.*	(1) *All P_1s are P_2s.*
(2) *Sarah doesn't live with a smoker.*	(2) *m is not a P_1.*
∴ *Sarah doesn't have an above-average risk of heart disease.*	∴ *m is not a P_2.*

COUNTEREXAMPLE:

(1) *Anyone who is a mother is female.*

(2) *Sarah is not a mother.*

∴ *Sarah is not a female.*

DESCRIBING AN INVALIDATING POSSIBILITY: (Smoking is not the only risk factor.) Sarah doesn't live with a smoker but loves to eat Big Macs and other high-fat foods. She also comes from a family with a history of heart disease.

3.

	Invalid Pattern
(1) *If dinner guests are coming, then we need more food.*	(1) *If G, then F.*
(2) *If we need more food, then we need to go to the store.*	(2) *If F, then S.*
(3) *Dinner guests aren't coming.*	(3) *Not G.*
∴ *We don't need to go to the store.*	∴ *Not S.*

COUNTEREXAMPLE:

(1) *If the Statue of Liberty is in San Francisco, then it is in California.*

(2) *If the Statue of Liberty is in California, then it is in the United States.*

(3) *The Statue of Liberty is not in San Francisco.*

∴ *The Statue of Liberty is not in the United States.*

DESCRIBING AN INVALIDATING POSSIBILITY: (We might need food even though the guests aren't coming.) The guests aren't coming. We had to take an unexpected trip out of town, but we do need food anyway because we didn't get a chance to shop.

5.

	Invalid Pattern
(1) *If the American people feel economically secure, then they will press for tax cuts.*	(1) *If S, then C.*
(2) *The American people don't feel economically secure.*	(2) *Not S.*
∴ *The American people won't press for tax cuts.*	∴ *Not C.*

COUNTEREXAMPLE:

(1) *If the Martin Luther King Memorial is in Hawaii, then it is in the United States.*

(2) *The Martin Luther King Memorial is not in Hawaii.*

∴ *The Martin Luther King Memorial is not in the United States.*

DESCRIBING AN INVALIDATING POSSIBILITY: Even if they don't feel economically secure, the American people could still press for tax cuts because they don't believe the government will use tax revenues to assure their future economic well being.

7.

	Invalid Pattern
(1) *All good friends are compassionate people.*	(1) *All P_1s are P_2s.*
(2) *All good friends are honest people.*	(2) *All P_1s are P_3s.*
∴ *All compassionate people are honest.*	∴ *All P_2s are P_3s.*

COUNTEREXAMPLE:

(1) *All mothers are animals.*

(2) *All mothers are female.*

∴ *All animals are female.*

DESCRIBING AN INVALIDATING POSSIBILITY: Even if good friends were compassionate and honest (at least toward those with whom they are friends), still, someone who is compassionate but not a good friend might be dishonest. For example, if you were unhappy, such a person might tell you lies to flatter you and make you feel happy.

9.

	Invalid Pattern
(1) *Anyone who is good at science is good at math.*	(1) *All P_1s are P_2s.*
(2) *Anyone who is good at math is intelligent.*	(2) *All P_2s are P_3s.*
∴ *Anyone who is intelligent is good at science.*	∴ *All P_3s are P_1s.*

COUNTEREXAMPLE:

(1) *Anyone who is in North Dakota is in the Midwest.*

(2) *Anyone who is in the Midwest is in the United States.*

∴ *Anyone who is in the United States is in North Dakota.*

DESCRIBING AN INVALIDATING POSSIBILITY: (There are different ways of being intelligent.) An artist such as Andy Warhol could have been quite intelligent (in dealing with the art world) without being particularly good at science.

Exercise 4.2 (p. 94)

1. In the United States there is little connection between whether a state has capital punishment and the homicide rate. Some states with death penalties have high homicide rates, and some states without the death penalty have low homicide rates. This suggests that the existence or absence of the death penalty does not markedly affect the homicide rate. If so, then eliminating capital punishment is unlikely to increase the homicide rate. Furthermore, even if abolishing capital punishment did tend to increase the homicide rate, demographic factors such as a drop in the percentage of young males in the population could outweigh this tendency.

3. Driving cars might make people aggressive, but it is certainly questionable whether this activity should be discouraged. Training for work in the military or security fields might make people more aggressive, but such activity is (unfortunately) necessary and permissible.

5. Stock car and other types of racing put spectators (bystanders) at some risk. Occasionally, accidents cause cars to become airborne and crash into the stands, injuring people. The rights of the spectators are not violated. Their voluntary decision to subject themselves to this risk by buying tickets would seem to preclude such "rights." Similarly, if someone sneaks behind barricades to get closer to a building demolition, the risk posed to them by the activity does not violate their rights. What seems crucial in these cases is that the bystanders are not "innocent." They know (or should know) the risks inherent in being near where the activity is being conducted. In another class of cases, the benefits of an action might clearly outweigh the health risk to bystanders. Shutting down a water system might risk the health of those who are forced to live (temporarily) without water, but if the system is contaminated the health benefits to those "bystanders" outweigh the health risks.

7. At any given time, Social Security is not used by most people in the sense that they are actually getting benefits. People pay into the system, however, in expectation of future benefits. Other aspects of government are like insurance that is never used (but might be). People should buy fire insurance even though most of them will never use it. Similarly, some military expenses might serve as insurance even if they are never used in

a military conflict. Even when people don't get direct benefit—they may never drive on a freeway or U.S. highway in Maine, nor even buy products that are shipped over this highway—it can be reasonably argued that they should pay gasoline taxes or extra transportation costs on what they buy. These are used to build highways.

9. Even if Asian and European countries have much higher average scores on science and math exams, it doesn't follow that the United States should adopt the educational methods of these countries. First, the United States does well by its best students. Furthermore, the higher average scores in Asia and Europe might be due in part to social and cultural factors rather than educational methods. Finally, there are features of American education that are valuable even though they don't produce high average science and math scores. For example, in contrast to Japanese education, schools in the United States might be seen as encouraging unconventional but potentially creative students.

11. Even if a practice could help cure disease without causing harm it might not be the best available practice, and for this reason should not be continued. The practice of treating many low-income patients in emergency rooms no doubt contributes to the cure of the disease in some of these patients without causing harm, but a better system of medical insurance might be even more effective in identifying and treating low-income patients.

Exercise 4.3 (pp. 98–99)

A1. The conclusion follows, but the first premise is surely false.

A3. The conclusion does not follow.

B1. *(1) If Los Angeles is in Texas, then Los Angeles is in the Lone Star State.*

(2) Los Angeles is in Texas.

∴ *Los Angeles is in the Lone Star State.*

B3. *(1) No bankers are overweight.*

(2) All overweight people will have a heart attack.

∴ *No bankers will have a heart attack.*

C1a. Misuse of terms

C1c. Sensible use of terms

C1e. Misuse of terms

C2a. Inconsistent

C2c. Consistent

Exercise 4.4 (pp. 106–111)

A1. (1) *Any activity that makes people aggressive should be discouraged.*

(2) *Football makes people aggressive.*

∴ *Football should be discouraged.*

The conclusion follows from the premises (with the provisions discussed in the chapter about arguments containing "should"). But Premise 1 has counterexamples, which were pointed out in the answer to Exercise 4.2, #3.

A3. (1) *If the government's antiviolence policies are effective, then youth violence will begin to decline.*

(2) *Youth violence is beginning to decline.*

∴ *The government's antiviolence policies are effective.*

The conclusion doesn't follow from the premises. It could be that violence beginning to decline for some reason other than the government's antiviolence effort. Perhaps it is declining because the number of violence-prone young men is becoming smaller because of demographic changes or cultural factors.

A5. (1) *If the average couple has more than two children, the population will rise drastically.*

(2) *We should prevent the population from rising drastically.*

∴ *We should prevent any couple from having more than two children.*

There is a subtle shift in wording that makes this argument invalid. The first premise says that if the average couple has more than two children, the population will rise drastically. The conclusion says that we should prevent any couple from having more than two children. All that would follow from these premises is that we should prevent the average couple from having more than two children. This would require much less drastic measures on the part of government than would the stated conclusion. The premises could also be called into question.

A7. (1) *If we allow doctors to determine the gender of a fetus whenever parents request it, then (some) parents will abort a fetus simply because of its gender.*

(2) *We shouldn't allow parents to abort a fetus simply because of its gender.* (IMPLICIT)

∴ *We shouldn't allow doctors to determine the gender of a fetus when parents request it.*

The conclusion follows from these premises (at least if we allow "value arguments" resembling *modus tollens*). But premise 1 assumes that when doctors determine the sex of a fetus, they will give this information to parents. It would be possible to have a policy that allows doctors to make this determination (for example, to detect sex-linked diseases) but that doesn't generally make this information available to parents. Premise 2 sounds persuasive, but keep in mind how strong an assertion this must be in order for the argument to be valid. The premise can't merely assert that allowing parents to abort a fetus because of its sex is a bad thing. Rather, it must assert that we must prevent this state of affairs—using abortion for sex selection—from coming about. In reply, a critic could admit that sex selection by means of abortion is a bad consequence that we would hope to minimize. However, the benefits of allowing doctors to determine the sex of a fetus (especially in detecting sex-linked disease) outweigh the risk that some parents will misuse information concerning the sex of the fetus.

A9. *(1) All tax increases are unjustified at this time.*

(2) User fees to get into national parks are not taxes.

∴ *Increasing user fees into national parks is justified.*

The conclusion does not follow from the premises. Even if tax increases are unjustified, we need not assume that an increase in other government fees (assuming they are not taxes) is thereby justified. Both tax increases and fee increases might be unjustified.

A11. *(1) People should pay taxes to support only parts of the government they use.*

(2) People without children don't use the schools. (IMPLICIT)

∴ *People without children shouldn't be required to pay for schools.*

The conclusion follows from the stated premise, plus the implicit premise that people without children don't use the schools. Both the explicit and implicit premises are doubtful. Arguably, government can function only if individuals are willing to pay for at least some benefits to others that they themselves will not directly use. Projects in some distant part of the country are "traded off" for projects close to home.

Further, it is plausible to assume that if we interpret "use" in a slightly broader way than direct personal use (by a person or at least by his or her family), then people without children do use the schools, contrary to the implicit premise. After all, the economic well-being of a community depends to a significant degree on the general educational level of its citizens, and a person benefits from ("uses") the economic resources of the community.

B1. *(1) The predicted bad effects of global warming are well into the future.*

(2) If so, then the occurrence of bad effects of global warming is uncertain.

(3) *If the occurrence of bad effects of global warming is uncertain, then we should not take expensive precautions (which might be unnecessary).*

∴ *We should not take expensive precautions (which might be unnecessary).*

The conclusion follows from the premises as the argument is reconstructed, but Premises 1 and 3 are doubtful. Many models of climate change (whether as the result of human activity or of significant natural variation) don't indicate a full century of lead time. This suggests that it will impact people who are already alive and not just those "well into the future."

But Premise 3 is the most vulnerable. Just because something is uncertain—just because we *might* have "wiped ourselves out" or devised a yet unimagined technological fix—this doesn't mean that these occurrences are likely. Even if there were some hope of technological advance, this doesn't mean that we should not take precautions (even if they are expensive). People regularly buy insurance, even though the prospects of an accident or other mishap is uncertain or slight, especially when the costs should it occur are very great. Furthermore, merely because the full effects of global warming may be in the more distant future, there might be a much shorter window of opportunity to do something about it.

Chapter 5

Exercise 5.1 (pp. 115–117)

A1. A; A3. $A \rightarrow B$; A5. $A \rightarrow (B \vee C)$; A7. $(A \& B) \rightarrow (C \vee D)$; B1. $\neg\neg A$ or alternatively A; B3. $A \vee B$; B5. $\neg (A \vee B)$, alternatively, $\neg A \& \neg B$; C1. From problem A1 in Exercise 3.1:

(1) $A \rightarrow B$. (2) A.	A: *The Netwizard desktop computer runs VideoMaker.*
∴ B.	B: *The Netwizard computer can meet my computing needs.*

From problem A3 in Exercise 3.1:

(1) $\neg A \rightarrow \neg B$. (2) $\neg B \rightarrow \neg C$.	A: *The Hacker laptop does run VideoMaker software.*
∴ $\neg A \rightarrow \neg C$.	B: *I can create DVDs and video for the Web.*
	C: *The Hacker1000 does meet my needs.*

[NOTE: Instead of treating B as a single statement we could treat it as a conjunction with (D & E) substituted for B throughout.]

From problem A5 in Exercise 3.1:

(1) $A \vee B$.
(2) $\neg B$.

∴ A.

A: *I should buy an Econoplasma high-definition TV.*
B: *I should buy a Primeoview high-definition plasma TV.*

C2. From problem C1 in Exercise 3.1:

(a) *(1)* $A \vee B$.
(2) $\neg B$.

∴ A.

A: *We should permanently cut taxes.*
B: *We should (use this opportunity to) preserve Social Security and expand medical coverage.*
C: *We will be unable to fund Social Security and expand medical care when the need inevitably arises.*
[Hint: This premise is needed for Reconstruction (b).]

(c) *(1)* B.
(2) $D \,\&\, E$.

∴ $\neg A$.

D: *We have an obligation to those who paid into Social Security.*
E: *It would be inhumane to leave our citizens without medical insurance.*

D1. *(1)* $A \vee B$.
(2) $B \rightarrow C$.
(3) $\neg C$.

∴ A.

D3. *(1)* $A \rightarrow B$.
(2) $B \rightarrow C$.
(3) $\neg C \vee D$.
(4) $\neg D$.

∴ $\neg A$.

Exercise 5.2 (pp. 122–123)

A1. $A \rightarrow \neg B$

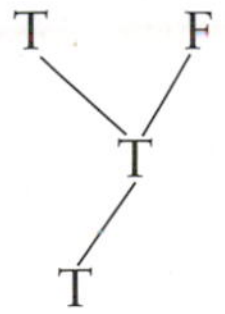

T F — Initial Assignment
T — *Row 2 Negation*
T — *Row 1 Conditional*

A3. $\neg (A \& \neg B)$

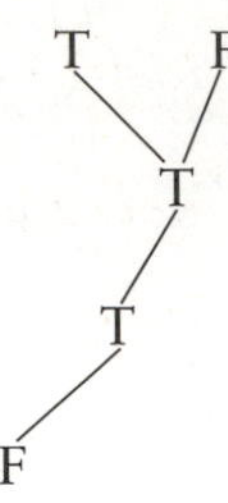

Initial Assignment

Row 2 Negation

Row 1 Conjunction

Row 1 Negation

A5. $\neg (A \leftrightarrow B)$

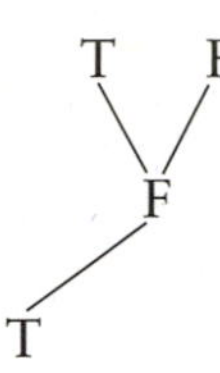

Initial Assignment

Row 2 Biconditional

Row 1 Negation

B1. $A \rightarrow \neg B$

Initial Assignment

Row 2 Negation

Row 3 Conditional

C1. $A \rightarrow (B \vee C)$

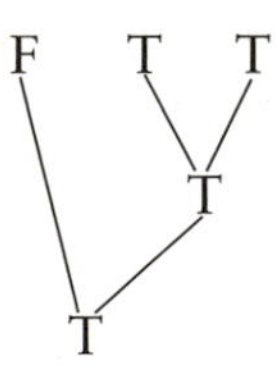

Initial Assignment

Row 1 Disjunction

Row 3 Conditional

C3. $(A \vee B) \rightarrow (C \& D)$

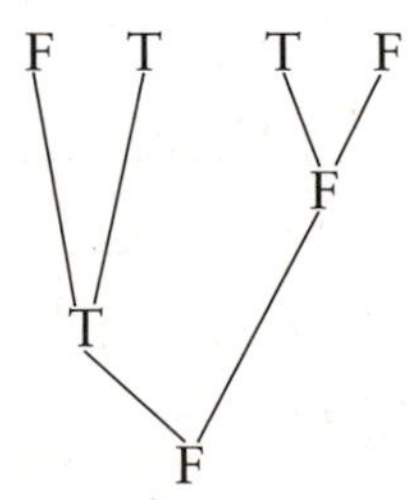

Initial Assignment

Row 2 Conjunction

Row 3 Disjunction

Row 2 Conditional

C5. $(\neg A \rightarrow B) \vee (\neg D \rightarrow C)$

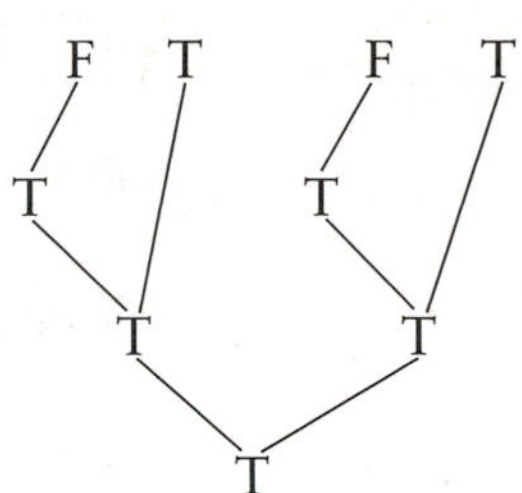

Initial Assignment

Row 2 Negation

Row 1 Conditional

Row 1 Disjunction

C7. $\neg ((A \vee \neg B) \,\&\, C)$

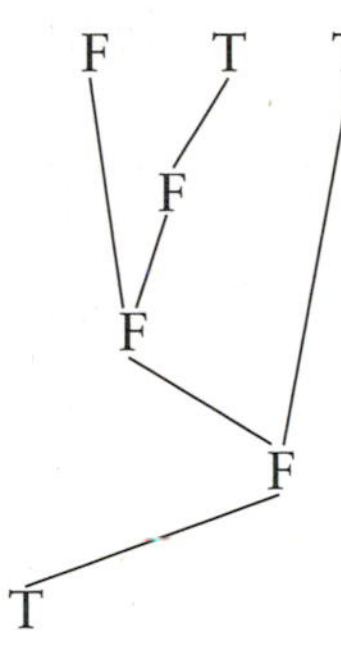

Initial Assignment

Row 1 Negation

Row 4 Disjunction

Row 3 Conjunction

Row 2 Negation

Exercise 5.3 (pp. 128–130)

A2.

Initial Assignments			Premises			Conclusion
A	B	C	$A \rightarrow B$	$B \rightarrow C$	A	C
T	T	T	T	T	T	T
T	T	F	T	F	T	F
T	F	T	F	T	T	T
T	F	F	F	T	T	F
F	T	T	T	T	F	T
F	T	F	T	F	F	F
F	F	T	T	T	F	T
F	F	F	T	T	F	F

Note that all premises are true in the first line only, and the conclusion is also true in this situation. So the argument is valid.

B1.

Initial Assignments		Premises		Conclusion
A	B	$\neg A \rightarrow B$	A	B
T	T	T	T	T
T	F	T	T	F
F	T	T	F	T
F	F	F	F	F

Invalid. Note the second line where the premises are all true and the conclusion false.

C1.

Initial Assignments		Premises		Conclusion
A	B	$A \to \neg B$	B	$\neg A$
T	T	F	T	F
T	F	T	F	F
F	T	T	T	T
F	F	T	F	T

Valid. Note that only the third line has (all) the premises true. The conclusion is also true in this situation.

C3.

Initial Assignments		Premise	Conclusion
A	B	$A \to B$	$B \to A$
T	T	T	T
T	F	F	T
F	T	T	F
F	F	T	T

Invalid. Note that on the third line the single premise is true, but the conclusion is false.

C9.

Initial Assignments			Premises			Conclusion
A	B	C	$A \to \neg B$	$\neg B \vee C$	A	C
T	T	T	F	T	T	T
T	T	F	F	F	T	F
T	F	T	T	T	T	T
T	F	F	T	T	T	F
F	T	T	T	T	F	T
F	T	F	T	F	F	F
F	F	T	T	T	F	T
F	F	F	T	T	F	F

Invalid. Note that in the fourth line all the premises are true and the conclusion is false.

C13.

Initial Assignments			Premises			Conclusion
A	B	C	$A \leftrightarrow B$	$B \to C$	$\neg C$	A
T	T	T	T	T	F	T
T	T	F	T	F	T	T
T	F	T	F	T	F	T
T	F	F	F	T	T	T
F	T	T	F	T	F	F
F	T	F	F	F	T	F
F	F	T	T	T	F	F
F	F	F	T	T	T	F

Invalid. Note the last line in which all the premises are true and the conclusion is false.

Exercise 5.4 (pp. 136–138)

A1. *All men are human.* $(x)\ (Mx \rightarrow Hx)$

All women are human. $(x)\ (Wx \rightarrow Hx)$

∴ *All men are women.* $\therefore (x)\ (Mx \rightarrow Wx)$

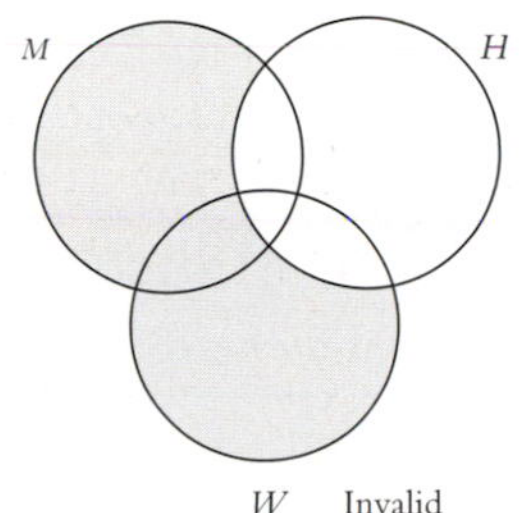

A3. *All dogs are mammals.* $(x)\ (Dx \rightarrow Mx)$

All mammals are animals. $(x)\ (Mx \rightarrow Ax)$

Zeke is a dog. Dz

∴ *Zeke is an animal.* $\therefore (x)\ Az$

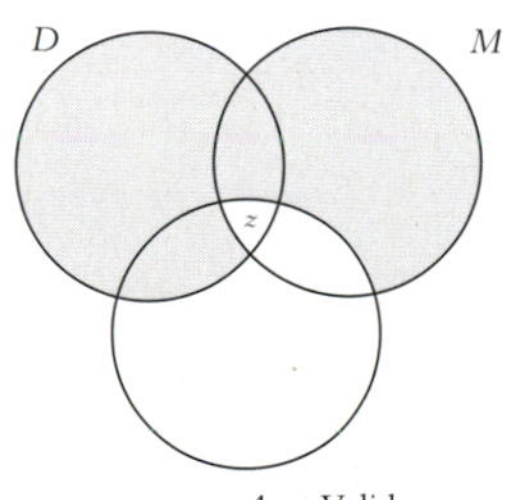

A5. *All men are human.* $(x)\ (Mx \rightarrow Hx)$

All women are human. $(x)\ (Wx \rightarrow Hx)$

Madonna is not a man. $\neg Mm$

∴ *Madonna is not a woman.* $\therefore \neg Wm$

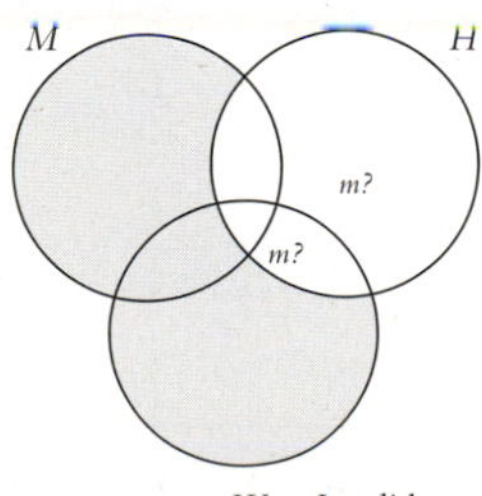

B1.	*No dogs are fish.*	*(x) (Dx → ¬ Fx)*
	All salmon are fish.	*(x) (Sx → Fx)*
	∴ *No dogs are salmon.*	∴ *(x) (Dx → ¬ Sx)*

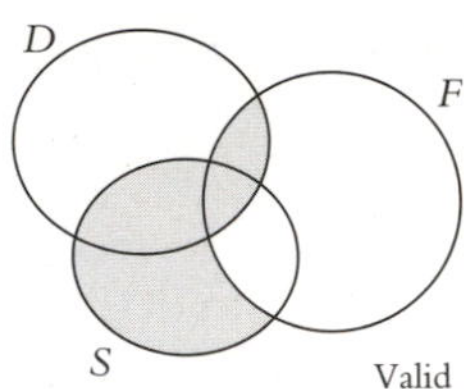

B3.	*No women are men.*	*(x) (Wx → ¬ Mx)*
	No men are mothers.	*(x) (Mx → ¬ Nx)*
	∴ *No women are mothers.*	*(x) (Wx → ¬ Nx)*

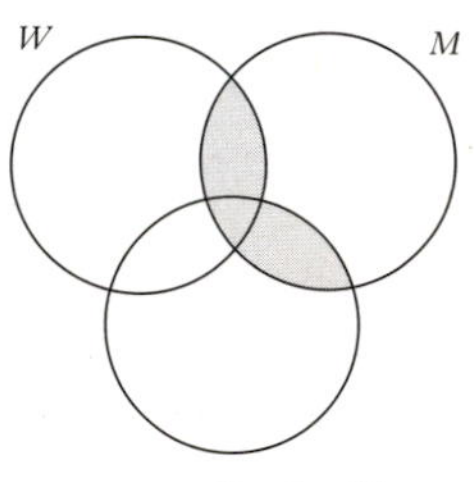

B5.	*No men are women.*	*(x) (Mx → ¬ Wx)*
	Every female vocalist is a woman.	*(x) (Fx → Wx)*
	Madonna is a female vocalist.	*Fm*
A5.	∴ *Madonna is not a man.*	∴ ¬ *Mm*

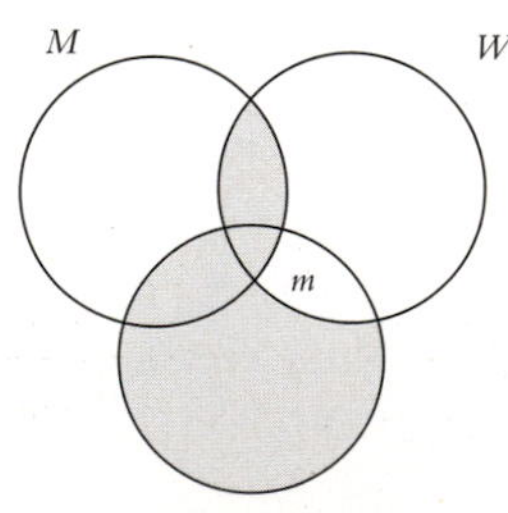

C1.	*All products high in fat are unhealthy.*	*(x) (Fx → Ux)*
	Some cuts of beef are high in fat.	(∃x) *(Bx & Fx)*
	∴ *Some cuts of beef are unhealthy.*	∴ (∃x) *(Bx & Ux)*

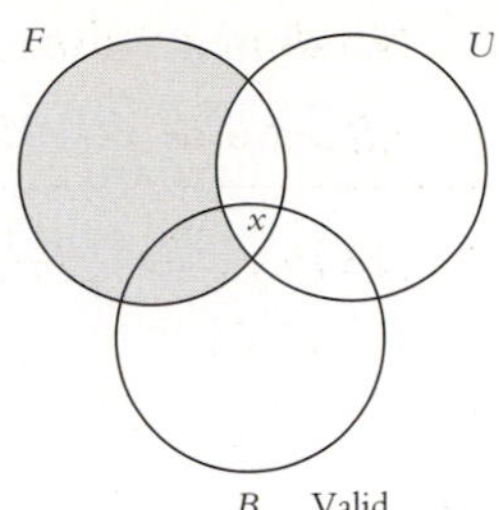

C3. *All bank presidents are human.* $(x)\ (Bx \rightarrow Hx)$

Some men are not bank presidents. $(\exists x)\ (Mx\ \&\ \neg\ Bx)$

∴ *Some men are not human.* ∴ $(\exists x)\ (Mx\ \&\ \neg\ Hx)$

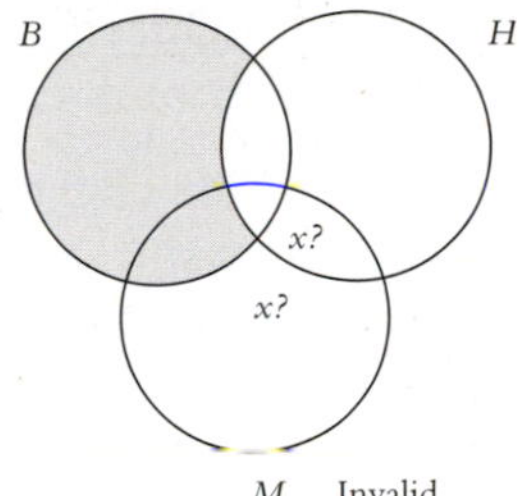

C5. *No boring job is satisfying.* $(x)\ (Bx \rightarrow \neg\ Sx)$

Some well-paying jobs are boring. $(\exists x)\ (Wx\ \&\ Bx)$

∴ *Some well-paying jobs are not satisfying.* ∴ $(\exists x)\ (Wx\ \&\ \neg\ Sx)$

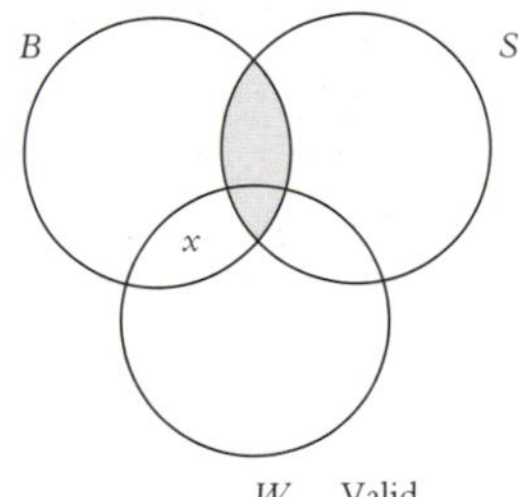

Chapter 6

Exercise 6.1 (pp. 148–151)

A1. False dilemma. Perhaps this is persuasive because we like to have our options simplified: Either you find a way to save a lot or you should forget about it. You don't look for a third alternative. What's wrong with saving a little? (*Note*: *If–then* in the passage can be treated as an "or." "If not *A*, then *B*" is logically equivalent to "*A* or *B*.")

A3. False dilemma. It would be persuasive because the thought that you might be part of the problem distracts you from considering that there are more alternatives than these two. A third alternative is that you are *both* part of the solution and part of the problem.

A5. Straw man. The opposition is portrayed as making a weaker argument against prayer than might be made. Even if, properly interpreted, the constitution calls for separation of church and state, this might be compatible with individual, voluntary prayer in public schools.

A7. False dilemma and slippery slope. There are many choices between these two extremes. Furthermore, if cigarettes and "self-abuse" at 15 led to being a moral and physical wreck at 48, then there would be a lot of moral and physical wrecks. The illustration was probably effective in its day because the prospect of becoming dissipated and then outcast would have been frightening enough to distract the reader's attention from the implausibility of the argument.

A9. Straw man. You might be distracted by the weak claim attributed to the opponent that there is no strategy whatever to deal with the root cause of terrorism and that we will lose. But the opponent, in saying that we can't win this war, might be taking the more defensible position that the conflict against terrorism isn't the kind of conflict that is either won or lost. Remember the "false dilemma" element of straw man arguments. The arguer is saying: either accept my position or accept the weak position I am attributing to the opposition. There might be a more defensible middle ground.

Exercise 6.2 (pp. 157–159)

A1. Denying the antecedent. This resembles a valid argument.

A3. Affirming the consequent. *(If we're nice guys, then we'll finish last. We'll finish last. Therefore, we're nice guys.)* This resembles a valid argument.

A5. Begging the question. If this persuaded anyone, it would be because the premise is stated in slightly different words from the conclusion, making it less apparent that no additional reason is being given for the conclusion.

A7. Denying the antecedent. This resembles a good argument.

C1. Denying the antecedent. This resembles a good argument, but the pattern is faulty.

C3. Affirming the consequent. This resembles a good argument, but the pattern is faulty.

C5. False dilemma. There are more choices than being either hip or smart.

C7. Slippery slope and false dilemma. The speaker probably believes the steps in the slope are connected just because she doesn't want to take the first one (living in the dorm). The only alternative she sees is the expensive apartment because she doesn't want to look for other alternatives.

Exercise 6.3 (pp. 165–166)

1. Appeal to pity
3. Prejudicial language
5. Appeal to force
7. Appeal to force

Exercise 6.4 (pp. 173–175)

B1. Straw man, false dilemma, begging the question.
B3. Appeal to force, denying the antecedent.
B5. Attacking the person, prejudicial language, slippery slope.
B7. Attacking the person, slippery slope, false dilemma (either we let development ruin us or we resist and save our community). Appeal to force in last sentence is debatable. It depends on whether voting is taken as deciding to believe or as acting.

Exercise 6.5 (pp. 175–176)

1. It might be claimed that this is the fallacy of appeal to pity. The question of whether this is a fallacy hinges on what the jury is deciding (or should decide). If the decision is simply one of guilt or innocence, then the appeal is fallacious. If the question is whether the accused should be imprisoned, then the appeal to pity is not fallacious.

3. The arguer raises for us the issue of whether this argument begs the question. In our discussion of this fallacy, we pointed out that an argument shouldn't use a premise that is just as doubtful, and doubtful on similar grounds, as the conclusion. We assume that the arguer is speaking on behalf of taxpayers to someone who thinks the government should provide free childcare to parents. The point of the argument is that people are more inclined to claim they have a right to something if they ignore the question of why someone else should have an obligation to provide it for them. In this sense, for many audiences, the premise that I have no obligation to give you something would be a reason for believing that you do not have a right to it. For such an audience, the argument would not be question-begging, even though the premise could be disputed.

5. The question is whether this is a fallacious attack on the person. If Franklin gave reasons for living in certain ways, independent of any attempt to set an example, then an assessment of his philosophy of life should focus on these reasons. Perhaps Franklin wasn't able to follow his own advice concerning how one should live, but his advice would work for many other people. Still, since Franklin had his own rules available to him as guides for living, if his own life was not happy, then this raises the question of how useful or workable his rules would be for others.

7. This example raises a puzzle concerning how a scientific theory is confirmed. The passage seems to say: "If the theory is correct, then we would expect these continental movements. The continental

movements did occur. So the theory is correct." But this would be the fallacy of affirming the consequent. So what kind of argument *should* we be making when we confirm a theory? This issue is touched upon in Chapter 10.

Chapter 7

Exercise 7.1 (pp. 187–188)

A1. The term "man" could refer to the human species or to individual human beings. "Free" could mean "having no constraints" or "having the power to do what one wants." It is probably true that the human species was, at some time in the distant past, free in the sense that it had no elaborate social constraints, but it was not free in the second sense. Individual human beings are or have been enslaved (so not all are free in the first sense); nor is anyone born free in the second sense. Everyone faces some constraints or limitations in their lives.

A3. The expression "indirect suicide" is vague. If we interpret it in such a way that a person who plays "Russian roulette" with a loaded gun participates in indirect suicidal behavior, the statement is true. If eating fatty red meat turns out to be as unhealthy as is sometimes suggested, then this too could be considered indirectly suicidal. But it is unclear, even with recent health warnings, that eating red meat should be "strongly condemned." If we specify the term in this broad way, the statement is false.

A5. The term "war" is ambiguous. It could mean either "an extensive armed conflict" or "a concerted public effort to eliminate or alter some unacceptable condition." Since the "war on poverty" was not a war in the first sense, interpreting it in this way would make the statement true. But it would be false if interpreted in the second sense.

A7. In this context, "equal" is ambiguous. It could mean equal in rights or equal in terms of some other conditions—for example, equal income, equal interest in a lively night life, and so on. The statement is most clearly true if the first clause is interpreted in the first sense and the last clause in the second sense. Using either interpretation in both clauses renders the statement false.

A9. "Treat students equally" is ambiguous in this context. In one sense, equal treatment might involve exactly the same educational experience. In another sense, equal treatment could be interpreted to allow for differences as long as students had equal opportunity or equal legal rights. Interpreted in the first way, the sentence is true. Schools can't (and shouldn't) treat students exactly the same (regardless of interests, talents, and so on). But it is false given the second interpretation because students can be given (roughly) the same opportunities or legal rights. Further, the second interpretation is vague.

B1. RECONSTRUCTION:

(1) *The United States is ruled by the people.*

(2) *All countries ruled by the people are democracies.*

∴ *The United States is a democracy.*

ASSESSMENT: "Ruled by the people" is vague, but following the Principle of Charitable Interpretation, we could allow that the degree of citizen participation in the U.S. would count as "ruled by the people." "Democracy" is also vague—it surely covers countries that are less than ideally democratic. The degree to which the U.S. is ruled by the people (premise 1) is adequate to satisfy this particular criterion for being democratic that is stated in premise 2, so the argument need not be seen as an equivocation on such a charitable interpretation. However, the second premise is doubtful in that there are probably other criteria for being a democracy in addition to being ruled by the people. A country with mob rule, lacking a legal system, would not qualify as democratic.

B3. RECONSTRUCTION:

(1) *If space is expanding, it is finite.*
[ALTERNATIVELY: *Either space is not expanding or it is finite; "A unless B" is interpreted as "A or B."*]

(2) *Space is not finite.*

∴ *Space is not expanding.*

ASSESSMENT: Equivocation makes the argument invalid. The term "finite" can be interpreted in at least two ways. In the first sense, something is finite if it has a boundary. But there is another sense in which something could be bounded, like the surface of the earth, but still we could travel indefinitely without reaching a boundary—we could just circle the earth endlessly. Similarly, space could be expanding, but no path in space needs to be in a boundary. It could be infinite, but bounded. So the sense of "finite" that makes Premise 2 true might not make Premise 1 true.

B5. RECONSTRUCTION:

(1) *We can't confidently predict the job market.*

(2) *If we can't confidently predict the job market, then we can't form a reasonable idea about what to do with our lives.*

(3) *If we can't form a reasonable idea about what to do with our lives, then we shouldn't go to college.*

∴ *We shouldn't go to college.*

ASSESSMENT: Equivocation makes the argument invalid. The expression "confidently predict the job market" is vague. It is true that we can't precisely predict all the particulars about future employment opportunities. And all bets are off if nuclear terrorism occurs. But some general predictions can be made about broad trends, and this might be all a person needs in order to form a reasonable idea of what to do with his or her life. So the sense of the phrase "confidently predict the job market" that would make Premise 1 true would probably make Premise 2 false. Similarly, the phrase "reasonable idea" could be seen as shifting in meaning from Premise 2 to Premise 3.

B7. RECONSTRUCTION:

(1) *If happiness involved freedom, then newborn children would be free (or would become free as they grow older).*

(2) *Newborn children are not free (nor do they become free as they grow older).*

∴ *Happiness does not involve freedom.*

ASSESSMENT: Two senses of "freedom" can be distinguished. Children are free, as Rousseau suggests, when they are subjected to few, if any, social expectations. As we grow up, society increasingly expects us to play socially defined roles. The author of the passage, B. F. Skinner, stresses a second sense of freedom, acting without constraint of physical environment or genetic endowment. According to Skinner, no one is free in this way. But if he asserted this conclusion without explaining his special meaning of "freedom," he would be guilty of misleading definition.

Exercise 7.2 (pp. 197–199)

1. A figure is a <u>square</u> *if and only if*
   (1) It has four sides; and
   (2) Its sides are equal in length.

3. A law is <u>just</u> *if and only if* it was passed democratically.

5. An event is a <u>traffic gridlock</u> *if and only if*
   (1) It involves total standstill of traffic;
   (2) It lasts at least fifteen minutes; and
   (3) It extends eight blocks or more in any direction.

7. Something is a <u>work of art</u> *if and only if*
   (1) It is man-made; and
   (2) Some society or sub-group of a society has conferred on it the status of candidate for appreciation.

9. A person has <u>(positive) liberty</u> *if and only if* he or she is self-directed.

(*Note:* Berlin offers what seem to be several conditions, but they are essentially the same though they are expressed in different ways. It is somewhat arbitrary which one is stated in the reconstruction.)

11. A death is a death with dignity *if and only if*

    (1) The dying person is treated with esteem and respect by himself or by others as is shown in the care and concern about seeing that no further discomfort, anguish or alteration of the physical body, appearance or condition occurs; and

    (2) This esteem and respect is carried over to the person once deceased.

Exercise 7.3 (pp. 203–205)

A1. COUNTEREXAMPLE: A parallelogram can have four equal sides but not be square.

A3. COUNTEREXAMPLE: Prisoners in adjacent cells live close to each other but may not constitute a society.

A5. COUNTEREXAMPLE: Some people have several compulsions. A person might believe that time spent gambling or drinking fine wines is worthwhile and still be a compulsive video gamer.

A7. COUNTEREXAMPLE: A person might be intelligent but have never taken the Stanford-Binet IQ tests or have been ill when taking the tests and got a score lower than 130.

A9. COUNTEREXAMPLE: At one point in history the belief that the sun goes around the earth was accepted by most people and was supported by some evidence—the sunrise—but was not true.

A11. COUNTEREXAMPLE: A person who recklessly exposes himself to certain death in order to try to do the impossible act of holding back floodwaters that threaten a town is not courageous but foolhardy.

B1. The theory does not elucidate. "Follows from" is unclear. It could mean either that the conclusion is brought to mind by the premises or that its truth is guaranteed by the premises.

B3. Theory does elucidate. "Happiness" is surely better understood than "good," although it too requires some explanation.

B5. The theory does not really elucidate. "Fair" is somewhat more clear than "just," but it is still an ethical concept over which there would be considerable disagreement.

B7. Theory does elucidate. Although it uses technical terms, their meanings are independent of the meaning of "arc."

B9. The theory elucidates only a little. "Transmission of information" is somewhat clearer than "communicates," but not much.

B11. The theory does not really elucidate. It is debatable whether "find worthy or valuable" is more clear than "appreciate."

C1. Although the conditions are not contradictory, they might be incompatible if as a matter of social psychology, people don't really want to do what we help them to do to realize their potential. After all, not everyone wants to exert the effort to get the most out of their education. It seems likely that at least some people will not do what is necessary to realize their potential unless society intervenes to force or at least manipulate them into activities that help them to do so.

Exercise 7.4 (pp. 207–214)

A1. CONCEPTUAL THEORY: Something is <u>right</u> *if and only if* it is in the interest of the stronger.

CRITICISM: The expression "interest of the stronger" needs elucidation. If we interpret "stronger" to mean political rulers, as Plato points out in *The Republic,* then one important issue is whether we are talking about the real interest of the rulers or what they believe is in their interest. Even though justice may be in the real interest of rulers, counterexamples can be found in which what rulers believe is in their interest is not right. Hitler presumably believed that the concentration camps were in his (and Germany's) best interest, but that did not make them right.

A3. CONCEPTUAL THEORY: An action is <u>morally right</u> *if and only if* it produces more good than any available alternative. Something is <u>good</u> *if and only if* it produces pleasure in normal individuals.

CRITICISM: This version of utilitarianism faces counterexamples. An act might produce more good than any alternative but might distribute the goods so unfairly that some other act would be morally preferable (for example, telling a joke that thoroughly amuses most of those present but humiliates one person). Even giving the death penalty to a person known by a few insiders to be innocent (a scapegoat) might prevent an angry mob from rioting. In such a case, this alternative produces more pleasure than any alternative, but it is not just. Furthermore, proving a complex mathematical theory may be a good even if it does not produce (bodily) pleasure in a normal person or even in the mathematician who does so. The concept of pleasure and the methods of measuring it need elucidation. It is probably too narrow a concept to cover all things that are good.

A5. CONCEPTUAL THEORY: Something is <u>human</u> *if and only if*

(1) Its IQ is at least twenty;
(2) It has self-awareness;
(3) It has self-control;
(4) It has a sense of time; and
(5) It is capable of relating to others.

CRITICISM: The theory is not elucidating. The way in which humans have self-awareness and self-control, but other animals do not, is hardly more clear than is the distinction between humans and animals to begin with. Furthermore, there is a possible counterexample: there may well be extraterrestrial beings who satisfy the conditions but are not human.

B1. CONCEPTUAL THEORY: A work of art is <u>modern</u> *if and only if* it was created recently.

ARGUMENT:

(1) The Museum of Modern Art should show only modern art.

(2) A work of art is modern only if it was created recently (in this century). (FROM THEORY)

(3) French Impressionist works of art were not created recently.

∴ *The Museum of Modern Art should not show French Impressionists.*

CRITICISM: The term "modern" reflects the style of the art, not the precise point in time at which it was created. In this sense of style, recent works can be done in traditional styles and not be modern in the stylistic sense. Native American totem art is not of the "modern" style even though it is still being created today.

B3. CONCEPTUAL THEORY: An argument is <u>good</u> *if and only if* it has a true conclusion.

ARGUMENT:

(1) All valid arguments are good arguments.

(2) All good arguments have a true conclusion. (IMPLICIT FROM THEORY)

∴ *All valid arguments have a true conclusion.*

CRITICISM: The conceptual theory about the goodness of an argument underlies the second, implicit premise. But this theory could be challenged by pointing out that certain deductive arguments—the valid ones—are good structurally even though they may have a false conclusion and that good inductive arguments, as we will see in Chapter 8, need not have a true conclusion. If the theory is faulty, then Premise 2 is questionable, and the soundness of the argument is in doubt. Furthermore, Premise 1 is weak if "good" is taken as meaning "without defect." A valid argument could have the defect of false premises and conclusion. Incidentally, the argument itself is an example of a valid argument with a false conclusion.

Chapter 8

Exercise 8.1 (pp. 219–220)

A1. Particular
A3. Generalization, statistical
A5. Generalization, universal
A7. Generalization, statistical
A9. Particular
A11. Generalization, universal
A13. Generalization, universal
B1. Inductive, argument with statistical premise
B3. Inductive, argument with statistical premise
B5. Inductive, sampling argument, then application with argument from statistical premise or deductive argument
B7. Deductive
B9. Deductive; Inductive, sampling argument (perhaps inductive, argument with statistical premise at the end of the passage)

Exercise 8.2 (pp. 229–231)

A1. *(1) More than half (six out of ten) of her teachers were women.*

(likely) More than half of teachers at her university are women.

The sample might be unrepresentative. She could be studying in fields with a high percentage of female faculty that is uncharacteristic of the university as a whole. A better sample could be obtained by getting data from a random sample of students; or better yet, the university office of institutional research would have data about the composition of the whole university faculty.

A3. *(1) An insufficient number of those sampled said that they would vote for Roosevelt.*

(likely) An insufficient number of voters would vote for Roosevelt to elect him.

The sample is not representative; the less well-to-do would be less likely to read *Literary Digest* or to have a telephone or an automobile, especially during the Depression. A random sample of addresses for registered voters (those likely to vote) would have produced better results, but the data would have been difficult to obtain for the country as a whole. This is a "classic" example of a very large sample that fails to support an inductive inference because it is not representative.

A5. (1) *Being female was not associated with greater life expectancy than being male [in the sample of three countries: Uganda, Rwanda, and Nigeria].*

(likely) *Being female is not associated with greater life expectancy than being male.*

The sample might not be representative (and is small). These African countries have had high rates of HIV/AIDS and periods of warfare, which could have affected females more than men or made them more susceptible to death in childbirth.

A7. (1) *(In the sample) The number of bank robberies increased.*

(likely) *The number of bank robbers increased.*

Shift in the unit of analysis. The premise concerns the number of robberies; the conclusion changes to the number of robb*e*rs. But the number of robbers could remain the same or even go down if they were committing more robberies.

A9. (1) *In most (all?) high school math and college algebra courses Al took, he did poorly.*

(likely) *In most future college math course Al would take, he would do poorly. [That is, Al will not succeed as a math major.]*

Those courses may not have been very well taught and hence may not be representative of other courses Al might take as a math major. The sample, however, is pretty good in this case, especially given the cumulative nature of much math learning.

A11. (1) *A very small percentage of the unvaccinated Cook County children care for by Homefirst in Chicago and unvaccinated Amish children in rural Lancaster Pennsylvania become autistic.*

(likely) *A very small percentage of (all) unvaccinated children become autistic.*

Although the sample is large, two communities might not be representative of the whole population to which the passage generalizes. Those children born while under the care of a health organization promoting home birth and those born into the Amish life style, could well have mothers who provided a prenatal or early childhood environment (besides resisting vaccination) that warded off autism.

B1. Suppose it were argued that the percentage of minority group members in the United States is not increasing. The United States Census report provides an estimate of the number of minority members for selected minority groups. If we didn't have the census figures, and we needed to develop a sampling procedure to determine the number of minority group members in the United

States, we would face several serious difficulties. First, there is the problem of whom to count as a minority group member. We could use self-identification as a member of a group such as "African-American" or "Latino," but this approach is made problematic by the large number of individuals of mixed race or ethnicity, and by the likely resistance of some individuals to be categorized in terms of race or ethnicity. Still, self-identification could give us a rough estimate. Second there is the problem of selecting a sampling frame—a list from which to select a random sample. Randomized dialing of phone numbers omits those who don't have phones or don't answer, and these categories might lead to over- or under-representation of minority group members. Even using census report figures is problematic because some urban minorities are apt to be undercounted because of a more mobile lifestyle—they might not be home much—or because they avoid government agents (for example, undocumented immigrants).

B3. An interview with individuals in randomly selected households selected from the city data base of residences in the neighborhood would be appropriate. Such an interview might be more easily done by telephone, given the emotional nature of the debate, though obtaining the telephone number of the household would be difficult. Care must be taken to avoid oversampling of one gender, perhaps by randomly asking for either a male or a female respondent from the household.

B5. A survey of an appropriately large, randomly selected sample could be drawn, in which the proportion of landline and cell numbers in the sample was proportional to the number of distinct phone numbers in each phone exchange found in the target area. Random digit could be drawn for numbers within each of the exchanges. Special care should be taken to determine what the respondents understood about the concept of global warming. As mentioned above for B1, a phone survey might have some degree of bias if those who don't have phones, can be reached at multiple phone numbers, or are not inclined to answer are more likely to favor one side of the issue or the other.

Exercise 8.3 (p. 235–236)

1. COUNTERARGUMENT:

(1) *Few drivers are drunk at 9:30 on Sunday morning.*

(2) *Armand was in an auto fatality at 9:30 on Sunday morning.*

(likely) *Armand's death was not the result of the driver drinking.*

3. COUNTERARGUMENT:

(1) *Most clerical jobs have lower wages.*

(2) *American cities with a strong service economy have a great many clerical jobs.*

(likely) *American cities with a strong service economy have lower wages.*

Exercise 8.4 (pp. 239–241)

1. Statistical Argument

(1) *America is a democracy.*

(2) *Most Democracies will not long permit substantial differences in wealth.*

(likely) *America will not long permit substantial differences in wealth.*

Deductive Argument

(1) *Roughly 59 percent of America's wealth is owned by the top 5 percent of households.*

(2) *If (1), then there is a substantial difference in wealth in America.* (IMPLICIT)

(3) *America will not long permit substantial differences in wealth.*

(4) *If America will not long permit substantial differences in wealth and there is a substantial difference in wealth in America, then legislation to alter this atleast somewhat will be produced.*

∴ *Legislation to alter substantial difference in wealth in America at least somewhat will be produced.*

The statistical argument can be criticized by the following counter argument

(1) *America is a strong promoter of free market capitalism.*

(2) *Most countries that promote free market capitalism will long permit substantial differences in wealth.*

(likely) *America will long permit substantial differences in wealth.*

3. Sampling Argument (Among other arguments that generalize)

(1) *A fifth of the 1500 women surveyed at Harvard (said they) had been forced into sexual activity.*

(likely) *Sex is forced on 19 percent (about a fifth) of all college women.*

Deductive Argument

(1) *Sex is forced on about a fifth of all college women.*

(2) *If is sex is forced on about a fifth of all college women, then forced sex is a major problem at college.* (IMPLICIT)

∴ *Forced sex is a major problem at college.* (IMPLICIT *suggested by the statement "That percentage was 'frighteningly high,'. . . .")*

The deductive argument is valid as reconstructed though in itself the passage doesn't reach a forceful policy proposal. The first premise (the conclusion of the sampling argument) can be criticized. It is unclear whether the sample was random or not. If it was drawn from those using the health services, for example, they might be unrepresentative of the whole population. It is also unclear whether the article wishes to generalize to a larger college population outside Harvard. If so, the sample must be taken from other colleges and universities as well, because there might be a higher rate of forced sexual activity on a campus where most students come from other states and countries with different sexual expectations, in contrast to community colleges with predominance of local students.

Chapter 9

Exercise 9.1 (pp. 249–252)

1. Texting might contribute to some traffic accidents. But a possible X-factor is the prevalence of texting among the young, who are relatively inexperienced drivers and tend to be less careful.
3. Although flu shots might cause some lowering of flu-related deaths, this might be relatively insignificant compared to other changes that might be made by those concerned enough to get flu shots regularly such as quitting smoking and getting more exercise. This concern with good health might be the X-factor that causes most of the increased longevity.
5. The increased TV watching and lowered test scores might both result from changes in the family. Children might be getting less attention or support, and this is the cause of both.

Exercise 9.2 (p. 260)

In exercise 9.1 #3, it was claimed that it is likely that taking flu shots every year causes people to live longer. To conduct a controlled experiment, we could solicit several hundred volunteers and randomly assign them to an experimental group and a control group. Those in the experimental group would be given a flu shot every year, and those in the control group would receive no flu shot. We could track these subjects for a long time (this study would require tracking the subjects for many decades in order to get a sufficient number of deaths from each group to compare the averages) and compare the average age at death of the members of the two groups. Although this longitudinal study would provide good evidence, it would be difficult to carry out, both because of possible ethical concerns over putting the control group at risk and a likely participant loss, particularly in the control group over time (perhaps because they felt that the risk was too great).

Exercise 9.3 (pp. 263–265)

1. A difference between the captain of a ship and the president of a country that makes the conclusion less likely is that the captain is supposedly an expert at handling his ship in all situations. An elected president may not be an expert at statecraft and may be unfamiliar with the kinds of crises that might confront him.

3. The implicit conclusion is that a government can't go on spending more than it takes in. One difference between a family and a government that makes the conclusion less likely is that a family has little or no control over the economic system in which it operates. For example, a government could affect the rate of interest on its debts through monetary policy, but a family could not. Furthermore, the premise that a family can't go on spending more than it takes in is somewhat doubtful. A family could do this for a long time, as long as it can pay the interest on its debt.

5. Rented tuxedos sometimes do fit. It is only if you abide by the myth of the perfect fit that you might think otherwise. Similarly, analogies might fit very well indeed.

Exercise 9.4 (p. 274)

1.

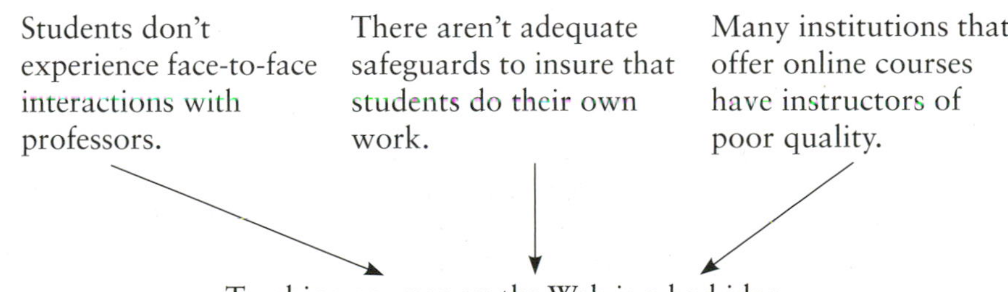
Students don't experience face-to-face interactions with professors.
There aren't adequate safeguards to insure that students do their own work.
Many institutions that offer online courses have instructors of poor quality.
Teaching courses on the Web is a bad idea.

Assessment:
Blunting a Consideration. Evidence would need to determine that instructors on the Web are poorer on the whole than those who teach classes face-to-face. Indeed, the quality of web courses might be higher during the initial stage of development than at some later point if web courses become widespread. Also it is not clear that the safeguards are especially inadequate. Cheating is a problem in other teaching modes as well.

The passage does not offer any considerations in favor of teaching courses on the Web, but we might add that the Web can provide education to "place bound" students who can't attend regular classes, web-based learning allows for flexible scheduling of course work, and furthermore, e-mail interaction with faculty, while not face-to-face, may be more personal than sitting in a large lecture hall in a standard university setting.

3.

Convergent Argument

Many adopted children want to know the identity of their birth parents.

Counter-considerations

Fewer women will complete their pregnancy if anonymous adoptions aren't legally guaranteed.

(Many) adoptive parents prefer that the adopted child focus on them as parents rather than divide concern with birth parents.

Conclusion: Adopted children should have the legal right to know the identity of their birth parents.

Alternatively: The argument in the passage might be reconstructed with the conclusion that adopted children should not have the legal right to know the identity of their birth parents. In which case, the two considerations on the right above would be placed on the left and the balance line would be shifted in the other direction.

Assessment:

Blunting Considerations. The stigma of having put up a child for adoption is not as great as it might have been in the past. To change the law (at least for future adoptions) might not affect whether pregnancies would be carried to term as suggested.

Promoting a Consideration: It is not just a matter of adopted children wanting to know for frivolous reasons (as might be suggested in the passage) but for sound psychological and even health reasons. Recent advances in medicine makes knowing the biological family's medical history particularly important.

Chapter 10

Exercise 10.1 (pp. 286–290)

A1. Statement (ii) explains Statement (i).

A3. Statement (ii) explains Statement (i).

A5 Statement (i) explains Statement (ii).

B1. WHAT IS EXPLAINED: Why so many banks are failing.
THEORY: Deregulation has resulted in bankers taking more risks.

B3. WHAT IS EXPLAINED: German genocide during the Holocaust.
THEORY: Two versions:
INTENTIONALIST: Hitler and his closest aides had an explicit long-term plan for extermination.
FUNCTIONALIST: The decision was the result of a struggle among rivals to gain Hitler's approval (not the result of a long-term plan).

B5. WHAT IS EXPLAINED: Why the U.S. Constitution survived.
THEORY: The Constitution was frequently altered to confer benefits and handicaps more in harmony with the social balance of power.

B7. WHAT IS EXPLAINED: Why there has been a temperature increase of about 0.5 degree over the last 100 years.
THEORY: The earth is subject to continual temperature oscillations (climate does not stay the same for long).

The theory is put forward as an alternative to the Greenhouse theory, which is meant to explain significant temperature increase. The author contends that the actual increase is not as significant as the Greenhouse theory predicts. Her theory accounts for changes in temperature as normal oscillations rather than the buildup of greenhouse gases.

B9. WHAT IS EXPLAINED: Why the Christian faith obtained (so remarkable) a victory (that is, why it spread and became established in much of Europe and the Mediterranean).
THEORY: There were five underlying causes: (a) a more inviting but nevertheless inflexible and intolerant zeal; (b) the doctrine of future life; (c) miraculous power ascribed to the primitive church; (d) pure and austere morals; and (e) connection to politics within the Roman Empire.

Exercise 10.2 (pp. 293–297)

Passage 1:

Initial Theory Being Evaluated
Younger Americans are reacting in a perfectly rational manner to their circumstances.

Alternative Theories
The regularity could be explained by the (four) alternative theories mentioned:
i. TV watching has produced cynicism
ii. Reagan/Bush presidencies fostered government-bashing
iii. Breakdown of the traditional family
iv. Incessant political scandals

Others might be added, such as: economic prosperity has fostered a more individualistic (libertarian) attitude that is suspicious of collective political action.

Regularity Being Explained by Both Initial Theory and Alternatives	Predicted Regularities That Might Not Occur
Generation X is politically apathetic.	If the initial theory is true, candidates that explicitly mentioned the issues cited in the passage would get a larger percentage of the Generation X vote. If, as the theory suggests Generation X acts particularly rationally, then we would not expect the risky investment in housing and high accumulation of personal debt that generation X exhibited later in life.

Passage 3

Initial Theory Being Evaluated	Alternatives
Suicide is caused by detachment from a social group or "anomie." When we are members of a group with well-defined norms, we have a sense of belonging and knowing expectations of the group.	Regularity 1 could be explained by pointing out that Catholicism (especially in the nineteenth century) strongly disapproved of suicide. Regularity 2 could be explained by the fact that many people live alone because they have serious problems, e.g., alcoholism or serious mental disorders.

Regularity Being Explained by Both Initial Theory and Alternatives	Predicted Regularities That Might Not Occur
1. Catholics have lower (recorded) suicide rates than Protestants. 2. Married persons living with a spouse have a lower (recorded) suicide rate than people living alone.	The initial theory predicts that youths living at home should have a lower suicide rate than other segments of society. There would be a relatively high suicide rate for those who move to a new social setting so that they are in transition between two sets of norms and expectations.

Exercise 10.3 (pp. 299–302)

A1. (i) Theory: Psi phenomena (true psychics) exist.
(ii) Criticism: Psychics don't break the bank in Las Vegas casinos (make a notable difference to casino profits).
(iii) Defense: Few psychics would be expected to be good, consistent gamblers, and we probably won't find out about those few who did win from casinos.

(iv) The defense does seem *ad hoc*. Great success at gambling would seem to be a good way at gaining popular (if not scientific) support for the position. The opportunity for quick wealth would surely be an incentive for many psychics to become good, consistent gamblers.

A3. (i) Theory: Darwinian evolutionary theory.
(ii) Criticism: Transitional evolutionary forms ("missing links") are extremely rare.
(iii) Defense: Darwinian theory should be altered by a nongradualistic theory of evolution in which there are long periods of stasis (no change) and short periods of rapid evolutionary change.
(iv) The response need not be seen as *ad hoc* depending on how well the nongradualist account can be supported.

A5. (i) Theory: Creationism (earth was created by God a relatively short time ago.)
(ii) Criticism: Radioisotope dating suggests the earth is very old.
(iii) Defense: Add to creationism the following items: radioisotope decay has not been constant, samples of decay products tested may be systematically contaminated by extra portions of that from which they decayed (the parent) or extra portions of decay product itself (the daughter), and God might have created the misleading array of radioisotopes.
(iv) The defense seems ad hoc, especially the last item. It is unrealistic to believe that the effects of contamination would systematically correlate with dating determined by other means such as historical records and tree rings. Why should we assume God would deceive us in this way?

B1. We might test the theory that personal space exists (or that it is tied to various characteristics) by determining whether people consistently react (for example, move away or say something) whenever another person (especially a stranger) enters the region.

B3. It is unclear how we could test the theory that God created the world with the (misleading) fossils in it since any evidence (or at least any fossil evidence) is irrelevant. It is not clear what other kind of evidence would be relevant unless there was evidence that all techniques for dating fossils had been altered as well.

B5. The theory that the dead communicate by phone with the living can't easily be tested, especially when it includes the claim that the call ends when someone realizes that he is speaking to a dead person. We would have to have some other way of communicating with the dead in order to determine whether the messages are indeed accurate.

Exercise 10.4 (pp. 303–312)

Passage 1

Theory: Handguns in private hands (in the United States) protect property and lives.
Regularity: Criminals in the United States engage in murder, rape, and robbery at a higher rate than other countries, but the United States has a lower burglary rate than these other countries.

Sample Criticism
Alternative Theory: Much of the violent crime in the United States is related to drugs. Both the drug trafficker and especially the addict act precipitously and often violently without the premeditation needed for successful burglary. The United States may have better alarm systems, security, and other protection against burglary than other countries.

Doubtful Prediction: The burglary rate is lowest in those areas with the highest gun ownership.

Passage 3
Theory: (International) politics is becoming feminized.
Regularity: Countries are becoming less inclined to use power around the world as freely as they have.

Sample Criticism
Alternative Theory: The threat of nuclear weapons (and more recently chemical and biological weapons as well) has made wide-scale military action more risky. The failure of the United States in Vietnam and Russia in Afghanistan have weakened resolve. The civil and ethnic conflicts around the world are difficult and dangerous to settle, and hence make the larger nations increasingly reluctant to intervene.

Doubtful Prediction: The United States will be less likely to go to war. The wars in Afghanistan and Iraq indicate that the U.S. is still willing to fight a war even though there are more women in the military and in important high position in government.

Chapter 11

Exercise 11.1 (pp. 327–336)

C1. ("Gender Tests May Not Be Worth Risk of Misuse"):
One of Goodman's arguments can be reconstructed in this way:

> (1) *If doctors are allowed to inform parents of the gender of their fetus, then it is possible that some parents will have an abortion because of the gender of the fetus.*

(2) This possibility should not be allowed.

∴ Doctors should not be allowed to inform parents of the gender of their fetus.

We should keep in mind that in order for the conclusion to follow, we must interpret the second premise as asserting more than mere disapproval of parents' aborting a fetus because of its gender. Rather, this premise must assert that we mustn't allow this possibility no matter what good consequences might follow from allowing doctors to give this information to parents. For example, such information would allow parents a role in a decision of whether to abort a fetus because of a sex-linked disease. And, in general, it might be an unwise policy to allow doctors to restrict the information they give to patients. No particular fallacy is involved here.

A second argument, supporting a suggestion by John Fletcher, whom she quotes, can be reconstructed as follows:

(1) Any genetic knowledge that is not related to disease should be kept from patients.

(2) Genetic knowledge about gender of fetuses is not related to disease.

∴ Genetic knowledge about gender of fetuses should be kept from patients.

The conclusion follows, but Premise 1 is doubtful. Even if patients might misuse information, most of us would be hesitant to allow physicians to withhold information about ourselves or our offspring that they acquired in the process of examining us, even if it were not related to disease. We value freedom of information so highly in principle that we are willing to put up with some significant abuse of information within our society in order to not compromise this principle.

INDEX